ENVIRONMENTAL VALUES, 1860-1972

MAN AND THE ENVIRONMENT INFORMATION GUIDE SERIES

Series Editor: Seymour M. Gold, Associate Professor, Department of
Environmental Horticulture, University of California, Davis, California

Also in this series:

AIR POLLUTION—*Edited by George Hagevik***

ENVIRONMENTAL DESIGN—*Edited by Wolfgang F. E. Preiser and
Steven Parshall***

ENVIRONMENTAL ECONOMICS—*Edited by Warren E. Johnston***

ENVIRONMENTAL EDUCATION—*Edited by William B. Stapp and
Mary Dawn Liston*

ENVIRONMENTAL LAW—*Edited by Mortimer D. Schwartz**

ENVIRONMENTAL PLANNING—*Edited by Michael J. Meshenberg**

ENVIRONMENTAL POLITICS AND ADMINISTRATION—*Edited by
Nedjelko D. Suljak***

ENVIRONMENTAL TOXICOLOGY—*Edited by Robert Rudd***

HUMAN ECOLOGY—*Edited by Gary H. Winkel and Emilie O'Mara***

NOISE POLLUTION—*Edited by Clifford R. Bragdon**

WASTEWATER MANAGEMENT—*Edited by George Tchobanoglous,
Robert Smith, and Ronald Crites*

WATER POLLUTION—*Edited by Allen W. Knight and Mary Ann Simmons***

*in press
**in preparation

The above series is part of the
GALE INFORMATION GUIDE LIBRARY

The Library consists of a number of separate Series of guides covering
major areas in the social sciences, humanities, and current affairs.

General Editor: Paul Wasserman, Professor and former Dean, School of Library
and Information Services, University of Maryland

ENVIRONMENTAL VALUES, 1860-1972

A GUIDE TO INFORMATION SOURCES

*Volume 4 in the Man and the Environment
Information Guide Series*

Loren C. Owings

*Collection Development Librarian, Peter J. Shields Library
University of California, Davis*

Gale Research Company
Book Tower, Detroit, Michigan 48226

Library of Congress
Cataloging in Publication Data

Owings, Loren C
   Environmental values, 1860-1972.

   (Man and the environment information guide series;
v. 4) (Gale information guide library)
   1. Human ecology--United States--Bibliography.
2. Nature--Bibliography. 3. Outdoor life--United States--
Bibliography. I. Title.
Z5861.093 [GF503] 016.30131 73-17539
ISBN 0-8103-1343-X

Copyright © 1976 by
Loren C. Owings

CONTENTS

Contents

VITA

Loren C. Owings is a collection development librarian at the Peter J. Shields Library at the University of California, Davis. He received his A.B., M.A., and M.L.S. from the University of California, Berkeley. Owings has been an editorial consultant for AMS Press (1971-72) and is a consulting editor for AGRI-CULTURAL HISTORY.

FOREWORD

The rapidly expanding scope and sophistication of literature in the area of environmental studies has created the need for an authoritative, annotated guide to the range and quality of information sources. New legislation, publications, developing techniques, and increasing levels of public involvement in environmental issues have created a need for government, industry, organizations, and individuals to seek more authoritative information on man-environment relationships. This information can be used to rationalize proposed public or private actions, resolve issues, and measure the impact of past actions on man and the environment.

The objective of this series is to provide an authoritative and systematic guide to significant information sources on selected topics for use by scholars, students, scientists, reference librarians, consultants, professionals, and citizens. The scope and scale of each volume are directed toward accommodating both the immediate and continuing needs of users in addition to establishing a chronological benchmark of the literature on each topic.

This series is concerned with the cause and effect relationships of man's impact on the urban and natural environment. It emphasizes the human problems, issues, and implications of these relationships that can be used to study or solve environmental problems. The series is intended to be a primary reference for people not familiar with the location and organization of information sources in the area of environmental studies. It should also serve as a basic reference for advanced students or professionals who need an annotated and selected sample of the current literature.

Each volume is prepared by a noted authority on the topic. The annotations and selection of references have been carefully reviewed to present an objective and balanced array of thought and practice. The organization of each volume is tailored to emphasize the way information is organized in this multidisciplinary and rapidly evolving field.

This volume is the most authoritative and comprehensive reference work on environmental values ever published. It is a landmark in the reference literature that brings together a diverse set of information sources from the humanities, and social and natural sciences. The scope, historical perspective, and focus offer a rare insight into the human values that have shaped American thinking on many environmental issues during the period of 1860 to 1972.

The volume presents a compendium of reference material and ideas invaluable to the scholar and practitioner. It contains a unique array of periodical literature, government documents, historical collections, and teaching materials on environmental values. The introductions, annotations, and sources have been carefully selected to give the reader a conceptual and pragmatic grasp of this important field of study.

The sensitive and scholarly nature of annotations do justice to this romantic period and capture the spirit of the environmental movement during these formative years. The classification and cross-referencing of materials presents an integrated view of time, space, and events that is rare in literature.

As the fourth volume in this series, ENVIRONMENTAL VALUES continues the standard of scholarly excellence and utility that will be followed in nine additional volumes now in preparation. When the entire series is completed in 1976, it will represent the most authoritative and comprehensive guide to the man-environment literature ever published.

Seymour M. Gold, Series Editor
November 1975

INTRODUCTION

The theme of this bibliography is the historical development of attitudes toward, and concern for, nature in the United States. From this development there has emerged a demonstrable environmental ethic. This ethic seems to be accepted at the moment by a minority of Americans; however, it is a very vocal and active minority which has exerted, and continues to exert, an influence which is perhaps disproportionate to its size. The ideological basis of this group of conservationists, preservationists, "nature-lovers," and ecologically oriented citizens is to be found in a series of esthetic, philosophical, literary, and emotional responses to their natural world. These components include a simple love of natural beauty, a sense of man's ecological and spiritual relationship to and need for nature, the struggle to preserve and defend wilderness against encroachment and despoilment, a questioning of urban-industrial values, and a concomitant movement to return to a simpler, more "natural" way of life.

In recent years, many books and articles have been written that deal wholly or in part with the components listed above. The thrust of some has been the search for an environmental or ecological ethic that can rationalize man's proper relationship to the natural world of which he is a part. Indeed, the modern ecology movement, espoused by many of today's youth and symbolized by such catch-phrases as "The Whole Earth" and "The Greening of America," is, in part at least, an expression of this attitude; yet, the ideas of this movement derive from the concerns shared by several generations of Americans. A proper understanding of today's environmental problems, then, can only be found in the context of the historical development of America's attitudes toward nature.

Any bibliography that seeks to trace this development must perforce be highly selective because of the magnitude of the topic and the vast quantities of literature available. Due to the limitations of time and space, this bibliography covers roughly the period from 1860 through 1972.

It should be stressed that this is not a guide to the literature of the conservation movement, especially as that term relates to the conserving of natural resources--soil, water, timber, and minerals--largely for economic reasons. The focus is neither economic nor political, but deals with the generalized concepts outlined above. Several other exclusions should also be noted: first, studies of wildlife conservation and, second, modern works detailing the degradation of our environment through air and water pollution, visual blight, overcrowding of human populations, and other elements of what may be termed human ecology are omitted.

In general, the bibliography includes books, parts of books, articles, documents, pamphlets, bibliographies, and reference works, but excludes unpublished theses and dissertations. With few exceptions, fiction and poetry are also not included. Wherever they have come to the editor's attention, recent reprints and paper editions are noted.

I am glad to acknowledge the assistance and encouragement of Mr. J. Richard Blanchard and Mr. Nelson Piper, both of the Peter J. Shields Library of the University of California, Davis. I greatly appreciate their releasing me from part of my duties in order that this work could be brought to completion.

Loren C. Owings
April 1975

Chapter 1

MAN AND NATURE IN AMERICA:

GENERAL WORKS

Chapter 1

MAN AND NATURE IN AMERICA: GENERAL WORKS

Chapter 1 presents a selected list of books and articles bearing on the theme of man and nature in America. Four separate sections are included: general, historical treatments of the man-nature theme; literary and cultural studies; American nature and the religious impulse; and modern works on environmental perception of natural areas. General bibliographies and reference books, not otherwise noted in Chapters 1 through 10, are listed in Chapter 11.

A. GENERAL STUDIES

Ekirch, Arthur A., Jr. MAN AND NATURE IN AMERICA. New York and London: Columbia University Press, 1963. viii, 231 p. Notes, pp. 195-212.

> Ekirch evidently wrote this book out of a deep personal concern for man and the environment, which he felt were in danger of destruction from either nuclear warfare or overpopulation. According to the author, these dangers are the outgrowths of the industrial-military state which is single-mindedly pursuing economic growth and material progress without regard for the effects upon the environment. Thus, the book is not so much a scholarly treatise as a polemical tract urging the point of view that man must learn to live in harmony with nature, not exploit it. In surveying American attitudes toward nature, Ekirch discusses the ideas of Emerson, Thoreau, George Perkins Marsh, and others, including some utopian socialists. Curiously, Aldo Leopold is ignored. Available in a paper edition.

Glacken, Clarence J. "Reflections on the Man-Nature Theme as a Subject for Study." In FUTURE ENVIRONMENTS OF NORTH AMERICA; Being the Record of a Conference Convened by the Conservation Foundation in April 1965 at Airlie House, Warrenton, Virginia, edited by Frank Fraser Darling, pp. 355-71. Garden City, N.Y.: Natural History Press, 1966.

> Glacken notes that most of his scholarly life has been spent study-ing the history of the man-nature theme. In short compass, he discusses the derivation of the theme within the context of the

history of ideas, with specific references to the American scene.
He then turns to contemporary environmental concerns and discusses
at some length certain ideas of enduring value that will play a
role in the increasing influence of urbanism upon the natural world.
A thoughtful and valuable essay.

_____. TRACES ON THE RHODIAN SHORE; NATURE AND CULTURE IN
WESTERN THOUGHT FROM ANCIENT TIMES TO THE END OF THE EIGH-
TEENTH CENTURY. Berkeley and Los Angeles: University of California Press,
1967. xxviii, 763 p. Bibliography, pp. 715-48.

Although only portions of this masterful work bear on the American
scene and none of it on the period under study, TRACES ON THE
RHODIAN SHORE is excellent background reading for a proper
understanding of the role of nature and culture--particularly its
religious implications--in western thought.

_____. "Man Against Nature: An Outmoded Concept." In THE ENVIRON-
MENTAL CRISIS: MAN'S STRUGGLE TO LIVE WITH HIMSELF, edited by
Harold W. Helfrich, Jr., pp. 127-42. New Haven and London: Yale Univer-
sity Press, 1970.

The concept of man against nature is not universal, but is largely
limited to western thought. Glacken discusses the historical evolution of the concept. He then argues that it is no longer (if it
ever was) a practical concept. Glacken is a professor of geography at the University of California, Berkeley.

_____. "Man's Place in Nature in Recent Western Thought." In THIS LITTLE
PLANET, edited by Michael Hamilton, pp. 163-201. New York: Scribner,
[1970].

Glacken examines the views of a selected number of scientists,
philosophers, and theologians (dating roughly from the end of the
eighteenth century) relative to the question, "Is man a significant
force in modifying the surface of the earth?" Major figures include Charles Lyell, Count Buffon, James Hutton, Charles Darwin,
George P. Marsh, and John Ruskin.

Hoffer, Eric. "A Strategy for the War With Nature." SATURDAY REVIEW
49 (February 5, 1966): 27-29, 73-75.

Hoffer sees nature as man's enemy and holds no brief for nature
lovers who "had no share in the world's work and did not know
nature at close quarters." The author ranges over the whole of
human history in support of his thesis that humanization of man
developed in spite of "nature."

Huth, Hans. NATURE AND THE AMERICAN; THREE CENTURIES OF CHANG-

ING ATTITUDES. Berkeley and Los Angeles: University of California Press, 1957. xvii, 250 p. Illustrated, with plates. Notes, pp. 213-27. Bibliography, pp. 229-40. Paperback ed., 1972.

A fascinating study of the development of America's appreciation of nature. Huth traces the developments that led to the conservation movement. However, the book's focus is much broader, for it deals with the growth of the esthetics of appreciation, the search for scenery in the United States, and the development of summer vacationing, resorts, and city parks. The book is strengthened by the author's choice of illustrations, including sixty-four plates. This is an outstanding work, well-written and documented.

Jackson, John B. AMERICAN SPACE: THE CENTENNIAL YEARS: 1865-1876. New York: Norton, 1972. 254 p. Plates. Bibliography, pp. 241-45.

A history of the ways the American landscape--both rural and urban--was transformed during a very critical period in our history. Jackson was for seventeen years the editor of the journal, LANDSCAPE.

_____. LANDSCAPES: SELECTED WRITINGS OF J.B. JACKSON. Edited by Ervin H. Zube. [Amherst]: University of Massachusetts Press, 1970. 160 p.

Includes essays and notes from LANDSCAPE, published between 1951 and 1968, and several lectures presented at the University of Massachusetts during 1965-66.

_____. "The Life and Death of American Landscapes: Jefferson, Thoreau, and After." LANDSCAPE 15 (Winter 1965-66): 25-27.

An interesting and valuable discussion of the two major proponents of nonurban philosophies of man in the environment. Jackson characterizes Jefferson as the leading voice of an agrarian utopianism, while Thoreau is given credit for translating into native terms the Romantic view of the landscape. These two positions are seen as the dividing line separating the critics of the American city. Reprinted in Jackson's LANDSCAPES, above, pp. 1-9.

Krutch, Joseph Wood. "Man, Nature and the Universe." AUDUBON 64, no. 3 (May/June 1962): 130, 132-33.

Krutch sees man as a cohabitor of the planet with all other living beings. Man has neither the moral right nor the obligation to banish all nature "to make room for man, his machines, and constructions."

McDermott, John J. "Nature Nostalgia and the City: An American Dilemma." SOUNDINGS 55, no. 1 (Spring 1972): 1-20.

McDermott develops the thesis that urban America has been seduced by nature, that is, by a series of nature metaphors growing out of our past. The author sees this as an unfortunate fact, since it results in an unconscious distaste for urban values and urban metaphors.

McEvoy, James III. THE AMERICAN PUBLIC'S CONCERN WITH THE ENVIRONMENT, A STUDY OF PUBLIC OPINION. Environmental Quality Series, no. 4. Davis: Institute of Governmental Affairs, University of California, February 1970.

Sociologist McEvoy uses the data accumulated in twelve surveys to plot the American public's concern with environmental questions. He points to the phenomenal increase in membership of major conservation organizations, and the increase in media coverage of environmental problems as just two indicators of this concern.

Mumford, Lewis. "The Renewal of the Landscape." In his THE BROWN DECADES: A STUDY OF THE ARTS IN AMERICA, 1865-1895, pp. 59-106. New York: Harcourt, Brace, 1931.

A thoughtful essay on America's discovery of the values of the natural landscape. Mumford singles out Thoreau as a seminal influence on this growing movement. George P. Marsh and Frederick Law Olmsted are also discussed.

Nash, Roderick. WILDERNESS AND THE AMERICAN MIND. Rev. ed. New Haven and London: Yale University Press, 1973. xvi, 300 p. Bibliography, pp. 274-88.

For annotation see Chapter 5, Section A: General and Historical.

Nye, Russell B. "The American View of Nature." In his THIS ALMOST CHOSEN PEOPLE, ESSAYS IN THE HISTORY OF AMERICAN IDEAS, pp. 256-304. [East Lansing]: Michigan State University Press, 1966.

A most valuable essay. Nye's theme is "the duality of the American attitude toward nature." This duality can best be seen in the contrast between the multiple-use advocates and the preservationists who see transcendent moral and spiritual values in American nature. The essay is comprehensive in scope, covering from the colonial period to the present.

Rosenkrantz, Barbara Gutmann, and Koelsch, William A., eds. AMERICAN HABITAT: A HISTORICAL PERSPECTIVE. New York: Free Press, 1973. x, 372 p. Illustrated.

A very useful compilation of selections illustrating "the interrelatedness of historical and ecological experience." The editors have divided the book into four sections: the first deals with public policy and the environment; the second samples varied usages of the environment; the third is a collection of twelve paintings by nineteenth-century American landscape artists; the last section is concerned with environmental values. Each section is introduced by an essay by the editors.

Schmitt, Peter J. BACK TO NATURE: THE ARCADIAN MYTH IN URBAN AMERICA. New York: Oxford University Press, 1969. xxiii, 230 p. Notes, pp. 191-221.

A fascinating and well-written study of the "back to nature" movement that developed in the urban middle class during the last decades of the nineteenth century. Schmitt traces this movement through the 1920s, showing how it was manifested in literature, camping and youth activities such as the Boy Scouts, the growth of city parks, country homes, outdoor magazines and popular "wilderness novels," the development of nature study, landscape gardening, and enthusiasm for country life. Out of this urban response to nature, there began the drive to conserve nature for the enjoyment of urban dwellers.

Slosson, Edwin E. "Back to Nature? Never! Forward to the Machine." INDEPENDENT 101 (January 3, 1920): 5-6, 37-40.

Slosson (1865-1929), author, lecturer, former chemistry professor and literary editor of the INDEPENDENT, has been called "the outstanding interpreter of science to the non-technical public (DICTIONARY OF AMERICAN BIOGRAPHY, vol. 17, p. 21)." In this article he attacks the "cult of naturalism" that praises the country but denounces the city and is filled with admiration for cliffs and forests, but denigrates skyscrapers and laboratories. Slosson saw this mode of thought as a reactionary movement, "antagonistic to progress." In his view, nature had to be conquered, not admired or imitated.

Udall, Stewart L. THE QUIET CRISIS. Introduction by John F. Kennedy. New York: Holt, Rinehart, and Winston, 1963. xiii, 209 p. Plates (some in color).

The story of America's attitudes toward the land and treatment of natural resources, with a strong plea for their conservation. A well-written, popular history.

Weimer, David R., ed. CITY AND COUNTRY IN AMERICA. New York: Appleton-Century-Crofts, 1962. xi, 399 p. Illustrated. Paper.

Selections from the writings of a wide spectrum of authors. Juxtaposition of essays illustrates the varied attitudes toward city and country in United States history from the eighteenth to the twentieth centuries.

White, Morton, and White, Lucia. THE INTELLECTUAL VERSUS THE CITY,
FROM THOMAS JEFFERSON TO FRANK LLOYD WRIGHT. Publications of
the Joint Center for Urban Studies. Cambridge, Mass.: Harvard University
Press and M.I.T. Press, 1962. x, 270 p. Notes, pp. 243-62.

> A stimulating study of varying degrees of "ambivalence and ani-
> mosity" exhibited by a group of America's foremost intellectual
> figures. The authors seek to define and explicate "this powerful
> tradition of anti-urbanism" in our history. They find that the
> history of the tradition falls into two fundamental phases: a pre-
> Civil War stage in which romanticism was used to attack the city
> for being too civilized; and a later stage in which the criticism
> found the city "undercivilized." Major figures examined are
> Franklin, Crevecouer, Jefferson, Emerson, Thoreau, Melville,
> Hawthorne, Poe, Henry Adams, Henry James, William Dean
> Howells, Frank Norris, Theodore Dreiser, William James, Jane
> Addams, Robert Park, John Dewey, Josiah Royce, George Santa-
> yana, Frank Lloyd Wright, and Lewis Mumford. Although the focus
> of the book is the city and its foes, much of the argument involves
> exposure of what the authors see as romantic and wrong-headed
> notions that the city should either be abandoned for decentral-
> ization, or that the city is inherently bad because it is not
> "natural."

B. LITERARY AND CULTURAL STUDIES

This section focuses on the belle-lettristic works dealing with the influence
of physical nature on American literature. Six literary and intellectual histories, described in the following paragraphs, touch upon literature and the
environment but have been excluded.

Three works--Henry Nash Smith's VIRGIN LAND, THE AMERICAN WEST AS
SYMBOL AND MYTH (Cambridge, Mass.: Harvard University Press, 1950),
Edwin Fussell's FRONTIER: AMERICAN LITERATURE AND THE WEST (Princeton, N.J.: Princeton University Press, 1965), and Lucy L. Hazard's THE
FRONTIER IN AMERICAN LITERATURE (New York: Crowell, 1927)--have in
common the concept of the American frontier. All were influenced by Turner's
frontier hypothesis. Smith and Fussell use myth, symbol, and metaphor in
literary sources to define American attitudes toward the frontier and its ultimate
influence in our culture; Hazard traces the representation of the frontier in
literature from the colonial period to the 1920s. However, they are not concerned directly with love or appreciation of wild nature and its representation
in literature.

Three other works--R.W.B. Lewis's THE AMERICAN ADAM: INNOCENCE,
TRAGEDY AND TRADITION IN THE NINETEENTH CENTURY (Chicago: Uni-
versity of Chicago Press, 1955), Charles L. Sanford's THE QUEST FOR PARA-
DISE: EUROPE AND THE AMERICAN MORAL IMAGINATION (Urbana:
University of Illinois Press, 1961), and Roy H. Pearce's THE SAVAGES OF

AMERICA: A STUDY OF THE INDIAN AND THE IDEA OF CIVILIZATION
(Baltimore: Johns Hopkins Press, 1965)--are literary studies in the history
of ideas. Both Lewis and Sanford are concerned to some extent with the im-
plantation of a paradisiacal myth in America. Lewis postulates the idea of
the American as a new Adam, while Sanford traces the quest for paradise in
American culture. Sanford does devote a chapter to the role natural scenery
played in developing a sense of national consciousness in literature, science,
and the arts. However, his discussion focuses upon the early nineteenth century, prior to the coverage of this bibliography. Pearce studies the history
of savagery and civilization in the 1850s, focusing upon the attitudes of white
immigrants toward the Indian. Although these six books are perceptive and
stimulating, with important implications for the study of American culture, they
do not bear directly upon the theme of this bibliography.

No effort is made to trace bibliographically the many literary studies showing
the role nature played in the writing of individual authors, particularly novel-
ists and poets. The reader interested in these is referred to the bibliographies
and reference books listed in Chapter 7: American Nature Writing.

Beers, Henry A. "The Modern Feeling for Nature." In his POINTS AT ISSUE,
AND SOME OTHER POINTS, pp. 129-59. New York: Macmillan, 1904.

    See next item.

    _____. "Aesthetic Botany." In his POINTS AT ISSUE, AND SOME OTHER
POINTS, pp. 163-79. New York: Macmillan, 1904. Reprint ed., 1967.

    In these two essays, the author describes the increasing role of
    nature in modern literature. The first essay deals largely with
    English authors. "Aesthetic Botany" is a discussion of plants,
    flowers, and trees as they appear in recent literature, particularly
    American.

Bennett, Meridan H. "The Scenic West: Silent Mirage." COLORADO
QUARTERLY 7, no. 1 (Summer 1959): 15-25.

    The author sees the scenery of the Rocky Mountain West as an
    inhibitor of literature. "Scenery is only meaningful in artistic
    expression when viewed, as it were, through the legs of the
    crowd."

Canby, Henry Seidel. "Back to Nature." YALE REVIEW, n.s. 6 (July 1917):
755-67.

    An exploration of the relationship between that "back to nature"
    impulse, then current, and its manifestation in American literature.
    Canby saw the "vast rush of nature in American literature" as a
    "search for tradition, and its capture." He believed that the
    nature experience was deep within the American consciousness and
    that, as tradition, it was uniquely American. This article was re-

printed in his DEFINITIONS, FIRST SERIES. ESSAYS IN CON-
TEMPORARY CRITICISM (New York: Harcourt, Brace, 1922,
pp. 92-108).

_____. "Back From Nature." SATURDAY REVIEW OF LITERATURE 3, no. 28
(February 5, 1927): 557, 560.

A short, provocative piece on what Canby felt was the declining
influence of nature upon American literature. Reprinted in the
author's AMERICAN ESTIMATES (New York: Harcourt, Brace,
1929, pp. 46-49).

Clough, Wilson O. THE NECESSARY EARTH: NATURE AND SOLITUDE IN
AMERICAN LITERATURE. Austin: University of Texas Press, 1964. xii, 234
p. Bibliography, pp. 213-18.

Clough states in his preface that his book is more of an essay
than an "exercise in research scholarship." He divides the book
into three divisions: the first deals with the first impact upon
European men on the American environment and the beginning of
the "American experience"; the second covers the growing aware-
ness by native authors of the possibilities of the frontier as a
"source of metaphor" in the definition of a "national expression";
the third considers the extent to which that metaphorical usage still
continues into the twentieth century. The author argues that the
frontier experience of solitude as reflected in literature from
colonial times to Wallace Stevens has had a significant impact
upon American literature and life.

Culmsee, Carlton F. MALIGN NATURE AND THE FRONTIER. Utah State
University Monograph Series, vol. 7, no. 2. Logan: Utah State University
Press, 1959. 45 p.

Using primarily literary sources, the author describes the change
in the American view of nature from one of a "doting mother,
a loving mistress," to that of enemy. The transition period is
the middle and late nineteenth century.

Foerster, Norman. NATURE IN AMERICAN LITERATURE: STUDIES IN THE
MODERN VIEW OF NATURE. New York: Macmillan, 1923. xiii, 324 p.
Reprint ed., 1958.

Foerster's is the pioneer study of nature in American literature.
A chapter each is devoted to Bryant, Whittier, Emerson, Thoreau,
Lowell, Whitman, Lanier, Burroughs, and Muir.

Hicks, Philip Marshall. THE DEVELOPMENT OF THE NATURAL HISTORY
ESSAY IN AMERICAN LITERATURE. Philadelphia: [University of Pennsylvania],
1924. 167 p. Bibliography, pp. 165-67.

See annotation for this item in Chapter 7, Section A2: Histories
and Special Studies.

Marx, Leo. THE MACHINE AND THE GARDEN: TECHNOLOGY AND THE
PASTORAL IDEAL IN AMERICA. New York: Oxford University Press, 1964.
392 p. Illustrated.

Using literary and historical sources, Marx deals with the tensions
in American culture and the "American experience" between the
pastoral ideal and an urban-industrial reality. The author examines the writings of a number of major and minor authors, including Jefferson, Thoreau, Melville, and Mark Twain to explicate
his theme. A most valuable treatment.

Tracy, Henry Chester. AMERICAN NATURISTS. New York: Dutton, 1930.
viii, 282 p.

The word "naturist" was coined by Liberty Hyde Bailey, and is
used here to mean "an ardent lover and observer of the life out-
of-doors." Tracy views American nature writing as unique and
fine, owing little or nothing to European traditions. The author
claims that we have not recognized our own outstanding naturists
as a distinct group, different from other essayists and scientists,
and very worthwhile reading and studying. Tracy's book is basi-
cally an appreciation of this group of men and women. Major
figures include the eighteenth- and early nineteenth-century
writers (the Bartrams, Alexander Wilson, and Audubon), Thoreau,
Burroughs, Muir, Olive Thorne Miller, Maurice Thompson, W.
T. Hornaday, Theodore Roosevelt, Liberty Hyde Bailey, William
Beebe, Ernest Thompson Seton, and Mary Austin.

C. NATURE AND THE RELIGIOUS IMPULSE

There is no single work that deals with the historical development of religious
attitudes toward nature in America. Peter J. Schmitt devotes a very short
chapter in his BACK TO NATURE: THE ARCADIAN MYTH IN URBAN AMERI-
CA (see main entry in Section A: General Studies, above) to religion and
nature from the 1890s to approximately 1930. The following is an illustrative
listing of books and articles that bear upon the subject.

General

White, Lynn. "The Historical Roots of Our Ecological Crisis." SCIENCE 155,
no. 3767 (March 10, 1967): 1203-7.

This is an important essay on the religious roots of our ecological
crisis. White asserts that our historical knowledge of ecological
change is still so "rudimentary" that we as yet know little about

its patterns and effects. History can, however, help us see some of the presuppositions that underlie modern science and technology. White presents a brief overview of the western traditions of technology and science, and, in particular, "the medieval view of man and nature." Man's exploitive attitude toward nature, he says, is not a recent result, but has its roots deep in our historical past. This attitude is "rooted in...Judeo-Christian teleology." The author describes Christianity as "the most anthropocentric religion the world has seen," a religion in which all creation was made for man's purposes. Western science in its early years was conditioned by Christian beliefs and may be seen as "an extrapolation of natural theology." Thus, modern science reflects the tenets of that dogma which asserts "man's transcendence of, and rightful mastery over, nature." White doubts that our problems can be avoided by "more science and more technology." The author concludes that the crisis will not be ameliorated until the Christian dogma of man's absolute mastery over nature is rejected. Any remedy, therefore, will have to be essentially religious in nature.

Theological Studies

Baer, Richard A., Jr. "Conservation: An Area for the Church's Concern." CHRISTIAN CENTURY 86, no. 2 (January 8, 1969): 40-43.

A call to action by a theologian from Earlham College. Baer feels the church is badly in need of a "twentieth century theology of nature and of a land ethic"; however, he says that even though more study is needed in some areas, enough evidence is available now for action. Theologians must learn to write for the popular press instead of panning it. He feels that a new organization of churchmen committed to the ecological ethic must begin to speak to and for the millions of Christians in America who do not as yet see the connection between their faith and the need to preserve our natural heritage. See also his earlier article in the same periodical: "Land Misuse: A Theological Concern," vol. 83, no. 41 (October 12, 1966): 1239-41.

Barbour, Ian G., ed. EARTH MIGHT BE FAIR, REFLECTIONS ON ETHICS, RELIGION AND ECOLOGY. Englewood Cliffs, N.J.: Prentice-Hall, 1972. vii, 168 p.

The primary purpose of this book is "the articulation of an ecological theology and an ecological ethic." The nine essays are: "Explanation in Science and Theology," by Frederick Ferre; "Science and God's Action in Nature," by John J. Compton; "Changing Concepts of Nature," by Daniel Day Williams; "Tao Now: An Ecological Testament," by Huston Smith; "The Uniqueness of the Earth," by William G. Pollard; "The Whole Earth is the Lord's: Toward a Holistic Ethic," by Harold K. Schilling; "Science

and Ethical Decision: Some New Issues," by Roger L. Shinn;
and "Attitudes Toward Nature and Technology," by Ian G. Barbour.
Barbour also contributes a twelve-page introduction.

Elder, Frederick. CRISIS IN EDEN: A RELIGIOUS STUDY OF MAN AND
HIS ENVIRONMENT. Nashville and New York: Abingdon Press, 1970.
172 p. Bibliography, pp. 163-67.

> A study of two contrasting views of nature. The author calls the
> two, "Inclusionist" and "Exclusionist." The first view is espoused
> by those who see man as a part of nature; the second conceive
> of man as standing apart from, and superior to, nature. Represen-
> tative figures used by the author to contrast the points of view
> are Loren Eiseley, Rachel Carson, Edmund Sinnott, Ian McHarg,
> and Aldo Leopold (inclusionists); and Pierre Teilhard de Chardin,
> Herbert Richardson, and Harvey Cox (exclusionists). Elder opts
> for the inclusionist philosophy and proposes a new asceticism
> composed of three fundamental elements: restraint, an emphasis
> upon quality of existence, and reverence for life.

The Faith-Man-Nature Group. CHRISTIANS AND THE GOOD EARTH: AD-
DRESSES AND DISCUSSIONS AT THE THIRD NATIONAL CONFERENCE OF
THE FAITH-MAN-NATURE GROUP. F/M/N Papers, No. 1. Alexandria,
Va.: [1968]. 190 p.

> See next item.

_____. A NEW ETHIC FOR A NEW EARTH. Edited by Glenn C. Stone.
F/M/N Papers, No. 2. [New York]: Friendship Press for the Faith-Man-
Nature Group and the Section on Stewardship and Benevolence of the Nation-
al Council of Churches, [1971]. 176 p. Bibliography, pp. 163-72.

> The Faith-Man-Nature Group, a little-known organization associ-
> ated with the National Council of Churches since 1963, has been
> grappling with the ecological crisis and the problems of develop-
> ing a truly creative theological response. The group held two
> major conferences in 1967 and 1969; the first produced CHRISTIANS
> AND THE GOOD EARTH, and the second brought forth A NEW
> ETHIC FOR A NEW EARTH. H. Paul Santmire has written of
> the deliberations of these two conferences in a valuable article,
> "The Struggle for an Ecological Theology," in CHRISTIAN CEN-
> TURY (volume 87, March 4, 1970, pp. 275-77).

Santmire, H. Paul. BROTHER EARTH: NATURE, GOD AND ECOLOGY IN
TIME OF CRISIS. New York and Camden, N.J.: Thomas Nelson, 1970.
236 p. Notes, pp. 201-32.

> Conceived as "a study in the theology of nature, not a study in
> 'natural theology.'" Of particular relevance are the first two
> chapters in which the author deals with nature in its American

historical context and in its contemporary setting. Santmire discusses Emerson, Thoreau, John Muir, and Liberty Hyde Bailey. He describes what he calls the "cult of the Simple Rustic Life" which manifests itself today in mass produced nature prints, Andrew Wyeth paintings, popular magazines on outdoor life (camping, boating, fishing, and hunting), conservation groups, Walt Disney films, youth groups, etc. This cult is juxtaposed to the "cult of Compulsive Manipulation." These two cults are analogous to nineteenth-century attitudes of adoration and exploitation of nature. Thus, the overall American attitude toward nature has been, and continues to be, contradictory.

Miscellaneous Works on Nature and Religion

Bailey, Liberty Hyde. THE HOLY EARTH. The Background Books. New York: Macmillan, 1915. vi, 171 p.

Bailey argues that the earth is divine "because man did not make it" and that man's relation to the earth must be a spiritual one. See also the annotation for this book in Chapter 10, Section A: Commentaries.

Borland, Hal G. COUNTRYMAN: A SUMMARY OF BELIEF. Philadelphia and New York: Lippincott, 1965. 160 p.

A very personal statement of the author's philosophy of nature framed in twelve essays corresponding to months of the year. The setting is Borland's upland Connecticut farm about which he records his impressions of nature's cycle of birth, growth, decay, and death--analogous to the rhythm of the seasons. Although the author discovers no final answers to the questions of life and death, he exhibits a deep serenity in this enduring pattern and in his own deep love for nature.

Burroughs, John (1837-1921)

John Burroughs's views on religion and nature can be found in the essays listed below and in Clifford Osbourne's work, also cited below. References are to individual volumes of the "Wake Robin Edition" of Burroughs's complete writings, rather than to the periodicals in which they originally appeared.

THE LIGHT OF DAY, RELIGIOUS DISCUSSIONS AND CRITICISMS FROM THE NATURALIST'S POINT OF VIEW. Complete Writings, vol. 10. New York: Wm. H. Wise, 1924.

"The Gospel of Nature." In his TIME AND CHANGE. Complete Writings, vol. 15, chap. 13. New York: Wm. H. Wise, 1924.

"Religion." In his FIELD AND STUDY. Complete Writings, vol. 20, pp. 241-51. New York: Wm. H. Wise, 1924.

ACCEPTING THE UNIVERSE. Complete Writings, vol. 21. New York: Wm. H. Wise, 1924.

Virtually all of the fifteen chapters in Volume 21 deal in some way with nature and religious belief, science and evolution, etc. Of special interest is the essay "The Faith of a Naturalist," which appears in this volume as Chapter 7.

"Ruminations." In his UNDER THE MAPLES. Complete Writings, vol. 22, chap. 11. New York: Wm. H. Wise, 1924.

Osbourne, Clifford H. THE RELIGION OF JOHN BURROUGHS. Boston and New York: Houghton Mifflin, 1930. x, 105 p.

"A study of the evolution of John Burroughs's stand on religion, showing the changes in his attitude from youth and early manhood to later years." Contains copious quotations from Burroughs's writings.

Gray, William Cunningham. MUSINGS BY CAMPFIRE AND WAYSIDE. Chicago, New York, and Toronto: Fleming H. Revell, 1902. 337 p. Illustrated.

Gray was a leading Presbyterian layman and editor of the Presbyterian paper THE INTERIOR (later, THE CONTINENT) from 1870 until his death in 1901. Under Gray's leadership, the paper became the leading voice of midwest Presbyterianism. MUSINGS is a new edition of a work originally published as CAMP-FIRE MUSINGS, LIFE AND GOOD TIMES IN THE WOODS (1894). Gray loved nature, especially the forests of the northern United States, Canada, and Alaska. MUSINGS contains chapters set in the "northern woods," Alaska, and the southern United States. Gray was both an accurate observer of natural phenomena and an excellent prose stylist. All of the writing is informed by his own brand of religious philosophy. The work attained a modest popularity and is cited with some frequency by contemporary authors.

Hamblin, Stephen F. MAN'S SPIRITUAL CONTACT WITH THE LANDSCAPE. Boston: Richard G. Badger, Gorham Press, 1923. 312 p. Plates. Bibliography, pp. 293-312.

This work is probably sui generis. The author states that he wrote most of the fourteen chapters out of doors, in calendar form. They relate to topics such as running water, the sea, the mountains, trees, the sky, etc. The writing is extremely discursive and is filled with quotations of nature poetry. The author's purpose was to illustrate man's spiritual relationship to, and dependence upon, nature by reference to nature literature, primarily poetry. The bibliography is actually a list for further reading.

Kirkham, Stanton Davis. RESOURCES: AN INTERPRETATION OF THE WELL-ROUNDED LIFE. New York and London: Putnam, 1910. ix, 236 p.

In this book, devoted to prescriptive thoughts on the conduct of life, Kirkham places a good deal of value upon nature as a spiritual resource.

_____. OUTDOOR PHILOSOPHY, THE MEDITATIONS OF A NATURALIST. New York and London: Putnam, 1912. xii, 214 p.

Contemplative essays on religion and nature philosophy inspired by Kirkham's outdoor life. For other titles by Kirkham, see Chapter 7, Section C: Nature Writing Since Thoreau.

Quayle, William Alfred (1860-1925)

Quayle, Methodist bishop, lecturer, and author, wrote more than a score of books, including poetry, sermons, literary essays, and nature books. Quayle's purpose in writing about nature subjects was, as he put it, "to people other hearts with love of flower and woodland path and drifting cloud...and to make men and women more the lovers of this bewildering world fashioned in loveliness by the artist hand of God." Four of his most popular books are listed below. For biographical information, see William W. Sweet's sketch in THE DICTIONARY OF AMERICAN BIOGRA-PHY (volume 15, p. 298).

IN GOD'S OUT-OF-DOORS. Cincinnati: Jennings and Pye; New York: Eaton and Mains, 1902. 232 p. Illustrated, with plates.

THE PRAIRIE AND THE SEA. Cincinnati: Jennings and Pye; New York: Eaton and Mains, 1905. 341 p. Illustrated, with plates.

WITH EARTH AND SKY. New York and Cincinnati: Abingdon Press, 1922. 181 p.

OUT-OF-DOORS WITH JESUS. New York and Cincinnati: Abingdon Press, 1924. 223 p.

Rutledge, Archibald. "The Faith of a Naturalist." AMERICAN FORESTS 41, no. 12 (December 1935): 666-69, 694, 710-11.

A personal statement of belief by a well-known poet and nature writer. For additional titles by Rutledge, see Chapter 7, Section C: Nature Writing Since Thoreau.

Van Dyke, Henry (1852-1933)

> Presbyterian minister, poet, essayist, university professor, and diplomat, Van Dyke was a religious leader of wide influence and an author of prominence (he was elected president of the National Institute of Arts and Letters). During his tenure as pastor of the Brick Presbyterian Chruch in New York City (1883-99), he was known as the "fishing preacher" because of his passion for angling and his ability for communicating that love in magazine essays and books. From 1899 to 1923, he held a chair in English literature at Princeton University. Van Dyke's outdoor essays and sketches are characterized by gentle humor and an unintrusive religious point of view. Although stylistically in the genteel tradition, his work is still quite readable. The three books listed below represent his major contribution to outdoor literature.

> LITTLE RIVERS, A BOOK OF ESSAYS IN PROFITABLE IDLENESS. New York: Scribner, 1895. viii, 291 p. Illustrated, with plates. Reprint ed., 1973.

> FISHERMAN'S LUCK AND SOME OTHER UNCERTAIN THINGS. New York: Scribner, 1899. 247 p. Plates. Reprint ed., 1973.

> DAYS OFF AND OTHER DIGRESSIONS. New York: Scribner, 1907. 322 p. Plates. Reprint ed., 1973.

D. ENVIRONMENTAL PERCEPTION OF NATURAL AREAS

The following is a select list of recent titles on environmental perception of natural areas--landscapes, natural beauty, and wilderness. Behavioral studies are excluded. For older works on perception of the American natural environment, see Chapter 2.

Bibliographies

Cerny, James W. LANDSCAPE AMENITY ASSESSMENT BIBLIOGRAPHY. Exchange Bibliography, no. 287. Monticello, Ill.: Council of Planning Librarians, 1972. 8 p. Paper.

> Consists of a four-page essay and bibliography of forty-five titles. The author, a geographer at Clark University, says that most of the material relating to landscape amenity assessment as an aspect of environmental quality is less than ten years old. Cerny uses the word "amenity" here to indicate a range of responses to landscape such as "intangible," "beautiful," or "aesthetic." Not annotated.

Harrison, James D. THE PERCEPTION AND COGNITION OF ENVIRONMENT. Exchange Bibliography, no. 516. Monticello, III.: Council of Planning Librarians, 1974. 79 p. Paper.

An annotated revision of Harrison's earlier, and shorter, bibliography (Exchange Bibliography, no. 93, 1969). The emphasis is again upon urban areas, and as such, its usefulness is limited. It is divided into two parts: the first is an annotated topical arrangement of books and articles covering (1) Personality and Perception; Psychological and Philosophical Views; (2) Attitude Formation; (3) Environmental Sensitivity and Selection; (4) Environmental Effects and Behavioral Manipulation; (5) Strategies of Change; (6) Measurement and Scaling; and (7) Reviews and Collections. The second part is an unannotated listing by author arrangement.

Marsh, John. SCENERY EVALUATION AND LANDSCAPE PERCEPTION: A BIBLIOGRAPHY. Exchange Bibliography, no. 304. Monticello, III.: Council of Planning Librarians, 1972. 9 p. Paper.

Heavy emphasis upon Canadian and British sources, although still useful for American users. Not annotated.

Books and Articles

Lowenthal, David. "Nature and the American Creed of Virtue." LANDSCAPE 9, no. 2 (Winter 1959-60): 24-25.

Geographer-historian Lowenthal refutes the idea of the "balance of nature" as espoused by many conservationists. He takes the position that it is right to remake nature to suit ourselves; we are seeking our good, not nature's.

_____. "Not Every Prospect Pleases: What Is Our Criterion for Scenic Beauty?" LANDSCAPE 12, no. 2 (Winter 1962-63): 19-23.

Lowenthal examines the notions that make any landscape seem pleasant or unpleasant. He also takes issue with the contemporary "wilderness cult" for its ideology that only what is natural is good.

_____. "Assumptions Behind the Public Attitudes [Toward the Environment]." In ENVIRONMENTAL QUALITY IN A GROWING ECONOMY, ESSAYS FROM THE SIXTH RFF FORUM, by Henry Jarrett, pp. 128-37. Baltimore: Published for Resources for the Future, Inc. by Johns Hopkins Press, 1966.

The author examines the perception of the American environment, the variability of human experience, the historical evidence of American responses to the landscape, etc.

_____. "The American Scene." GEOGRAPHICAL REVIEW 58, no. 1 (January 1968): 61-88.

In this essay, Lowenthal is concerned with environmental perception, specifically with scenery. He discusses images, stereotypes, questions of size and scale, formlessness, and other attributes of the American scene. He concludes that for planning and design to be effective they must take into account how we feel and think about the environment. A very valuable essay.

_____. "Recreation Habits and Values: Implications for Landscape Quality." In CHALLENGE FOR SURVIVAL: LAND, AIR, AND WATER FOR MAN IN MEGALOPOLIS, edited by Pierre Dansereau, pp. 103-17. New York and London: Columbia University Press, 1970.

An address presented as part of a symposium sponsored by the New York Botanical Garden on April 25-26, 1968. Lowenthal's essay is much in the same vein as his previous writings on the environment. He makes the following points: wilderness must inevitably give way to overcrowding; humanized nature is as "moral" as wilderness; "people care most about those aspects of the outdoors with which they are familiar"; and it is necessary to show people that nature can be found and appreciated in the city and backyard as well as the great outdoors. The author sketches what he sees as the five traits of contemporary outdoorsmen. The outdoorsman (1) "observes nature mainly to court and classify"; (2) "is there to improve himself"; (3) "is organized"; (4) "is a good citizen"; and (5) "is a masochist." Charles C. Morrison, Jr., a fellow geographer, criticizes Lowenthal's contentions on pp. 118-28.

Lowenthal's essay was also published in August 1968 under the title "Daniel Boone is Dead," in NATURAL HISTORY (volume 77, no. 7), and in a slightly edited version titled, "To Love at a Distance is Not Enough," in LANDSCAPE ARCHITECTURE (volume 59, October 1968).

Lucas, Robert W. "Wilderness Perception and Use: The Example of the Boundary Water Canoe Area." NATURAL RESOURCES JOURNAL 3, no. 3 (January 1964): 394-411.

The author is an economic geographer and his article is based upon research conducted for the Lake States Forest Experiment Station, U.S. Forest Service in St. Paul, Minnesota. The first part of the report discusses briefly the historical background to wilderness as a resource and its various uses. The second and third parts present the results of the research relative to perception of the wilderness resource in the Boundary Waters Canoe Area, and how that resource is influenced through environmental perception by resource managers and recreationists. A valuable article.

Shepard, Paul, Jr. "The Cross Valley Syndrome." LANDSCAPE 10, no. 3 (Spring 1961): 4-8.

An examination of human attraction to a form of landscape--the water gap. Shepard suggests that one reason for this attraction is a deep-seated tendency to equate earth forms to human forms.

_____. MAN IN THE LANDSCAPE: A HISTORIC VIEW OF THE ESTHETICS OF NATURE. New York: Knopf, 1967. xx, 290 p. Sources and references, pp. 275-90.

Shepard, a biologist, has written a fascinating and valuable history of environmental perception. He traces the history of western man's attitude toward the environment from classical times to the present, utilizing myths, pastoral image, sense of place, and urban nostalgia for a lost rural world. The American response centers upon a discussion of U.S. gardens, public parks, cemeteries, and the discovery of scenery, including landscape painting, tourism, and vacationing.

Tuan, Yi-Fu. "Man and Nature: An Eclectic Reading." LANDSCAPE 15, no. 3 (Spring 1966): 30-36.

A very rewarding and substantive bibliographic essay. Tuan discusses the terms "landscape," "scenery," and "nature" with reference to the books and articles cited. These range over many cultures and disciplines.

_____. "Attitudes Toward Environment: Themes and Approaches." In ENVIRONMENTAL PERCEPTION AND BEHAVIOR, edited by David Lowenthal, chap. 1. University of Chicago, Department of Geography Research Paper, no. 109. Chicago: University of Chicago, Department of Geography, 1967.

Tuan outlines a number of approaches to the study of man's attitude toward his environment.

Chapter 2

TRAVEL REPORTS ON SCENERY

AND THE SEARCH FOR THE PICTURESQUE

Chapter 2

TRAVEL REPORTS ON SCENERY
AND THE SEARCH FOR THE PICTURESQUE

Included in this chapter are books and articles showing the growing appreciation of this country's natural scenery by its citizens. This particular type of writing was well developed prior to the period covered by this bibliography; however several factors contributed to its accelerated growth after the Civil War. The improvement of transportation facilities, particularly the transcontinental railroad; the growth of resort centers in scenic regions such as the Adirondacks, the Catskills, and the White Mountains; the development of an infant travel industry, often sponsored by the railroads and resorts; and the "back to nature" movement itself--all these contributed to a growing wanderlust on the part of the more affluent classes to visit the picturesque wonders of America.

For the most part, early travel reports do not show any special concern for the preservation of natural beauty. There are exceptions, but the primary expression was one of wonder and delight. Gradually, exceptions become more common and one can discern a growing interest in preserving natural beauty for the future. This interest came to fruition in the national parks movement, which is treated in Chapter 4.

Only the more significant and representative examples of this enormous body of literature are included. Very few travel accounts by foreign visitors are listed because the focus of this chapter is what Americans themselves thought and wrote about natural scenery. No effort has been made to survey the exploration literature of the West. Tourist guides are included only on a very selective basis.

A. BIBLIOGRAPHIES

Bartlett, Richard A. GREAT SURVEYS OF THE AMERICAN WEST. American Exploration and Travel Series, vol. 38. Norman: University of Oklahoma Press, 1962. xxiii, 408 p. Illustrated, with maps. Bibliography, pp. 377-90.

> Much of the literature relating to the wonders of the American West occurs in survey reports resulting from government expeditions.

No attempt has been made to list these. Bartlett's book provides
a good starting point and contains a useful bibliography.

Clark, Thomas D., ed. TRAVELS IN THE NEW SOUTH. 2 vols. American
Exploration and Travel Series, vol. 36. Norman: University of Oklahoma
Press, 1962.

> An excellent annotated bibliography of accounts of southern travel
> published between 1865 and 1955. Many reports of scenery are
> included.

Coulter, Ellis M. TRAVELS IN THE CONFEDERATE STATES: A BIBLIOGRA-
PHY. American Exploration and Travel Series, vol. 11. Norman: University
of Oklahoma Press, 1948. xiv, 289 p.

> Does essentially the same thing as Clark's book (above) for the
> period 1861 to 1865. Much less emphasis is given to scenic re-
> porting than in Clark.

Dellenbaugh, Frederick S. "Travelers and Explorers, 1846-1900." In THE
CAMBRIDGE HISTORY OF AMERICAN LITERATURE, Vol. 3, chap. 14. New
York: Putnam; Cambridge: Cambridge University Press, 1921.

> Unsystematic and unanalytical, this bibliographic essay is largely
> a recital of titles. The accompanying bibliography of over a
> thousand titles is contained in Volume 4, pp. 681-728.

U.S. National Park Service. A BIBLIOGRAPHY OF NATIONAL PARKS AND
MONUMENTS WEST OF THE MISSISSIPPI RIVER. Compiled at the Western
Museum Laboratories of the National Park Service with assistance provided by
the Work Projects Administration and the Civilian Conservation Corps. 2 vols.
Mimeographed. [Berkeley, Calif.?]: 1941.

> The bibliographies in these two volumes were prepared and distrib-
> uted separately; consequently they have separate forewords and are
> paged separately. The tables of contents have no page references
> and there is no index. Despite these drawbacks, the bibliography
> is an invaluable source of information about national parks and
> monuments. The compilations were begun in 1936. Included are
> books, parts of books, articles, documents, proceedings, reports,
> and newspaper stories. For the most part, fiction, poetry, and
> maps are excluded. The arrangement is by region. The larger
> or more well-known parks and monuments are subdivided by cate-
> gory--history, travel, description, geology, flora and fauna,
> Indians, archaeology, etc. Several parks are represented by sub-
> stantial bibliographies, and two, Yellowstone (200 p.) and Yosemite
> (134 p.), are large and comprehensive to 1936.

> Because many of the "scenic" wonders of the western United States
> have been included within the National Parks system, this bibliog-
> raphy is an exceptionally valuable but little-known source for

thousands of publications that bear on scenery, as well as other aspects of the parks and monuments. Many of the items have brief annotations.

B. SPECIAL STUDIES

Betts, Ritchie G. "The Rediscovery of America by the Automobile." OUTING 42, no. 2 (May 1903): 167-76. Illustrated with photos.

A contemporary article on the impact of the automobile upon scenic touring.

Bredeson, Robert C. "Landscape Description in Nineteenth Century American Travel Literature." AMERICAN QUARTERLY 20, no. 1 (Spring 1968): 86-94.

An insightful article. Bredeson describes three modes of "seeing" the American landscape that were current in nineteenth-century travel literature. He calls them "the fashionable, the informative, and the utilitarian."

Chittenden, Hiram M. "Sentiment versus Utility in the Treatment of National Scenery." PACIFIC MONTHLY (Portland, Ore.) 23 (January 1910): 29-38.

"Ordinarily the demands of utility are imperative and scenic beauty where it stands in the way must yield." Chittenden, a lieutenant-colonel in the Army Corps of Engineers, cites what he calls "rare" examples in our national parks where the reverse is true. The author presents several unique engineering ideas, including cutting off the overflow of Niagara Falls during the night and storing the water in Lake Erie for power development. Chittenden sided with the city of San Francisco in the Hetch Hetchy Reservoir controversy.

Huth, Hans. NATURE AND THE AMERICAN: THREE CENTURIES OF CHANGING ATTITUDES. Berkeley and Los Angeles: University of California Press, 1957. xvii, 250 p. Illustrated, with plates. Notes, pp. 213-27. Bibliography, pp. 229-40.

Chapters 5-9 deal in part with travels, landscape reporting, and the picturesque. See also the annotation for this title in Chapter 1, Section A: General Studies.

Jones, Howard Mumford. "American Landscape." In his O STRANGE NEW WORLD, AMERICAN CULTURE: THE FORMATIVE YEARS, chap. 10. New York: Viking, 1964.

Discussion of landscape description in literary works and its pictorialization in art of the eighteenth and nineteenth centuries.

_____. "Landscape and Microscope." In his THE AGE OF ENERGY: VARIETIES OF AMERICAN EXPERIENCE, 1865-1915, chap. 7. New York: Viking, 1971.

Jones describes four great categories of response to the American landscape: "a sense of delight and terror, a belief in limitless natural resources..., a greed to possess as much land as possible, and a curiosity to find out what makes nature 'work'." In illustrating these categories, Jones discusses George Perkins Marsh and the effect and implications of his book, MAN AND NATURE. He also examines some of the more well known nature writers--Muir, Burroughs, Clarence King, and Frank Bolles--and briefly looks at the rise of the conservation movement.

Pomeroy, Earl. IN SEARCH OF THE GOLDEN WEST: THE TOURIST IN WESTERN AMERICA. New York: Knopf, 1957. xii, 233 p. Plates.

A documented, well-written social history. Describes the various resorts and scenic tourist attractions as well as the attributes and attitudes of the hordes of "argonauts" who visited scenic wonders of the West.

Rhodes, Harrison. "American Holidays: The Sea Shore." HARPER'S MONTHLY MAGAZINE 129 (June 1914): 3-15.

See next item.

_____. "American Holidays: Fresh Water and Inland Valleys." HARPER'S MONTHLY MAGAZINE 129 (July 1914): 211-21.

See next item.

_____. "American Holidays" Springs and Mountains." HARPER'S MONTHLY MAGAZINE 129 (September 1914): 536-47.

These pieces are devoted to a discussion of the scenes of American vacations. Emphasis is upon the social and cultural aspects. Presented in a rambling mode with great literary pretense, the pieces are nevertheless valuable as contemporary views of how the affluent and upper-middle classes spent their vacations and of their attitudes toward scenery.

Shepard, Paul, Jr. "The Nature of Tourism." LANDSCAPE 5, no. 1 (Summer 1955): 29-33.

An interesting commentary upon the nature of tourism, primarily in the United States. Shepard points out that "boobism," or insensitivity to landscape, is not a creation of the twentieth century, but has roots in the past.

Wooley, Mary E. "The Development of the Love of Romantic Scenery in America." AMERICAN HISTORICAL REVIEW 3, no. 1 (October 1897): 56-66.

Traces the development from the time of the earliest settlements
to the beginning of the American Revolution. Roderick Nash
challenges her assertion that the love of romantic scenery became
fully established between 1780 and 1785. (See Nash's WILDER-
NESS AND THE AMERICAN MIND, p. 55n.)

C. THE ESTHETICS OF LANDSCAPE

Leopold, Luna B. "Landscape Esthetics: How to Quantify the Scenics of a
River Valley." NATURAL HISTORY 78, no. 8 (October 1969): 35-45.

Leopold describes a "new language of numbers" that measures the
appeal of landscape without using economic or sentimental values.

Sargent, Charles S. "The Love of Nature." GARDEN AND FOREST 5,
no. 218 (April 28, 1892): 193-94; no. 219 (May 4, 1892): 205-6; no. 220
(May 11, 1892): 218-19; no. 230 (July 20, 1892): 337-38.

Sargent, a noted botanist and director of the Arnold Arboretum at
Harvard, writes of the love of nature and natural beauty. Scenery
is not the whole of natural beauty: a true nature lover is one who
does not need magnificent scenery, but can also exercise his admiration within narrow limits. Thus, the more one knows a place
or thing, the more one cares for it. The author argues for appreciation of the natural microcosm in all its infinite variation as well
as for the macrocosmic effects. A most interesting and valuable
treatment.

Shaler, Nathaniel S. "The Landscape as a Means of Culture." ATLANTIC
MONTHLY 82 (December 1898): 777-85.

An unusual essay on the esthetics of landscape viewing. Shaler
demonstrates his own criteria for landscape appreciation. One must
attain a relationship with the land, study the view from different
perspectives, and, above all, do it alone. A truly contemplative
mood is necessary for the art of seeing into nature. Shaler explains
the stages for the novitiate: seek first the humanized views in and
around towns; explore rural scenery; and third, learn to understand
truly primitive landscapes. The author was for many years professor of geology at Harvard University and Dean of the Lawrence
Scientific School.

D. TRAVEL REPORTS BY REGION

What follows is a selective, regional compilation of travel reports, regional
histories, special studies, and bibliographies. Alphabetical arrangement is
maintained within regions; where included, bibliographies appear at the end
of each regional section. Older titles are usually available in major research
libraries. For the most part, only books have been included because they are

easier to trace in the bibliographic record. Periodical accounts, however, are voluminous and many are important; yet, a truly significant selection would have called for a compilation beyond the bounds of manageability.

1. The East, General

Ferris, George T., ed. OUR NATIVE LAND; OR, GLANCES AT AMERICAN SCENERY AND PLACES, WITH SKETCHES OF LIFE AND ADVENTURE. New York: D. Appleton, 1882. xvi, 615 p. Illustrated. Map.

> A lavishly illustrated gift book. Extolls the virtues of "America the Beautiful." Sold by subscription. Reissued in 1886, 1889, and 1891. Later issues replace the word "Adventure" in the subtitle with the word "Character."

Jackson, Helen Hunt. BITS OF TRAVEL AT HOME. Boston: Roberts Brothers, 1878. vi, 413 p.

> Mrs. Jackson, a well-known author and poet in her day, is now remembered mainly for two works: A CENTURY OF DISHONOR and RAMONA. She wrote a number of other works including several travel reports. In this work, she recounts her impressions of New England, California (including Yosemite), and the Southwest. A popular work, it was reprinted in 1894 and 1909.

Steele, David McConnell. VACATION JOURNEYS EAST AND WEST: DESCRIPTIVE AND DISCURSIVE STORIES OF AMERICAN SUMMER RESORTS. New York and London: Putnam, 1918. xiv, 240 p. Plates. Map.

> Reprinted in part from various periodicals. Steele, a Philadelphia clergyman, writes of his experiences at various resorts from the White Mountains to the Canadian Rockies. A good deal of landscape description is included.

Sweetser, Charles H., comp. BOOK OF SUMMER RESORTS, EXPLAINING WHERE TO FIND THEM, HOW TO FIND THEM, AND THEIR ESPECIAL ADVANTAGES, WITH DETAILS OF TIME TABLES AND PRICES. A COMPLETE GUIDE FOR THE SUMMER TOURIST. New York: "Evening Mail" Office, 1868. Various pagings. Illustrated. Folding maps, "Advertisements for Tourists."

> Devoted to the eastern states from Virginia to Canada, this is a very useful pocket-size guide compiled by the editor of the New York EVENING MAIL. Contains five folding maps and twenty-seven illustrations in over 500 pages. The guide is divided into chapters covering lakes, rivers and mountains; springs and falls; seaside resorts; Canadian resorts; and a chapter on time tables.

2. The Appalachian Region, General

Bryant, William Cullen, ed. PICTURESQUE AMERICA: OR, THE LAND WE
LIVE IN. A DELINEATION BY PEN AND PENCIL OF THE MOUNTAINS,
RIVERS, LAKES, FORESTS, WATER-FALLS, SHORES, CANONS, VALLEYS,
CITIES, AND OTHER PICTURESQUE FEATURES OF OUR COUNTRY. WITH
ILLUSTRATIONS ON STEEL AND WOOD, BY EMINENT AMERICAN ARTISTS.
2 vols. New York: D. Appleton, 1872-74. 568 p., 576 p. Frontispiece.
Illustrated, with plates. 33 cm.

> This work may be considered the pictorial culmination of the nine-
> teenth-century search for the picturesque. No other book in this
> genre compares in the magnitude of conception or in the excellence
> of design and production. Conceived by George S. Appleton and
> Oliver B. Bunce, the enterprise required the services of twenty-
> eight writers and more than thirty artists and engravers and was
> undoubtedly one of the costliest publishing ventures up to that
> time. The artists were sent to all points of the country, from
> Maine to Washington, and from Southern California to Florida,
> although the bulk of description is confined to the region east of
> the Mississippi. PICTURESQUE AMERICA consists of two weighty,
> brown leather-covered volumes (10 x 13 inches), with gilt-edged
> pages and marbled endpapers. Bryant's contribution was limited to
> writing the preface and reading the proof-sheets. The original
> edition was also issued in forty-eight parts in four portfolios be-
> tween 1872 and 1874. Other editions appeared as follows: a
> four-volume edition in 1881-85 by Cassell, Petter, Galpin & Co.,
> London; a three-volume edition (paged continuously) in 1892 by
> D. Appleton, New York; a one-volume revised edition in 1894
> by Appleton; and another four-volume edition by Cassell & Co.
> between 1894 and 1897.

THE HOME BOOK OF THE PICTURESQUE; OR AMERICAN SCENERY, ART,
AND LITERATURE. COMPRISING A SERIES OF ESSAYS BY WASHINGTON
IRVING, W.C. BRYANT, FENIMORE COOPER, MISS COOPER, N.P. WILLIS,
BAYARD TAYLOR, H.T. TUCKERMAN, E.L. MAGOON, DR. BETHUNE, A.B.
STREET, MISS FIELD, ETC. WITH THIRTEEN ENGRAVINGS ON STEEL...
ENGRAVED EXPRESSLY FOR THIS WORK. New York: Putnam, 1852. 188 p.

> Although this work falls outside the chronological scope of this
> bibliography, it is included because of its historical importance
> and because of its popular success. It was reprinted in the same
> year by Leavitt and Allen under the title HOME AUTHORS AND
> HOME ARTISTS, and in 1868 it appeared in modified form with
> more engravings under the title A LANDSCAPE BOOK (see below).
> The book was reprinted in 1967 by Scholar's Facsimiles and Reprints
> with a valuable introduction by Motley F. Deakin.

Hows, John Augustus, illustrator. FOREST SCENES BY WILLIAM CULLEN
BRYANT, HENRY WADSWORTH LONGFELLOW, FITZ-GREENE HALLECK,
ALFRED B. STREET. New York: Hurd and Houghton, 1864. 95 p. Illus-

trated, with plates.

Nature poetry illustrated with engraved scenes of eastern American views. It was also published separately with the titles A FOREST HYMN, IN THE WOODS WITH BRYANT, LONGFELLOW AND HALLECK, and FOREST PICTURES IN THE ADIRONDACKS.

James, Henry. THE AMERICAN SCENE. Introduction and notes by Leon Edel. Bloomington and London: Indiana University Press, 1968. xxiv, 486 p. Notes on chronology and itinerary, pp. 466-82.

First published in London in 1907 and one week later in the United States by Harper. Eleven chapters were also serialized in various American magazines during 1907. A new edition was published in 1946 by Scribner with an introduction by W.H. Auden. The 1907 American edition omitted Section VII of the essay on Florida. Although the bulk of THE AMERICAN SCENE is not concerned with the landscape, two chapters, "New England: An Autumn Impression" and "New York and the Hudson: A Spring Impression," contain observations and reflections on scenery.

Kitchin, William Copeman. A WONDERLAND OF THE EAST, COMPRISING THE LAKE AND MOUNTAIN REGION OF NEW ENGLAND AND EASTERN NEW YORK. "See America First" Series. Boston: Page Co., 1920. xvi, 331 p. Plates. Maps.

Subtitled "A book for those who love to wander among beautiful lakes and rivers, valleys and mountains, or in places made famous by historic men and events; to which is added an afterword on the worth-while in this wonderland of the East, with some suggestions to motor-tourists on how best to find it."

A LANDSCAPE BOOK, BY AMERICAN ARTISTS AND AMERICAN AUTHORS; SIXTEEN ENGRAVINGS ON STEEL, FROM PAINTINGS BY COLE, CHURCH, CROPSEY, DURAND, GIGNOUX, KENSETT, MILLER, RICHARDS, SMILLIE, TALBOT, WEIR. New York: Putnam, 1868. 108 p.

BIBLIOGRAPHY

Stockbridge, Helen E., comp. "A Bibliography of the Southern Appalachian and White Mountain Regions." PROCEEDINGS OF THE SOCIETY OF AMERICAN FORESTERS 6, no. 2 (1911): 173-254.

Arranged in nine classes by author: national forest movement; topography and resources in general; botany; forests and forestry-forest influences; water resources; climatology; geology; mines and mineral resources; and soils. The section on topography contains an excellent listing of nearly 500 travel accounts, guide books, scenic descriptions--articles, books, and state documents--relating to the White Mountains, the Green Mountains, and the Appalachian region to the south of New England. The bibliography also appears separately as an offprint.

3. Maine

Carter, Robert. A SUMMER CRUISE ON THE COAST OF NEW ENGLAND. Boston: Crosby and Nichols, 1864. viii, 261 p.

Chapter 30 describes the author's visit to Mount Desert Island and to Bar Harbor. The visit was made during the summer of 1858 while he was on vacation from his position as Washington correspondent for the NEW YORK TRIBUNE. Though the bulk of the book is devoted to fishing experiences and to descriptions of the crew, Chapter 30 is valuable for the response of an urbanite to the wilderness of Mount Desert.

Hubbard, Lucius L. THE WOODS AND LAKES OF MAINE. A TRIP FROM MOOSEHEAD LAKE TO NEW BRUNSWICK IN A BIRCH-BARK CANOE. Boston: J. R. Osgood, 1884. xvi, 223 p. Illustrated.

An excellent and authoritative book on the Maine woods. Hubbard also wrote a guide book to the Moosehead Lake area in 1879 that went through four editions.

Street, George E. MOUNT DESERT: A HISTORY. Edited and revised by Samuel A. Eliot. Boston and New York: Houghton Mifflin, 1926. x, 339 p. Frontispiece. Plates. Map. Bibliography, pp. 317-28.

The first edition, also edited by Eliot, was published in 1905. Dr. Street collected the materials in the book which, after his death in 1903, were edited by Eliot. The new edition has been corrected and somewhat condensed and a new chapter added. Most of the material is of local and geneological interest; however, the chapters on social conditions, the history of summer colonies, and the bibliographical notes and references are of permanent value. The references contain additional material of interest including guide books, articles, and local histories.

Winthrop, Theodore. LIFE IN THE OPEN AIR, AND OTHER PAPERS. Boston: Ticknor and Fields, 1863. iv, 374 p. Frontispiece. Portrait.

Includes a humorous and somewhat florid account of a trip made in the 1850s through the Adirondacks into the Maine woods to Mount Katahdin and finally down the Penobscot River. Winthrop was accompanied by the painter Frederick E. Church, here given the pseudonym, "Iglesias." Includes an introductory note by George W. Curtis.

4. The Catskills

Evers, Alf. THE CATSKILLS FROM WILDERNESS TO WOODSTOCK. Garden City, N.Y.: Doubleday, 1972. xiv, 821 p. Illustrated. Facsimiles. Photos. Maps. Notes, pp. 723–77. Bibliography, pp. 781–86.

> The Catskill Mountain region is one of the most storied locales in the United States. Evers, a writer, folklorist, and town historian of Woodstock, narrates the history of the Catskills. Based upon an enormous amount of research in regional archives, contemporary accounts, local newspapers, as well as published works of visitors, this book is the definitive account.

Longstreth, Thomas M. THE CATSKILLS. New York: Century Co., 1918. 321 p. Map. Plates. Bibliography, pp. 316–17. Reprint ed., 1970.

> The author and a young companion hiked the greater part of the Catskills in the spring and again in the summer of 1917. Of particular interest is a description of a day spent with John Burroughs. The book is both an appreciation of, and a guidebook to, the Catskills.

Rockwell, Charles. THE CATSKILL MOUNTAINS AND THE REGIONS AROUND. THEIR SCENERY, LEGENDS, AND HISTORY; WITH SKETCHES IN PROSE AND VERSE BY COOPER, IRVING, BRYANT, COLE AND OTHERS. Rev. ed. New York: Taintor Brothers, 1867. xii, 351 p. Plates.

> The author, pastor of a Reformed Dutch Church in the Catskills, brought together a great deal of local history from the writings of others with interpolations of his own. Rockwell's descriptions of the Catskills, the region's weather, natural history, and scenery are of some interest. The book went through several later editions.

Van Zandt, Roland. THE CATSKILL MOUNTAIN HOUSE. New Brunswick, N.J.: Rutgers University Press, 1966. xxii, 416 p. Colored plates. Figures. Maps. Plans. Notes, pp. 347–80. Bibliography, pp. 381–97.

> The story of the most celebrated resort hotel in New York, and one of the great scenic wonders of the East. Built in 1824, the hotel was expanded during the nineteenth century and finally closed in 1942. The Mountain House was destroyed by fire in 1963.

5. The White Mountains

Drake, Samuel Adams. THE HEART OF THE WHITE MOUNTAINS, THEIR LEGEND AND SCENERY. With illustrations by W[illiam]. H[amilton]. Gibson. New York: Harper, 1882. xii, 318 p. Illustrations. Portraits. Maps. 30 1/2 cm.

> The author's descriptions and impressions were derived from three

visits. The narrative is often vivid and nearly always interesting. The engravings from illustrations by William Hamilton Gibson are dramatic and well chosen, if somewhat somber in tone.

Kilbourne, Frederick W. CHRONICLES OF THE WHITE MOUNTAINS. Boston and New York: Houghton Mifflin, 1916. xxxiii, 433 p. Illustrated.

Presents a detailed account of the region's history, including Indian legends, early settlements, discovery and exploration, travel accounts, hotels and resorts, and trails. Although there is no formal bibliography, the author provides considerable documentation in the body of the text.

King, Thomas Starr. THE WHITE HILLS: THEIR LEGENDS, LANDSCAPE AND POETRY. Boston: Crosby, Nichols, 1860. xv, 403 p. Illustrated. Map.

Illustrated with forty engravings of White Mountain views, this book was intended as a guide to, and an appreciation of, the "noble landscapes." The "poetry" in the title is not restricted to the local variety, but includes standard American nature verse as well as European poetry. Two chapters (on exploration and vegetation) were contributed by Edward Tuckerman. Reprinted several times.

Sweetser, Moses Foster. A GUIDE TO THE WHITE MOUNTAINS. Edited and revised by John Nelson. With maps and panoramas. Boston and New York: Houghton Mifflin, 1918. xv, 387 p. Folding plates.

First published in Boston in 1876 under the title THE WHITE MOUNTAINS: A HANDBOOK FOR TRAVELERS, this guide was extremely popular, going through many editions. The revised edition by John Nelson in the most useful.

Ward, Julius H. THE WHITE MOUNTAINS: A GUIDE TO THEIR INTERPRETATION. New York: D. Appleton, 1890. viii, 258 p. Plates. Folding map.

A very personal and appealing interpretation of the mountains, their scenic description and the emotions felt by the author while touring the region. "It is written in illustration of the modern interpretation of Nature which has been taught us by Emerson and Wordsworth and Ruskin, and is an attempt to express the enrichment of human life that comes from the knowledge of the harmony that exists between mountains and ourselves, when they are approached through the sympathetic imagination" (Preface). The mood created by certain passages is reminiscent of the writing of John Muir.

BIBLIOGRAPHY

Bent, Allen H. A BIBLIOGRAPHY OF THE WHITE MOUNTAINS. Boston: Published for the Appalachian Mountain Club by Houghton Mifflin, 1911. vii, 114 p. Frontispiece. Portraits.

A valuable and comprehensive list. Includes "classics," guide books, magazine articles, incidental references to fiction, poetry, maps, engravings, and a list of newspapers containing notices of the mountains. No specific references to newpaper articles. Especially valuable is the indexing of articles that appeared in the Club's journal, APPALACHIA, which receives only haphazard indexing elsewhere. Entries, although complete in every other way, do not list publishers.

Downes, William Howe. "The Literature of the White Mountains." NEW ENGLAND MAGAZINE 4 (August 1891): 717-30.

A bibliographical essay.

6. The Adirondack Mountains

Carson, Russell Mack Little. PEAKS AND PEOPLE OF THE ADIRONDACKS. Garden City, N.Y.: Doubleday, Page, 1927. xxii, 269 p. Illustrated. Portraits. Maps on endpapers.

Composed of sketches about forty-six peaks of the Adirondacks that rise to an elevation of 4,000 feet or more. Included is information on their names, records of first ascents, and trail history, as well as anecdotes of the men and women involved in the mountaineering history of the region. Tables provide information on rated Adirondack views, first recorded ascents, heights, and order of naming of the various peaks. The book was sponsored by the Adirondack Mountain Club.

Donaldson, Alfred Lee. A HISTORY OF THE ADIRONDACKS. 2 vols. New York: Century Co., 1921. Plates. Portraits. Folding maps and charts. Bibliography, Vol. 2, pp. 229-363.

A labor of love by a noted collector of Adirondackiana. This work will probably remain the definitive history for the period it covers.

Emerson, Ralph Waldo. "The Adirondacs." In MAY-DAY AND OTHER PIECES, pp. 43-62. Boston: Ticknor and Fields, 1867.

Based upon an excursion in August 1858 made by Emerson, James Russell Lowell, Louis Agassiz, W. J. Stillman, and others. Their summer camp was later known as the "Philosopher's Camp." Emerson dedicated the poem to his "fellow travelers." A fascinating account of the excursion by a participant may be read in:

> Stillman, William J. "The Philosopher's Camp. Emerson, Agassiz, Lowell and Others in the Adirondacks." THE CENTURY 46, no. 4 (August 1893): 598-606.

Headley, Joel Tyler. THE ADIRONDACK: OR LIFE IN THE WOODS. New ed., enl. New York: Scribner, Armstrong, 1875. xi, 416 p. Plates. Map.

> First published in 1849, this best-selling book went through many editions, the last being in 1875. The author, an ex-minister and journalist, became an immensely popular writer. THE ADIRONDACK was the best descriptive book on the mountains to appear in the 1850s. It is filled with fishing stories.

Longstreth, Thomas M. THE ADIRONDACKS. New York: Century Co., 1917. viii, 370 p. Folding map. Plates.

> Based on a trip through the mountains made by the author and a companion, this book is interesting if a trifle "literary."

Lossing, Benson J. THE HUDSON, FROM THE WILDERNESS TO THE SEA. New York: Virtue and Yorston, 1866. vii, 464 p. Illustrated. Reprint ed., 1972.

> Illustrated with 306 wood engravings from drawings by the author. In the summer of 1859, the author, his wife, and some friends began a tour from the headwaters of the Hudson in the Adirondacks to the sea. The author's pen and pencil sketches in this volume were published originally in the London ART-JOURNAL during 1860 and 1861. Lossing was a careful observer and his depiction of scenes along the river has historical value.

Murray, William Henry Harrison. ADVENTURES IN THE WILDERNESS, OR CAMP-LIFE IN THE ADIRONDACKS. Boston: Fields, Osgood, 1869. vi, 236 p. Illustrated.

> Published with variant titles. Although others had written and described the wonders of the Adirondacks, notably J.T. Headley (above), Murray's work was the most influential in popularizing the area. His ADVENTURES takes the form of anecdotal guide to the mountains with information on camping, fishing, hunting, and appropriate equipment. It has been called mostly fiction, and is so classified in the ADIRONDACK BIBLIOGRAPHY (below). Murray's many books about the region of the Adirondacks resulted in the sobriquet "Adirondack Murray." Warder Cadbury's introduction to the edition of the ADVENTURES published by Syracuse University Press (see next item) is the most useful and scholarly biographical source on Murray's life and work.

_____. ADVENTURES IN THE WILDERNESS. Edited by William K. Verner. With an introduction and notes by Warder H. Cadbury. Syracuse, N.Y.: The Adirondack Museum/Syracuse University Press, 1970. 75 p., vi, 236 p. Appendix, pp. 77-95. Illustrated. Map in pocket.

This is a splendid book. The original edition is reprinted and photographically enlarged for easier reading. Cadbury contributes a lengthy introduction with contemporary illustrations and his research uncovered sources that are not found in the ADIRONDACK BIBLIOGRAPHY (below). Included in an appendix is a "Reply to His Calumniators," written by Murray and published in the NEW YORK DAILY TRIBUNE on October 23, 1869.

_____. LAKE CHAMPLAIN AND ITS SHORES. Boston: De Wolfe, Fiske & Co., 1890. 261 p. Frontispiece.

An advertisement and an appreciation. Murray narrates the history and describes the scenic qualities of the area. Yachting, camping, and fishing opportunities are described. Of special interest is a chapter, "The Great National Park," in which Murray calls for national park status for a huge area of land from Niagara Falls to the Maine coast.

_____. "Reminiscences of My Literary and Outdoor Life." THE INDEPEN-DENT 57 (July 28, 1904): 194-200; (August 4, 1904): 277-80.

"Reminiscences" was completed only weeks before Murray's death.

Although eulogic in tone, an important source of information about Murray's life and work as a Congregational minister in Boston, a noted sportsman, writer, and lecturer is:

Radford, Harry V. ADIRONDACK MURRAY: A BIO-GRAPHICAL APPRECIATION. New York, Montreal, and London: Broadway Publishing Co., 1905. 84 p. Plates.

Warner, Charles Dudley. IN THE WILDERNESS. Boston: Houghton, Osgood, 1878. 176 p.

Warner, a minor essayist of the Gilded Age, wrote a number of sketches of adventure, hunting, and fishing in the Adirondacks. IN THE WILDERNESS contains a number of his more interesting essays. The book appears in numerous editions and in his COM-PLETE WRITINGS (1904), Volume 6.

White, William Chapman. ADIRONDACK COUNTRY. Introduction by L. Fred Ayvazian, M.D.; afterword by Ruth M. White. New York: Knopf, 1967. ix, 325 p. Illustrated. Map.

First edition published in 1954. This is the best introduction to the history, geography, and natural history of the region. Donald-son's work (above) remains the standard comprehensive account.

BIBLIOGRAPHY

Adirondack Mountain Club. Bibliography Committee. ADIRONDACK BIBLIOG-
RAPHY: A LIST OF BOOKS, PAMPHLETS AND PERIODICAL ARTICLES PUB-
LISHED THROUGH THE YEAR 1955. Gabriels, N.Y.: Adirondack Mountain
Club, Inc., 1958. xviii, 354 p. Map. (Distributed by New York University
Press.)

> One of the most useful and comprehensive bibliographies of its
> kind. Brief annotations are given for some titles and reference to
> book reviews is often provided for significant works. Topics in-
> clude general history, geography, natural history, social and eco-
> nomic history, health and medicine, religious history, education,
> recreation, clubs and private preserves, biography, art and litera-
> ture, and juveniles.

_____. ADIRONDACK BIBLIOGRAPHY SUPPLEMENT, 1956-1965. A LIST OF
BOOKS, PAMPHLETS AND PERIODICAL ARTICLES. Introduction by William
K. Verner. Blue Mountain Lake, N.Y.: Adirondack Museum, 1973. xl,
198 p. Map. (Distributed by Syracuse University Press.)

> The introduction by Verner, curator of the Adirondack Museum,
> is a valuable thirty-two-page historical, bibliographical essay.

7. Niagara Falls

Dow, Charles Mason. ANTHOLOGY AND BIBLIOGRAPHY OF NIAGARA
FALLS. 2 vols. Albany, N.Y.: Published by the State of New York,
J.B. Lyon, Printers, 1921. xvi, 1423 p. Illustrated, with plates (some
colored). Photos. Maps.

> This is a monumental and valuable work. The author was President
> of the Commission of the State Reservation at Niagara from 1903 to
> 1914 and an active conservationist. The alphabetical list of titles
> is contained in Volume 2, pp. 1269-1423. The bulk of the work
> is arranged in classified order by chapter. Within each chapter
> the arrangement is chronological with the date and author in the
> margin for easy reference. Many of the titles have both the
> compiler's own annotations and a selection from the work. Twelve
> chapters are arranged as follows: Niagara Discovered: The French
> Period; Other Eighteenth Century Accounts: The English Period;
> Travelers' Original Accounts, 1801-1840; Travelers' Original Ac-
> counts since 1840; Niagara--Historical and Reminiscent; Flora and
> Fauna; Science, Geology and Physics; Music, Poetry, Fiction;
> Maps and Pictures; Industrial Niagara; Preservation of the Falls;
> Open Road Guides, Railroads, Canals, Bridges. Although Dow
> did not claim his work to be exhaustive, it is as nearly so as one
> man could hope for.

8. The Southern Appalachians

Frome, Michael. STRANGERS IN HIGH PLACES: THE STORY OF THE GREAT
SMOKY MOUNTAINS. Garden City, N.Y.: Doubleday, 1966. ix, 394 p.
Maps. A Camping and Hiking Appendix, bibliography, and notes, pp. 357-86.

Probably the best and most comprehensive book on the region yet
published. Frome's history of the Great Smokies is well written
and thoroughly documented. Altogether a fascinating and valuable
work.

Pangborn, Joseph Gladdings. PICTURESQUE B. AND O., HISTORICAL AND
DESCRIPTIVE. Chicago: Knight and Leonard, 1882. 152 p. Illustrated.

Describes the scenery and history of the territory along the route
of the Baltimore and Ohio Railroad. Clark, in TRAVELS IN THE
NEW SOUTH, (Volume 1, p. 430; see Chapter 2, Section A:
Bibliographies), called it "a better than usual commercial publication for this period." It contains seventy engravings of paintings
by Thomas Moran. Pangborn (1844-1914), journalist, railroad
official, author, and traveler, worked for the NEW YORK TIMES
and the KANSAS CITY TIMES before becoming associated with the
B. & O. as an advertising agent. For biographical information
see THE NATIONAL CYCLOPEDIA OF AMERICAN BIOGRAPHY,
Volume 16, pp. 282-83.

Taylor, Bayard. AT HOME AND ABROAD: A SKETCH-BOOK OF LIFE,
SCENERY, AND MEN. New York: Putnam, 1860. 500 p.

Collected travel pieces published earlier in periodicals. Of
particular interest are Taylor's impressions of the Mammoth Cave in
Kentucky written in 1855.

Warner, Charles Dudley. ON HORSEBACK. A TOUR IN VIRGINIA, NORTH
CAROLINA AND TENNESSEE, WITH NOTES OF TRAVEL IN MEXICO AND
CALIFORNIA. Boston and New York: Houghton Mifflin, 1883. 331 p.

Graphic scenes of Southern Appalachian countrysides and human
society. Warner climbed Mt. Mitchell, the highest mountain in
the East. See Chapter 2, Section A: Bibliographies, for Clark,
TRAVELS IN THE NEW SOUTH, no. 493.

9. Transcontinental Reports

Bowles, Samuel. OUR NEW WEST. RECORDS OF TRAVEL BETWEEN THE
MISSISSIPPI RIVER AND THE PACIFIC OCEAN. OVER THE PLAINS--OVER
THE MOUNTAINS--THROUGH THE GREAT INTERIOR BASIN--OVER THE
SIERRA NEVADAS--TO AND UP AND DOWN THE PACIFIC COAST...
Published by subscription only. Hartford, Conn.: Hartford Publishing

Co.; New York: J.D. Dennison; Chicago: J.A. Stodard, 1869. xx, 528 p.
Map. Illustrated. Portraits.

Bowles, the well-known editor of the Springfield, Massachusetts,
REPUBLICAN, traveled to the West during the summers of 1865
and 1868. Bowles, immensely impressed by the uniqueness of the
western scenery, visited Yosemite Valley and the Colorado Rockies.
His observations about the value of wild lands for the use of public
parks are valuable. He also recommended similar park lands be
set aside in the East, specifically, Niagara Falls, the Adirondacks,
and in the mountain and lake country of Maine. Much of an
earlier work entitled ACROSS THE CONTINENT: A SUMMER'S
JOURNEY TO THE ROCKY MOUNTAINS, THE MORMONS, AND
THE PACIFIC COAST, WITH SPEAKER COLFAX (1865) has been
incorporated in the present volume.

Buel, James William. AMERICA'S WONDERLANDS. A PICTORIAL AND
DESCRIPTIVE HISTORY OF OUR COUNTRY'S SCENIC MARVELS AS DELIN-
EATED BY PEN AND CAMERA. Boston: J.S. Round; New York: Hunt &
Eaton, Williams & Cox, W.W. Wilson; Philadelphia: Historical Publishing
Co.; Richmond, Va.: B.F. Johnston; San Francisco: J. Dewing; Vancouver:
MacGregor, 1893. 503 p. Illustrated, with colored plates. 23 1/2 x 32 cm.

Published by subscription. Buel (1849-1920), whose career included jobs as librarian, clerk, attorney, newspaper editor and
reporter, and successful author, wrote dozens of books. Until
1897, the aggregate sales of his books exceeded 6 million. In
1890 Buel, subsidized by his publishers and given free passage on
the nation's railroads, embarked upon a nationwide trip accompanied by three photographers. Using a specially designed railway
coach, he and his companions toured the country from Maine to
Alaska. The resulting book, AMERICA'S WONDERLANDS, contains 500 views of scenic attractions accompanied by an interpretation by Buel.

Ludlow, Fitz Hugh. THE HEART OF THE CONTINENT: A RECORD OF
TRAVEL ACROSS THE PLAINS AND IN OREGON, WITH AN EXAMINATION
OF THE MORMON PRINCIPLE. New York: Hurd and Houghton, 1870. vi,
568 p. Plates. Portraits.

Ludlow (1836-70), a well-known author, editor, and New York
drama critic in the 1850s and 60s, traveled overland to California
for his health in 1863. Many of the chapters in this book appeared
originally in the ATLANTIC MONTHLY. Ludlow was a good
observer, interested not only in macrocosmic effects of scenery,
but in the smaller details of nature. The book is well written,
the style easy and not rhetorical as in many nineteenth-century
travel reports. Ludlow's route took him through the Pike's Peak
area, north to Salt Lake City, west to San Francisco and east to
Yosemite, where he spent seven weeks. He rode horseback into
Oregon as far as the Columbia River before returning to San Fran-

cisco by steamer. HEART OF THE CONTINENT is a notable
and valuable travel account.

Murphy, Thomas D. THREE WONDERLANDS OF THE AMERICAN WEST,
BEING THE NOTES OF A TRAVELER, CONCERNING THE YELLOWSTONE
PARK, THE YOSEMITE NATIONAL PARK, AND THE GRAND CANYON OF
THE COLORADO RIVER, WITH A CHAPTER ON THE OTHER WONDERS OF
THE GREAT AMERICAN WEST. WITH SIXTEEN REPRODUCTIONS IN COLOR
FROM ORIGINAL PAINTINGS BY THOMAS MORAN. "See America First"
Series. Rev. ed. Boston: Page Co., 1913. xiv, 184 p. Plates. Maps.

This is a slightly corrected version of the first edition published
in 1912. In addition to the Moran reproductions, it contains
thirty-two "duogravures from photographs."

Richardson, Albert D. BEYOND THE MISSISSIPPI: FROM THE GREAT RIVER
TO THE GREAT OCEAN. LIFE AND ADVENTURE ON THE PRAIRIES, MOUN-
TAINS, AND PACIFIC COAST...1857-1867. Hartford, Conn.: American
Publishing Co., 1867. xvi, 572 p. Illustrated.

Issued by subscription only. Includes more than 200 illustrations
and engravings from photos and sketches. Richardson, an able
journalist and, later, chief correspondent for the NEW YORK
TRIBUNE, compiled the book from his reports to the papers. The
book was extremely popular.

Steele, David M[cConnell]. GOING ABROAD OVERLAND: STUDIES OF
PLACES AND PEOPLE IN THE FAR WEST. New York and London: Putnam,
1917. x, 197 p. Frontispiece. Plates. Folding map.

Based upon three transcontinental trips, these studies were written
as articles for the PHILADELPHIA PRESS. The author, a Philadelphia clergyman, was both a good traveler and an excellent observer. His studies include the Grand Canyon, Lake Tahoe, Glacier
National Park, Yellowstone, Yosemite, and Rocky Mountain National
Park. Steele's avowed purpose was to acquaint easterners with
the beauties of the West.

Thayer, William M. MARVELS OF THE NEW WEST, A VIVID PORTRAYAL
OF THE STUPENDOUS MARVELS IN THE VAST WONDERLAND WEST OF THE
MISSOURI RIVER. Norwich, Conn.: Henry Bill Publishing Co., 1890. xxxvi,
715 p. Maps. Engravings.

Sold by subscription only, this "book of marvels" is drawn largely
from the writings of visitors to the West, government and railroad
survey reports, and tourist guides. The first section or "book" is
entitled "Marvels of Nature" and is copiously illustrated with
engravings of scenes of mountains, deserts, forests, rock forma-
tions, etc. Intended for the edification of the eastern stay-at-
home, this book stresses pictorially the curiosities of nature. It

is of little value except as an example of a genre of scenery
reporting for the gullible and wonder-hungry easterner.

10. Yellowstone Park

The travel and descriptive literature of the Yellowstone region is voluminous.
The Yellowstone bibliography (below), for example, contains seventy-nine pages
of titles relating to the history, travel, and description of Yellowstone National
Park from 1868 to 1936. The works chosen for this section are a small but
representative selection of materials. Several of the titles in Chapter 2,
Section D 9: Transcontinental Reports, also contain relevant observations on
Yellowstone, as do such works as PICTURESQUE AMERICA (above) and PICTUR-
ESQUE CALIFORNIA (below).

Baker, Ray Stannard. "A Place of Marvels. Yellowstone Park As It Now
Is." CENTURY MAGAZINE 66, no. 4 (August 1903): 481-91.

> Baker was an excellent reporter. In addition to scenic descriptions,
> vividly drawn, he provides a humorous look at tourists in the park.

Chittenden, Hiram Martin. THE YELLOWSTONE NATIONAL PARK, HISTORI-
CAL AND DESCRIPTIVE. New ed., enl. Cincinnati: Stewart & Kidd, [1918].
vii, 350 p. Plates. Maps. Reprints eds., 1949, 1964.

> The author, a retired army officer, spent two tours of duty in
> Yellowstone. His love for the park's wilderness areas is apparent.
> First published in 1895, the present edition contains two sections,
> one historical, the second descriptive. The latter part deals with
> scenery, geology, natural history, and natural resources. Several
> tours for ·prospective visitors are suggested.

Haupt, Herman, Jr. THE YELLOWSTONE NATIONAL PARK. A COMPLETE
GUIDE TO AND DESCRIPTION OF THE WONDROUS YELLOWSTONE REGION
OF WYOMING AND MONTANA TERRITORIES OF THE UNITED STATES OF
AMERICA. New York and Philadelphia: J.M. Stoddart, 1883. 190 p.
Illustrated. Folding map.

> Appendices provide information on railroad fares, trip expenses,
> locations and times of eruption of the principal geysers, park rules,
> minerals, and park elevations.

Hayden, Ferdinand V. "Wonders of the West II: More about the Yellowstone."
SCRIBNER'S MONTHLY MAGAZINE 3, no. 4 (February 1872): 388-96.

> Hayden led the first official government survey expedition into the
> Yellowstone area in 1871. He describes the Grand Canyon of the
> Yellowstone, Yellowstone Lake, and the Geysers.

Langford, Nathaniel P. "The Wonders of the Yellowstone." SCRIBNER'S
MONTHLY MAGAZINE 2, no. 1 (May 1871): 1-17; 2, no. 2 (June 1871):
113-28. Illustrated.

Langford made a trip to the Yellowstone in the summer of 1870 and,
in this series, he describes the major scenic features. He later
enlisted in the drive to create a national park. Illustrated with
views by Thomas Moran.

Stanley, Edwin J. RAMBLES IN WONDERLAND, OR UP THE YELLOWSTONE,
AND AMONG THE GEYSERS AND OTHER CURIOSITIES OF THE NATIONAL
PARK. New York: D. Appleton, 1878. vii, 179 p. Folding map. Plates.

The author's "rambles" took place during the months of August
and September 1873. The fifth and last edition, published in 1898,
contains directions for tourists wishing to visit the park.

BIBLIOGRAPHY

U.S. National Park Service. "A Bibliography of Yellowstone." In A BIBLI-
OGRAPHY OF NATIONAL PARKS AND MONUMENTS WEST OF THE MISSIS-
SIPPI...vol. 1, pp. iii-200. [Berkeley, Calif.?]: 1941. Mimeographed.

A comprehensive and invaluable bibliography with occasional
annotations. The section on history, travel, etc., is the major
source for scenic and descriptive materials. Contains books,
periodical and newspaper articles, and government documents.
Omits poetry, maps, and most fiction. Coverage to 1936.

11. The Rocky Mountains

Bishop, Isabella Lucy (Bird). A LADY'S LIFE IN THE ROCKY MOUNTAINS.
Introduction by Daniel Boorstin. Norman: University of Oklahoma Press, 1960.
xxiii, 253 p.

A classic, sympathetic account by one of the most celebrated
women travelers of the nineteenth century. Mrs. Bishop visited
the Rockies in the autumn and early winter of 1873 on her return
from the Hawaiian Islands to England. First published in the
English periodical LEISURE HOUR in 1878, the account was published in book form by John Murray in London in 1879. G.P.
Putnam's Sons brought out the American edition in the same year.

Bowles, Samuel. THE SWITZERLAND OF AMERICA. A SUMMER VACATION
IN THE PARKS AND MOUNTAINS OF COLORADO. Springfield, Mass.:
Samuel Bowles & Co.; Boston: Lea & Shepard, 1869. iv, 166 p.

Bowles, a careful observer, was immensely impressed by the
Colorado Rockies and their environs. This work, along with his

two other western "reports," has value as an example of a culti-
vated New Englander's response to the wonders of the West. (See
also Bowles, Samuel. OUR NEW WEST, Chapter 2, Section 9:
Transcontinental Reports.)

Gage, Emma A. WESTERN WANDERINGS AND SUMMER SAUNTERINGS.
Baltimore: Lord Baltimore Press, The Friedenwald Co., 1900. 262 p. Frontispiece. Illustrated.

Originally appeared as letters written for the EVENING CAPITAL
(Annapolis, Maryland), of which the author's father was editor. The
descriptions, somewhat genteel in character, are based upon observations made in Colorado; Kansas City, Missouri; and Omaha,
Nebraska.

Ingersoll, Ernest. KNOCKING ROUND THE ROCKIES. New York: Harper,
1883. viii, 220 p. Illustrated.

Extracted and reworked from material published in various magazines.

_____. THE CREST OF THE CONTINENT: A RECORD OF A SUMMERS
RAMBLE IN THE ROCKY MOUNTAINS AND BEYOND. Chicago: R.R.
Donneley & Sons, 1885. 344 p. Frontispiece. Illustrated. Folding map.

Ingersoll (1852-1946) received his training at Harvard under Agassiz
and for a time he was a collaborator at the Smithsonian. After
joining the Hayden Survey as a naturalist, he worked for the NEW
YORK TRIBUNE as a western correspondent in 1874. Later, he
joined the TRIBUNE's editorial staff, and also acted as natural
history editor for FOREST AND STREAM. Ingersoll wrote many
pieces during the 1870s and 1880s for the periodical press, traveling
widely in the West to gather material. He spent three months
collecting material for THE CREST OF THE CONTINENT, his most
popular book, which, between 1885 and 1901, went through forty-
two printings. It is probable that as many as 100,000 copies were
sold. Ingersoll wrote many popular natural history books and some
juveniles, but none achieved the popularity of the two works listed
here. In 1969 the Rio Grande Press brought out a facsimile reprint,
photographically enlarged, with an added introduction, a new
index, and a section of photographs of narrow-gauge railroad loco-
motives, cars, stations, etc., belonging to the Denver & Rio
Grande Western Railroad.

Taylor, Bayard. COLORADO: A SUMMER TRIP. New York: Putnam, 1867.
185 p.

Another in a long series of travel books by Taylor. The amount of
space devoted to scenic description is small compared to that given
to his concern for the state's social, political, and economic development.

12. The Grand Canyon and the Southwest

Baker, Ray Stannard. "The Great Southwest." CENTURY MAGAZINE 64, no. 1 (May 1902): 5-51; 64, no. 2 (June 1902): 213-25. Illustrated with half-tones.

Excellent reportage concerning the scenery of the area, its inhabitants, economic growth potential, etc.

Dellenbaugh, Frederick S. THE ROMANCE OF THE COLORADO RIVER. New York and London: Putnam, 1902. xxxv, 399 p. Illustrated, with photos and maps. Reprint ed., 1962.

Dellenbaugh was a member of Powell's second Colorado River expedition (1871-73). As the party's artist, he made sketches for the geologists and assisted in map-making. In this book, he traces the history of the discovery and exploration of the River, including his own part.

_____. A CANYON VOYAGE: THE NARRATIVE OF THE SECOND POWELL EXPEDITION DOWN THE GREEN-COLORADO RIVER FROM WYOMING, AND THE EXPLORATIONS ON LAND IN THE YEARS 1871 and 1872. Foreword by William H. Goetzmann. New Haven and London: Yale University Press, 1962. xxxvi, 277 p. Illustrated, maps.

First published in 1908 and reprinted in 1926, this book was awarded the John Burroughs Medal in 1932 "for the best literary work relating to nature."

Krutch, Joseph Wood. GRAND CANYON; TODAY AND ALL ITS YESTER-DAYS. New York: William Sloane, 1958. 276 p. Illustrated.

Beautifully written. Geological description, human history, exploration, discussion of the problems of preservation versus recreation, and other topics--all informed by Krutch's familiar concern for ecology.

Powell, John Wesley. "The Cañons of the Colorado." SCRIBNER'S MONTH-LY MAGAZINE 9, nos. 3-5 (January-March 1875): 293-310, 394-409, 523-37.

See next item.

_____. "An Overland Trip to the Grand Cañon." SCRIBNER'S MONTHLY MAGAZINE 10, no. 6 (October 1875): 659-78.

This is the first account by Powell of his two famous Colorado River expeditions. Powell merged the accounts for publication in the popular press. The articles were brought together in book form in 1875 and published by the Smithsonian Institution under the title EXPLORATION OF THE COLORADO RIVER OF THE WEST AND ITS TRIBUTARIES.

BIBLIOGRAPHIES

Edwards, Elza Ivan. THE ENDURING DESERT: A DESCRIPTIVE BIBLIOGRAPHY.
Foreword by Russ Leadabrand. [Los Angeles]: Ward Ritchie Press, 1969. xiii,
306 p.

> An invaluable work, THE ENDURING DESERT is restricted to
> Southern California and excludes books on the Colorado River.
> It contains more than 2000 items, including books and magazine
> articles. The arrangement is alphabetical by author. Annotations
> vary in length from a paragraph to several pages. The author
> published an earlier bibliography of Southern California deserts in
> 1958 called DESERT VOICES.

Farquhar, Francis P. THE BOOKS OF THE COLORADO RIVER AND THE
GRAND CANYON; A SELECTIVE BIBLIOGRAPHY. Early California Travels,
vol. XII. Los Angeles: Glen Dawson, 1953. xi, 75 p.

> A very helpful little book. Farquhar lists some 170 books; the
> annotations are always useful and often provide critical insight
> into the relative importance of the titles. Part IV, "The Grand
> Canyon Appreciated," is particularly valuable for travelers' re-
> sponses to "scenic wonders."

13. Yosemite

Travel literature and scenic reports concerning the Yosemite region are numerous.
Only the more significant examples of this writing have been selected, the
emphasis being upon early works, culminating with John Muir's YOSEMITE.
For additional material, the reader should consult the bibliographies by Farquhar
and the National Park Service noted below. Scenic reports of California in
general are omitted because this literature is voluminous and essentially promotional in nature. The bibliographies by Cowan and Rocq, although not organized
for this purpose, may be consulted for such materials:

> Cowan, Robert Ernest, and Cowan, Robert Granniss. A BIBLIOG-
> RAPHY OF THE HISTORY OF CALIFORNIA, 1510-1930. San
> Francisco: John Henry Nash, 1933. iv, 825 p.
>
> > A descriptive bibliography arranged by main entry with
> > a title and subject index, plus a chronological index.
> > Issued separately in three volumes, paged continuously.
> > A supplementary volume by Robert Granniss Cowan was
> > published in 1964 by Torrez Press (Los Angeles). This
> > fourth volume continues the pagination of the original three.

> Rocq, Margaret Miller. CALIFORNIA LOCAL HISTORY; A BIBLI-
> OGRAPHY AND UNION LIST OF LIBRARY HOLDINGS. Edited

for the California Library Association. 2nd ed., rev. and enl.
Stanford, Calif.: Stanford University Press, 1970. xv, 611 p.
Map.

> Arranged by county, subdivided by city, with separate
> sections for statewide, northern and central California,
> and southern California. Author index.

YOSEMITE REPORTS

Bromley, Isaac H. "The Wonders of the West--I: The Big Trees and the
Yosemite." SCRIBNER'S MONTHLY MAGAZINE 3, no. 3 (January 1872):
261-77.

> Bromley, a well-known journalist for the NEW YORK TRIBUNE,
> spent five days in Yosemite in 1871 in company with six others,
> two of whom are referred to as "the Governor" and "the Congress-
> man." His account is lively and humorous ("it beats all how
> common Congressmen were that season"). His descriptions of
> Yosemite scenery are, to some extent, conventional. The Big
> Trees disappointed him at first because he had already anticipated
> his sensations; however, his responses to Yosemite Valley are
> interesting. His impressions of that spectacle would remain "while
> memory lasts."

Bunnell, Lafayette Houghton. DISCOVERY OF THE YOSEMITE, AND THE
INDIAN WAR OF 1851, WHICH LED TO THAT EVENT, by Lafayette Houghton
Bunnell, M.D., of the Mariposa Battalion, One of the Discoverers, Late
Surgeon Thirty-Sixth Regiment Wisconsin Volunteers. Chicago: Fleming H.
Revell, 1880. 331 p. Illustrated. Map.

> Strictly speaking, Bunnell's book is not a travel report of scenery;
> however, it is included because his account is the principal source
> of information about the discovery of Yosemite Valley. Bunnell
> suggested the name "Yosemity" and was responsible for naming
> many of the natural features in the area. Although freshness of
> impression was somewhat diminished by the passage of twenty-nine
> years, Bunnell succeeded in conveying some of his original excite-
> ment and awe at the sight of the valley. The grandeur of Yosemite
> deeply affected the young doctor (he was twenty-seven when he
> visited the valley) and, although he was not a remarkable prose
> stylist, his sincere emotional response is effectively communicated
> to the modern reader. The book went through three subsequent
> editions, the last in 1911. The first edition was reprinted in 1972.
> Full bibliographic description and notes may be found in YOSEMITE,
> THE BIG TREES AND THE HIGH SIERRA: A SELECTIVE BIBLIOG-
> RAPHY, by Francis P. Farquhar, see below.

Finck, Henry T. THE PACIFIC COAST SCENIC TOUR, FROM SOUTHERN CALIFORNIA TO ALASKA, THE CANADIAN PACIFIC RAILWAY, YELLOW-STONE PARK AND THE GRAND CANON. New York: Scribner, 1891. xiv, 309 p. Plates. Map.

> The author states his belief that climate and scenery "make up fully one half of human happiness." The scenery of the western half of the United States was incomparably better and grander than that of the East. This scenic tour begins in southern California in January and moves north with the spring, pivoting in Alaska and returning to the East via one of the three transcontinental rail lines.

Hittel, John S. YOSEMITE: ITS WONDERS AND ITS BEAUTIES, WITH IN-FORMATION ADAPTED TO THE WANTS OF TOURISTS ABOUT TO VISIT THE VALLEY. ILLUSTRATED WITH TWENTY PHOTOGRAPHIC VIEWS....San Francisco and New York: H.H. Bancroft, 1868. viii, 59 p. Plates. Map.

> According to Francis P. Farquhar, this was the first Yosemite guide book.

Hutchings, James M. SCENES OF WONDER AND CURIOSITY IN CALIFOR-NIA. San Francisco: Hutchings & Rosenfield, [1860]. 236 p. Illustrated.

> Later editions appeared in 1861, 1862, 1865, 1870, 1871, 1872, 1875, and 1876; subtitle varies. Editions after 1861 are enlarged with more engravings. Hutchings was the pioneer publicist of the Sierra and made his home in Yosemite Valley, where he engaged in hotel operations, publishing, and guiding. He was, between 1880 and 1884, the Guardian of Yosemite Valley and the Mariposa Big Trees. Between 1856 and 1861, he published in San Francisco HUTCHINGS' CALIFORNIA MAGAZINE, an illustrated monthly.

————. IN THE HEART OF THE SIERRAS. THE YOSEMITE VALLEY, BOTH HISTORICAL AND DESCRIPTIVE; AND SCENES BY THE WAY. THE HIGH SIERRA, WITH ITS MAGNIFICENT SCENERY, ANCIENT AND MODERN GLA-CIERS, AND OTHER OBJECTS OF INTEREST; WITH TABLES OF DISTANCES AND ALTITUDES, MAPS, ETC. Published at the Old Cabin, Yosemite Valley and at Pacific Press Publishing House, Oakland, California, 1886. xii, 496 p. Frontispiece. Portrait. Illustrations. Maps.

> In this work, Hutchings tells of his experiences in the valley and covers all aspects of Yosemite and the Big Trees that would interest tourists. Profusely illustrated. Later editions appeared in 1887 and 1888; an undated subsequent edition appeared with the subtitle TOURIST'S EDITION. A GUIDE TO CALIFORNIA'S NATURAL ATTRACTIONS.

Kneeland, Samuel. THE WONDERS OF THE YOSEMITE VALLEY AND OF CALIFORNIA. 3rd ed., rev. & enl. Boston: Alexander Moore, Lee &

Shepard; New York: Lee, Shepard & Dillingham, 1872. xiii, 98 p. Photos.
Figures. Maps.

> The author's descriptions of Yosemite were accurate and his photo-
> graphs excellent. Kneeland's work was influential in popularizing
> Yosemite.

Muir, John. THE YOSEMITE. New York: Century Co., 1912. x, 284 p.
Plates. 3 folding maps.

> Although THE YOSEMITE is not vintage Muir, it is still an excel-
> lent descriptive guide to the park. It was intended by the pub-
> lishers as a handbook for the carriage trade and is a mixture of
> scenic description, natural history, park history, and suggested
> excursions. A paper edition with notes and introduction by Fred-
> eric R. Gunsky (Anchor Books, 1962) is a convenient and useful
> revision of the original edition.

PICTURESQUE CALIFORNIA AND THE REGION WEST OF THE ROCKY MOUN-
TAINS, FROM ALASKA TO MEXICO. Edited by John Muir. 2 vols. San
Francisco: J. Dewing, 1887.

> The title page for Volume 2 (1888) appeared with the title PIC-
> TURESQUE CALIFORNIA: THE ROCKY MOUNTAINS AND THE
> PACIFIC SLOPE. This work was issued by subscription and in a
> variety of formats. Jacob Blanck, in his BIBLIOGRAPHY OF
> AMERICAN LITERATURE, indicates that he has been unable to
> establish a sequence for what appear to have been the thirty-two
> separate parts of this work, some issued in portfolios instead of
> bound volumes. Muir contributed seven chapters, including sec-
> tions on Yosemite and the Sierra Nevada. PICTURESQUE CALIF-
> ORNIA is heavily illustrated with engravings and has become a
> collectors' item.

Thayer, James Bradley. A WESTERN JOURNEY WITH MR. EMERSON. Boston:
Little, Brown, 1884. 141 p.

> In April 1871 Emerson, with nine others, left Boston on a western
> journey across the plains through Salt Lake City, San Francisco,
> Yosemite Valley, and back to Boston. Thayer, related to Emerson
> by marriage, was the trip's historian. Of particular interest is the
> author's account of Emerson's meeting with John Muir in Yosemite
> Valley.

BIBLIOGRAPHIES

Farquhar, Francis P. YOSEMITE, THE BIG TREES AND THE HIGH SIERRA:
A SELECTIVE BIBLIOGRAPHY. Berkeley and Los Angeles: University of
California Press, 1948. xi, 104 p. Illustrated, with facsimiles.

Although restricted to a relatively small number of titles, the annotations are excellent and the descriptive bibliographical details are valuable. See also the author's HISTORY OF THE SIERRA NEVADA (Berkeley and Los Angeles: University of California Press in Collaboration with The Sierra Club, 1965. xiv, 262 p. Illustrated. Maps).

U.S. National Park Service. "A Bibliography of Yosemite." In A BIBLIOG-RAPHY OF NATIONAL PARKS AND MONUMENTS WEST OF THE MISSISSIPPI vol. 1, compiled at the Western Museum Laboratory of the National Park Service with Assistance Provided by the Works Projects Administration and the Civilian Conservation Corps., pp. iii-134. [Berkeley, Calif.?]: 1941. Mimeographed.

A comprehensive and invaluable bibliography with occasional annotations. Classified arrangement. The sections on geography, travel and description, and history are especially rewarding for titles of scenic reports. Coverage is to 1936.

14. Alaska and the Pacific Northwest

Ballou, Maturin M. THE NEW ELDORADO: A SUMMER JOURNEY TO ALASKA. Boston: Houghton Mifflin, 1889. xii, 355 p.

Ballou (1820-95), editor, journalist, traveler, and author, was the founder of GLEASON'S PICTORIAL, later BALLOU'S MONTH-LY MAGAZINE. He was also the first editor of the BOSTON DAILY GLOBE. Ballou wrote a number of books--fiction, history and biography, and travel. From 1882 until his death, Ballou took many trips, which led to his writing several books. THE NEW ELDORADO was a popular, if undistinguished, travel book. Later editions were published with the title BALLOU'S ALASKA. A TOURIST'S EDITION OF "THE NEW ELDORADO."

Burroughs, John. "Alaska, Narrative of the Expedition." In HARRIMAN ALASKA EXPEDITION. ALASKA: NARRATIVE, GLACIERS, NATIVES, edited by C. Hart Merriam, pp. 1-118. Harriman Alaska Series, vol. 1. New York: Doubleday, Page, 1902.

Burroughs was the historian of the expedition organized and financed in 1899 by Edward Harriman. The expedition consisted of the Harriman family, a scientific party of twenty-five members (including John Muir, C. Hart Merriam, G.K. Gilbert, George Bird Grinnell, and Charles A. Keeler), a group of artists, photographers, stenographers, doctors, nurses, and a chaplain. It left New York in May, crossed the country by rail, and took passage in a specially outfitted steamer. Burroughs was overwhelmed by the trip's rigors and, although he was impressed by the scenery, he apparently preferred the humanized landscape of the Catskills and his Hudson River home.

Hallock, Charles. OUR NEW ALASKA; OR, THE SEWARD PURCHASE VIN-
DICATED. New York: Forest and Stream Publishing Co., 1886. viii, 209 p.
Illustrated. Folding map. Reprint ed., 1970.

> Hallock, founder and editor of FOREST AND STREAM and a noted
> conservationist, here describes his travels in Alaska, pointing out
> the "visible resources" of the region and urging their development.
> "I would popularize home excursions among our votaries of fashion
> --Yosemite, Alaska, and the Yellowstone--as the primary and
> proper thing to 'do' before attempting the Old World Tour...."

Muir, John. TRAVELS IN ALASKA. Boston and New York: Houghton
Mifflin, 1915. ix, 326 p. Plates.

> Alaska was Muir's second love (his first being Yosemite and the
> Sierra Nevada) and this book describes the events of three trips
> he made in 1879, 1880, and 1890. The narration is drawn from
> unpublished notes and from letters written to the SAN FRANCISCO
> BULLETIN between 1879 and 1881. Although Muir carefully worked
> over his material for publication, it imparts a rare vividness of
> impression and description. Muir died in 1914 and the manuscript
> was arranged for publication by Mrs. Marion Randall Parsons who
> assisted him during the final months of his life. TRAVELS IN
> ALASKA is one of the finest Alaskan travel books to be found in
> a very large body of literature.

Putnam, George Palmer. IN THE OREGON COUNTRY; OUT-DOORS IN
OREGON, WASHINGTON, AND CALIFORNIA TOGETHER WITH SOME
LEGENDARY LORE, AND GLIMPSES OF THE MODERN WEST IN THE MAK-
ING. Introduction by James Withycombe, Governor of Oregon. New York
and London: Putnam, 1915. xxi, 169 p. Plates.

> The author, a transplanted easterner, was the grandson of the
> founder of the publishing house. IN THE OREGON COUNTRY
> is a glowing semipromotional work, mainly of Oregon. It empha-
> sizes description of Oregon's great natural resources, its scenery,
> and its prospects for growth.

Winthrop, Theodore. THE CANOE AND THE SADDLE, ADVENTURES AMONG
THE NORTHWESTERN RIVERS AND FORESTS AND ISTHMANIA. Boston:
Tichnor & Fields, 1863, 375 p.

> A narrative of travel and scenic reporting in Washington Territory
> in 1853. Later editions appeared in 1866, [190?] and 1913.
> Winthrop was also the author of LIFE IN THE OPEN AIR (see
> Chapter 3, Section D 3: Maine).

BIBLIOGRAPHY

For a listing of materials relating to the Alaskan national parks and monuments, see the section "Territorial Parks and Monuments" (Glacier Bay National Monument, Katmai National Monument, Mt. McKinley National Park, Old Kasaan National Monument, and Sitka National Monument) in A BIBLIOGRAPHY OF NATIONAL PARKS AND MONUMENTS WEST OF THE MISSISSIPPI RIVER, prepared by the U.S. National Park Service, vol. 2 ([Berkeley, Calif.?]: 1941).

E. PICTURE BOOKS

The book of scenic views has been with us for a long time and traces its origins to the early nineteenth-century "gift book." The modern variety, often disparagingly called "the coffee-table book," has thrived in the last few years. Except as a measurement of the exploitation of modern America's interest in nature, they have little value. There are two series, however, that have more to offer the serious student. The "Exhibit Format" books published by the Sierra Club and "The Earth's Wild Places" books published by the Friends of the Earth provide a documentary expression of preservationist concerns by photographic display and textual explication. All are beautifully designed and produced. Most of the Sierra Club books have been reprinted in paper editions.

Sierra Club Books

Adams, Ansel, and Newhall, Nancy. THIS IS THE AMERICAN EARTH. Exhibit Format Series, vol. 1. San Francisco: Sierra Club, 1960. xvii, 89 p. Illustrated.

Wright, Cedric. WORDS OF THE EARTH. Foreword by Ansel Adams. Edited by Nancy Newhall. Exhibit Format Series, vol. 2. San Francisco: Sierra Club, [1960]. 93 p. Illustrated. 35 cm.

Adams, Ansel. THESE WE INHERIT; THE PARKLANDS OF AMERICA. Exhibit Format Series, vol. 3. San Francisco: Sierra Club, [1962]. 103 p. 42 plates. 35 cm.

Porter, Eliot. "IN WILDERNESS IS THE PRESERVATION OF THE WORLD," FROM HENRY DAVID THOREAU. Selections and photographs by Eliot Porter. Introduction by Joseph Wood Krutch. Exhibit Format Series, vol. 4. San Francisco: Sierra Club, [1962]. 167 p. Colored illustrations. 35 cm.

_____. THE PLACE NO ONE KNEW: GLEN CANYON ON THE COLORADO. Edited by David Brower. Exhibit Format Series, vol. 5. San Francisco: Sierra Club, [1963]. 170 p. Colored illustrations. Bibliography, p. 170. 35 cm.

Hyde, Philip, and Leydet, Francois. THE LAST REDWOODS; PHOTOGRAPHS AND STORY OF THE VANISHING SCENIC RESOURCE. Foreword by Stewart L. Udall. Exhibit Format Series, vol. 6. San Francisco: Sierra Club, 1963. 127 p. Illustrations (some in color). Folding colored map. Bibliography, pp. 126-27. 32 cm.

Newhall, Nancy. ANSEL ADAMS: VOLUME ONE, THE ELOQUENT LIGHT. Exhibit Format Series, vol. 7. San Francisco: Sierra Club, [1963]. 175 p. Illustrated. 35 cm.

Leydet, Francois. TIME AND THE RIVER FLOWING: GRAND CANYON. Edited by David Brower. Exhibit Format Series, vol. 8. San Francisco: Sierra Club, [1964]. 174 p. Colored illustrations. Map. 36 cm.

Muir, John. GENTLE WILDERNESS; THE SIERRA NEVADA. Photographs by Richard Kauffman. Edited by David Brower. Exhibit Format Series, vol. 9. San Francisco: Sierra Club, [1964]. 167 p. Colored illustrations. Facsimiles. 35 cm.

   The text from Muir was condensed from MY FIRST SUMMER IN THE SIERRA NEVADA.

Brower, David, ed. NOT MAN APART; LINES FROM ROBINSON JEFFERS. Photographs of Big Sur Coast by Ansel Adams and others. Exhibit Format Series, vol. 10. San Francisco: Sierra Club, [1965]. 159 p. Illustrations (some in color). Facsimile. 36 cm.

Manning, Harvey. THE WILD CASCADES, FORGOTTEN PARKLAND. Photographs by Ansel Adams and others. With lines from Theodore Roethke. Foreword by William O. Douglas. Exhibit Format Series, vol. 11. San Francisco: Sierra Club, [1965]. 128 p. Illustrations (some in color). Colored map. Bibliography, p. 128. 36 cm.

Hornbein, Thomas F. EVEREST, THE WEST RIDGE. Photographs from the American Mount Everest Expedition by its leader, Norman G. Dyhrenfurth. Introduction by William E. Siri. Edited by David Brower. Exhibit Format Series, vol. 12. San Francisco: Sierra Club, [1965]. 198 p. Colored plates. Map. Bibliography, p. 12. 34 cm.

Porter, Eliot. SUMMER ISLAND: PENOBSCOT COUNTRY. Edited by David Brower. Exhibit Format Series, vol. 13. San Francisco: Sierra Club, [1966]. 200 p. Illustrations (some in color). Map on lining papers. 35 cm.

Jett, Stephen C. NAVAJO WILDLANDS; "AS LONG AS THE RIVERS SHALL RUN." Photographs by Philip Hyde. Foreword by David Brower. Edited by Kenneth Brower. Exhibit Format Series, vol. 14. San Francisco: Sierra Club, [1967]. 160 p. Colored illustrations. Folding map. 35 cm.

Wenkam, Robert. KAUAI AND THE PARK COUNTRY OF HAWAII. Foreword by David Brower. Edited by Kenneth Brower. Exhibit Format Series, vol. 15. San Francisco: Sierra Club, [1967]. 158 p. Illustrations (some in color). Maps (some in color). 35 cm.

Bohn, Dave. GLACIER BAY, THE LAND AND THE SILENCE. Edited by David Brower. Exhibit Format Series, vol. 16. San Francisco: Sierra Club, [1967]. Photos. Illustrations (some in color). Bibliography, pp. 159–63. 36 cm.

Krutch, Joseph Wood. BAJA CALIFORNIA AND THE GEOGRAPHY OF HOPE. Photographs by Eliot Porter. Foreword by David Brower. Edited by Kenneth Brower. Exhibit Format Series, vol. 17. San Francisco: Sierra Club, [1967]. 174 p. Colored illustrations. Folding map. 35 cm.

Johnston, Nancy. CENTRAL PARK COUNTRY, A TUNE WITHIN US. Photographs by Nancy and Retta Johnston. Text by Mireille Johnston. Introduction by Marianne Moore. Edited, with a foreword, by David Brower. Exhibit Format Series, vol. 18. San Francisco: Sierra Club, 1968. 151 p. Colored illustrations. 36 cm.

GALAPAGOS: THE FLOW OF WILDNESS. Photographs by Eliot Porter. Introduction by Loren Eiseley. Edited by Kenneth Brower. 2 vols. Exhibit Format Series, vols. 19–20. San Francisco: Sierra Club, 1968. 36 cm.

GRAND CANYON OF THE LIVING COLORADO. Photographs and a journal by Ernest Braun. Contributions by Colin Fletcher, Allen J. Malmquist, Roderick Nash, and Stewart Udall. Foreword by David Brower. Edited by Roderick Nash. [San Francisco]: Sierra Club/Ballantine Books, [1970]. 143 p. Illustrated, with facsimiles, maps, and colored plates. 25 cm.

Abbey, Edward. SLICKROCK; THE CANYON COUNTRY OF SOUTHWEST UTAH. Photographs and commentary by Philip Hyde. Exhibit Format Series (unnumbered volume). San Francisco: Sierra Club, [1971]. 143 p. Colored illustrations and maps. Bibliography, p. 143. 35 cm.

Friends of the Earth Books

Wenkam, Robert. MAUI; THE LAST HAWAIIAN PLACE. Foreword by David Brower. Introduction by Charles A. Lindbergh. Edited, with sketches, by Kenneth Brower. Earth's Wild Places, vol. 1. San Francisco: Friends of the Earth, 1970. 158 p. Illustrations (some in color). Photos. Maps. 35 cm. (Distributed by McCall Publishing Co., New York.)

Knight, Max. RETURN TO THE ALPS. Photographs by Gerhard Klammet. Edited, with a foreword and selections from Alpine literature, by David R.

Brower. Earth's Wild Places, vol. 2. San Francisco: Friends of the Earth; New York: McCall Publishing Co., [1970?]. 160 p. Illustrated. Map. Colored plates. 36 cm.

Brower, Kenneth, ed. THE EARTH AND THE GREAT WEATHER: THE BROOKS RANGE. Foreword by David Brower. Introduction by John P. Milton. Earth's Wild Places, vol. 3. San Francisco: Friends of the Earth, [1971]. 188 p. Illustrations (some in color). Map. 36 cm. (Distributed by McCall Publishing Co., New York.)

Hay, John. THE PRIMAL ALLIANCE: EARTH AND OCEAN. Lines from THE ATLANTIC SHORE, by John Hay. Photographs of Big Sur Coast by Richard Kauffman. Foreword by David R. Brower. Edited by Kenneth Brower. Earth's Wild Places, vol. 4. San Francisco: Friends of the Earth, [1971]. 144 p. Colored illustrations. 35 cm.

Gussow, Alan. A SENSE OF PLACE: THE ARTIST AND THE AMERICAN LAND. Introduction by Richard Wilbur. Foreword by David R. Brower. Earth's Wild Places, vol. 6. San Francisco: Friends of the Earth, [1972]. 160 p. Illustrations (some in color). 36 cm.

Chapter 3

AMERICAN LANDSCAPE PAINTING

Chapter 3

AMERICAN LANDSCAPE PAINTING

This chapter surveys the sources of artistic response to the American landscape from the later years of the Hudson River School to the death of Winslow Homer in 1910. Included are reference works on American art (indexes, encyclopedias, and biographical dictionaries), histories of American art and especially of landscape painting, histories, catalogs, treatises, and biographical studies of the Hudson River School, its "sub-schools," and derivative painters. Similar treatment is afforded those artists who were active in the American West. Although there are exceptions, most major American artists since Homer have moved away from the expression of values in landscape to other forms which are not directly concerned with nature.

A.   REFERENCE WORKS

ART INDEX. New York: H.W. Wilson. 1929--.

> "An author and subject index to domestic and foreign art periodicals and museum bulletins." Subjects include archaeology, architecture, art history, arts and crafts, city planning, fine arts, graphic arts, industrial design, interior design, landscape design, photography and films and related fields. Three-year cumulations were offered from 1929 to 1953; two-year cumulations are available for the years 1953 (November) to date.

Encyclopedias

ENCYCLOPEDIA OF WORLD ART. 15 vols. New York: McGraw-Hill, [1959-68].

> "All articles have been translated into English from the original language...and correlated with the final editorial work of the Italian edition." Includes bibliographies. This is a scholarly work, but because of its European origin, it is not as useful for some American painters as the following encyclopedias.

McGRAW-HILL DICTIONARY OF ART. 5 vols. Edited by Bernard S. Myers. New York: McGraw-Hill, 1969.

> More American artists are noted in this work than the one above. Includes bibliographies.

PRAEGER ENCYCLOPEDIA OF ART. 5 vols. New York, Washington, London: Praeger, 1971.

> This English-language edition is an updated translation, with additional new material, of DICTIONNAIRE UNIVERSEL DE L'ARTE ET DES ARTISTES.

Biographical Dictionaries

Fielding, Mantle. DICTIONARY OF AMERICAN PAINTERS, SCULPTORS, AND ENGRAVERS. Addendum Containing Corrections and Additional Material on the Original Entries compiled by James F. Carr. New York: James F. Carr, 1965. vi, 529 p.

> Originally published in 1926, this has since become a standard work. The biographical data is substantial and accurate.

Groce, George C., and Wallace, David H. NEW YORK HISTORICAL SOCIETY'S DICTIONARY OF ARTISTS IN AMERICA, 1564-1860. New Haven, Conn.: Yale University Press, 1957. xxvii, 759 p.

> Arranged alphabetically by artist. Each entry is documented. Generally excludes artists born in 1841 or later. Artists are defined as painters, draftsmen, sculptors, engravers, lithographers, and allied artists. Total number of artists is between ten and eleven thousand. An exceptionally valuable source, especially for minor artists. "Key to Citations of Sources," pp. 713-59.

Mallet, Daniel Trowbridge. MALLET'S INDEX OF ARTISTS. INTERNATIONAL BIOGRAPHICAL. INCLUDING PAINTERS, SCULPTORS, ILLUSTRATORS, ENGRAVERS, AND ETCHERS OF THE PAST AND PRESENT. New York: Bowker, 1935. xxxiv, 493 p. Supplement. New York: Bowker, 1940. xxxviii, 319 p. Reprint eds., 1948.

> Alphabetical arrangement. Gives nationality, place and dates of birth and death. Code letters refer to list of sources where biographical information may be located.

Michigan State Library, Lansing. BIOGRAPHICAL SKETCHES OF AMERICAN ARTISTS. Compiled by Helen L. Earle. 5th ed., rev. and enl. Lansing, Mich.: 1924. 370 p. Bibliography, pp. 349-56. Reprint ed. Charleston, S.C.: Garnier & Co., 1972.

Although a considerable amount of biographical data herein is available in more modern sources, many minor artists, sculptors, illustrators, mural painters, stained glass designers, etchers, and miniature painters are covered by this work. In addition to the biography, there is a list of periodical references by artists on pp. 357-70.

Waters, Clara Erskine Clement, and Hutton, Laurence. ARTISTS OF THE NINETEENTH CENTURY AND THEIR WORKS; A HANDBOOK CONTAINING TWO THOUSAND AND FIFTY BIOGRAPHICAL SKETCHES. 2 vols. Boston: Houghton, Osgood, 1879.

International in coverage. The sketches are short, rarely longer than one page. The introduction contains resumes of the various American academies, societies, clubs, and schools devoted to the support of fine art. The work is dated but useful for information about little-known, regional artists.

B. AMERICAN ART, GENERAL

Eliot, Alexander. THREE HUNDRED YEARS OF AMERICAN PAINTING. Introduction by John Walker. New York: Time Inc., 1957. x, 318 p. Colored illustrations. Bibliography, pp. 312-14.

A useful nontechnical study.

Flexner, James Thomas. THAT WILDER IMAGE; THE PAINTING OF AMERICA'S NATIVE SCHOOL FROM THOMAS COLE TO WINSLOW HOMER. Boston, Toronto: Little, Brown, 1962. xxii, 407 p. Illustrated. Bibliography, pp. 375-94.

A comprehensive treatment of America's native school of painting. Flexner's object was to give it "its day in a fair court." This he has done in an objective manner. The writing is smooth and the documentation superb. Flexner's bibliography (divided into general sources and also by chapter) is the place to begin a search for historical material relating to the topic.

Isham, Samuel. THE HISTORY OF AMERICAN PAINTING. WITH TWELVE FULL-PAGE PHOTOGRAVURES AND ONE HUNDRED AND FORTY-ONE ILLUSTRATIONS IN THE TEXT. New ed., with supplemental chapters by Royal Cortissoz. New York: Macmillan, 1927. xvii, 608 p. Illustrated. Bibliography, pp. 593-600.

First published in 1905. Isham was a painter of note, and this work is "consistently a study of American painting from the painter's point of view." The bibliography was compiled by Henry Meier of the New York Public Library. This edition was reissued in 1936.

Larkin, Oliver W. ART AND LIFE IN AMERICA. Rev. and enl. ed. New York: Holt, Rinehart and Winston, 1960. xvii, 559 p. Illustrations (some in color). Bibliography, pp. 491-525.

> An introductory survey of the history of painting, sculpture, architecture, and, to some extent, photography. See especially Part 2, Chapters 16 to 18 for a summary of nineteenth-century landscape painting. First edition published in 1949.

Richardson, Edgar P. AMERICAN ROMANTIC PAINTING. Edited by Robert Freund. New York: E. Weyhe, 1944. 50 p. 168 plates on 84 leaves. 31 x 23 1/2 cm.

> Covers colonial times to 1876. An important reference history on the Romantic spirit in America.

Soby, James Thrall, and Miller, Dorothy C. ROMANTIC PAINTING IN AMERICA. New York: Museum of Modern Art, 1943. 143 p. Plates (some in color). Bibliographic footnotes.

> Of particular interest is the section entitled "The Triumph of Nature: The Hudson River School and the Glorification of the West," pp. 15-20.

Tuckerman, Henry T. BOOK OF THE ARTISTS. AMERICAN ARTIST LIFE, COMPRISING BIOGRAPHICAL AND CRITICAL SKETCHES OF AMERICAN ARTISTS: PRECEDED BY AN HISTORICAL ACCOUNT OF THE RISE AND PROGRESS OF ART IN AMERICA. New York: Putnam, 1867. xi, 639 p. Frontispiece. Reprint ed., 1967.

> A biographical history useful for a contemporary view of American art and artists. Reissued in 1870 and 1882.

C. STUDIES OF LANDSCAPE PAINTING

Born, Wolfgang. AMERICAN LANDSCAPE PAINTING: AN INTERPRETATION. New Haven, Conn.: Yale University Press, 1948. xiii, 228 p. Illustrated. Notes, pp. 217-21. Reprint ed., 1971.

> An important historical study; the first to survey the whole of American landscapes. Born includes townscapes, seascapes, and genre painting. He concluded that the artistic contributions of lesser-known artists have often been more important than those of the well-known.

Goodrich, Lloyd. "Landscape Painting in America." NORTH AMERICAN REVIEW 246, no. 1 (Autumn 1938): 96-117.

> Surveys American landscape painting from its eighteenth-century beginnings through the late nineteenth-century impressionists. Goodrich evaluates the paintings of the Hudson River School, George Inness, Alexander Wyant, Homer Martin, Winslow Homer, and Albert Ryder. A valuable treatment.

Scott, David W. "American Landscape: A Changing Frontier." THE LIVING WILDERNESS 33, no. 108 (Winter 1969): 3-13.

> A survey of landscape painting and painters. Illustrations follow page 7. Scott is Past Director of the National Collection of Fine Arts in Washington, D.C.

Shepard, Paul, Jr. "They Painted What They Saw." LANDSCAPE 3, no. 1 (Summer 1953): 6-11.

> American landscape painting and changing perspectives. Illustrated.

Van Dyke, John C. NATURE FOR ITS OWN SAKE: FIRST STUDIES IN NATURAL APPEARANCES. New York: Scribner, 1898. xx, 292 p.

> The author, a noted art critic and nature writer, discusses natural elements such as light, sky, clouds, water, land, and foliage that give form and color to landscape. Several editions are available.

Whitney Museum of American Art. A CENTURY OF AMERICAN LANDSCAPE PAINTING, 1880 to 1900. January 19 to February 25, 1938. Text by Lloyd Goodrich. New York: 1938. 30 p. 16 plates.

> Goodrich contributed a useful introduction to this exhibition catalog.

D. THE HUDSON RIVER SCHOOL, GENERAL

Howat, John K. THE HUDSON RIVER AND ITS PAINTERS. Preface by James Bidle. Foreword by Carl Carmer. New York: Viking, 1972. 207 p. Plates. Maps. Bibliography, pp. 193-201.

> A splendid pictorial exposition. Contains 100 plates, most of which are in color. Howat contributes a twenty-five-page historical introduction as well as notes to the plates. In addition, a facsimile of Bunce's THE HUDSON BY DAYLIGHT; MAP FROM NEW YORK BAY TO THE HEAD OF TIDEWATER...(1894), is included. A very interesting and informative production.

Mather, Frank Jewett, Jr. "The Hudson River School." MAGAZINE OF ART 27 (June 1934): 297-306.

> A critical, though not unsympathetic, estimate of the artists who made up the school.

Sears, Clara Endicott. HIGHLIGHTS AMONG THE HUDSON RIVER ARTISTS. Boston: Houghton Mifflin, 1947. xvii, 216 p. Plates. Bibliography, pp. 215-16.

> A well-written popular history of the Hudson River Artists. Illustrated with sixty-three black and white plates and one colored frontispiece. The illustrations are of paintings found in the gallery

of the Fruitlands and Wayside Museums in Harvard, Massachusetts, then owned by Miss Sears.

Sweet, Frederick A. THE HUDSON RIVER SCHOOL AND THE EARLY AMERICAN LANDSCAPE TRADITION. The Art Institute of Chicago, February 15 to March 25, 1945; Whitney Museum of American Art, New York, April 17 to May 18, 1945. [Chicago]: 1945. 123 p. Illustrated catalog.

The works of fifty artists were included in this exhibition arranged by Sweet and shown in Chicago and New York. One hundred sixty-three black and white reproductions and one colored are included. Sweet introduced the exhibition and provides notes on the individual artists.

Talbot, William S. "American Visions of Wilderness." BULLETIN OF THE CLEVELAND MUSEUM OF ART 56, no. 4 (April 1969): 151-66.

An interpretation of the visions of wilderness seen in the landscape painting of Cole, Church, Cropsey, Bierstadt, and Moran. Talbot points out that mid-nineteenth-century American landscape painting was unique because our landscape, compared with Europe's, was unique; it was, in fact, a "wilderness." That wilderness was both a link to the primordial state of nature and a promise for the future. To Americans, acquainted through literature--and especially poetry--with the idea of a rational, moral universe, scenery "had a direct effect on the mind and the intellect, for landscape reflected the natural order imposed by the Creator." Talbot illustrated his essay with thirteen reproductions. Reprinted in THE LIVING WILDERNESS 33, no. 108 (Winter 1969): 14-25.

Van Zandt, Roland. "The Catskills and the Rise of American Landscape Painting." NEW YORK HISTORICAL SOCIETY QUARTERLY 44 (July 1965): 257-81.

The focus of this historical study is the Catskill Mountains--the "cradle" of the Hudson River School--and the artists who came to make up that school. The author points out that the Catskills occupied "a strategic location close to the transportation facilities of the Hudson Valley and the social and commercial resources of New York City." In 1825 Thomas Cole, now the acknowledged founder of the Hudson River School, made his first visit to the mountains. His success in translating Catskill scenery into salable paintings established the movement and transformed the Catskills into "a nostalgic symbol of the primeval glories of American landscape." The mountains soon became a retreat for artists and affluent urban travelers. Painters discussed by the author include Cole, F.E. Church, Thomas Doughty, A.B. Durand, J.F. Kensett, A.D.O. Browere, S.R. Gifford, Jervis McEntee, A.H. Wyant, Jasper Cropsey, and Winslow Homer.

E.   INDIVIDUAL ARTISTS

1.   General

Champney, Benjamin (1817-1907)

Champney, Benjamin. SIXTY YEARS MEMORIES OF ART AND ARTISTS.
Woburn, Mass.: 1900. 178 p. Frontispiece. Plates.

> Champney was a minor figure in the history of American landscape
> painting; but his autobiography, written in his old age, is an
> important source of information because of his association with
> many of the more prominent members of the Hudson River School.
> In 1850 Champney "discovered" the village of North Conway,
> New Hampshire, where he took up residence, spending his winters
> in Woburn, Massachusetts. Champney was joined in North Conway
> by his friend John F. Kensett and others. The village became a
> popular center for painters interested in the White Mountains. For
> biographical information see the sketch by Frederick W. Coburn
> in the DICTIONARY OF AMERICAN BIOGRAPHY (volume 3,
> pp. 609-10). The two articles listed below trace in somewhat
> greater detail Champney's activities in North Conway.

Hardy, Ruth G. "White Umbrellas on the Saco; American Mountain Painters,
II: Benjamin Champney, 1817-1907." APPALACHIA 24, no. 4 (December
1943): 453-59.

Hennessy, William G., and Scharf, Frederic A. "Benjamin Champney and
the American Barbizon, 1850-1857." ANTIQUES 84 (November 1963): 566-
69.

Church, Frederic Edwin (1826-1900)

Avery, Myron H. "The Artist of Katahdin; American Mountain Painters, III:
Frederic Edwin Church, 1826-1900." APPALACHIA 25, no. 2 (December
1944): 147-54.

> The author, an authority on Maine's highest peak, describes
> Church's trips to the mountain and the resultant paintings. A
> number of fascinating bibliographic details are included. The
> article is reprinted from the 1940 issue of IN THE MAINE WOODS.

Huntington, David C. THE LANDSCAPES OF FREDERIC EDWIN CHURCH:
VISION OF AN AMERICAN ERA. New York: George Braziller, [1966].
xii, 210 p. Illustrated, with colored plates and photos. Notes, pp. 198-204.

> Intended as an introduction to Church's life and work. Church
> studied with Thomas Cole, the founder of the Hudson River School.

Cropsey, Jasper Francis (1823-1900)

Talbot, William S. "Jasper F. Cropsey, Child of the Hudson River School." ANTIQUES 92, no. 5 (November 1967): 713-17.

> Cropsey in his early career was regarded as a worthy landscapist, but later suffered a decline in popularity because of his adherence to the style of the Hudson River School. Includes ten black and white reproductions. An informative article.

Durand, Asher Brown (1796-1886)

Durand, John. THE LIFE AND TIMES OF A.B. DURAND. New York: Scribner, 1894. ix, 232 p. Illustrated. Reprint ed., 1970.

> Durand was one of the major artists of the Hudson River School. He began his career as an engraver and when he turned to painting, his style, particularly the accurate rendering of the details of nature, reflected his early training. John Durand's biography of his father is the standard work, thorough and readable. See also the sketch by William Howe Downes in the DICTIONARY OF AMERICAN BIOGRAPHY (volume 5, pp. 535-38). The most recent and valuable assessment of Durand's place in American art is James Thomas Flexner's "God in Nature: Durand and the Esthetic of the Hudson River School," in his THAT WILDER IMAGE: THE PAINTING OF AMERICA'S NATIVE SCHOOL FROM THOMAS COLE TO WINSLOW HOMER, pp. 60-76 (see above). Another earlier treatment of Durand, which is still useful and contains eleven black and white reproductions, is Frederick A. Sweet's "Asher B. Durand, Pioneer American Landscape Painter," THE ART QUARTERLY 8, no. 1 (Winter 1945): 141-60.

Homer, Winslow (1836-1910)

Beam, Philip C. WINSLOW HOMER AT PROUT'S NECK. Foreword by Charles Lowell Homer. Boston: Little, Brown, [1966]. xxii, 282 p. Illustrated. Bibliography, pp. 265-72.

> The author tells the story of Homer's last years (1883-1910) at Prout's Neck, Maine, during which period the artist painted almost exclusively seascapes. The foreword was contributed by the artist's nephew. Beam consulted him for much biographical information.

Downes, William Howe. THE LIFE AND WORKS OF WINSLOW HOMER. Boston and New York: Houghton Mifflin, 1911. xxvii, 306 p. Frontispiece. Plates. Bibliography, pp. 291-95.

> Downes was for many years the art critic for the BOSTON EVENING TRANSCRIPT. Although the artist before his death declined

to furnish any biographical details to Downes, Homer's brothers supplied information to the author and "scrutinized" the finished product; therefore this may be considered the "official" biography. It tends to be pedestrian in style.

Flexner, James Thomas. "Winslow Homer." In his THAT WILDER IMAGE: THE PAINTING OF AMERICA'S NATIVE SCHOOL FROM THOMAS COLE TO WINSLOW HOMER, pp. 333-55. Boston: Little, Brown, 1962.

A valuable interpretive essay.

_____. THE WORLD OF WINSLOW HOMER, 1836-1910. Time-Life Library of Art. New York: Time Inc., [1966]. 190 p. Illustrated. Photos. Appendix. Bibliography, p. 185.

Not strictly a biography, for it contains much about the social and cultural era in which Homer lived and worked. In addition to a selection of Homer's paintings (many represented in color), a number of paintings by his contemporaries are also included. A popular, but useful work.

Gardner, Albert Ten Eyck. WINSLOW HOMER, AMERICAN ARTIST: HIS WORLD AND HIS WORK. New York: Clarkson N. Potter, 1961. xiv, 263 p. Illustrated. Bibliography. Chronology. Indexes of illustrations and museums and print collections.

The author has not written a new standard life, but rather attempts to relate Homer to the milieu in which he lived and worked. See also the essay by Gardner in the entry under U.S. National Gallery of Art, in this section.

Goodrich, Lloyd. WINSLOW HOMER. New York: Published for the Whitney Museum of American Art by the Macmillan Co., 1944. viii, 241 p. 63 p. of photos and reproductions. Chronology, pp. 228-29. Notes, pp. 229-34. Bibliography, pp. 234-36.

A critical, yet sympathetic, biography of Homer and an appreciation of his painting. Goodrich's work remains the definitive biography.

_____. WINSLOW HOMER. New York: George Braziller, 1959. 127 p. Illustrated. Chronology. Bibliography, pp. 117-22.

This is an introduction to Homer's art. It contains thirty-two pages of text and ninety-five pages of plates, some of which are colored.

U.S. National Gallery of Art. WINSLOW HOMER: A RETROSPECTIVE EXHIBITION. National Gallery of Art, Smithsonian Institution, November 23, 1958 to January 4, 1959; Metropolitan Museum of Art, January 29 to March 8,

1959. [Washington?]: 1958. 131 p. Illustrated.

This exhibition catalog contains an essay, "The Orientation of An American Painter: Winslow Homer in Paris--1867," by Albert Ten Eyck Gardner. Gardner proposes a new theory: that Homer's trip to Paris "was the most important event in his entire career as an artist." According to Gardner, Homer was exposed to Japanese prints, then exhibited at the Paris Exposition Universelle, which had a profound effect upon his later style, particularly his water colors. Gardner's essay also appears in the catalog of the exhibition held at the Boston Museum of Fine Arts in 1959.

Inness, George (1825-1894)

Goodrich, Lloyd. "George Inness and American Landscape Painting." THE ARTS 7, no. 2 (February 1925): 106-10.

Primarily a narrative of Inness's history as a painter set against the influences of his predecessors in the Hudson River School. Goodrich describes Inness as a painter who concentrated on senti- ment, "the least permanent of all elements in painting." See also the sketch by William Howe Downes in the DICTIONARY OF AMERICAN BIOGRAPHY (volume 9, pp. 487-89).

Inness, George R. LIFE, ART, AND LETTERS OF GEORGE INNESS. Intro- duction by Elliot Daingerfield. New York: Century Co., 1917. xxviii, 290 p. Illustrated. Portraits. Reprint ed., 1970.

This is the standard biography by the artist's son.

Ireland, LeRoy, comp. THE WORKS OF GEORGE INNESS. AN ILLUSTRATED CATALOGUE RAISONNE. Introduction by LeRoy Ireland. Preface by Donald B. Goodall. Foreword by Robert G. McIntyre. Austin and London: Published in cooperation with the University Art Museum [by the] University of Texas Press, 1965. xxiii, 476 p. Appendices: "An Inness Chronology," and "Inness Exhibitions." Bibliography, pp. 455-59.

Lists 1541 paintings by Inness, each illustrated in black and white. A separate section, not illustrated, lists several hundred paintings without chronology and without authentification.

McCausland, Elizabeth. GEORGE INNESS, AN AMERICAN LANDSCAPE PAINTER, 1825-1894. Springfield, Mass.: The George Walter Vincent Smith Art Museum, 1946. xvi, 87 p. Plates. Catalog. Bibliography, pp. 84-87.

An exhibition catalog and monograph. Miss McCausland's text (pp. 1-70) evaluates Inness's place in the American landscape tradition.

Kensett, John Frederick (1816-1872)

Howat, John. "John F. Kensett, 1816-1872." ANTIQUES 96, no. 3 (September 1969): 397-401.

> An interesting and informative essay on Kensett's life and art. Howat is currently writing a biography of the painter.

Johnson, Ellen H. "Kensett Revisited." ART QUARTERLY 20, no. 1 (Spring 1957): 71-92.

> A valuable biographical study. Kensett was an extremely successful landscape artist of the Hudson River School. The White Mountains, the Catskills, the Adirondacks, and the Green Mountains were his favorite wilderness locales.

Kilbourne, Frederick W. "A White Mountain Artist of Long Ago; American Mountain Painters, IV: John Frederick Kensett, 1816-1872." APPALACHIA 26, no. 4 (December 1947): 447-55.

> The author, a leading authority on the White Mountains, lived in Kensett's home town of Cheshire, Connecticut, and had access to local sources for this study of the artist.

Lewison, Florence. "John Frederick Kensett: A Tribute to Man and Artist." AMERICAN ARTIST 30, no. 8 (October 1966): 32-37, 72-75.

> Kensett stands out from his contemporaries because of the "poetic softness and simplicity of concept" in his paintings. The author states that these qualities flow from the artist's personal attributes. Kensett's basic contribution to American art was his awareness of the "effect of light on color." Includes eight reproductions.

Martin, Homer Dodge (1836-1897)

[Martin, Elizabeth Gilbert]. HOMER MARTIN, A REMINISCENCE, OCTOBER 28, 1836 - FEBRUARY 12, 1897. New York: William Macbeth, 1904. ix, 58 p. Illustrated.

> The author is the painter's wife. A very slight offering as biography, but important for interpretation.

Mather, Frank Jewett, Jr. HOMER MARTIN: POET IN LANDSCAPE. New York: Privately printed by F.F. Sherman, 1912. 76 p. Colored frontispiece. 8 plates.

> A critical and biographical essay. Only 250 copies were printed. See also Mather's sketch in the DICTIONARY OF AMERICAN BIOGRAPHY (volume 12, pp. 338-40), wherein he refers to Martin as a painter of sentiment--"a poet as much as a painter."

Whittredge, Worthington (1820-1910)

Dwight, Edward H. "Worthington Whittredge, Artist of the Hudson River School." ANTIQUES 96, no. 4 (October 1969): 582-86.

> The article is largely descriptive of the painter's life, not analytical. Valuable for nine black and white reproductions.

Whittredge, Worthington. "The Autobiography of Worthington Whittredge, 1820-1910." Edited by John I.H. Baur. BROOKLYN MUSEUM JOURNAL (1942): 5-68.

> Whittredge was a leading member of the Hudson River School. The autobiography was completed in 1905, after being revised with the help of Whittredge's daughter. Although the editor has condensed parts, the document is a valuable source of information about many of the author's contemporaries. It was reprinted in book form with additional illustrations by Arno Press in 1969.

Wyant, Alexander Helwig (1836-1872)

Brewster, Eugene V. "Wyant, the Nature Painter." ARTS AND DECORATION 10, no. 4 (February 1919): 197-200, 234.

> This is a highly favorable estimate of Wyant. The author describes the painter as "the Thoreau of Art." Wyant's early paintings (from the 1860s) show the influence of the panoramic Hudson River School style. He later turned to scenes of smaller scope with intimate detail in his mountain paintings.

Clark, Eliot. SIXTY PAINTINGS BY ALEXANDER H. WYANT. New York: Privately printed, 1920. 144 p. Colored frontispiece. Illustrations.

> Contains black and white reproductions of sixty paintings on forty-six plates. Each painting is described by Clark. Size and location of each composition is given. Two hundred copies of this work were printed.

2. Special Studies

Baur, John I.H. "American Luminism." PERSPECTIVES USA, no. 9 (Autumn 1954): 90-98.

> A study of a group of nineteenth-century landscape artists who displayed in their paintings the special quality of the American atmosphere, thereby turning "it to a quietly poetic use." The group was not organized and lacked leaders. It began in the 1830s with obscure artists and reached its greatest expression in the 1860s. Baur touches upon many well-known artists (Kensett,

Bierstadt, Cropsey, Homer, and others) who, he says, exhibited
a liking for luminism.

Mather, Frank Jewett, Jr. ESTIMATES IN ART, SERIES II; SIXTEEN ESSAYS ON
AMERICAN PAINTERS OF THE NINETEENTH CENTURY. New York: Holt,
1931. xii, 337 p. Illustrated.

Essays dealing with landscape painters George Inness, Homer
Martin, Albert Ryder, and Winslow Homer.

Van Dyke, John C. AMERICAN PAINTING AND ITS TRADITION AS REPRE-
SENTED BY INNESS, WYANT, MARTIN, HOMER, LA FARGE, WHISTLER,
CHASE, ALEXANDER, SARGENT. New York: Scribner, 1919. x, 270 p.
Plates.

The author deals with the generation of painters that were active
from about 1878 to 1915.

F. WESTERN ARTISTS

1. General

Culmer, H.L.A. "Mountain Art." OVERLAND MONTHLY 2nd series, 24,
no. 142 (October 1894): 341-52.

The author, himself a painter of mountains, laments the nonexis-
tence of great mountain art. Briefly tracing the development of
the genre in Europe and America, Culmer points to two paintings
of Bierstadt and Moran which suggest to him that great mountain
art is possible. Illustrated with washes of Culmer's paintings of
mountain scenery in the Wasatch and Uinta Ranges of Utah.

Huth, Hans. "Wilderness and Art." In WILDERNESS: AMERICA'S LIVING
HERITAGE, edited by David R. Brower, pp. 60-66. Wilderness Conference,
7th session. San Francisco: Sierra Club, 1961.

In this brief survey, the author concludes that today's artist can
no longer be a leader in the field of conservation, for "nature
is no longer the axis about which he rotates."

McCracken, Harold. PORTRAIT OF THE OLD WEST. With a Biographical
Check-list of Western Artists. New York: McGraw-Hill, 1952. 232 p.
Plates (some in color).

A visual documentary of the West and western art, not a critical
or historical study, this book is intended for a popular audience.
Excludes artists born after 1875. Includes forty colored plates.
The checklist is useful for the student seeking biographical information.

Rossi, Paul A., and Hunt, David C. THE ART OF THE OLD WEST. From the Collection of the Gilcrease Institute. New York: Knopf, 1971. 335 p. Illustrations (some colored). 32 cm.

A running narrative places the more than 300 plates in historical perspective. The Indian, the cowboy, and the buffalo tend to crowd out other motifs, yet this is a valuable pictorial presentation. Contains a bibliography and a biographical section.

St. Louis City Art Museum. WESTWARD THE WAY: THE CHARACTER AND DEVELOPMENT OF THE LOUISIANA TERRITORY AS SEEN BY ARTISTS AND WRITERS OF THE NINETEENTH CENTURY. Edited by Perry T. Rathbone. St. Louis, Mo.: 1954. 280 p. Illustrated.

A well-produced volume based upon an exhibition at the City Museum. The exhibition was held in commemoration of the 150th anniversary of the Louisiana Purchase. Rathbone contributed introductory essays for the six sections of paintings. Each of the 224 paintings reproduced is underscored with a pertinent quotation from a travel account or other source. In addition to the catalog, a short biographical section on the artists is included.

Taylor, Rose Schuster. YOSEMITE INDIANS AND OTHER SKETCHES. San Francisco: Johnck & Seeger, 1936. 103 p. Illustrated.

Contains a section on early artists in Yosemite: Thomas A. Ayres, Thomas Hill, Albert Bierstadt, Chris Jorgensen, William Keith, and Thomas Moran.

2. Bierstadt, Keith and Moran

Bierstadt, Albert (1830-1902)

Hardy, Ruth G. "A Mountain Traveler; American Mountain Painters, VI: Albert Bierstadt (1830-1902). APPALACHIA 28, no. 1 (June 1950): 63-70.

Miss Hardy's essay, based partly upon accounts by Bierstadt's friends and contemporaries, is a discussion of the artist's love for mountains and his mountain paintings.

Haverstock, Mary Sayre. "Can Nature Imitate Art?" ART IN AMERICA 54 (January-February 1966): 73-80.

Devoted largely to the landscape painters Albert Bierstadt and Thomas Moran, both of whom discovered the beauty of western landscape as a result of their participation in government exploring expeditions. Their landscapes of scenic areas which later became national parks popularized the areas and influenced the movement to create parks. This essay is illustrated with a series of paintings and photographs, the intent of which is to show the striking similarities of view.

Hendricks, Gordon. A BIERSTADT; AN ESSAY AND CATALOGUE TO AC-
COMPANY A RETROSPECTIVE EXHIBITION OF THE WORK OF ALBERT
BIERSTADT. Fort Worth: Amon Carter Museum, [1972]. 48 p. Illustrations
(some colored).

> Hendricks briefly sketches the highlights of the artist's life and
> gives a running account of his trips and the paintings that resulted
> from them. Neither a critical nor interpretive essay, the volume
> is valuable for details of Bierstadt's life. For example, the reader
> learns that Bierstadt accompanied Fitz Hugh Ludlow on his western
> trip in 1863. (See Ludlow's account in THE HEART OF THE CON-
> TINENT, cited in Chapter 2, Section D9: Transcontinental Reports.)
> Contains bibliographic references. Relatively little has been written
> about Bierstadt in recent years and there is no biography. See
> also Charles De Kay's singularly unsympathetic sketch in DICTIO-
> NARY OF AMERICAN BIOGRAPHY (volume 2, pp. 253-54).

Lewison, Florence. "The Uniqueness of Albert Bierstadt." AMERICAN ARTIST
28, no. 8 (September 1964): 28-33, 72-74.

> A useful short sketch of the artist's life and work. The author
> points out that, although Bierstadt's early acclaim derives from
> his huge canvases of western scenery, it is his smaller, detailed
> studies of nature that have greater meaning for our time.

Keith, William (1838-1911)

Cornelius, Brother Fidelis. KEITH, OLD MASTER OF CALIFORNIA. New
York: Putnam, 1942. xix, 631 p. Frontispiece. Plates (some in color).
Portraits. Notes and references, pp. 580-606. Supplement. Fresno: Academy
Literary Guild, 1956. xi, 296 p.

> William Keith was born in Scotland and died in California. His
> fame today rests largely upon his landscapes of California scenes.
> Keith met John Muir in 1872 and together they spent a number
> of outings in the Sierra and the mountains of Oregon and Washing-
> ton. Muir's contagious love of the Sierra undoubtedly influenced
> Keith's painting, particularly in his choice of scenery. Muir was
> also influential in popularizing Keith's work. Brother Cornelius
> of Saint Mary's College in Moraga, California, produced this
> monumental biography of the painter. The second volume is a
> supplement and a page-by-page correction of the main volume.

Neuhaus, Eugen. WILLIAM KEITH, THE MAN AND THE ARTIST. Berkeley:
University of California Press, 1938. xi, 95 p. Plates.

> The author knew Keith and has produced a useful monograph and
> introduction to the artist's work. Brother Cornelius's book, above,
> remains the definitive biography.

Moran, Thomas (1837-1926)

Fryxell, Fritiof, ed. THOMAS MORAN, EXPLORER IN SEARCH OF BEAUTY. East Hampton, N.Y.: East Hampton Free Library, 1958. xii, 84 p. Plates.

From the title page: "A biographical sketch; an account of the history and nature of THE THOMAS MORAN BIOGRAPHICAL ART COLLECTION in the Pennypacker Long Island Collection, at the East Hampton Free Library, New York; and selected articles and illustrations relating to the life of Thomas Moran." See also the article by Mary S. Haverstock (above).

Gerdts, William H. "The Painting of Thomas Moran: Sources and Style." ANTIQUES 85, no. 2 (February 1964): 202-5.

The author's aim was "to point out some of the sources on which [Moran] drew for his rich, colorful, painterly art and to consider the basis of his achievement." Includes nine black and white reproductions.

Jackson, William H. "Famous American Mountain Paintings, I: With Moran in the Yellowstone; A Story of Exploration, Photography and Art." APPALA-CHIA 21 (December 1936): 149-58.

Jackson, the famous photographer of the old West and a lifelong friend of Thomas Moran, recalls the trip he and the artist made to Yellowstone in 1871 as members of the Hayden Geological Survey.

Wilkins, Thurman. THOMAS MORAN, ARTIST OF THE MOUNTAINS. Norman: University of Oklahoma Press, 1966. xvi, 315 p. Plates (some in color). Appendix and bibliography, pp. 261-93.

Thomas Moran today is most famous for his paintings of national park scenes, many painted while he was a member of the Hayden Survey of 1871. Wilkin's book, well-written and reflecting metic-ulous scholarship, is the standard biography. His bibliography, comprehensive in scope and detail, should be consulted for the many titles of books, articles and manuscript sources about the artist's life and work.

Chapter 4

CONSERVATION AND THE PRESERVATION
OF NATURAL BEAUTY: THE NATIONAL PARKS

Chapter 4

CONSERVATION AND THE PRESERVATION
OF NATURAL BEAUTY: THE NATIONAL PARKS

Especially in its early years, conservation as a national movement has been
closely identified with the conserving of natural resources, primarily for
economic uses. In this chapter, and the two following, attention is drawn
to materials concerned with the noneconomic aspects of conservation. The
focus is on the esthetic, spiritual, and recreational values of wild nature and
its ideological and ecological bases.

There are thousands of books, articles, pamphlets, newspaper articles, and
government documents that deal with the national parks in the United States.
Many take the form of popular guides and promotional pieces and most are
outdated and out of print. No work adequately covers the historical development of the national parks; but there are a number of important individual
park histories, biographies and autobiographies, monographs, and scholarly
articles, as well as the publications of private conservation organizations.
Many of these are listed below. Chapter 4 is a highly selective list of publications showing the development of attitudes toward natural beauty and its
preservation in a national park system.

A. BIBLIOGRAPHIES

U.S. Department of the Interior. Library. READINGS ON NATURAL BEAUTY,
A SELECTED BIBLIOGRAPHY. Compiled by Signe Ruh Ottersen. Bibliography
No. 1. Washington, D.C.: July 1967. iii, 94 p. Mimeographed. Paper.

> Compiled in response to demands for information occasioned by the
> White House Conference on Natural Beauty in 1965. Most of the
> references appeared after 1964. Categories include: the environ-
> mental setting (general works, esthetics, and natural beauty);
> planning (city, rural, regional, and new towns); pollution; urban
> townscape; landscape architecture; historic preservation; rural land-
> scape; outdoor recreation; transportation and citizen action. Un-
> annotated. A useful earlier bibliography is:

U.S. Department of the Interior. Library. READINGS ON
THE PRESERVATION OF NATURAL BEAUTY. Compiled by
Reference Services. [Washington, D.C.]: 1964. 47 p.
Mimeographed. Paper.

U.S. National Park Service. A BIBLIOGRAPHY OF NATIONAL PARKS AND
MONUMENTS WEST OF THE MISSISSIPPI RIVER. Compiled at the Western
Museum Laboratories of the National Park Service with Assistance Provided by
the Work Projects Administration and the Civilian Conservation Corps. 2 vols.
[Berkeley?]: 1941. Mimeographed.

> The bibliographies in these volumes were prepared and distributed
> separately; consequently, they have separate forewords and are
> paged separately (for a total of over 1000 pages). The tables of
> contents have no page references and there is no index. Despite
> these drawbacks, the bibliography is an invaluable source of in-
> formation about western parks and monuments. The compilations
> were begun in 1936 so, with some exceptions, that is the cutoff
> date. Included are books, parts of books, articles, documents,
> proceedings, reports, and newspaper stories. For the most part,
> fiction, poetry, and maps are excluded. The arrangement is by
> region. The larger or more well-known parks and monuments are
> subdivided by category--history, travel, description, geology, flora
> and fauna, Indians, archaeology, etc. Several parks are repre-
> sented by substantial bibliographies, of which the Yellowstone (200
> p.) and the Yosemite (134 p.) are large and comprehensive to
> 1936.

B. GENERAL

Brockman, Christian Frank, and Merriam, Lawrence C., Jr. RECREATIONAL
USE OF WILD LANDS. 2nd ed. with two especially prepared chapters by
William R. Catton, Jr. and Barney Dowdle. New York: McGraw-Hill, 1973.
xii, 329 p. Maps. Bibliography. References.

> This is an extensive revision of the 1959 edition. Two new chap-
> ters have been added: "The Recreational Visitor: Motivation,
> Behavior, Impact," by sociologist William R. Catton, Jr., and
> "Economics of Outdoor Recreation," by Barney Dowdle. Although
> intended as an introduction to its subject, the book is thorough in
> scope, covering (albeit in brief compass) the historical development
> of interest in recreational use of wild lands by various government
> agencies. Seven of the seventeen chapters deal directly with this
> development and include discussion of the creation of national
> parks and forests, state parks, the Outdoor Recreation Resources
> Review Commission, the Bureau of Outdoor Recreation, and the
> National Wilderness Preservation System. A separate chapter each
> is devoted to the roles of the national park system, the national
> forests, other federal agencies, and state and local groups.

Hays, Samuel P. CONSERVATION AND THE GOSPEL OF EFFICIENCY: THE PROGRESSIVE CONSERVATION MOVEMENT, 1890-1920. Harvard Historical Monographs, 40. Cambridge, Mass.: Harvard University Press, 1959. 297 p. Bibliography, pp. 277-82.

> Hays devotes a short section (pp. 189-98) to a discussion of the issues dividing the conservationists and the "preservationists."

Huth, Hans. NATURE AND THE AMERICAN: THREE CENTURIES OF CHANG-ING ATTITUDES. Berkeley and Los Angeles: University of California Press, 1957. xvii, 250 p. Illustrated, with plates. Notes, pp. 213-27. Bibliography, pp. 229-40.

> A generalized study of America's appreciation of nature. Chapters 9-12 deal with the growth of the national parks. See also the annotation for this item in Chapter 1, Section A: General Studies.

Nash, Roderick. "John Muir, William Kent, and the Conservation Schism." PACIFIC HISTORICAL REVIEW 36 (November 1967): 423-33.

> In this informative article, Nash focuses upon the single example of the varying attitudes toward wilderness that can exist within conservationist circles. The author describes Kent's role as Califor-nia conservationist and congressman, his support for Hetch Hetchy reservoir, and Muir's dedication to the defeat of the project. Al-though Kent donated to the federal government a tract of coastal redwoods in Marin County and insisted that it be designated The Muir Woods National Monument, his friendship with Muir came to an end over the Hetch Hetchy issue.

_____. WILDERNESS AND THE AMERICAN MIND. Rev. ed. New Haven and London: Yale University Press, 1973. xvi, 300 p. Bibliography, pp. 274-88.

> Chapters 6-8 and 10 deal in part with the creation and growth of the national park system, especially within the context of the idea of wilderness. See also the annotation for this item in Chapter 5, Section A: General and Historical.

Richardson, Elmo R. THE POLITICS OF CONSERVATION: CRUSADE AND CONTROVERSIES, 1897-1913. University of California Publications in History, vol. 70. Berkeley and Los Angeles: University of California Press, 1962. ix, 207 p. Notes, pp. 163-86. Bibliography, pp. 189-97.

> Although valuable as a treatment of the political issues of the conservation movement from 1897 to 1913, Richardson's book has little to offer the student of national parks and natural beauty.

Swain, Donald C. FEDERAL CONSERVATION POLICY, 1921-1933. Univer-sity of California Publications in History, vol. 76. Berkeley and Los Angeles:

University of California Press, 1963. 221 p. Bibliographical note, pp. 173-79. Notes, pp. 183-207.

> Swain devotes a valuable chapter, "The Preservation of Natural Beauty" (pp. 123-43), to the development of the National Park Service, its activities, policies, and its struggles with the U.S. Forest Service for control of scenic and recreational areas.

U.S. President's Council on Recreation and Natural Beauty. FROM SEA TO SHINING SEA: A REPORT ON THE AMERICAN ENVIRONMENT--OUR NATURAL HERITAGE. Washington, D.C.: Government Printing Office, 1968. 304 p. Illustrated. Paper.

> On May 4, 1966, President Johnson established the President's Council on Recreation and Natural Beauty, chaired by Vice-President Humphrey, and the Citizen's Advisory Committee on Recreation and Natural Beauty, chaired by Laurence S. Rockefeller. FROM SEA TO SHINING SEA is their joint report. The two groups had three objectives: to "outline progress in environmental programs since the 1965 White House Conference on Natural Beauty" (see White House Conference on Natural Beauty, Washington, 1965, cited below in Section E: Conference Reports); to "make proposals and recommendations to stimulate federal, state, local, and private action to enhance the quality of our environment and [natural beauty]"; and to provide a guide for further action on the part of officials, groups, and private citizens. Much of the report proposes long-term goals and covers aspects of environmental concern. Only seventy-two pages deal specifically with "Rural Areas" ("The Countryside," "Waterways," and "Recreation and Wildlands"). Part IV lists books, periodicals, pamphlets, and films. It also includes a list of local, state, federal, and private organizations "which can help."

C. GUIDES TO NATIONAL PARKS

There are innumerable guides to the national parks. Listed below are some of the best and most comprehensive guides, as well as several that are historically significant. For additional titles, consult Chapter 2, Section D: Travel Reports by Region. See also A BIBLIOGRAPHY OF NATIONAL PARKS AND MONUMENTS WEST OF THE MISSISSIPPI RIVER, cited above in Section A: Bibliographies.

Allen, Edward Frank, ed. A GUIDE TO THE NATIONAL PARKS OF AMERICA. [New York]: Robert McBride, 1915. 286 p. Plates. Folding map. 16 cm. Rev. ed. [New York]: Robert McBride, 1918. 338 p. Plates. Folding maps. 16 cm.

> Insofar as the editor can determine, the first edition of Allen's book was the first guide book to include all national parks in its

schedule of trips and information. The author was the editor of
TRAVEL.

Butcher, Devereux. EXPLORING OUR NATIONAL PARKS AND MONUMENTS.
6th ed., rev. Boston: Houghton Mifflin, 1969. xiii, 369 p. Illustrated.
Maps. Bibliography, pp. 360-66.

   A thoroughly competent and accurate guide to the parks and monuments in each of its editions. The book is sponsored by the National Parks and Conservation Association.

Matthews, William H. III. A GUIDE TO THE NATIONAL PARKS, THEIR
LANDSCAPE AND GEOLOGY. Foreword by Paul M. Tilden. 2 vols. Garden City, N.Y.: Natural History Press, 1968.

   A useful compendium of information by a professor of geology.
   The two volumes are a guide to the thirty-two parks (not monuments) with primary emphasis upon their landforms and geologic
   history. Each park's scenic features are described and a section
   on what to do and see is included. At the end of each chapter
   is a brief summary of the park's size, attractions, season, accomo-
   dations, services, programs, and special features. Volume One
   covers western parks; Volume Two, eastern. Each volume contains
   the same introductory chapters on the national park system, "science and scenery," and guidelines for enjoying and protecting
   them. Concluding each volume is a glossary of terms and a bibliography, which is useful for geological information, but slights
   other aspects.

Mills, Enos A. YOUR NATIONAL PARKS. With Detailed Information for
Tourists by Laurence F. Schmeckebier. Boston and New York: Houghton
Mifflin, 1917. xxi, 531 p. Illustrated, with plates. Maps. Bibliography,
pp. 417-21.

   Mills was a famous wilderness guide, author, and resort owner.
   His efforts were instrumental in the creation of the Rocky Mountain
   National Park in 1915. His book is well written, informative,
   and, for its time, comprehensive in its historical description of
   the parks and national monuments extant in 1917. For other works
   by Mills, see Chapter 7, Section C: Nature Writing Since
   Thoreau.

Muir, John. OUR NATIONAL PARKS. Boston and New York: Houghton
Mifflin, 1901. 382 p. Illustrated. Maps.

   Made up of sketches from the ATLANTIC MONTHLY written by
   Muir to popularize the scenic wonders of the West. Muir devotes
   a chapter each to Yellowstone, Sequoia, and General Grant National Parks, and to "Forest Reservations of the West"; the other
   six chapters describe various scenic parts of Yosemite. For a list

of other works by Muir, see Chapter 7, Section C: Nature Writing Since Thoreau.

Tilden, Freeman. THE STATE PARKS, THEIR MEANING IN AMERICAN LIFE. Foreword by Conrad L. Wirth. New York: Knopf, 1962. xvi, 496, xi p. Illustrated. Maps.

Similar in form and content to the author's book on the national parks, although now outdated for the newer parks.

_____. THE NATIONAL PARKS. A Revised and Enlarged Edition of the Classic Book on the National Parks with New Information & Evaluation on All of the National Parks, National Monuments, & Historic Sites. Foreword by George B. Hartzog, Jr. New York: Knopf, 1968. xviii, 562, xix p. Illustrated. Maps.

Originally published in 1951. A fascinating guide and compendium of information on the parks, their history, geography and meaning. Profusely illustrated. In many ways the best of the guides.

Yard, Robert Sterling. THE BOOK OF THE NATIONAL PARKS. New York: Scribner, 1919. xv, 420 p. Illustrated. Maps and diagrams.

The author, formerly an author and editor, was pressed into service as Chief of the Educational Division of the National Park Service by Stephen Mather, the Director. Yard did a magnificent job of popularizing and promoting the use of the parks. He was later to become the first president of The Wilderness Society in 1935. This book is a pioneer effort to combine popular writing style and scientific content for the average American interested in visiting the parks.

D. HISTORY

Books and Articles

Hampton, H. Duane. HOW THE U.S. CAVALRY SAVED OUR NATIONAL PARKS. Bloomington and London: Indiana University Press, 1971. 246 p. Illustrated. Map. Bibliography, pp. 190-206. Notes, pp. 207-42.

Although Yellowstone, the nation's first national park, had been created in 1872, the Department of the Interior was ill-equipped because of inadequate appropriations to defend the park against poachers, trespassing, and recurring vandalism. In 1886 the Secretary of the Interior asked the U.S. Army for troops to protect Yellowstone. Hampton tells the story of the army's administration of Yellowstone and other later military management in Yosemite, General Grant, and Sequoia national parks, until the creation of the National Park Service in 1916. More than half the book covers the history of the Yellowstone occupation.

Huth, Hans. "Yosemite: The Story of An Idea." SIERRA CLUB BULLETIN 33, no. 3 (March 1948): 47-78.

A significant essay. Huth disputes the idea that the establishment of Yellowstone in 1872 sparked the movement for a national park system. He analyzes the historical background of the cession of Yosemite Valley to California by Congress in 1864 and states that the national park idea was engendered by this Congressional action. Huth chronicles the growth of the appreciation of natural beauty in his NATURE AND THE AMERICAN, cited above in Section B: General.

James, Harlean. ROMANCE OF THE NATIONAL PARKS. New York: Macmillan 1939. xiv, 240 p. Illustrated. Map.

Although this book is not documented and has neither bibliography nor footnotes, it is still a remarkably good popular history, informed by Miss James's special knowledge gained as a result of her long tenure as Executive Secretary of the American Planning and Civic Association.

Johnson, Robert Underwood. REMEMBERED YESTERDAYS. Boston: Little, Brown, 1929. xxi, 624 p. Plates. Facsimiles.

This is a reprint, with minor alterations, of the first edition published in 1923. Johnson was the conservation-minded editor of THE CENTURY. For a description of his conservation alliance with John Muir and the fight for Hetch Hetchy, see pp. 279-316.

Mills, Enos A.

Mills was a key figure in the creation of the Rocky Mountain National Park, a noted conservationist, lecturer, and nature writer. For a list of his writings and an introductory annotation, see Chapter 7, Section C: Nature Writing Since Thoreau.

Muir, John

Many of Muir's works are concerned with national parks--their preservation and their natural beauty. For a list of his writings, bibliographies and critical works about Muir, see Chapter 7, Section C: Nature Writing Since Thoreau.

Nash, Roderick. "The American Invention of National Parks." AMERICAN QUARTERLY 22, no. 3 (Fall 1970): 726-35.

A discussion of the historical development of the national park idea in America and the reasons for its implementation.

"The National Parks; Six Chapters in the History of An American Idea." THE AMERICAN WEST 6, no. 5 (September 1969).

A special issue edited by Donald C. Swain, and illustrated with photographs by Ansel Adams. It contains the following articles: "Introduction," by George B. Hartzog, Jr.; "The Founding of the National Park Service," by Donald C. Swain; "'Will Anyone Come Here for Pleasure?'," by Richard A. Bartlett; "Harding, Coolidge, and the Lady Who Lost Her Dress (Ten Years as Yellowstone's First Superintendent)," by Horace M. Albright; "The Man Who 'Owned' Grand Canyon," by Douglas Hillman Strong; "Pilgrim's Pride," by T.H. Watkins; and "The Last of the Redwoods," by Michael Mc-Closkey.

Olmsted, Frederick Law. "The Yosemite Valley and the Mariposa Big Trees, a Preliminary Report (1865)...With an Introductory Note by Laura Wood Roper." LANDSCAPE ARCHITECTURE 43, no. 1 (October 1952): 12-25.

This hitherto unpublished report of the Yosemite Commission (appointed by Governor Frederick F. Low in 1864) was never sent to the state legislature. The only extant copy was located in Olmsted's office in 1952. The report, written by Olmsted, is a fascinating document because, in addition to examining the philosophical and historical background for public parks and discussing the psychological and physical value of scenery to America, Olmsted also detailed a plan to conserve the natural beauty of Yosemite while opening it to the public.

Roosevelt, Nicholas. CONSERVATION: NOW OR NEVER. New York: Dodd, Mead, 1970. x, 238 p.

The title of this book is misleading, for it is not so much a plea for conservation as it is a valuable history of the conservation movement by one who was active in it. Roosevelt, a cousin of Theodore Roosevelt, has had a distinguished career as a journalist and editorial writer, as a public servant and diplomat, and as a conservationist and author. He has long been involved in the struggle to preserve scenic areas in the United States and has known personally many of the leading participants in that continuing struggle. His book is both a narration of the events in which he took a part, and a more generalized history. In terms of the preservation movement, the author might be called a moderate, for he doesn't condone the indiscriminate locking up of wilderness for its own sake, and he takes a charitable position toward the state highway commissions, the U.S. Forest Service, and other government agencies—all of which have been roundly criticized by ardent preservationists.

Shankland, Robert. STEVE MATHER OF THE NATIONAL PARKS. 3rd ed., rev. and enl. New York: Knopf, 1970. xii, 370, xxiii p. Illustrated. Map. Bibliography, pp. 365-70.

Mather was the first director of the National Park Service and is justifiably known as the "father" of the Service. During his tenure (1917-28), Mather ably and energetically pursued a policy of proselytizing for the Park idea among businessmen, government and Congressional leaders, and members of the press. Shankland's is the only biography of Mather and is a valuable contribution. The volume was first published in 1951; this edition "has been reissued and enlarged by the publisher."

Strong, Douglas H. "The Rise of American Esthetic Conservation: Muir, Mather, and Udall." NATIONAL PARKS MAGAZINE 44, no. 269 (February 1970): 5-9.

A brief historical sketch of the fight for esthetic conservation between the preservationists and multiple-use proponents.

Swain, Donald C. "The Passage of the National Park Service Act of 1916." WISCONSIN MAGAZINE OF HISTORY 50, no. 1 (Autumn 1966): 4-17.

The National Park Service Act of August 1916 was the achievement of a collaboration of "aesthetic conservationists," sympathetic federal legislators and journalists, and particularly of Stephen T. Mather, then assistant to the Secretary of the Interior, and his own young assistant, Horace M. Albright. Swain points out that the creation of the Park Service marks the emergence of that group within the conservation movement variously described as "nature-lovers," "aesthetic conservationists," and "preservationists." Much of the material in his article was later used by the author in his biography of Albright, cited below.

. WILDERNESS DEFENDER: HORACE M. ALBRIGHT AND CONSER-VATION. Chicago and London: University of Chicago Press, 1970. xii, 347 p. Illustrated. Bibliography, pp. 323-32.

Horace Albright has had a distinguished career as a conservationist and public administrator. After graduation from the University of California, he accepted a post in Washington in 1913 as a clerk to the Secretary of the Interior. In 1915 Albright became Stephen Mather's assistant in the job of unifying the administration of the national parks. After serving as Superintendent of Yellowstone and as Assistant Director of the National Park Service, he succeeded Mather as Director in 1929 and held that post until his retirement from the Service in 1933. Swain's biography is a well balanced and judicious treatment of Albright's public career. It is based heavily upon manuscripts, oral history transcripts, and interviews with Albright and those who were associated with him. An important and lively account.

Histories of Individual Parks

Campbell, Carlos C. BIRTH OF A NATIONAL PARK IN THE GREAT SMOKY
MOUNTAINS; AN UNPRECEDENTED CRUSADE WHICH CREATED, AS A GIFT
OF THE PEOPLE, THE NATION'S MOST POPULAR PARK. Preface by Horace
M. Albright. Rev. ed. [Knoxville: University of Tennessee Press, 1969].
155 p. Illustrated.

> The author is Secretary of the Great Smoky Mountains Conservation
> Association, for whom this history was written. According to
> Albright, Campbell "was in the midst of the struggle to create"
> the park. Although there are occasional references to local news-
> paper stories and to a few other sources, the history is largely
> undocumented. Another account, well written and thoroughly
> documented, may be read in:
>
> > Frome, Michael. STRANGERS IN HIGH PLACES: THE
> > STORY OF THE GREAT SMOKY MOUNTAINS. Garden
> > City, N.Y.: Doubleday, 1966.

Chittenden, Hiram Martin. THE YELLOWSTONE NATIONAL PARK, HISTORI-
CAL AND DESCRIPTIVE. New ed., enl. Cincinnati: Stewart & Kidd, [1918].
vii, 350 p. Plates. Maps.

> The author, a retired army officer, spent two tours of duty in
> Yellowstone. His love for the Park's wilderness areas is apparent.
> The present edition of the work first published in 1895 contains
> two sections, one historical, the second descriptive. The latter
> part deals with the scenery, geology, natural history, and its
> natural resources. Several tours for prospective visitors are de-
> scribed. Since its publication, Chittenden's work has become a
> classic work on Yellowstone and has been reprinted several times.
> The last edition, edited and with an introduction by Richard A.
> Bartlett, was published by the University of Oklahoma Press in
> 1964 and is still in print.

Jackson, W. Turrentine. "The Creation of Yellowstone National Park."
MONTANA, MAGAZINE OF WESTERN HISTORY 7 (July 1957): 52-66.

> The author is a noted historian of the American West. The editor
> has not examined this article.

Russell, Carl Parcher. ONE HUNDRED YEARS IN YOSEMITE; THE ROMANTIC
STORY OF EARLY HUMAN AFFAIRS IN THE CENTRAL SIERRA NEVADA.
Stanford, Calif.: Stanford University Press; London: Humphrey Milford at the
Oxford University Press, 1931. xvi, 241 p. Illustrated, with plates. Appen-
dix of documents, pp. 169-202. Chronology, pp. 203-16. Bibliography, pp.
217-30. Maps on endpapers. Rev. ed. with subtitle THE STORY OF A
GREAT PARK AND ITS FRIENDS. Berkeley and Los Angeles: University of
California Press, 1947. xviii, 226 p. Illustrated. Folding map. Chronology
and sources, pp. 179-93. Bibliography, pp. 197-213.

Russell was one of the foremost naturalists in the Park Service
when he wrote his history. The first edition was published while
he was a field naturalist, and the book quickly established itself
as the standard history of Yosemite. The second edition is a
revised and partly rewritten history based upon new materials not
previously available. The first edition is still useful for the documents on Yosemite history which are reprinted in the appendix.
Russell later became Superintendent of Yosemite.

Smith, Charles D. "The Appalachian National Park Movement, 1885-1901."
NORTH CAROLINA HISTORICAL REVIEW 37 (January 1960): 38-65.

Not examined by the editor.

Watkins, T.H., ed. THE GRAND COLORADO, THE STORY OF A RIVER
AND ITS CANYONS. Photographs by Philip Hyde. Palo Alto, Calif.:
American West Publishing Co., 1969. 310 p. Illustrations (some in color).
Maps and diagrams.

The volume includes contributions by William E. Brown, Jr.,
Robert C. Euler, Helen Hosmer, Roderick Nash, Roger Olmsted,
Wallace Stegner, Paul S. Taylor, and Robert A. Weinstein. This
is an excellent, lavishly produced pictorial history of the Colorado
River and its canyons. The text includes chapters on ethnography,
geology, exploration, reclamation and dam building, scenic reports
by visitors, conservation and preservation, and the development of
the national parks and monuments.

E. CONFERENCE REPORTS

Conservation Foundation. NATIONAL PARKS FOR THE FUTURE, AN APPRAIS-
AL OF THE NATIONAL PARKS AS THEY BEGIN THEIR SECOND CENTURY
IN A CHANGING AMERICA. Washington, D.C.: 1972. viii, 254 p.

An interesting assessment of the many problems facing the national
parks now and in the future, along with outlines of specific reme-
dies. The report grew out of a National Parks Centennial Symposium held in Yosemite during 1972.

GOVERNORS' CONFERENCE ON THE CONSERVATION OF NATURAL RE-
SOURCES IN THE WHITE HOUSE, MAY 13-15, 1908, 60th Cong., 2d sess.,
House Document, no. 1425 (Serial 5538). Washington, D.C.: Government
Printing Office, 1909. 451 p.

President Theodore Roosevelt called this conference on conservation,
the first such presidential meeting in American history, to examine
the need for conserving our natural resources. Of the many reports and addresses, only two were concerned with preservation of
natural beauty. J. Horace McFarland, President of the American
Civic Association, spoke on the value of natural scenery (pp. 153-

57) and Dr. George F. Kunz, President of the American Scenic and Historic Society, addressed the conference on "The Preservation of Scenic Beauty" (pp. 408-19).

McFarland assailed the conference's disproportionate concern for conservation of material resources alone. "It is the love of country that has lighted and that keeps glowing the holy fire of patriotism. And this love is excited, primarily, by the beauty of the country." McFarland urged that the use of our mineral and timber resources not be damaging to scenic resources. "The scenic value of all the national domain yet remaining should be jealously guarded as a distinctly important natural resource, and not as a mere incidental increment." McFarland's remarks were reprinted in AMERICAN FORESTS (volume 14, August 1908, pp. 457-59) and in the SIERRA CLUB BULLETIN (volume 7, no. 1, January 1909, pp. 64-69).

Kunz informed the conference that the purpose of the "Scenic Society" was "to encourage the regard for the beautiful without [checking] the development of forests, mines, or railroads or the rational use of water for power, irrigation, or municipal use." Yet it was clear that we had wasted our resources, polluted our streams, and ravaged our scenery. He therefore supported government regulation and supervision of the individual or corporate use of natural resources. In describing his own Society's activities, Kunz pointed out that scenic and historic "resources" can bring revenue in the form of tourist dollars. He urged that the governors each set aside "some site of scenic beauty" to "mark the hundredth anniversary of steam navigation."

National Conservation Commission. REPORT, Vol. 1, 60th Cong., 2d sess., Senate Document, no. 676 (Serial 5397-99). Washington, D.C.: Government Printing Office, 1909. 276 p.

The Commission, appointed by Theodore Roosevelt, was an outgrowth of the Governors' Conference called by the president in May 1908 (cited above). Gifford Pinchot was the chairman. No esthetic conservationists were called to the Commission and its report makes no recommendations for preservation of natural beauty. "National parks" appears in the report twice, each time in connection with forest reserves and their production and use. The report was devoted exclusively to natural (material) resources. J. Horace McFarland took note of this omission in his article "Shall We Have Ugly Conservation?" (THE OUTLOOK, volume 91, March 13, 1909, pp. 594-98) and strongly denounced the Commission for its lack of foresight.

"Our National Parks: A Conference; The Proposed National Park Service." LANDSCAPE ARCHITECTURE 6, no. 3 (April 1916): 101-23.

Addresses and letters presented at the meeting of the American Society of Landscape Architects, held in Boston on February 14,

1916. The National Park Service Act became law in August of that year.

U.S. National Conference on Outdoor Recreation. PROCEEDINGS, 68th Cong., 1st sess., Senate Document, no. 151 (Serial 8249). Washington, D.C.: Government Printing Office, 1924. 1v, 244 p.

Held in Washington on May 22–24, 1924, the Conference was called by President Coolidge to assist the administration in formulating a national policy on outdoor recreation. The proceedings contain much information on conservation and recreation. The following addresses are especially relevant: "Scenic Resources of the United States," by Robert Sterling Yard, Executive Secretary of the National Parks Association (pp. 45–49); "National Provision for the Enjoyment of Our Scenic Resources," by Henry Vincent Hubbard, of the American Society of Landscape Architects (pp. 58–61); "The Appalachian Trail," by Benton MacKaye, of the Regional Planning Association of America (pp. 124–27); and "Shall We Protect Niagara Falls for Posterity," by J. Horace McFarland, President of the American Civic Association (pp. 137–44).

U.S. National Conference on Outdoor Recreation, 2d. PROCEEDINGS, 69th Cong., 1st sess., Senate Document, no. 117 (Serial 8549). Washington, D.C.: Government Printing Office, 1926. v, 175 p.

Held in Washington, D.C., on January 20–21, 1926. The Conference proceedings contain much information in the form of addresses and resolutions regarding general recreation policy, conservation, national and state parks, outdoor education and nature study, wilderness conservation (see remarks by Aldo Leopold, pp. 61–65), wildlife management, and pollution. Delegates of note addressing the conference included T. Gilbert Pearson, Arthur Newton Pack, Ernest Thompson Seton, John C. Merriam, Stephen T. Mather, Aldo Leopold, and Herbert Hoover.

White House Conference on Conservation, Washington, D.C., 1962. OFFICIAL PROCEEDINGS, May 24 to 25, 1962. Washington, D.C.: Government Printing Office, [1963]. iv, 103 p. Illustrated. Paper.

Compared to the last such conference in 1908, this one accomplished relatively little, for "no conclusions were drawn...and no recommendations or resolutions were offered." It met in plenary sessions only. Its stated purpose was "to stimulate the exchange of ideas about the future course of American conservation policy." The conference used panel discussions followed by questions from the audience to stimulate the exchange. This is a relatively unimportant source. There is little emphasis upon national parks or wilderness areas, the stress being upon resources and policy.

White House Conference on Natural Beauty, Washington, D.C., 1965.

BEAUTY FOR AMERICA; PROCEEDINGS, May 24 to 25, 1965. Washington, D.C.: Government Printing Office, 1965. v, 782 p. Paper.

"These proceedings present the edited and in some cases revised transcript....Also included...are the action recommendations of the Conference, President Johnson's address to the Congress of February 8, 1965 and a number of additional statements submitted for the record by participants." An index and list of participants facilitates the use of the material, which was the prelude to the great "clean-up" of America.

F. PARK POLICY AND INSTITUTIONAL STUDIES

Everhart, William C. THE NATIONAL PARK SERVICE. New York, Washington, and London: Praeger, 1972. xii, 276 p. Illustrated. Chart. Map. Bibliography, pp. 261-63.

This is a successful, short administrative study by a veteran member of the Service. Everhart reviews the origin and history of the agency, as well as its organization, functions, and goals. In addition, he discusses such issues as preservation and/or use, protection, and concessionaires. He describes the life of park employees and outlines relationships with Congress, with other federal agencies, and with conservation organizations. A very useful current list of the 284 park areas is given in an appendix. Largely replaced by Ise's and Everhart's books is Jenks Cameron's THE NATIONAL PARK SERVICE: ITS HISTORY, ACTIVITIES AND ORGANIZATION (Brookings Institution, Washington, D.C., Institute for Government Research, Service Monographs of the United States Government, no. 11. New York and London: Appleton, 1922. xii, 172 p. Tables. Folding map. Bibliography, pp. 141-66).

Ise, John. OUR NATIONAL PARK POLICY: A CRITICAL HISTORY. Baltimore: Published for Resources for the Future, Inc. by Johns Hopkins Press, 1961. xiii, 701 p. Illustrated. Maps.

This book is one of a series of studies of land use and management sponsored by Resources for the Future. Its purpose is to trace the development of a unified national park policy and its emphasis is upon administrative history and detail. The author divided the book into three parts. The first deals with the history and development of the early parks from 1872 to 1916; the second covers the administrative history of the Park Service through the various directorships from 1916 to 1959; while the third part examines special problems like wildlife, concessionaires, financing, and wilderness areas. Though there is no formal bibliography, Ise's documentation is impressive; the footnotes show a heavy reliance upon government documents. A valuable, though heavily detailed, study.

Lee, Ronald F. PUBLIC USE OF THE NATIONAL PARK SYSTEM, 1872-2000. [Washington, D.C.]: National Park Service, United States Department of the Interior, January 1, 1968. 93 p. Paper.

> A useful survey, although obsolete in terms of policy objectives. Lee, a retired official with thirty-two years in the Park Service, was a special adviser to the director when he wrote this pamphlet.

G. VIEWS, ATTITUDES, AND PROMOTIONAL MATERIALS

The following listing comprises a representative selection from a very large number of titles reflecting views and attitudes toward natural beauty and the national parks in America from 1910 to 1972. Included are a number of promotional materials frankly intended to "sell" the parks. For older scenic reports and attitudes, see Chapter 2, Section D: Travel Reports by Region, especially those relating to Yellowstone, Yosemite, and the Grand Canyon.

Abbey, Edward. DESERT SOLITAIRE: A SEASON IN THE WILDERNESS. New York: McGraw-Hill, 1968. xiv, 269 p. Illustrated.

> A beautifully written personal appeal for the preservation of wilderness in our national parks. Abbey recounts his experiences as a seasonal ranger in Arches National Monument and states his own opposition to the Park Service's policy of making our parks and monuments more accessible to greater numbers of people. The author is in favor of eliminating automobiles from many parks. A controversial proposal cogently presented.

Albright, Horace M., and Taylor, Frank J. "OH, RANGER!" A BOOK ABOUT THE NATIONAL PARKS. Rev. ed. New York: Dodd, Mead, 1947. xvi, 299 p. Illustrated.

> One of the most popular books ever written about the national parks. Since it was first published by Stanford University Press in 1928, the book has gone through four editions and thirteen printings, finally going out of print in 1949. "OH RANGER!" grew out of material accumulated by Albright while he was superintendent of Yellowstone, and which was worked over by Taylor and supplemented by him. Basically an informal, humorous, and anecdotal book for tourists, it has little significance beyond its great popularity.

Brooks, Paul. "The Pressure of Numbers." ATLANTIC MONTHLY 207, no. 2 (February 1961): 54-56.

> Brooks's essay discusses the pressures of increasing numbers of visitors to the parks and offers some tentative solutions. See annotation for Butcher, Devereux, below.

Bryce, James. "National Parks--The Need of the Future." THE OUTLOOK 102 (December 14, 1912): 811-15.

> James Bryce, later Lord Bryce, was a famous scholar, diplomat, and author of the landmark study of American institutions, THE AMERICAN COMMONWEALTH (1889). He delivered this perceptive address to the eighth annual convention of the American Civic Association on November 20, 1912. Bryce's theme was the growing need to preserve scenic beauty in the United States for its future citizens. The author was, at this time, the British ambassador to the United States.

Butcher, Devereux. "Resorts or Wilderness." ATLANTIC MONTHLY 207, no. 2 (February 1961): 45-61.

> Butcher's essay is a contribution to a special section of the ATLANTIC entitled "Our National Parks in Jeopardy." Although somewhat dated, the essay is valuable as a representative statement about the deteriorating quality of the park system. The author, former executive secretary of the National Parks Association and a strong preservationist, states that the goal of park-minded citizens should be to maintain the parks, as much as possible, "as nature made them." That, he felt sure, was the meaning of the Congressional mandate to "'leave them unimpared.'" To document his assertion of deteriorating quality, Butcher surveyed conditions in Mount McKinley, The Everglades, Yellowstone, Grand Canyon, Grand Teton, and Yosemite Parks.
>
> The series, in which Butcher's was the lead article, provoked considerable response. It can be found in the April 1961 issue (pp. 36-37) and in the May issue (pp. 27-28).

Craig, James B. "Natural Beauty--The Follow Through." AMERICAN FORESTS 71, no. 10 (October 1965): 12-15, 54-55.

> This article reviews the events of the joint meeting of the American Forestry Association and the National Council of State Garden Clubs held in Grand Teton National Park. See also the annotation for Train, Russell, below.

Darling, Frank Fraser, and Eichorn, Noel D. THE NATIONAL PARKS; REFLECTIONS ON POLICY. Washington, D.C.: The Conservation Foundation, 1967. 80 p. Illustrated.

> The report of a study made by the authors "into some of the social-political-ecological problems of the national parks of the United States."

De Voto, Bernard. "Let's Close the National Parks." HARPER'S MAGAZINE 207 (October 1953): 49-52.

> De Voto, in a tone of outrage and indignation, described the

terrible condition of the national parks in 1953, citing the lack
of Congressional funds as the primary reason for neglect of the
parks. De Voto suggested that, to make the miniscule appropria-
tion last, the National Park Service should close Yellowstone,
Rocky Mountain, Yosemite, and Grand Canyon Parks--"close
and seal them [and] assign the Army to patrol them" for the use
of more enlightened future visitors. De Voto hoped that such
deprivation would cause the public to demand of Congress the
necessary appropriations to maintain the parks in an acceptable
manner.

Dolan, Edwin. "Why Not Sell the National Parks?" NATIONAL REVIEW
23, no. 13 (April 6, 1971): 362-65.

In what is described as a "modest proposal," the author in fact
puts forward in some detail a revolutionary proposal to auction
off the national parks to private interests, allowing them to be
used for recreational or purely commercial purposes. The author's
contention is that the present subsidy of the parks by federal tax
funds is unfair to great numbers of citizens who get no use from
them. Dolan reviews the arguments of preservationists and wilderness enthusiasts for maintaining governmental control and then
proceeds to negate them, largely in economic terms. He states,
for example, that although wilderness does possess spiritual value,
it definitely can be expressed in monetary terms. This is a most
provocative and controversial argument.

Eliot, Charles W. "The Need of Conserving the Beauty and Freedom of
Nature in Modern Life." NATIONAL GEOGRAPHIC MAGAZINE 26, no. 1
(July 1914): 67-73.

Eliot, president emeritus of Harvard University, wrote persuasively
of the need of urban dwellers for the uplifting experience of nature.
He argued for more city parks, arboretums, and botanical gardens,
as well as national parks.

Goldman, Don. "National Parks and the Ecology of Beauty." AMERICAN
FORESTS 72, no. 11 (November 1966): 18-21, 46, 48, 50, 52.

In stressing the uniqueness of the national park concept, the
author examines the idea of natural beauty as both physical
environment and human experience. Mere protection of natural
beauty in the park context is not enough, says the author, and
he calls for an ecological study of park landscapes.

Grosvenor, Gilbert H. "The Land of the Best." NATIONAL GEOGRAPHIC
MAGAZINE 29, no. 4 (April 1916): 327-430.

A popular, promotional survey of the scenic spots of the United
States with special emphasis on the national parks. Grosvenor
was editor of the NATIONAL GEOGRAPHIC and a friend of

Stephen Mather, then Assistant Secretary of the Interior in charge of the parks. The article includes historic and picturesque urban and semirural areas as well as wild lands.

[Johnson, Robert Underwood.] "The Neglect of Beauty in the Conservation Movement." THE CENTURY 79, no. 4 (February 1910): 637-38.

Johnson, editor of THE CENTURY magazine, used this forum for years to advance the cause of conservation. He and John Muir formed an alliance to promote the cause of making Yosemite a national park. In this brief editorial, Johnson takes issue with Gifford Pinchot and his followers for not recognizing the importance of natural beauty as a criterion for establishing national parks and monuments.

McFarland, J. Horace. "Our National Parks." LANDSCAPE ARCHITECTURE 5, no. 3 (April 1915): 148-50.

A letter read at the Boston meeting of the American Society of Landscape Architects, February 24, 1915. McFarland was President of the American Civic Association.

_____. "Twenty Years of Scenery-Saving in America." LANDSCAPE ARITECTURE 20, no. 4 (July 1930): 301-7.

McFarland, past-president of the American Civic Association, describes briefly the success of that organization in its efforts to save scenic resources.

Mather, Stephen T. "Our National Parks for the American People." MUNSEY'S MAGAZINE 63, no. 3 (April 1918): 661-75.

An effort to popularize the parks by the Director of the National Park Service. Pages 661-72 are photos of national park scenery.

Merriam, Lawrence C., Jr. "National Park System Growth and Outlook." NATIONAL PARKS AND CONSERVATION MAGAZINE 46 (December 1972): 4-12.

The author is Vice-Chairman of the Board of Trustees of the National Parks and Conservation Association. The article is an excellent short review of the major points of park system history as well as an analysis of current problems. One of these is the recreation versus preservation conflict in terms of the mission of the National Park Service. See also RECREATIONAL USE OF WILD LANDS, of which Merriam was a coauthor, cited under Brockman, Christian Frank, in Section B: General, above.

Neuberger, Richard L. "How Much Conservation?" SATURDAY EVENING POST, June 15, 1940, pp. 12, 89-90, 92, 94-96.

In this somewhat ambiguous article, Neuberger, who was later
to become U.S. Senator from Oregon, discusses the place of
national parks in the Pacific Northwest. He adduces arguments
for and against tourism and recreation versus lumbermen, stock-
men, and mine owners. Neuberger seemingly sought to balance
the rights of the individual against the public good, but his arguments seemed to the editor to favor individual rights.

Rinehart, Mary Roberts. "Sleeping Giant." LADIES HOME JOURNAL 39
(May 1921): 20-21, 80, 83.

Discussion of the national parks as a refuge for people seeking
wilderness and an exhortation to the American people (who, col-
lectively, are the "Sleeping Giant") to remain awake in order to
beat down attempts to commercialize the parks and steal their
natural resources.

Train, Russell. "America the Beautiful." AMERICAN FORESTS 71, no. 10
(October 1965): 16-19, 46-47, 49-50.

Keynote address to the 90th Annual Meeting of the American
Forestry Association by the president of the Conservation Foundation. The topic was the preservation of natural beauty in the
United States. This article and that by James B. Craig, above,
reflect the interest in a beautiful America which was being promoted by the Johnson administration.

Udall, Stewart. "National Parks for the Future." ATLANTIC MONTHLY
207, no. 6 (June 1961): 81-84.

Written in response to the ATLANTIC's series noted above (in
the annotation for Butcher, Devereux). Secretary Udall, six
months into his administration of the Interior Department, reviews
the conditions in the National Parks (brought about largely by
war-time neglect), discusses the Park Service's "Mission 66"
project, and calls for the development of new national, state,
and regional parks to aid in relieving pressure on the system.

_____. "Address." In TOMORROW'S WILDERNESS, edited by Francois
Leydet, pp. 205-19. Wilderness Conference, 8th session. San Francisco:
Sierra Club, 1963.

Udall reviews the record of the Kennedy administration since
1961: the development of new national parks, acquisition of
new land, the loss of opportunities, and the inevitable failures.
He also discusses three obsolete assumptions: "that man must
destroy nature in order to 'conquer' it"; "that science alone can
solve all our problems"; and "that the population explosion is
inevitable."

U.S. Department of the Interior. NATIONAL PARKS PORTFOLIO. Text and picture selection by Robert Sterling Yard. [New York: Scribner, 1916]. 9 pamphlets, with 4 pages of introductory text, in a paper wrapper. Illustrated. Map on inside of wrapper.

See next item.

U.S. National Park Service. THE NATIONAL PARKS PORTFOLIO. By Robert Sterling Yard. 2nd ed. Washington, D.C.: Government Printing Office, 1917. 260 p. Illustrated. Map. Loose in flexible paper cover. 3rd ed., 1921. 266 p. Illustrated. Map. 4th ed., 1925. 270 p. Illustrated. Map. 5th ed., 1928. 270 p. Illustrated. Map. 6th ed., revised by Isabelle F. Story, 1931. 274 p. Illustrated. Map.

Robert Shankland, in his book STEVE MATHER OF THE NATIONAL PARKS (1970, pp. 97-99), relates that Mather wheedled $43,000 out of western railroads and, with $5,000 of his own money, put together the nine pamphlets that comprised the first edition of the PORTFOLIO. Although each of the original pamphlets bore the inscription "Department of the Interior, Franklin K. Lane, Secretary," the first PORTFOLIO was a private venture. Mather and Yard mailed at government expense 275,000 copies to a select group of professional people, business leaders, university staff members, and other influential individuals whom Mather hoped would promote the use of the parks. The PORTFOLIO was overwhelmingly well received and the newly formed Park Service was able to collect a price for all editions after the first. The format changed, with the third edition, to bound books. The PORTFOLIO, in its six editions, is the all-time best seller of the National Park Service.

Yard, Robert Sterling. "The People and the National Parks." SURVEY GRAPHIC 48, no. 13 (August 1922): 547-53, 583.

An excellent contemporary assessment of the parks and their significance to America by the Executive Secretary of the National Parks Association. Yard felt that the parks could no longer be considered as travel resorts for the affluent few. "They have become part of the general popular conception of the greatness of America."

H.   ORGANIZATION PUBLICATIONS

What follows is a list of materials published or prepared by those conservation organizations that have had, or continue to have, a major impact upon the creation and preservation of national parks. Not included here are the publications of organizations such as the American Society of Landscape Architects, the American Forestry Association, the Izaak Walton League, the National Audubon Society, and other associations too numerous to mention here. Chapter 11 contains a list of publications of the major national organizations functioning in the areas of conservation and environmental preservation.

AMERICAN PLANNING AND CIVIC ANNUAL. Washington, D.C.: American Planning and Civic Association, 1929-57. Title varies.

The American Civic Association was formed in 1904 by the union of the American Park and Outdoor Art Association and the American League for Civic Improvement. In 1935 the A.C.A. joined with the National Conference on City Planning to become the American Planning and Civic Association. J. Horace McFarland became the Association's first president in 1904 and served for twenty years. The Association promoted the ideals of civic beauty in America, the preservation and development of landscape, the protection of national parks, comprehensive city planning, and better use of land for both city and country. The Association was a pioneer in the advocacy of national parks and the creation of the National Park Service. The ANNUAL is a good source for following the activities of the Association. It contains generally short essays on national parks and forests, wilderness areas, regional planning, scenic highways, roadside improvements, local parks and gardens, state parks, housing projects, and civic progress. The early volumes contain articles by such notables as Stephen Mather, Horace Albright, Albert Shaw, J.H. McFarland, and F.L. Olmsted, Jr. The section on national parks contains essays and reports by officials of the National Park Service. Most volumes have a biographical section, entitled "Who's Who in Civic Achievement," at the end.

American Scenic and Historic Preservation Society. ANNUAL REPORTS. Albany, N.Y.: 1895-1925.

The Society was founded by Andrew H. Green of New York City in 1895. At that time, Green was one of the commissioners of the State Reservation at Niagara. The Society began its existence as the Trustees of Scenic and Historic Places and Objects under a charter granted by the New York State Legislature; the name was changed in 1898 to Society for the Preservation of Scenic and Historic Places and Objects, and in 1901 to its present name. The Society was made up of "substantial, respected, and well-known citizens" (J. Pierpont Morgan was its honorary president), to whom "adequate power and authority" were granted by the legislature to act as a quasi-public body to "acquire, hold, maintain, improve, and administer historic places and objects and picturesque areas of natural scenery." The Society gradually extended its activities beyond New York State boundaries and took an active role in supporting the preservation of scenery and the establishment of the national parks. For a statement of purpose, see the 19th Annual Report, March 24, 1914. See also the Society's successor publication, SCENIC AND HISTORIC AMERICA, published quarterly from 1929 to 1931.

[Boone and Crockett Club]. HUNTING AND CONSERVATION: THE BOOK OF THE BOONE AND CROCKETT CLUB. Edited by George Bird Grinnell and Charles Sheldon. New Haven: Yale University Press, 1925. xiv, 548 p. Illustrated.

> This is the sixth in a series of books sponsored by the Club. It contains fourteen contributions dealing with hunting and conservation. The following are relevant to the scope of this bibliography: "Saving the Redwoods," "The Establishment of Mt. McKinley National Park," and "The Beginnings of Glacier National Park," all by Madison Grant; "Importance of Natural Conditions in National Parks," by Barrington Moore; and "The National Recreation Conference [1924]," by G.B. Grinnell. As in previous volumes by the Club, appendices offer material relating to the Club's conservation activities and goals. Reprinted in 1970. See also BRIEF HISTORY OF THE BOONE AND CROCKETT CLUB, WITH OFFICERS, CONSTITUTION AND A LIST OF MEMBERS FOR 1910, edited by George B. Grinnell (New York: Forest and Stream, n.d. 71 p.).

NATIONAL PARKS AND CONSERVATION MAGAZINE. Washington, D.C.: National Parks and Conservation Association. June 1919--. Title varies.

> Formerly called BULLETINS then NEWS BULLETINS then, from 1939-70, NATIONAL PARKS MAGAZINE. The Association began as the National Parks Association in 1919, just three years after the establishment of the National Park Service. Its avowed purpose was and is the protection of national parks against commercial exploitation and to promote public understanding and support. Since 1970, the Association has broadened its function to include the more general aspects of environmental preservation.

SAVE-THE-REDWOODS LEAGUE BULLETIN. San Francisco: Save-the-Redwoods League, 1918--.

> A California group primarily interested in the preservation of coastal and Sierra redwoods, principally in California. It has been successful in acquiring stands of trees through gift and purchase and then donating them for public use as parks. It cooperates with state and other organizations in its work.

SIERRA CLUB BULLETIN. San Francisco: Sierra Club, 1893--.

> The frequency varies: semiannual, 1893-1905, 1907-13; annual, 1906, 1914-27; bimonthly, 1928-December 1946; eleven times a year, January 1947-May 1951; and ten times a year, June 1951 to date. A FIFTY-SEVEN YEAR INDEX, 1893-1949, compiled by Dorothy H. Bradley and George Shochat, was published by the Club in 1952. Although in its early years the Sierra Club, in practical terms and in the interests of its members, was primarily a mountaineering organization devoted to the exploration and recreational enjoyment of the Sierra Nevada and other mountains in the

West, it rapidly became involved in conservation issues. Beginning during John Muir's presidency and continuing today, the Sierra Club has become almost synonymous with esthetic preservation. Without doubt it has been the single most influential private organization in the United States devoted to the preservation of wilderness, national parks, and, most recently, to the pursuit of environmental quality. There is no formal history of the Club; however, two titles are useful: Holway R. Jones' JOHN MUIR AND THE SIERRA CLUB: THE BATTLE FOR YOSEMITE (San Francisco: Sierra Club, 1965) is a detailed study of Muir's and the Club's battle to save Hetch Hetchy, and the Handbook Edition of the SIERRA CLUB BULLETIN (volume 52, no. 11, December 1967, 63 p.) offers information about the Club, its history, officers, publications, by-laws, organization, and structure, and a useful chronology of activities during 1892-1967. An earlier edition appeared in November 1947 as volume 32, no. 10 of the BULLETIN.

[The Wilderness Society]. THE LIVING WILDERNESS. Washington, D.C. 1935--.

Prior to 1945 LIVING WILDERNESS was published on an irregular basis; since December 1945 it has appeared quarterly. The Society, along with the Sierra Club, has been actively dedicated to the creation and preservation of wilderness areas in the United States. Much of its work has been concerned with the creation of areas in U.S. Forests and National Parks. Through its educational program and its publications, the Society seeks also to promote and explain the values of wilderness in our civilization. For additional material relating to The Wilderness Society, see numerous entries in Chapter 5: Conservation and the Idea of Wilderness.

Chapter 5

CONSERVATION AND THE IDEA OF WILDERNESS

Chapter 5

CONSERVATION AND THE IDEA OF WILDERNESS

Contemporary wilderness preservation grew out of the conservation movement
and today has its own advocates, organizations, and special pleaders. It developed in opposition to the actions of Americans who regard wilderness as a
luxury, or as just another natural resource to be used for the material or economic benefit of our society. Preservationists, in pursuit of their goals, have
engaged in law suits, lobbying, and public relations activities, and have thus
incurred the wrath of the lumbering industry, power companies, mining companies, and other special interest groups. Despite many setbacks and name-calling
by opponents, preservationist organizations such as The Wilderness Society, The
Sierra Club, and The Audubon Society, which devote a major part of their
activity to programs of wilderness protection and environmental education, have
brought the problem of a diminishing American wilderness to the attention of
the public.

Included in this chapter are histories of wilderness in American civilization,
works on the idea of wilderness--its values, uses, and place in today's world--
and the writings of well-known figures who played important roles in the defense of wilderness. Because the movement for the creation of the national
parks is closely related to wilderness preservation, the reader is referred to the
preceding chapter for relevant titles.

No effort has been made to detail the fight to create and preserve individual
wilderness areas. This literature is extremely voluminous. In part, it can be
traced by a close reading of such journals as THE LIVING WILDERNESS, THE
SIERRA CLUB BULLETIN, THE AUDUBON MAGAZINE, and the published
reports of the Wilderness Conferences sponsored by the Sierra Club.

A. GENERAL AND HISTORICAL

In addition to the works below and in Chapter 4, readers interested in pursuing
the study of wilderness should consult the following: Chapter 2, Section D:
Travel Reports by Region, for early titles reflecting American views of nature
(that chapter also contains a list of books on wilderness scenery by the Sierra
Club and The Friends of the Earth); Chapter 3 for pictorial representations of

wilderness in landscape painting; Chapter 7 for the works of many nature writers who have written about wilderness, notably Henry David Thoreau, John Muir, and Sigurd F. Olson; and Chapter 9 for books on the wilderness aspects of camping and outdoor life.

"The Adirondacks." AMERICAN HERITAGE 20, no. 5 (August 1969): 44–63, 96–98.

> The text (pp. 44–48, 96–98) is a brief overview of the history of the Adirondack wilderness, and concludes with a warning of the unlikelihood of the area remaining "forever wild." An "Adirondack Exhibition" (pp. 49–63) contains fifteen color reproductions of paintings by Thomas Cole, Winslow Homer, and others.

Bent, Allen H. "The Mountaineering Clubs of America." APPALACHIA 14 (December 1916): 5–18.

> A brief survey of the founding of the major mountaineering clubs in the United States and Canada.

Broome, Harvey. "Origins of the Wilderness Society." LIVING WILDERNESS 10, no. 5 (July 1940): 13–15.

> The Society was organized in 1935. The author, one of the founders, briefly sketches its origins.

_____. "Decades of the Wilderness Society: Thirty Years." LIVING WILDERNESS 29, no. 91 (Winter 1965–66): 15–26.

> A brief survey of the history of the society from 1935 to 1965. Includes photographs and a list of officers.

Jones, Holway R. JOHN MUIR AND THE SIERRA CLUB: THE BATTLE FOR YOSEMITE. San Francisco: Sierra Club, 1965. xvii, 207 p. Illustrated. Photos. Maps. Appendices. Bibliography, pp. 195–200.

> Traces the development of Yosemite National Park, the founding of the Sierra Club, and the fight for the preservation of Hetch Hetchy Valley. A very valuable and detailed account, based heavily upon manuscripts and archival material.

Nash, Roderick. "The Cultural Significance of the American Wilderness." In WILDERNESS AND THE QUALITY OF LIFE, edited by Maxine E. McCloskey and James P. Gilligan, pp. 66–73. Wilderness Conference, 10th session. San Francisco: Sierra Club, 1969.

> The wildness of the New World, contrasted with the humanized natural scene in Europe, became a cultural asset to Americans, something uniquely different, and was a vital element in the new nation's art, literature, and music.

_____. "A Home for the Spirit." AMERICAN WEST 8, no. 1 (January 1971): 40-47.

Subtitled "A Brief History of the Wilderness Preservation Move-
ment--The Story of an Idea Given the Strength of Law." Some
of the ideas in this article were incorporated in the revised edition
of his WILDERNESS AND THE AMERICAN MIND (cited below).

_____. WILDERNESS AND THE AMERICAN MIND. Rev. ed. New Haven
and London: Yale University Press, 1973. xvi, 300 p. Bibliography, pp.
274-88.

Since the first edition appeared in 1967, this work has become the
classic account of American attitudes toward wilderness from the
seventeenth century to the present. Nash traces the transformation
from fear and dislike of wilderness, through stages of exploitation
and incipient conservation, to a growing concern for its preservation. The revised edition has been enlarged to consider more
fully origins and implementation of the Wilderness Preservation
System. Nash has also added a new chapter, "Wilderness, Culture
and the Counterculture," which describes the values of a growing
number of Americans--alienation from our technological society and
discovery of spiritual values in wilderness. In an epilogue, the
author notes the increasing danger to our wilderness areas from
public overuse. This book is an indispensable prelude to any
serious study of the environment in American history.

Netboy, Anthony. "Wilderness and the American." AMERICAN FORESTS 75,
no. 4 (April 1969): 12-15, 48, 50-51.

The first part of Netboy's article describes the wilderness existing
in colonial America, its gradual diminishment, and the consequent
awakening of a nature nostalgia and growth of "the wilderness
cult." The remainder of the essay is devoted to a chronicling of
the preservation movement and a description and characterization
of its leaders, "acolytes," and their "monumental greed." Thoreau,
Muir, Robert Marshall, and Aldo Leopold are characterized without
subtlety as enthusiasts lacking a requisite "social sense." The
author closes on a "prophetic" note, envisioning the United States
in the year 2000, opening its national parks and wilderness areas
to "multiple use"--timber cutting, hunting, reservoir-building, and
mass recreational use.

Nye, Russell B. "The American View of Nature." In his THIS ALMOST
CHOSEN PEOPLE, ESSAYS IN THE HISTORY OF AMERICAN IDEAS, pp.
256-304. [East Lansing]: Michigan State University Press, 1966.

See the annotation for this item in Chapter 1, Section A: General
Studies.

Olson, Sigurd F. "Six Decades of Progress." AMERICAN FORESTS 68, no. 10 (October 1962): 16-19.

> Olson, who was intimately involved in the battle to preserve the Quetico-Superior wilderness area, briefly traces the history of that struggle.

Sutton, Ann, and Sutton, Myron. THE APPALACHIAN TRAIL, WILDERNESS ON THE DOORSTEP. Philadelphia and New York: Lippincott, 1967. 180 p. Illustrated.

> Designed to focus attention on the Trail and gain support for its maintenance, the book traces historical and physical development of the Trail and discusses organizations supporting the Trail. See also the titles by Benton MacKaye in Chapter 6, Section B: Books and Articles.

Thompson, Roger C. "Politics in the Wilderness: New York's Adirondack Forest Preserve." FOREST HISTORY 6, no. 4 (Winter 1963): 14-23.

> This essay is a reworking of the author's doctoral dissertation in forestry at Syracuse University, 1962. Thompson discusses the history of the Adirondack Forest Preserve within the context of inherent difficulties and contradictions that stem from managing timber, water, and recreational resources as long as the Preserve is constitutionally "forever wild."

Verner, William K. "Wilderness and the Adirondacks--An Historical View." LIVING WILDERNESS 33, no. 108 (Winter 1969): 27-47.

> Verner briefly sketches the history of wilderness preservation in the Adirondacks (illustrated by reproductions of paintings in the Adirondack Museum), and proposes a radical restructuring of the area to preserve a wilderness core.

B. PERSONAL VIEWS OF WILDERNESS

Brooks, Paul. ROADLESS AREAS. New York: Knopf, 1964. xiii, 259 p. Illustrated. Map.

> Descriptions of trips into wild areas from New England to Washington, as well as to England and Africa. The point of view is that of a wilderness enthusiast exhorting the faithful. Chapters have appeared in several periodicals. Illustrated with drawings by the author.

_____. THE PURSUIT OF WILDERNESS. Boston: Houghton Mifflin, 1971. xiii, 220 p. Illustrated. Maps.

> Most of the essays originally appeared in slightly different form in

the ATLANTIC, HARPER'S, HORIZON, AUDUBON, SIERRA CLUB BULLETIN, and the NEW YORK TIMES; all deal with efforts to preserve wilderness areas in the United States and Africa.

Broome, Harvey, "A Journal of the Wilderness." LIVING WILDERNESS, 1949-65.

> Broome published his "Journal" in eight parts, each with its own subtitle, in eight different issues of LIVING WILDERNESS:
>
>> "...Mountain Notebook 1941." LW 14, no. 30 (Autumn 1949): 6-11.
>>
>> "...Mountain Notebook 1942." LW 14, no. 31 (Winter 1949-50): 17-23.
>>
>> "... Mountain Notebook 1943-1944." LW 16, no. 38 (Autumn 1951): 1-9.
>>
>> "...Spring in a Mountain Notebook." LW 17, no. 40 (Spring 1952): 9-17.
>>
>> "...Summer in a Mountain Notebook." LW 17, no. 41 (Summer 1952): 1-7.
>>
>> "... Winter in a Mountain Notebook." LW 17, no. 43 (Winter 1952-53): 14-19.
>>
>> "...Mountain Notebook 1950." LW 29, no. 90 (Autumn 1965): 3-13.
>
> From 1941 to 1950 Broome kept a journal of his activities in the Smoky Mountains. The subject matter varies, but in general the entries contain reflections on nature, wilderness, and descriptions of the Smokies. There are many references to nature writers and to people in the wilderness movement, notably Robert Marshall, Sterling Yard, and others. An interesting and charming series.

_____. FACES OF THE WILDERNESS. Missoula, Mont.: Mountain Press Publishing Co. in cooperation with The Wilderness Society, Washington, D.C., 1972. xiii, 271 p. Illustrated.

> A personal record of trips to various American wilderness areas from the Adirondacks to the Sierra. The author was one of the eight organizers of the Wilderness Society and president from 1957 until his death in 1968.

Douglas, William O. MY WILDERNESS: THE PACIFIC WEST. Garden City, N.Y.: Doubleday, 1960. 206 p. Illustrated. Maps on endpapers.

> See next item.

_____. MY WILDERNESS: EAST TO KATAHDIN. Garden City, N.Y.: Doubleday, 1961. 290 p. Illustrated. Maps on endpapers.

Douglas's books comprise a personal and loving account of twenty-two wilderness areas. See also the annotations for these items and other Douglas books in Chapter 7, Section C: Nature Writing Since Thoreau.

Kent, Rockwell. WILDERNESS; A JOURNAL OF QUIET ADVENTURE IN ALASKA. Drawings by the author. Introduction by Dorothy Canfield. New York: Putnam, 1920. xvii, 217 p. Reprint ed., with a new preface by the author. New York: Modern Library, 1930. xiii, 243 p. Illustrated. Rev. ed., Including Extensive Hitherto Unpublished Passages from the Original Journal. Los Angeles: Wilderness Press, 1970. xxi, 204 p. Illustrated. (Distributed by Ward Ritchie Press, Los Angeles.)

Kent and his nine-year-old son, Rockwell, landed on Fox Island, a small island in Resurrection Bay, southwest of Seward, Alaska, in August 1918, and left there in the following March. Most of the book was written on the island and later supplemented by a few letters written to friends. The Kents refurbished a small cabin (formerly inhabited by goats) and resided there for eight months—painting, chopping wood, writing, reading, and making excursions to Seward for mail and provisions. Their existence was primitive and austere, subject to violent storms and bitterly cold weather. In spite of hazardous conditions, the Kents relished their life there, coming reluctantly away, spiritually refreshed and physically strengthened. The book is a classic adventure. The 1970 edition contains a new (third) preface by the senior Kent, as well as a letter to art critic Christian Brinton, written as an introduction to an exhibition catalog of the artist's "wilderness" drawings.

Leopold, Aldo. ["Remarks on the Need for Wilderness Conservation"]. In U.S. National Conference on Outdoor Recreation, 2d. PROCEEDINGS, 69th Cong., 1st sess., Senate Document, no. 117 (Serial 8549), pp. 61-65. Washington, D.C.: Government Printing Office, 1926.

An early plea for wilderness preservation and an adumbration of Leopold's later ideas. Wilderness, he said, is the "fundamental recreational resource." Being neither a crop nor a renewable resource, wilderness must be safeguarded from economic exploitation. Leopold felt that outdoor recreation was being "overpromoted," for its future availability would depend on its conservation now. Wilderness areas should be developed in parks and forests in all parts of the country, not just in the West, because the person of moderate means could not be expected to travel long distances to enjoy it. Leopold's suggestion that the Conference sponsor a national wilderness policy was disregarded.

_____. "Wilderness." In his SAND COUNTY ALMANAC AND SKETCHES HERE AND THERE, pp. 188-201. New York: Oxford University Press, 1949.

Leopold has written elsewhere of the importance of wilderness preservation; this essay, however, summarizes his major ideas and is the most accessible. Additional references to Leopold's thought may be read in Chapter 6, Section B: Books and Articles, and in the following two items:

Bradley, Harold C. "Aldo Leopold--Champion of Wilderness." SIERRA CLUB BULLETIN 36, no. 5 (May 1951): 14-18.

Nash, Roderick. "Aldo Leopold: Prophet." In his WILDERNESS AND THE AMERICAN MIND, rev. ed., pp. 182-99. New Haven and London: Yale University Press, 1973.

Bradley's essay is a moving tribute to a friend. Annotation for Nash's essay on Leopold may be read in Chapter 6, Section B: Books and Articles.

McPhee, John. ENCOUNTERS WITH THE ARCHDRUID. New York: Farrar, Straus and Giroux, 1971. 245 p.

The "archdruid" is David Brower, former executive director of the Sierra Club, and now President of The Friends of the Earth, a new conservation group with an international focus, which he founded. The author, who traveled extensively with Brower on many outings, recounts three specific trips made in company with three ideological foes: a mining geologist for Kennecott Copper, a developer of island properties on the southeastern coast, and the Commissioner of the Bureau of Reclamation. McPhee does not intrude in his narrative of the expeditions, allowing the principals to speak for themselves. Brower is at the center of the book, and a balanced account of his role in the conservation/preservation movement is given here. The book is well written and impartial. It originally appeared in the spring 1971 issues of THE NEW YORKER.

Marshall, Robert (1901-39)

Robert Marshall was, at the time of his death, Chief of the U.S. Forest Service Division of Recreation and Lands. His early experiences in the Adirondacks, where his family owned a summer home, led him to choose a career in forestry. He graduated in 1924 from the New York State College of Forestry and he later took an M.F. from Harvard and a Ph.D. from Johns Hopkins. Marshall was a true lover of the wilderness. He worked for its appreciation and preservation through his activities in the Forest Service, his writings, and, finally, his efforts to found and financially endow the Wilderness Society. Marshall was not an "armchair" enthusiast, but a noted explorer of wilderness areas (see ALASKA WILDERNESS, below) and a rugged exemplar of strenuous outdoor life. In addition to his two books, his more significant essays and a bibliography of his writings (prepared by his brother) are listed below. No published biography exists.

"The Wilderness as a Minority Right." [U.S. Forest] SER-
VICE BULLETIN 12, no. 35 (August 27, 1928): 5-6.

"The Problem of the Wilderness." SCIENTIFIC MONTHLY 30
(February 1930): 141-48.

> Alarmed by the continued erosion of American wilderness,
> Marshall devoted this essay to thoughtful examination of
> the relative advantages and disadvantages of wilderness
> preservation. He described in detail the physical bene-
> fits of wilderness experience (health and adventure), as
> well as the mental (psychological release) and esthetic.
> He saw only three disadvantages: the danger of fires in
> undeveloped areas, direct economic loss of locking up
> forests, and the fact that only a minority of Americans
> would indulge in wilderness recreation. He concluded,
> however, that all these disadvantages would be minimized
> by "forethought and some compromise." Marshall called
> for immediate action through government planning and
> new programs and, finally, the unity of all "friends of
> the wilderness" to further the goal.

"Journal of the Exploration of the North Fork of the Koyukuk by
Al Retzlaf and Bob Marshall." THE FRONTIER: MAGAZINE OF
THE NORTHWEST (Missoula, Mont.) 11 (January 1931): 162-75.

ARCTIC VILLAGE. New York: Harrison Smith and Robert Haas,
1933. 399 p. Illustrated.

> Based on letters written from Alaska to friends in the
> states, the volume is primarily concerned with the social
> life and customs of an Eskimo village. The book was a
> Literary Guild selection in June 1933 and was reprinted
> as a Penguin Book in 1940.

"The Universe of the Wilderness is Vanishing." NATURE MAGA-
ZINE 29 (April 1937): 235-40.

> A major exposition of Marshall's philosophy of wilderness
> and its use.

"Looking for Adventure, and Peace." LIVING WILDERNESS 11,
no. 17 (June 1946): 1-4.

"Impressions from the Wilderness." NATURE MAGAZINE 44, no.
9 (November 1951): 481-84.

> Written about 1930, this essay was found among the
> author's unpublished papers. In it, Marshall attempts
> to explain his "lust for the primeval" by recalling his
> experiences during a walk through a portion of the

Selway National Forest in Idaho, now organized as The
Selway-Bitteroot Wilderness Area.

ALASKA WILDERNESS, EXPLORING THE CENTRAL BROOKS RANGE.
2nd ed., edited and with an introduction by George Marshall.
Foreword by A. Starker Leopold. Berkeley and Los Angeles: University of California Press, 1970. xl, 173 p. Illustrated. Maps.

ALASKA WILDERNESS, edited by the author's brother,
is based on Marshall's journals, diaries, and letters written during the explorations conducted from 1929 through
the spring of 1939. George Marshall's handling of the
material is smooth and the narrative of exploration, mountain climbing, the hazards of storms, and encounters
with wild animals is engrossing. The first edition was
published in 1956 under the title ARCTIC WILDERNESS.
The second edition was also issued as a paperback.

Marshall, George. "Robert Marshall as a Writer." LIVING
WILDERNESS 16, no. 38 (Autumn 1951): 14-20.

_____. "Bibliography of Robert Marshall, 1901-1939." LIVING
WILDERNESS 16, no. 38 (Autumn 1951): 20-23. "Supplement."
LIVING WILDERNESS 19, no. 49 (Summer 1954): 31-35.

Nash, Roderick. "The Strenuous Life of Bob Marshall." FOREST
HISTORY 10, no. 3 (October 1966): 18-25.

This article is similar to Chapter 12 in the author's WIL-
DERNESS AND THE AMERICAN MIND (see Chapter 5,
Section A: General and Historical).

Meader, Frederick Putnam. WILDERNESS ESSAYS. n.p., [1972?]. Paper.
Mimeographed.

Meader, with his wife Elaine and their young son, emigrated to the
wilds of the Brooks Range in Alaska in 1960 to live an austere life.
The Meaders have "come out" periodically for lecture engagements
and have produced a documentary film of their wilderness life. The
three essays in this collection (two of which are reprinted from periodicals) are statements of Meader's view of modern man and his own
commitment to the values of very primitive existence.

Muir, John

All of Muir's books are listed in Chapter 7, Section C: Nature
Writing Since Thoreau.

Murie, Margaret E. TWO IN THE FAR NORTH. Illustrated by Olaus J.

Murie. New York: Knopf, 1962. xii, 438 p.

> A fascinating semiautobiographical account of the Muries' life.
> When this memoir was written, the author's husband was a biologist
> for the U.S. Fish and Wildlife Service in Alaska. He later be-
> came an officer in the Wilderness Society.

Murray, William Henry Harrison. ADVENTURES IN THE WILDERNESS. Edited
by William K. Verner. Introduction and notes by Warder H. Cadbury. [Syra-
cuse]: The Adirondack Museum/Syracuse University Press, 1970. 75 p., vi, 236 p.
Appendix, pp. 77-95. Illustrated. Map in pocket.

> Published in several editions, with variant titles. See the annota-
> tion for this item in Chapter 2, Section D6: The Adirondack
> Mountains.

Olson, Sigurd F. "Quetico-Superior Elegy." LIVING WILDERNESS 13, no.
24 (Spring 1948): 5-12.

> Olson describes a canoe trip into the Quetico-Superior area made
> by himself and Robert Marshall in August 1937. Olson acted as
> guide; Marshall was on an official tour of inspection for the Forest
> Service. For biographical information and a list of Olson's books,
> see Chapter 7, Section C: Nature Writing Since Thoreau. Addi-
> tional articles by Olson appear in Section C: The Idea of Wilder-
> ness: Philosophy, Value, and Use, below. An interesting sketch
> of Olson's life and philosophy of nature may be read in
>
> > Huyck, Dorothy Boyle. "Sig Olson: Wilderness Philos-
> > opher." AMERICAN FORESTS 71, no. 5 (May 1965):
> > 46, 72, 74.

[Yard, Robert Sterling]. "Robert Sterling Yard, 1861-1945." LIVING WIL-
DERNESS 10, nos. 14-15 (December 1945).

> This is a memorial issue devoted to Yard, the first president and
> permanent secretary of the Wilderness Society. Reminiscences and
> an article by Yard, and a bibliography of his writings, are included.

C. THE IDEA OF WILDERNESS: PHILOSOPHY, VALUE, AND USE

Bradley, Charles C. "Wilderness and Man." SIERRA CLUB BULLETIN 37,
no. 10 (December 1952): 59-67.

> An address presented at Montana State College Faculty Forum,
> January 17, 1952, this is an examination of the scientific, con-
> servationist, and recreational values of wilderness.

Brower, David R. "De Facto Wilderness: What is Its Place?" In WILDLANDS
IN OUR CIVILIZATION, edited by David R. Brower, pp. 103-10. San Francisco: Sierra Club, 1964.

De facto wilderness is, in Brower's view, all wilderness that was not then (in 1959) included in national parks or was otherwise unprotected.

_____. "Wilderness--Conflict and Conscience." In WILDLAND IN OUR CIVILIZATION, edited by David R. Brower, pp. 52-64, 73-74. San Francisco: Sierra Club, 1964.

Brower's theme is "How much right does one generation have to another generation's freedom?" In exploring this issue, he finds that our generation is speedily consuming the scenic and spiritual gifts of wilderness which might have been enjoyed by future generations.

California. University of. Wildland Research Center. WILDERNESS AND RECREATION--A REPORT ON RESOURCES, VALUES, AND PROBLEMS. Outdoor Recreation Resources Review Commission Study Report, 3. Washington, D.C.: 1962. x, 352 p. Tables. Charts. Photos. Maps.

A very useful study. Chapters 1 and 5, which deal with the evolution of wilderness concepts, the preservation idea, values, and the appeal of wilderness to vacationists, are especially important.

Clement, Roland C. "A Use for Wilderness." AUDUBON MAGAZINE 68, no. 2 (March-April 1966): 94-95.

The author, a staff biologist for the National Audubon Society, argues that wilderness is a place for man to find inspiration and spiritual regeneration. He takes issue with the position of David Lowenthal (see "Is Wilderness 'Paradise Enow'?" below).

Cook, Reginald L. "West of Walden: On the Wild Side." LIVING WILDERNESS 32, no. 102 (Summer 1968): 11-15.

Cook discusses Thoreau's vision of wildness and its implications for modern America. Originally delivered before the Thoreau Society, Concord, Massachusetts, on July 13, 1968.

Dasmann, Raymond F. A DIFFERENT KIND OF COUNTRY. New York and London: Macmillan, 1968. viii, 276 p. Illustrated. Maps. Bibliography, pp. 259-68.

Dasmann presents a strong argument for diversity in nature--man, animals, countries--and in thought. He argues that wilderness areas are essential for ecological research; once gone, they cannot be replaced. Diversity is really a product of evolution. To reduce diversity may well have serious consequences for all humanity.

Douglas, William O. A WILDERNESS BILL OF RIGHTS. Boston: Little,

Brown, 1965. 192 p. Illustrated.

> A revision and expansion of an article written for THE ENCYCLO-
> PEDIA BRITANNICA YEAR BOOK for 1965. Recommends changes
> in federal laws to insure the continued existence of wilderness
> areas.

Gordon, J. Berkeley. "Psychiatric Values of the Wilderness." THE WELFARE
REPORTER (New Jersey State Department of Institutions and Agencies) 6 (1952):
3-4, 15-16.

> An unusual article. Gordon related his own experiences in wil-
> derness areas, and states his belief that outings in primitive areas
> have definite therapeutic value in reducing tensions of urban life.

Harris, Frederick Brown. "The Sanctity of Open Spaces." LIVING WILDER-
NESS 22, no. 60 (Spring 1957): 5-8.

> Brown, a noted Methodist clergyman, wrote this sermon on conser-
> vation at the invitation of the Wilderness Society.

Krutch, Joseph Wood. "Wilderness As More Than a Tonic." In his IF YOU
DON'T MIND MY SAYING SO...ESSAYS ON MAN AND NATURE, pp.
367-75. New York: Sloane, 1964.

> A thoughtful essay prompted by the title of a 1962 Sierra Club
> book, IN WILDERNESS IS THE PRESERVATION OF THE WORLD.
> Krutch places the title in the context originally given it by
> Thoreau and explicates its meaning in both Thoreau's world and
> our own time. The essay also appears in his THE BEST NATURE
> WRITING OF JOSEPH WOOD KRUTCH (New York: William
> Morrow, 1969, pp. 255-63).

Lindbergh, Charles A. "The Wisdom of Wilderness." LIFE 63, no. 25 (Decem-.
ber 22, 1967): 8-10

> A personal belief in a nature teleology. "There is in wildness a
> natural wisdom that shapes all earth's experiments with life."

Lowenthal, David. "Is Wilderness 'Paradise Enow'? Images of Nature in
America." COLUMBIA UNIVERSITY FORUM 7, no. 2 (Spring 1964): 34-40.

> A critique of modern "nature worship" and the "wilderness cult."
> Man must not, Lowenthal says, concentrate exclusively on wilder-
> ness to the abandonment of man. Nature must be viewed unsenti-
> mentally as an impersonal and unpredictable force. See also Clem-
> ent, Roland C., above, and Simmons, I.G., below.

Luten, Daniel B. "Engines in the Wilderness." LANDSCAPE 15, no. 3

(Spring 1966): 25-27.

> Luten, a geographer, discusses motorized intrusion into wilderness
> areas. This is the result, he says, of the wilderness enthusiast's
> efforts to communicate the areas' beauties. Central to the discus-
> sion is the proposition that wilderness is necessary to gratify human
> "wanderlust."

McCloskey, Michael. "Wilderness Movement at the Crossroads, 1945-1970."
PACIFIC HISTORICAL REVIEW 41, no. 3 (August 1972): 346-61.

> McCloskey, Executive Director of the Sierra Club, reviews the
> progress of the wilderness preservation movement since 1945, and
> warns of its problems in the future.

McConnell, Grant. "Conservation and Political Realism." In WILDERNESS:
AMERICA'S LIVING HERITAGE, edited by David R. Brower, pp. 163-68.
San Francisco: Sierra Club, 1961.

> McConnell, a political scientist, discusses the growing feeling of
> powerlessness to affect public policy. Specifically, he is con-
> cerned with this problem as it affects the conservation movement.

Mauk, Charlotte E. "The Paradox of the Pioneer Spirit." LIVING WILDER-
NESS 23, no. 65 (Summer-Fall 1958): 1-6.

> A plea for recognition of the fragility of wilderness.

Menninger, Karl. "Human Needs in Urban Society." ARCHITECTURAL REC-
ORD 126 (July 1959): 197-200.

> Menninger, a renowned psychiatrist, states that one of man's needs
> is the "maintenance of contact with non-human nature." Thus,
> more wilderness or near-wilderness is "essential to the mental health
> of both child and adult."

Merton, Thomas. "The Wild Places." THE CENTER MAGAZINE (A Publication of the Center for the Study of Democratic Institutions, Santa Barbara,
California) 1, no. 5 (July 1968): 40-44.

> A thoughtful essay about ambivalences in America's attitudes towards
> nature. Father Merton, Trappist monk and author, examines the
> ideas of Thoreau, Muir, the American Puritans, Aldo Leopold, and
> Roderick Nash. The essay is reprinted in THE ECOLOGICAL CON-
> SCIENCE: VALUES FOR SURVIVAL (A Spectrum Book), edited by
> Robert Disch, pp. 37-43 (Englewood Cliffs, N.J.: Prentice-Hall,
> 1970).

Nash, Roderick. "Can We Afford Wilderness?" In ENVIRONMENT, MAN,
SURVIVAL: GRAND CANYON SYMPOSIUM, 1970, edited by Leroy H. Wull-
stein et al., pp. 97-111. Salt Lake City: University of Utah, Department

of Biology, 1971.

> A very interesting essay. In developing the idea that man must assume responsibility for preserving wilderness, Nash points out the possibilities for creating new wilderness areas and the need for a quota system to limit access to them.

Olson, Sigurd F. "Why Wilderness?" AMERICAN FORESTS 44, no. 9 (September 1938): 395-97, 429-30.

> Sigurd Olson has for many years been one of the foremost explicators of the wilderness idea and a staunch supporter of wilderness preservation. His own experiences as a guide in the Quetico-Superior region and later as an ecologist give him a unique perspective on the concept and value of wilderness. In this penetrating analysis, Olson describes the need of some men for wilderness, "a way of life...as deeply rooted...as the love of home and family." He understands this deep craving and claims there are only two kinds of experience that can satisfy it: "the way of wilderness or the way of war." Olson differentiates between the "picnickers and strollers," between such naturists as John Burroughs, who eschewed the wilderness urge, and men like Joseph Conrad and Jack London who knew and loved wild places. Olson sees the need for the wilderness experience as an atavistic surge of feeling, common to the race and deeply rooted in our heritage. For a list of Olson's books, see Chapter 7, Section C: Nature Writing Since Thoreau.

_____. "The Preservation of Wilderness." LIVING WILDERNESS 13, no. 26 (Autumn 1948): 1-8.

> Originally prepared for the Inter-American Conference on the Conservation of Renewable Natural Resources held in Denver, September 7-20, 1948.

_____. "The Spiritual Aspects of Wilderness." In WILDERNESS: AMERICA'S LIVING HERITAGE, edited by David R. Brower, pp. 16-25. San Francisco: Sierra Club, 1961.

> An extremely thoughtful and valuable essay. Olson chose as his theme the explication of Thoreau's famous statement "In wildness is the preservation of the world." Swift changes in the world have left a gap between the ancient rhythms to which man still moves and the new and conflicting pressures and ideologies of the current technological era. Olson points to spiritual satisfactions derived from wilderness experiences. "The past still haunts our dreams," he writes, and we surround ourselves with symbols and artifacts of an earlier and simpler life. Nature nostalgia is simply the need to experience again what "simplicity really means, the importance of the natural and the sense of oneness with the earth...." If we are to maintain the human spirit, Olson says we

must bridge the gap between the ancient rhythms and the new demands of our technological life.

_____. "The Meaning of Wilderness for Modern Man." CARLETON MISCEL-LANY 3, (Summer 1962): 99-113.

A very perceptive account of man's need for wild places and what is happening to them under pressure of an ever-expanding urban sprawl. Olson's remarks were part of an American Studies Seminar held at Carleton College in 1961.

_____. "The Spiritual Need." In WILDERNESS IN A CHANGING WORLD, edited by Bruce M. Kilgore, pp. 212-19. San Francisco: Sierra Club, 1966.

This is an extension of the author's earlier essay, "Spiritual Aspects of Wilderness" (above). Olson says that the wilderness experience brings silence, a contemplative attitude of mind and soul, and leaves one with a feeling of "oneness and unity with life and the universe, of the eternal essence, and the perception of reality." This perception brings a richness, a warmth to man's spirit; without it, without the preservation of wilderness, our culture and ourselves will be destroyed.

Roosevelt, Nicholas. "What Wilderness?" In his CONSERVATION: NOW OR NEVER, pp. 72-83. New York: Dodd, Mead, 1970.

A brief discussion of the difficulties in administering wilderness areas.

Scoyen, Eivind T. "National Park Wilderness." In WILDERNESS: AMERICA'S LIVING HERITAGE, edited by David R. Brower, pp. 185-93. San Francisco: Sierra Club, 1961.

Scoyen, then Associate Director of the National Park Service, defines wilderness in the national parks and discusses its care, use, and preservation.

Simmons, I. G. "Wilderness in the Mid-Twentieth Century U.S.A." TOWN PLANNING REVIEW 36 (January 1966): 249-56.

The author, an Englishman, has written an informative and reasoned study of the place of wilderness in the United States. He examines at some length the reasons put forward for wilderness preservation, including ecological, esthetic, recreational, and moral uses. Simmons also points out the danger of subjecting wilderness preservation to economic analysis, seeing the evil of people serving the economy rather than vice versa. The author concludes that population control is vital if wilderness, among other things, is to survive, for wilderness has a function even for people who do not use it. "If it vanishes, then all men are diminished." This is a very stimulating refutation of the position advocated by David Lowenthal (see Lowenthal, David, above).

Stegner, Wallace. "The War Between the Rough Riders and the Bird Watchers." SIERRA CLUB BULLETIN 44, no. 5 (May 1959): 4-11.

Reprinted as the Introduction to WILDLANDS IN OUR CIVILIZA-TION, edited by David R. Brower (San Francisco: Sierra Club, 1964). Stegner, using the Wilderness Bill then pending in the Congress as the focus, discusses amusingly and convincingly the points of issue between preservationists and those who wish the wilderness to remain unprotected and thus open to multiple-use.

_____. "The Wilderness Idea." In WILDERNESS: AMERICA'S LIVING HERI-TAGE, edited by David R. Brower, pp. 97-102. San Francisco: Sierra Club, 1961.

Stegner argues for the preservation of wilderness as an idea, a "resource in itself." Wilderness has conditioned the American people, formed our character and shaped our history. By destroy-ing it we will be destroying a part of ourselves. Roderick Nash has called this essay "the classic statement of the relationship of wilderness to man's spirit." The essay originally appeared as a letter, dated December 3, 1960, written to David E. Pesonen at the University of California's Wildland Research Center and was included in the Center's report WILDERNESS AND RECREATION, pp. 34-36 (see California. University of. Wildland Research Center, above). It also appeared in Stegner's THE SOUND OF MOUN-TAIN WATER (Garden City, N.Y.: Doubleday, 1969, pp. 145-53).

Udall, Stewart L. "To Save the Wonder of the Wilderness." NEW YORK TIMES MAGAZINE, May 27, 1962, pp. 22-23, 39-40.

Using the Wilderness Bill then under debate in the House of Repre-sentatives as a springboard, Secretary Udall discusses the value of protecting American wildlands from commercial greed.

Wernick, Robert. "Speaking Out: Let's Spoil the Wilderness." SATURDAY EVENING POST 238 (November 6, 1965): 12, 16.

The burden of Wernick's argument is that many wilderness advocates are hysterical and that their wilderness lust is not compatible with the needs or wishes of the overwhelming majority of American citizens.

Wilderness Conferences (1949-   )

Since 1949, the Sierra Club has sponsored a biennial series of wilderness conferences. The edited proceedings are published by the Club in book form; each has a distinctive title. The proceedings of the first three biennial conferences, held in Berkeley, California, were summarized in mimeographed form and distributed by the Club. The fourth and fifth proceedings appeared separately as printed pamphlets (the fifth conference was also reported in full in the SIERRA CLUB BULLETIN for June 1957). From 1955 through 1969, the conferences were held in San Francisco. Contributors to the proceedings included notable figures in conservation, wilderness preservation, government, education, science, and the arts. The reports are unique and important sources of information about trends and developments in all aspects of wilderness. Beginning with the Twelfth Biennial Conference in September 1971, the Sierra Club held its conferences in Washington, D.C. The Conference report was published in abridged form as a "Sierra Club Battlebook." An excellent compilation of thirty-two addresses and essays from the various conferences is VOICES FOR THE WILDERNESS (Sierra Club/ Ballantine Book), edited by William Schwarz (New York: Ballantine Books, [1970]. xiv, 366 p. Paper).

Brower, David R., ed. THE MEANING OF WILDERNESS TO SCIENCE. Wilderness Conference, 6th Session. San Francisco: Sierra Club, 1960. xi, 129 p. Illustrated, with photos.

> Principal contributors are Daniel B. Beard, Stanley A. Cain, Ian McTaggert Cowan, Raymond B. Coweles, Frank Fraser Darling, Luna B. Leopold, Robert Rausch, and G.M. Trevelyan. Trevelyan's contribution is a reprint of the Third Rickman Godlee Lecture given before the University College and University College Hospital Medical School, London, in 1931, and is entitled "The Call and Claims of Natural Beauty."

_____. WILDERNESS: AMERICA'S LIVING HERITAGE. Wilderness Conference, 7th session. San Francisco: Sierra Club, 1961. xvi, 204 p. Photos.

> Topics include "Wilderness and the Molding of American Character" and "Wilderness and the American Arts."

_____. WILDLANDS IN OUR CIVILIZATION. San Francisco: Sierra Club, 1964. 175 p. Photos.

> Contributions by John Collier, Bruce M. Kilgore, A. Starker Leopold, Wallace Stegner, Lowell Sumner, Lee Merriman Talbot, and Howard Zahniser. Includes summaries of the proceedings of the first five conferences, 1949-57.

Leydet, Francois, ed. TOMORROW'S WILDERNESS. Wilderness Conference, 8th session. San Francisco: Sierra Club, 1963. 262 p. Photos.

Kilgore, Bruce M., ed. WILDERNESS IN A CHANGING WORLD. Wilderness Conference, 9th session. San Francisco: Sierra Club, 1966. 253 p. Photos.

Topics include "Wilderness in Crisis," "The Impact of Technology," "The Outlook for Wilderness," and "What Wilderness Means to Man."

McCloskey, Maxine E., ed. WILDERNESS: THE EDGE OF KNOWLEDGE. Wilderness Conference, 11th session. San Francisco: Sierra Club, 1970. xiv, 303 p.

Topics include: "The Role of Wildlife in Wilderness," "Alaska's Wilderness," "Alaska's Wilderness Wildlife," and "Wilderness Planning and People."

McCloskey, Maxine E., and Gilligan, James P., eds. WILDERNESS AND THE QUALITY OF LIFE. Wilderness Conference, 10th session. San Francisco: Sierra Club, 1969. xv, 267 p. Color plates.

Topics include "The Wilderness Act in Practice," "The Contribution of Wilderness to American Life," "Forgotten Wilderness," and "The Quality of American Wilderness."

Gillette, Elizabeth R., ed. ACTION FOR WILDERNESS. Sierra Club Battlebook, 7. San Francisco and New York: Sierra Club, 1972. 222 p. Paper.

Not the complete proceedings of the Twelfth Biennial Conference, the volume omits some speeches and includes supplementary articles. The publication marks a change in policy for the Sierra Club. Former Wilderness Conference reports were lavishly illustrated with dramatic photographs of wilderness and constituted fully edited, complete proceedings. The editor states in her foreword that this "is a book for those people who already 'believe'....The book is intended as a practical manual for activists, and activists-to-be, in their wilderness preservation campaigns."

Zahniser, Howard. "How Much Wilderness Can We Afford to Lose?" SIERRA CLUB BULLETIN 36, no. 4 (April 1951): 5-8.

From an address to the Second Wilderness Conference Dinner, March 30, 1951. Reprinted in WILDLANDS IN OUR CIVILIZATION, edited by David R. Brower, pp. 46-51 (San Francisco: Sierra Club, 1964). Zahniser, long active in the conservation movement, was then Executive Director of the Wilderness Society.

Zahniser, Howard, and Baker, Frederick S. "We Certainly Need a Sound

Philosophy: An Exchange of Letters." LIVING WILDERNESS 12, no. 23 (Winter 1947-48): 1-5.

An exchange of correspondence between Zahniser, then Executive Secretary of the Wilderness Society and editor of LIVING WILDER-NESS, and Frederick S. Baker, professor of forestry at the University of California, Berkeley. On a questionnaire circulated by the Wilderness Society in December 1945, Baker had criticized the aims and philosophy of the Society. The exchange of letters is informative in that it juxtaposes the values of proponents and opponents of the wilderness preservation philosophy.

Perception of Wilderness

The following is a brief list of titles reflecting the views of users, primarily vacationers, of wilderness areas. Additional titles of some relevance may be found in Chapter 1, Section D: Environmental Perception of Natural Areas.

Bultena, Gordon L., and Taves, Marvin J. "Changing Wilderness Images and Forestry Policy." JOURNAL OF FORESTRY 59, no. 3 (March 1961): 167-70.

An insightful study based upon research involving vacationers in the Quetico-Superior Wilderness Area. It discusses the motivations of visitors. See also the report to the Outdoor Recreation Resources Review Commission (cited under California. University of. Wildland Research Center, above).

Catton, William R., Jr., and Hendee, John C. "Wilderness Users...What Do They Think?" AMERICAN FORESTS 74, no. 9 (September 1968): 29-31, 60-61.

In the summer of 1965, the authors questioned 2,000 visitors to the Glacier Peak, Eagle Cap, and Three Sisters Wilderness Areas in the Oregon Cascades. Seventy-one percent of the visitors responded to the fifty-three-item questionnaire. Some of the findings are outlined in question and answer format. Among the significant findings are the following: wilderness users are better educated than most people; most visitors do not go alone, but few make trips with organized groups; more than half of the responding visitors were members of small family groups; and wilderness use is rapidly increasing.

Henning, Daniel. "Evaluations of the Backcountry." LIVING WILDERNESS 25, no. 74 (Autumn-Winter 1960-61): 15-20.

The author, a seasonal ranger-naturalist in Glacier National Park during the summer of 1955, asked the visitors he guided about their reasons for coming to the wilderness. Not a scientific survey, but still interesting.

MacKaye, Benton. "The Gregarious and the Solitary." LIVING WILDERNESS 5, no. 5 (March 1939): 7-8.

> MacKaye postulates the existence of two kinds of people: those who enjoy the outdoors "en masse" and those who prefer solitary adventures. From this, he describes the "two states of land" to go with the human categories. In order to avoid destructive pressures on the fragile wilderness areas appreciated by the "solitary" types, MacKaye suggests that the Wilderness Society promote the development of more recreational areas for the "gregarious," "if only to advance our benighted notions."

Penfold, Joseph W. "The Outdoors, Quality, and Isoprims." In WILDERNESS: AMERICA'S LIVING HERITAGE, edited by David R. Brower, pp. 109-16. San Francisco: Sierra Club, 1961.

> " 'Isoprims' can be drawn on a map to connect points of equal degree of primitiveness and can help us to understand the wilderness better, and what is happening to it, and the quality of experience which we can hope to find there."

Shafer, Elwood L., Jr., and Mietz, James. "Aesthetic and Emotional Experiences Rate High With Northeast Wilderness Hikers." ENVIRONMENT AND BEHAVIOR 1, no. 2 (December 1969): 187-97.

Stone, Gregory P., and Taves, Marvin J. "Research into the Human Element in Wilderness Use." PROCEEDINGS [of the] SOCIETY OF AMERICAN FORESTERS, 1956, pp. 26-32.

> Reprinted with the title "Camping in the Wilderness" in MASS LEISURE, edited by Eric Larrabee and Rolf Meyersohn, pp. 290-305 (Glencoe, Ill.: Free Press, 1958).

Chapter 6

CONSERVATION AND THE ECOLOGICAL ETHIC

Chapter 6

CONSERVATION AND THE ECOLOGICAL ETHIC

This chapter presents a selected list of books, parts of books, anthologies, conference reports, handbooks, articles, and bibliographies that stress an ecological
view of nature and its development in the conservation movement. The emphasis here is upon the ideological and philosophical background of the ecological
approach. Hence, strictly biological treatises on ecology and related sciences,
as well as materials relating to human ecology, are excluded.

In addition to the titles listed below, the reader is referred to other parts of
this bibliography for expressions of ecological concern. Chapter 1, Section
C: Nature and the Religious Impulse, contains several relevant works (for
example, those by White, Barbour, Baer, Elder, the Faith-Man-Nature Group,
and Santmire are useful). Chapters 4 and 5 include works on other aspects of
conservation.

Seven authors most often considered nature writers (and so classified here)--
Henry David Thoreau, Henry Beston, Hal Borland, John Hay, Joseph Wood
Krutch, John Muir, and Sigurd F. Olson--have written out of a deep ecological concern and love for nature. Their books, listed in Chapter 7, should
be consulted for a better understanding of the tradition of ecological thinking
in America.

A. BIBLIOGRAPHIES

McKinley, Daniel. "A Reader's Guide: Ecology for Bookworms." LAND-
SCAPE 15, no. 2 (Winter 1965-66): 30-33.

> A bibliographic essay emphasizing ecological works per se, but
> some titles listed in this bibliography are discussed. Originally
> appeared in SNOWY EGRET (volume 29, no. 2, Autumn 1965).

Sangster, Robert P. ECOLOGY: A SELECTED BIBLIOGRAPHY. Exchange
Bibliography, no. 170. Monticello, Ill.: Council of Planning Librarians,
1971. 27 p. Paper.

A highly selective bibliography which emphasizes recent books and articles. Less than half of the titles are annotated. On the whole, a useful compilation.

Watkins, Jessie B. ECOLOGY AND ENVIRONMENTAL QUALITY: A SELECT-ED AND ANNOTATED BIBLIOGRAPHY FOR BIOLOGISTS AND EARTH SCIEN-TISTS. Syracuse, N.Y.: Syracuse University Libraries, 1971. 127 p. Paper.

A useful compilation of materials available in the Syracuse University libraries. It is arranged by subject and alphabetically by author. Annotations are descriptive, not critical. Although the compilation is intended for use by biologists and earth scientists and therefore stresses those aspects of environmental quality of paramount interest to them, Mrs. Watkins has included a section of historic works on ecology and a significant selection of works dealing with the modern ecology movement.

B. BOOKS AND ARTICLES

Adams, Ansel. "Problems of Interpretation of the Natural Scene." SIERRA CLUB BULLETIN 30, no. 6 (December 1945): 47-50.

A brief but valuable contribution to the esthetics of conservation. Adams points to one weakness in man's appreciation of nature-- the emphasis upon scenery as a giant curiosity. The "integrity of experience" gained from our natural world is as important as the more obvious benefits. Includes sixteen photographs.

_____. "The Conservation of Man." JOURNAL OF THE AMERICAN INSTI-TUTE OF ARCHITECTS 45 (June 1966): 68-74.

"Adapted from the keynote address presented at the 1965 annual convention of the California Council, American Institute of Archi-tects, at Yosemite National Park." Adams reviews the gains and losses of the conservationists since the days of Theodore Roosevelt, remarks on the frustration he feels over "the drag and creep" toward the solution of environmental problems, and admonishes "architects, planners, artists...[and] all perceptive and creative men" to join in the conservation of man's environment.

Bailey, Liberty Hyde. THE HOLY EARTH. The Background Books. New York: Macmillan, 1915. vi, 171 p.

Bailey's book, one of the earliest statements of the ecological conscience in America, influenced the ideas of Aldo Leopold (see especially Leopold's GAME MANAGEMENT, pp. 21, 422 [New York and London: Scribner, 1933]). Chapter 10, Section A: Commentaries, may also be consulted for further discussion of Bailey and his works.

Carson, Rachel. UNDER THE SEA-WIND; A NATURALIST'S PICTURE OF OCEAN LIFE. New York: Oxford University Press, 1952. 314 p. Illustrated.

This is the new and corrected edition of the first edition published in 1941. Three sections describe the life of the shoreline, the open sea, and the bottom of the sea. Book One deals with part of the seacoast of North Carolina; Book Two discusses the ecology of the open sea, specifically related to the life history of an eel from coastal river to the sea bottom. Fictionalized animal person-ages advance the story without sentimentality. Contains a glossary of terms.

_____. THE EDGE OF THE SEA. Boston: Houghton Mifflin, 1955. 276 p. Illustrated.

The Atlantic coast of the United States is the setting for this ecological study of the shoreline and its plants and animals. Miss Carson's crystal-clear style and the illustrations by Bob Hines com-bine to produce an uncommonly fine treatment. Includes an ap-pendix on the classification of sea animals and plants.

_____. SILENT SPRING. Boston: Houghton Mifflin, 1962. 368 p. Illus-trated.

At first considered extremely controversial, the thesis that our environment is endangered by indiscriminate use of pesticides and herbicides is now generally accepted. The book was influential in furthering the modern ecology movement. A paper edition is available. Miss Carson, a dedicated marine biologist and cele-brated science writer, died in 1964. A well-written and fascinat-ing literary biography of Miss Carson, based on her letters and personal papers, is:

> Brooks, Paul. THE HOUSE OF LIFE: RACHEL CARSON AT WORK, WITH SELECTIONS FROM HER WRITINGS. Boston: Houghton Mifflin, 1972. xvi, 350 p. Illus-trated. Bibliography, pp. 339-43.

Charter, S P R. "Why Preserve Nature?" MAN ON EARTH (Olema, Calif.) 1, no. 2 (1965): 1-8.

Charter presents a subtle argument for the preservation of nature. He says that without an articulated organic need to preserve it, nature will not be preserved. He disposes of arguments often advanced by conservationists for preservation: esthetic reasons and the balance of nature (which he terms a myth). Technology, he says, has no need for conservation, except "on a moral and aesthet-ic plane," because of its faith that mankind's "devices" can replace natural resources. Charter argues that man is unquestionably a part of nature and by his own existence modifies nature, and therefore himself, through his technology. If man is to remain man, a part

of the "bio-mass," he must preserve nature. Charter's thesis is
similar to one advanced in more technical language by geographer
Daniel B. Luten in his essay, "Resource Quality and Value of the
Landscape," in NATURAL RESOURCES: QUALITY AND QUANTITY:
PAPERS PRESENTED BEFORE A FACULTY SEMINAR AT THE UNI-
VERSITY OF CALIFORNIA, BERKELEY, 1961-1965, edited by S.V.
Ciriacy Wantrup and James J. Parsons, pp. 19-34 (Berkeley and
Los Angeles: University of California Press, 1967).

Darling, Frank Fraser. "A Wider Environment of Ecology and Conservation."
DAEDALUS 96 (Fall 1967): 1003-19.

The theme of Darling's essay is "the breadth of concern of ecology
and conservation." He gives a brief overview of the approach and
concerns of American ecology, touching upon the work of Charles
Elton, Aldo Leopold, Homer Shantz, Paul Sears, and others. Although he praises the work that has been done, and the principles
of "wholeness" and interrelation, he feels that ecologists have not
yet devised adequate means of communicating their findings. Conservation frequently has been "ecology in action," and, although
many ecologists have been active in the movement, they tend to
be "nervous" in the ranks of zealous, often overemotional, preservationists. Darling acknowledges the excellent job performed by
organizations such as the Sierra Club, National Parks and Conservation Association, and the Wilderness Society in preserving
our natural heritage. He believes, however, that sound ecological
information should be made more readily available by professional
ecologists through their societies. He calls for an "intelligence
center" to serve the interests of conservation groups. In conclusion, the author calls for an extension of ecological concern into
the fields of "the human species and its environment."

Dasmann, Raymond F. THE DESTRUCTION OF CALIFORNIA. New York
and London: Macmillan, 1965. 247 p. Illustrated.

Relates the story of California's diminishing scenic and recreational
areas, the reduction of its prime agricultural land, the increase in
pollution, destruction of wildlife, and the loss of virgin timber.
The author, a well-known ecologist, pleads for a return to sanity
as California's population grows.

Iltis, Hugh H. "Whose Fight is the Fight for Nature?" SIERRA CLUB BULLE-
TIN 52, no. 9 (October 1967): 34-39.

A professional botanist challenges his colleagues to assume a larger
role in the conservation movement.

Krutch, Joseph Wood. "Conservation is Not Enough." AMERICAN SCHOLAR
23, no. 3 (Summer 1954): 295-305.

In this eloquently written plea, the author draws upon the ideas of Thoreau, Aldo Leopold, and others to develop the idea that what is lacking in conservation as a rational philosophy of land use and utilization of other natural resources, including animate beings, is love. Love for land, a willingness to grant the right of existence to other animate species regardless of their economic usefulness to man, and a respect for evolutionary diversity are the bases upon which Krutch would have man build a new ecological morality. The essay also appears in THE BEST NATURE WRITINGS OF JOSEPH WOOD KRUTCH, pp. 367-84 (New York: Morrow, 1969).

_____ . "Man's Ancient, Powerful Link to Nature--A Source of Fear and Joy." In his IF YOU DON'T MIND MY SAYING SO...ESSAYS ON MAN AND NATURE, pp. 336-48. New York: William Sloane, 1964.

The author examines the man-nature relationship and describes several dichotomies that characterize it: friendship-enmity, love-fear, use-misuse, avoidance-acceptance, and flight-return. These paradoxes are as old as civilization itself. Yet today the question of man's relation to nature is truly crucial; he now has the terrifying power to "banish" nature from the earth. Krutch argues for a love of nature built upon a reverence for our companionship with all living matter, for to renounce nature is to deny an integral part of our heritage. This essay originally appeared in LIFE (volume 51, December 1961, pp. 112-23). See also an earlier essay, "Human Life in the Context of Nature," in WILDERNESS: AMERICA'S LIVING HERITAGE (Wilderness Conference, 7th session), edited by David R. Brower, pp. 67-73 (San Francisco: Sierra Club, 1961) for a similar ecological statement of man's need for nature.

Leopold, Aldo (1886-1948)

Aldo Leopold began his professional career with the U.S. Forest Service in 1909. He served in Arizona and New Mexico for nearly fifteen years, where he developed special interests in game management, wilderness preservation, and recreational use of forest land. During that time, he was able to see some of his ideas for the establishment of wilderness preserves take root. In 1924, he became Assistant Director of the U.S. Forest Products Laboratory in Madison, Wisconsin, but in 1928 he left the Forest Service for a new career in wildlife management, a discipline just then emerging as a profession. In 1933, Leopold accepted a chair in game management created for him by the University of Wisconsin. He suffered a fatal heart attack in 1948 while fighting a grass fire in Wisconsin. Leopold's influence in the fields of ecology, wildlife management, and conservation has been widespread. Since his death, his ideas, especially those relating to the importance of wilderness preservation and the development of an ecological conscience in man, have gained great currency. Leopold termed himself a dissident in the sense that, like Thoreau, he found much of his thought to be in opposition to the materialistic goals of American society. For additional titles, see Chapter 5, Section B: Personal Views of Wilderness.

"The Conservation Ethic." JOURNAL OF FORESTRY 31, no. 6 (October 1933): 634-43.

> Portions of this essay appeared in A SAND COUNTRY ALMANAC under the title "The Land Ethic." See below.

"Conservation Esthetic." BIRD-LORE 40 (March-April 1938): 101-9.

> Reprinted in A SAND COUNTY ALMANAC, pp. 165-77. See below.

"The Ecological Conscience." BULLETIN OF THE GARDEN CLUB OF AMERICA, ser. 11, no. 4 (September 1947): 45-53.

> In this address to a meeting in Minneapolis, June 1947, Leopold defined the ecological conscience, with reference to four case histories, as the ethics of community life.

A SAND COUNTY ALMANAC AND SKETCHES HERE AND THERE. New York: Oxford University Press, 1949. xiii, 226 p. Illustrated.

> Consists of three sections: "A Sand County Almanac," "Sketches Here and There," and "The Upshot." The first section is a delightful record of Leopold's activities on his worn-out farm in Wisconsin and is filled with ecological ruminations and descriptions of the gradual reclamation of the land. "Sketches" is a collection of essays ranging over time and locale in which he describes events in his life which had bearing on conservation issues. The third part is a rationalization, in philosophical terms, of his dissent and consists of his best-known ecological essays: "Conservation Ethic," "Wildlife in American Culture," "Wilderness," and "The Land Ethic." The last essay (pp. 201-26) is one of the most profound statements of ecological principles applied to ethics ever written. This book is considered a classic in both nature writing and ecology. It would be difficult to exaggerate the importance of the work to the development of the modern ecology movement. Leopold's writings have earned him status equal to that of Thoreau, George Perkins Marsh, and John Muir. See also next item.

ROUND RIVER, FROM THE JOURNALS OF ALDO LEOPOLD. Edited by Luna B. Leopold. New York: Oxford University Press, 1953. 173 p. Illustrated. Reprint ed., 1972.

Journal entries cover the years 1922-37 and deal with outings to Mexico and Canada made by the author with his family and friends. Hunting and nature essays are included. The section entitled "Round River" consists of essays on conservation and ecology.

A SAND COUNTY ALMANAC WITH OTHER ESSAYS ON CON-SERVATION FROM "ROUND RIVER." New York: Oxford University Press, 1966. xv, 269 p. Illustrated.

Includes all the essays in the original SAND COUNTY ALMANAC, although rearranged, and eight essays from ROUND RIVER. See also above.

Nash, Roderick. "Aldo Leopold: Prophet." In his WILDERNESS AND THE AMERICAN MIND. rev. ed., pp. 182-99. New Haven and London: Yale University Press, 1973.

This is the best published assessment of Leopold's work, writing, and influence. See also Nash's earlier essay, "The Wisdom of Aldo Leopold," in WISCONSIN ACAD-EMY REVIEW (Wisconsin Academy of Sciences, Arts and Letters, volume 8, Fall 1961, pp. 161-67).

McHarg, Ian L. DESIGN WITH NATURE. New York: Published for the American Museum of Natural History by the Natural History Press, 1969. viii, 197 p. Illustrated. Maps and charts. Bibliographical footnotes.

McHarg demonstrates how a new ecological approach may be applied to actual environments to protect natural areas while planning and building new urban projects. Profusely illustrated with photographs, topographical maps, aerial surveys, and charts.

McHenry, Robert, and Van Doren, Charles, eds. A DOCUMENTARY HISTORY OF CONSERVATION IN AMERICA. New York: Praeger, 1972. xviii, 422 p.

A wide-ranging collection of 211 selections from articles, books, newspapers, government documents, and poetry. The sources cover conservation of natural resources, ecology, and preservation of natural beauty.

MacKaye, Benton (b.1879)

MacKaye is perhaps best known as the "father" of the Appalachian Trail, yet his work as a forester (M.A., Harvard, 1905), conservationist, regional planner, and wilderness advocate (he helped to found the Wilderness Society in 1935) places him at the forefront of the environmental preservation movement in the United States. Throughout his long life MacKaye has been concerned with the implementation of what he calls "geotechnics," the science of making the earth more habitable. To achieve this goal, MacKaye has sought to control and channel the forces of urbanism, employing regional planning, in order to preserve the environment while providing for creative and thoughtful metropolitan growth. His major work, THE NEW EXPLORATION (1928), was devoted to an examination of the problems of an exploding metropolitanism and its containment. The work was the first of its kind and, according to Lewis Mumford, it deserves a place next to Thoreau's WALDEN and George Perkins Marsh's MAN AND NATURE. For an additional work by MacKaye, see Chapter 5, Section C1: Perception of Wilderness. For biographical information, see Mumford's introduction to the 1962 edition of THE NEW EXPLORATION and the article by Penny Whitley listed below.

"An Appalachian Trail: A Project in Regional Planning." JOURNAL OF THE AMERICAN INSTITUTE OF ARCHITECTS 9 (October 1921): 325-30.

> This is the first published statement of MacKaye's idea for a trail that would follow the crest of the mountains from Maine to Georgia. He vigorously pursued his goals for the Appalachian Trail until its completion in 1937.

"Outdoor Culture, The Philosophy of Through Trails." LANDSCAPE ARCHITECTURE 17, no. 3 (April 1927): 163-71.

> An address to the New England Trail Conference in Boston, January 21, 1927. MacKaye outlines his proposal for an Appalachian Trail which was to be the exemplification of a philosophy of "outdoor culture" (an "ally" of regional planning) which aimed at a balance between the overcivilized, artifical aspects of urbanization and the natural environment. McKaye called for the development of a new American "Barbarian" to oppose the urban "civilizee." The Barbarian would capture the crestline of the Appalachian range, place it in public hands, and defend it from future encroachment by "Metropolitanism." The Trail would become the base for a "Barbarian invasion." Reprinted in FROM GEOGRAPHY TO GEOTECHNICS, pp. 169-79 (below).

"Wilderness Ways." LANDSCAPE ARCHITECTURE 19, no. 4 (July 1929): 237-49.

> "Based in part on a report for a Plan for Wilderness Ways in Massachusetts submitted to the Governor's Committee on the Needs and Uses of Open Spaces." An extension of MacKaye's earlier article, "Outdoor Culture, The Philosophy of Through Trails." He suggests the creation of wilderness belts in Massachusetts which would serve as buffers to an exploding "metropolitan glacier" and provide recreational outlets for primeval

wanderlust. "We must develop primeval influence as the ultimate source of culture as we would develop primeval timber as a source of industry."

"The Appalachian Trail: A Guide to the Study of Nature." SCIENTIFIC MONTHLY 34 (April 1932): 330-42.

A brief guide to the natural history of the Trail.

THE NEW EXPLORATION; A PHILOSOPHY OF REGIONAL PLAN-NING. Introduction by Lewis Mumford. Urbana: University of Illinois Press, 1962. xxv, 243 p. Illustrated. Maps.

Originally published in 1928 by Harcourt, Brace. This edition contains a valuable introduction by MacKaye's friend Lewis Mumford and an appendix consisting of an article, "The Townless Highway," reprinted from NEW REPUBLIC (March 12, 1930).

FROM GEOGRAPHY TO GEOTECHNICS. Edited, with an intro-duction, by Paul T. Bryant. Urbana, Chicago, and London: Uni-versity of Illinois Press, 1968. 194 p.

A collection of articles previously published elsewhere. Topics include regional planning, forestry conservation, ecological control of the landscape, and uses of wilder-ness. Geotechnics is defined as the science of making the earth more habitable for all living things. Bryant contributed a valuable seventeen-page introduction.

EXPLORATION NINE: A RETURN TO A REGION. Washington, D.C.: The Wilderness Society, 1969. vi, 50 p. Illustrated. Maps.

"Expedition Nine" was one of a score of "expeditions" made by MacKaye around his home in Shirley Center, Massachu-setts, in the spring of 1893. In this unique little book, the author retraces the route of that expedition, explaining the natural world within a small ecosystem. The publication was designed by an anonymous group of friends as a tribute to MacKaye on his ninetieth birthday.

Whitley, Penny. "Long, Long Trail Awinding." AMERICAN FORESTS 77 (February 1971): 16-18, 59.

Marsh, George Perkins. MAN AND NATURE. Edited, with an introduction, by David Lowenthal. Cambridge, Mass.: Harvard University Press, 1965. xxix, 472 p.

Originally published in 1864 under the title MAN AND NATURE;

OR, PHYSICAL GEOGRAPHY AS MODIFIED BY HUMAN ACTION,
Marsh's pioneer work on the destructive effects of human action
on the earth is here set forth in a new edition with a critical
introduction by Lowenthal. It was Marsh's original purpose to
indicate the type and extent of the changes caused by man in
the physical environment and to caution his readers not to inter-
fere with organic (ecological) arrangements in the natural world.
Marsh emphasized the existence of a balance in nature and man's
need to understand its workings. About half of MAN AND NA-
TURE is devoted to a study of woodlands in history, their functions,
and the effects of their destruction. Although the message of his
book was not heeded in his own time, Marsh is recognized as the
father of the conservation movement. Much of what he wrote in
the nineteenth century is applicable today. A revised edition of
MAN AND NATURE appeared in 1874 with the title THE EARTH
AS MODIFIED BY HUMAN ACTION (New York: Scribner, Armstrong) and a second edition of that title was printed by the same
publisher in 1885. Marsh, a Dartmouth graduate, lawyer, businessman, Congressman, state official, ambassador, and scholar, earned
enduring fame with MAN AND NATURE. Lowenthal's biography
of Marsh, below, was undertaken as a doctoral dissertation presented at the University of Wisconsin. It is an outstanding,
exhaustive study.

> Lowenthal, David. GEORGE PERKINS MARSH: VER-
> SATILE VERMONTER. New York: Columbia University
> Press, 1958. 442 p. Illustrated. Bibliography.

Marx, Leo. "American Institutions and Ecological Ideals." SCIENCE 170
(November 27, 1970): 945-52.

> Marx discusses the ecological ideal and its chances for success in
> the context of the dominant value structure in the United States.
> Reprinted in ENVIRONMENT AND AMERICANS: THE PROBLEM
> OF PRIORITIES, edited by Roderick Nash, pp. 90-123 (New York:
> Holt, Rinehart and Winston, 1972).

Nash, Roderick. "Can Government Meet Environmental Needs?" In TRANS-
ACTIONS OF THE THIRTY-SIXTH NORTH AMERICAN WILDLIFE AND NATURAL
RESOURCES CONFERENCE, pp. 6-15. Washington, D.C.: Wildlife Manage-
ment Institute, 1971.

> This insightful and valuable essay represents a radical new extension
> of Aldo Leopold's argument of ecological ethics. Nash asserts that
> government cannot meet environmental needs without a "basic
> change in society's ethical perspective," and that the "health" of
> the environment is basically a question of "values, morals and
> ethics." Nash negates the idea that technological progress leads
> to a satisfying life; in fact, he says, the opposite is true. He
> challenges the concept of private property when applied to the
> environment, for it is this concept that is at the heart of many

environmental problems. In an appeal for the extension of ethics
to conservation, Nash asserts that the same concepts of ethics that
now apply to human beings must be extended to all forms of life
on this planet.

_____, ed. THE AMERICAN ENVIRONMENT: READINGS IN THE HISTORY
OF CONSERVATION. Reading, Mass.: Addison-Wesley, 1968. xix, 236 p.
Illustrated. Bibliography, pp. 223-36. Paper.

This is a useful collection of documents, carefully chosen by the
editor to illustrate the development of the conservation movement.
Nash's selective bibliography is very useful.

Rakestraw, Lawrence. "Conservation Historiography: An Assessment." PACIFIC
HISTORICAL REVIEW 41, no. 3 (August 1972): 271-88.

Rakestraw defends the U.S. Forest Service against the imprecations
of such preservationist organizations as the Sierra Club and against
historians "unwilling" or unable to see the Forest Service as also
interested in preservation, recreation, etc. A challenging article.

Roosevelt, Theodore. THE WORKS OF THEODORE ROOSEVELT. National
Edition. 20 vols. New York: Scribner, 1926.

Prepared under the auspices of the Roosevelt Memorial Association,
Hermann Hagedorn, Editor. Each volume has a separate introduction by a well-known friend of Roosevelt. Titles relevant to his
role in conservation and his interest in natural history and nature
study are: HUNTING TRIPS OF A RANCHMAN and RANCH LIFE
AND THE HUNTING TRAIL, Volume 1; THE WILDERNESS HUNTER
and OUTDOOR PASTIMES OF AN AMERICAN HUNTER, I, Volume
2; OUTDOOR PASTIMES OF AN AMERICAN HUNTER, II and A
BOOK-LOVER'S HOLIDAYS IN THE OPEN, Volume 3; PAPERS
ON NATURAL HISTORY, Volume 5; and the AUTOBIOGRAPHY,
Volume 20.

_____. THEODORE ROOSEVELT'S AMERICA. SELECTIONS FROM THE
WRITINGS OF THE OYSTER BAY NATURALIST. Edited, with an introduction,
by Farida A. Wiley. Introductory essays by John Burroughs, Gifford Pinchot,
Henry Fairfield Osborn, and Ambrose Flack. Foreword by Ethel Roosevelt
Derby. New York: Devin-Adair, 1955. xxiii, 418 p. Illustrated.

The foreword is by Roosevelt's daughter. This very useful compilation is available in a paper edition. Also of interest is Cutright's
documentary biography of Roosevelt as a nature lover and amateur
naturalist. Cutright's book, below, corrects the common miscon-
ception of T.R. as a "butcher" of game animals.

Cutright, Paul Russell. THEODORE ROOSEVELT, THE
NATURALIST. New York: Harper, 1956. xiv, 297 p.
Illustrated. Notes, pp. 273-82. Bibliography, pp.
283-87.

Shaler, Nathaniel Southgate. MAN AND THE EARTH. New York: Fox, Duffield & Co., 1905. vi, 240 p. Reprint ed., 1967.

Shaler (1841-1906), professor of geology at Harvard and Dean of Lawrence Scientific School from 1891 to his death, wrote this book because he, like George Perkins Marsh, felt the need for a change in the way man views the earth and its resources. The greater part of MAN AND THE EARTH is a survey of the earth's natural resources and a discussion of their limits and probable future use, based upon previous human consumption. Included are chapters devoted to possible evolutionary changes in homo sapiens and speculative ending of life on earth in the far-distant future. In Chapter 10, "The Beauty of the Earth," Shaler hypothesizes about the manner in which man acquired an esthetic sense, and particularly an appreciation for beauty in natural landscapes. Chapters 11 and 13 contain Shaler's view of man as an agent of ecological change and his responsibility. Organic life, he wrote, is "united as in a commonwealth." Man alone is "the supremely successful weed" in this commonwealth, changing the harmony of nature to his own advantage. Shaler believed that certain species would inevitably disappear due to the agency of man; some harmless species would be lost due to shrinkage of habitat, while others, inimical to man, would be purposefully irradicated. Some animals, Shaler hoped, would be preserved for "further inquiry," particularly those mammals close to man's own path of evolution. Although he would disagree with the attitude that denies man the right to control nature for his benefit, Shaler did believe in man's kinship to nature and he stressed the need for an understanding of man's obligation to the earth. Though master of the earth, man must serve the higher interests of a "complete unity of nature."

Summer, Francis B. "The Need for a More Serious Effort to Rescue Fragments of Vanishing Nature." SCIENTIFIC MONTHLY 10 (March 1920): 236-48.

A lecture delivered before the California Academy of Sciences in San Francisco, December 3, 1919. The author proposed the setting aside of large tracts of land as sources of "scientific knowledge and of the highest esthetic enjoyment of mankind." Summer saw contemporary conservation as being too much concerned with natural resources and not enough with animal and plant life and natural scenery.

Talbot, Allan R. POWER ALONG THE HUDSON: THE STORM KING CASE AND THE BIRTH OF ENVIRONMENTALISM. New York: Dutton, 1972. 244 p. Bibliography, pp. 213-34. Maps.

The author summarizes the bitter battles over the Storm King project and the Hudson Expressway. Although Consolidated Edison Company won its suit to build a pumped-storage plant atop Storm King Mountain, the Hudson Expressway was defeated, and the coalition of preservationist associations came of age. This is an important book and should be read by all interested in the ideological bases of environmental controversy.

Ways, Max. "How to Think About the Environment." FORTUNE 81, no. 2 (February 1970): 98-101, 159-66.

A useful journalistic call for an ecological conscience in America.

C. CONFERENCE REPORTS

Darling, Frank Fraser, and Milton, John P., eds. FUTURE ENVIRONMENTS OF NORTH AMERICA; BEING THE RECORD OF A CONFERENCE CONVENED BY THE CONSERVATION FOUNDATION IN APRIL 1965, AT AIRLIE HOUSE, WARRENTON, VIRGINIA. Garden City, N.Y.: Natural History Press, 1966. xv, 767 p.

This is the record of a conference convened to consider the evidence and significance of man's influence upon North American environments. Its thirty-four prepared papers, introductory remarks, closing statement, and verbatim discussions, all stressing an ecological point of view, make this conference report a valuable successor to MAN'S ROLE IN CHANGING THE FACE OF THE EARTH (1956), listed below. Of the prepared papers, the following are relevant to the theme of this chapter: "Economics and Ecology," by Kenneth E. Boulding; "Economics and Environmental Aspects of Increasing Leisure Activities," by Marion Clawson; "Man in North America," by Raymond F. Dasmann; "The Special Role of National Parks," by Noel Eichorn; "Reflections on the Man-Nature Theme As a Subject for Study," by Clarence J. Glacken (see Chapter 1, Section A: General Studies, for annotation); "Ecological Impact and Human Ecology," by Pierre Dansereau; "Ecological Determinism," by Ian L. McHarg; "Preserving the Cultural Patrimony," by Christopher Tunnard; and "Closing Statement," by Lewis Mumford. The general discussions after each of the six sections in the book reflect significant disagreement and disputation on the content and role of modern ecology. A major criticism levelled by the economist Kenneth E. Boulding was that ecology was as yet an "unsophisticated science," largely committed to "bird watching," rather than to a more necessary study of human ecology.

Jarrett, Henry, ed. PERSPECTIVES ON CONSERVATION; ESSAYS ON AMERICA'S NATURAL RESOURCES. Baltimore, Md.: Published for Resources for the Future, Inc., by The Johns Hopkins Press, 1958. xii, 260 p.

Most of the material here is concerned with natural resources--history, consumption, limits, policy, and management--from the perspective of the last fifty years, and hence is not directly related to the theme of this chapter. Two essays, however, are relevant: "Ethics, Esthetics and the Balance of Nature," by Paul B. Sears, and "Our Need of Breathing Space," by Sigurd F. Olson.

Thomas, William L., ed. MAN'S ROLE IN CHANGING THE FACE OF THE EARTH. Chicago: Published for the Wenner-Gren Foundation for Anthropological Research and the National Science Foundation, by the University of Chicago Press, 1956. xxxviii, 1193 p. Illustrated. Maps.

> This is the record of the proceedings, contributed papers, and addresses of the seventy-five participants in the International Symposium on Man's Role in Changing the Face of the Earth, held in Princeton, New Jersey, in June 1955 and sponsored by the Wenner-Gren Foundation and the National Science Foundation. The book is dedicated to George Perkins Marsh, whose pioneer work in the field of man's influence on the environment may well be considered the ecological progenitor of the Symposium's theme. The book is arranged in four parts: "Retrospect," covering the prehistorical and historical contexts; "Process," which focuses upon man's effect upon the earth in its contemporary setting; "Prospect," which examines possible future changes in human ecology and the limits to consumption of resources; and "Summary Remarks." Although most of the papers deal with plant and animal ecology, human ecology, anthro-geography, economic geography, and other allied fields, a number consider the need for a new ecological ethic for the earth. Of particular relevance to this chapter are the following: "Introduction," by William L. Thomas; "The Agency of Man on Earth," by Carl O. Sauer; "Changing Ideas of the Habitable Earth," by Clarence J. Glacken; "The Natural History of Urbanism," by Lewis Mumford; "The Process of Environmental Change by Man," by Paul B. Sears; "Recreational Land Use," by Artur Glikson; "Man's Relation to the Earth in Its Bearing on His Aesthetic, Ethical and Legal Values," by F.S.C. Northrop; and "Prospect," by Lewis Mumford. All papers contain bibliographical references.

D. ANTHOLOGIES

Disch, Robert, ed. THE ECOLOGICAL CONSCIENCE: VALUES FOR SURVIVAL. A Spectrum Book. Englewood Cliffs, N.J.: Prentice-Hall, 1970. xv, 206 p. Suggested readings, pp. 205-6.

> A very useful anthology. The opening essay, an exposition by Barry Commoner of the ecological crisis, is followed by a section on the ecological conscience featuring articles by Ian McHarg, Thomas Merton, Aldo Leopold, and Paul Shepard, Jr. This second part is the most relevant. The remaining sections reprint articles on environmental policy, impact of technology, and "the metaphysics of ecology" (R. Buckminster Fuller, Alan Watts, and Gary Snyder).

Shepard, Paul, Jr., and McKinley, Daniel, eds. THE SUBVERSIVE SCIENCE; ESSAYS TOWARD AN ECOLOGY OF MAN. Boston: Houghton Mifflin,

1969. x, 453 p. Illustrated. Bibliography, pp. 439-53.

This is one of the most useful and valuable of the numerous anthologies on ecology, and the most pertinent to the theme of this bibliography. Shepard and McKinley have done an excellent job of bringing together essays which bear upon their theme--that the survival of man qua man is inextricably bound to the survival of all nature, and that man is morally obligated to assume an ethical stewardship over the earth. The editors preface each essay with an explanatory note, and Shepard contributes a substantive introduction, "Ecology and Man--A Viewpoint." Each essay contains the original references and there is a very valuable general bibliography at the end of the book.

E. ENVIRONMENTAL HANDBOOKS

De Bell, Garrett, ed. THE ENVIRONMENTAL HANDBOOK; PREPARED FOR THE FIRST NATIONAL ENVIRONMENTAL TEACH-IN. Ballantine/Friends of the Earth Book. New York: Ballantine Books, 1970. xv, 367 p. Bibliography, pp. 345-50. Paper.

Similar in intent and format to the Sierra Club publication, ECOTACTICS, below. De Bell's compilation grew out of a suggestion by David R. Brower (and was sponsored by his organization, The Friends of the Earth) that there should be a "source of ideas and tactics" for the National Environmental Teach-In, April 22, 1970. The selections include essays by college students and ecologically oriented "self-exiled non-students," older conservationist activists, and reprinted articles by "authorities." The book is arranged in four sections: "The Meaning of Ecology"; "Eco-Tactics--Part I," concerned with individual action; "Eco-Tactics--Part II," devoted to political action; and an Appendix containing a bibliography of books and films, membership information on Zero Population Growth and the Friends of the Earth, and "Eco-Notes."

Mitchell, John G., and Stallings, Constance L., eds. ECOTACTICS: THE SIERRA CLUB HANDBOOK FOR ENVIRONMENTAL ACTIVISTS. Introduction by Ralph Nader. New York: Pocket Books, 1970. 288 p. Paper.

Although already dated by the end of the Vietnam War, the energy crisis, and other developments, this handbook is still useful for activists and for historians of the environment. The contributors to this little book adopt an aggressive stance toward those whom they regard as enemies of the environment. Most of the writers are young activists. Among the more well-known names are Paul Brooks, N. Scott Momaday, Senator Philip Hart, Allan Gussow, and Representatives Richard Ottinger and Paul McCloskey. An appendix includes "The Activist's Checklist," a bibliography, a list of conservation and environmental organizations, a directory of key congressional committees and subcommittees, and a listing of key federal agencies.

Chapter 7

AMERICAN NATURE WRITING

Chapter 7

AMERICAN NATURE WRITING

American writing about nature encompasses a broad spectrum of works dealing
with the natural world and its influence upon man and his literature. In this
bibliography, however, we are concerned only with the nature, or natural
history, essay originated by Thoreau and brought to its modern development by
John Burroughs and his successors. No attempt has been made to trace bibliographically the influence of Emersonian romanticism upon the origin and development of the nature essay; hence, the works of Emerson and other transcendental-
ists (except Thoreau) are not included. Nature poetry is also excluded, so
that no reference is made to the poetry of Bryant, Whittier, Lowell, Whitman,
Frost, and others who have taken nature as a major theme. Also excluded are
the popular and semipopular treatments of birds, animals, insects, and physio-
graphic features of specific areas, although some titles in this genre will be
found in Chapter 8: Nature Study in America.

Although the treatment of nature writing in this chapter is selective, ignoring
many minor figures, it is comprehensive to the extent that writers cited are
covered in detail, with collected works, individual works, bibliographies,
studies of specific writers, biographies, and autobiographies included.

The chapter is divided into three parts: the first lists general works, the
second lists works by and about Henry David Thoreau, and the third lists
nature writing since Thoreau.

A. GENERAL WORKS

1. Bibliographies

Lillard, Richard G. "Books in the Field: Nature and Conservation." WILSON
LIBRARY BULLETIN 44 (October 1969): 159-77.

> A valuable bibliographic essay and list of books. Lillard discusses
> contemporary nature writing, its scope, subject matter, and charac-
> teristics. The author contrasts the nature book to the conservation

book and defines the latter as a relatively modern creation, one now more concerned with the ecological crisis created by man. A list of 148 books is included.

LITERARY HISTORY OF THE UNITED STATES: BIBLIOGRAPHY. Edited by Robert E. Spiller and others. 3rd ed., rev. New York: Macmillan; London: Collier-Macmillan, 1963. xxiv, 790 p.; SUPPLEMENT I. xvii, 268 p.

Reprints in one volume the bibliography of 1948 and the supplement published in 1959. The bibliography volume of the LHUS devotes less than half a page to "Nature Essays." John Burroughs, John Muir, Henry Van Dyke, William Beebe, Donald Culross Peattie, and Theodore Roosevelt are mentioned as writers, and the critical works of Norman Foerster and Philip M. Hicks are noted. The opening sentence of the section is indicative of this neglect: "As a genre, the nature essay has been surprisingly undeveloped." Individual bibliographies for the writers noted are included.

_____. SUPPLEMENT II. Edited by Robert E. Spiller and others. New York: Macmillan; London: Collier-Macmillan, 1972. xxiii, 366 p.

Teale, Edwin Way. "Great Companions of Nature Literature; A 100 Volume Nature Library." AUDUBON MAGAZINE 46, no. 6 (November-December 1944): 363–66.

Includes neither annotations nor introduction.

2. Histories and Special Studies

Barton, William G. "Thoreau, Flagg, and Burroughs." HISTORICAL COLLECTIONS OF THE ESSEX INSTITUTE 22 (1885): 53–80.

A comparative study of the nature writings of Thoreau, Wilson Flagg, and Burroughs. Barton uses essays by the three authors treating similar subjects in order to compare their approaches to both nature and its representation in literature. One of the very few analytical pieces on the writing of Flagg.

Carrington, James B. "Books for Days in the Open." THE BOOK BUYER 22 (April 1901): 212–15.

A list of about 100 titles and an introductory essay.

Foerster, Norman. NATURE IN AMERICAN LITERATURE; STUDIES IN THE MODERN VIEW OF NATURE. New York: Macmillan, 1923. xiii, 324 p. Reprint ed., 1958.

Foerster's is the pioneer study of nature in American literature, and has not yet been surpassed for its comprehensive view. A chapter each is devoted to the following authors: Bryant, Whittier, Emerson, Thoreau, Lowell, Whitman, Lanier, Muir, and Burroughs.

Halsey, Francis W. "The Rise of the Nature Writers." AMERICAN MONTHLY REVIEW OF REVIEWS 26, no. 5 (November 1902): 567-71.

The author reviews the growth of popular nature writing and superficially discusses several writers, including Burroughs, Seton, Chapman, and Ernest Ingersoll.

"Heirs of a Great Tradition." LIFE 51, no. 25 (December 22, 1961): 103-10.

A photo-story on modern popular naturalists with photographs by Alfred Eisenstadt. Covers the Murie brothers (Adolf and Olaus), Paul Errington, Edwin Way Teale, Roger Tory Peterson, Richard H. Pough, Sigurd Olson, Rachel Carson, and H. Albert Hochbaum.

Hicks, Philip Marshall. THE DEVELOPMENT OF THE NATURAL HISTORY ESSAY IN AMERICAN LITERATURE. Philadelphia: University of Pennsylvania, 1924. 167 p. Bibliography, pp. 165-67.

Hick's work, a published Ph.D. thesis in English done at the University of Pennsylvania, continues to be the only treatise on the origins and development of the natural history essay in American literature. The author defines his subject as "the literary expression of scientifically accurate observations of the life history of the lower orders of nature, or of other natural objects." Thus, he eliminates essays whose object is an expression of "an aesthetic or sentimental delight in nature in general," the travel narrative, and the descriptive sketch of scenery. Hicks briefly notes early treatment of natural history from 1584 to 1700, describes the beginning of the genre during the eighteenth century, and then concentrates in the remaining chapters on the nineteenth and early twentieth centuries. Authors examined are John and William Bartram, St. John de Crevecoeur, Alexander Wilson, Audubon, Thoreau, N.P. Willis, Hawthorne, Emerson, Wilson Flagg, T.W. Higginson, Lowell, Gail Hamilton, Charles D. Warner, Donald G. Mitchell, and John Burroughs. Burroughs receives major treatment, while John Muir, curiously, is not discussed. Although Hick's work is by no means a completely satisfactory study, it deserves to be reprinted.

LITERARY HISTORY OF THE UNITED STATES: HISTORY. Edited by Robert E. Spiller and others. 3rd ed., rev. New York: Macmillan; London: Collier-Macmillan, 1963. xxiv, 1511 p.

The discussion of nature writing and writers in the LHUS is perfunctory. Audubon, Thoreau, Burroughs, Muir, Clarence King, John Wesley Powell, Clarence E. Dutton, and Robert Frost are mentioned briefly, but no recognition is given to the genre as such, nor is there any discussion of its history, influences, and cultural significance.

Merwin, Henry Childs. "Books About Nature." SCRIBNER'S MAGAZINE 33, no. 4 (April 1903): 430-37.

> A critical essay on the state of nature writing. The author praises Thoreau, William Brewster, John Burroughs, Maurice Thompson, Wilson Flagg, and Bradford Torrey, but criticizes the "birdmen" who range the fields, not in search of birds, but for "copy." Too many nature books were, in his view, filled with trite description and homilies about nature.

Shinn, Charles H. "Recent Outdoor Literature. Part II--American." OVERLAND MONTHLY, n.s., 39, no. 3 (May 1902): 711-26.

> A wide-ranging, though uncritical, article.

Tracy, Henry Chester. AMERICAN NATURISTS. New York: Dutton, 1930. viii, 282 p.

> An important interpretation of American nature writing. Authors represented include the Bartrams, Alexander Wilson, Audubon, Thoreau, Burroughs, Muir, Hornaday, Theodore Roosevelt, Ernest T. Seton, L.H. Bailey, Mary Austin, and others. Tracy sees American nature writing as a unique literary genre, owing little or nothing to European influences.

West, Herbert Faulkner. THE NATURE WRITERS: A GUIDE TO RICHER READING. Foreword by Henry Beston. Brattleboro, Vt.: Stephen Daye Press, 1939. 155 p.

> Discussion of the works of some 200 writers from classical to contemporary times. English and American writers are emphasized. An introduction considers the role of nature in human history.

_____. "Nature Writers." In his THE MIND ON THE WING: A BOOK FOR READERS AND COLLECTORS, chap. 6. New York: Coward-McCann, 1947.

> A bibliographic essay. Interesting and useful. Not restricted to American authors.

B. HENRY DAVID THOREAU (1817-1862)

The works and thought of Henry David Thoreau have become central to any meaningful understanding of man and the environment in America today. His reputation as a nature writer, nonconformist, and critic of American industrial society has grown slowly but steadily since his death in 1862. He remains today one of the greatest individualists this country has ever produced. The force of his thought, often flinty, obdurate, and contrary, challenges our complacent belief in continuing material progress and economic growth. His message that we must "simplify" our lives and seek a proper, harmonious relationship with nature, makes him very contemporary. Thoreau's thought has profoundly influenced several generations of conservationists and preservationists, and his stature continues to grow.

The literature about Thoreau, both popular and scholarly, has grown to monumental proportions. The scholarly work alone is so prodigious that, according to Walter Harding, a noted Thoreau scholar, one must be an "extreme specialist" to hope to assimilate even a small part of it. Given this fact, the editor has provided minimal annotation of Thoreau's works and the major biographies and critical studies included here. Several excellent Thoreau bibliographies, reference books, and literary handbooks are listed to help provide a path through the proliferating maze of material.

1. General Bibliographies

AMERICAN LITERARY SCHOLARSHIP: AN ANNUAL. Durham, N.C.: Duke University Press, 1965--.

> Various editors. Each annual volume contains a first chapter, "Emerson, Thoreau, and Transcendentalism," written by various scholars, in which the literary scholarship of the past year is discussed in some detail. Coverage is from 1963.

LITERARY HISTORY OF THE UNITED STATES: BIBLIOGRAPHY. Edited by Robert E. Spiller and others. 3rd ed., rev. New York: Macmillan; London: Collier-Macmillan, 1963. xxiv, 790 p. SUPPLEMENT I. xvii, 268 p.

_____. SUPPLEMENT II. Edited by Robert E. Spiller and others. New York: Macmillan; London: Collier-Macmillan, 1972. xxiii, 366 p.

> The LHUS, with its two supplements, is a convenient source for Thoreau scholarship, containing brief selections in bibliographical-essay format. Relevant material is to be found in the main volume on pages 742-46. In SUPPLEMENT I, consult pages 197-99; in SUPPLEMENT II, see pages 264-67.

Modern Language Association of America. MLA INTERNATIONAL BIBLIOGRA-PHY. New York: 1921--.

> An annual classified list with author indexes. The title varies: from 1921-55 it was entitled AMERICAN BIBLIOGRAPHY: since 1956 it has appeared as MLA INTERNATIONAL BIBLIOGRAPHY. Selection is made from books and from a list of more than 1100 journals. No annotations.

2. Special Bibliographies

Advena, Jean Cameron. A BIBLIOGRAPHY OF THE THOREAU SOCIETY BULLETIN BIBLIOGRAPHIES, 1941-1969. A CUMULATION AND INDEX.

Edited by Walter Harding. Troy, N.Y.: Whitson Publishing Co., 1971. viii, 323 p.

Allen, Francis H., comp. A BIBLIOGRAPHY OF HENRY DAVID THOREAU. Boston and New York: Houghton Mifflin, 1908. xviii, 201 p. Frontispiece. Facsimile. Reprint ed., 1967.

   This is the standard bibliography, comprehensive to 1908. Lists all Thoreau's works--books, articles, and poetry, books containing selections from Thoreau, biographies and critical pieces about Thoreau, newspaper and periodical articles about Thoreau and his works, and a list of auction prices.

Burnham, Philip E., and Collins, Carvel. "Contribution to a Bibliography of Thoreau, 1938-1945." BULLETIN OF BIBLIOGRAPHY 19, no. 1 (September-December 1946): 16-18; no. 2 (January-April 1947): 37-39.

Harding, Walter R. A THOREAU HANDBOOK. [New York]: New York University Press, 1959. xviii, 229 p.

   Unquestionably the best introduction to a study of Thoreau's life, his writing, and sources for his thought, as well as for Thoreau scholarship up to the late 1950s. Of particular interest is a chapter devoted to the worldwide fame of Thoreau and his influence in literary, social, and political fields. Harding is the secretary of the Thoreau Society and the author of many critical works, including the latest and best biography of Thoreau the man (see Section B5: Biography and Criticism, below). The book is available in both hardcover and paper editions. It should be supplemented by Leary's bibliographic essay below.

Leary, Lewis. "Henry David Thoreau." In EIGHT AMERICAN AUTHORS: A REVIEW OF RESEARCH AND CRITICISM, edited by James Woodress, rev. ed., pp. 129-71. New York: Norton [1972].

   A revision of a similarly titled work edited by Floyd Stovall and published in 1956. Leary's bibliographic essay, according to Walter Harding, is the "best selective and annotated bibliography" and can be used as a supplement to Harding's A THOREAU HANDBOOK, above.

THOREAU SOCIETY BULLETIN (Geneseo, N.Y.). October 1941--.

   Since its inception, this quarterly has carried a running bibliography of Thoreau items and scholarship.

Wade, J. S. "A Contribution to a Bibliography from 1909 to 1936 of Henry David Thoreau." JOURNAL OF THE NEW YORK ENTOMOLOGICAL SOCIETY, 1939, pp. 163-203.

Duplicates White's bibliography, below, but each includes items not covered by the other.

White, William. A HENRY DAVID THOREAU BIBLIOGRAPHY, 1908-1937. Bulletin of Bibliography Pamphlets, no. 35. Boston: F.W. Faxon, 1939. 51 p.

"Reprinted from the BULLETIN OF BIBLIOGRAPHY, vol. 16, no. 5, January to April 1938, and following issues." Reprinted in 1971 in book form. See also Wade, J.S., above.

3. Collected Works

THE WRITINGS OF HENRY DAVID THOREAU. Manuscript Edition, 20 vols. Vols. 1-6, edited by F.B. Sanborn; Vols. 7-20, edited by Bradford Torrey and Francis H. Allen. Biographical sketch by Ralph Waldo Emerson. Photographs by Herbert W. Gleason. Boston and New York: Houghton Mifflin, 1906. 3 portraits. 101 photos. Autograph manuscript bound in 1st vol.

This is the only "complete" edition of Thoreau's writings. Volumes 1-6 contain A WEEK ON THE CONCORD AND MERRIMACK RIVERS; WALDEN; THE MAINE WOODS; CAPE COD, AND MISCELLANIES; EXCURSIONS, AND POEMS; FAMILIAR LETTERS. Volumes 7-20 contain the JOURNAL. Journal extracts, edited by H.G.O. Blake, EARLY SPRING IN MASSACHUSETTS, SUMMER, AUTUMN, and WINTER, were omitted. This edition was limited to 600 copies and the first volume of each set had a piece of Thoreau's autograph manuscript mounted and bound in. A second, "Walden," edition, in 12mo. and printed from the same plates, appeared the same year and was sold by subscription (see also next item). The Manuscript Edition has been reprinted and is still in print.

JOURNAL. [Walden Edition]. 14 vols. Edited by Bradford Torrey and Francis H. Allen. Foreword by Henry Seidel Canby. Boston: Houghton Mifflin, 1949.

Reprinted in a two-volume edition in 1962 with a foreword by Walter Harding.

A completely new edition of Thoreau's writings is currently being prepared at the Princeton University Press. This definitive edition is supported by the National Endowment for the Humanities and administered through the Center for Editions of American Authors of the Modern Language Association. The general editor is Walter Harding. Twenty-five to thirty volumes (including hitherto unpublished material) are projected and are scheduled to appear during the next eight to ten years. Since 1971, three volumes (WALDEN, THE MAINE WOODS, and REFORM PAPERS) have been published.

4. Individual Works

The various editions of Thoreau's works are legion. There are, for example, nearly 150 editions of WALDEN. The preferred text of each work will be the new Princeton University Press edition mentioned above (see Section B3: Collected Works). The three Princeton volumes now in print have been listed here; the first editions of all other works are listed.

A WEEK ON THE CONCORD AND MERRIMACK RIVERS. Boston and Cambridge: James Munroe; New York: George P. Putnam; Philadelphia: Lindsay and Blackiston; London: John Chapman, 1849. 413 p.

   Also available in several paper editions.

WALDEN. Edited by J. Lyndon Shanley. The Writings of Henry David Thoreau. Princeton, N.J.: Princeton University Press, 1971. 409 p. Illustrated.

   First published in 1854. Numerous paper editions available.

EXCURSIONS.... Boston: Ticknor and Fields, 1863. 319 p.

   Available in a paper edition.

THE MAINE WOODS. Edited by Joseph J. Moldenhauer. The Writings of Henry David Thoreau. Princeton, N.J.: Princeton University Press, 1972. 485 p.

   First published in 1864. Several paper editions are available.

CAPE COD.... Edited by Sophia E. Thoreau and William Ellery Channing. Boston: Ticknor and Fields, 1865. 252 p.

   Available in a paper edition.

A YANKEE IN CANADA, WITH ANTI-SLAVERY AND REFORM PAPERS.... Boston: Ticknor and Fields, 1866. 286 p.

   Several reprints, but no paper edition.

REFORM PAPERS. Edited by Wendell Glick. The Writings of Henry David Thoreau. Princeton, N.J.: Princeton University Press, 1973. 402 p.

EARLY SPRING IN MASSACHUSETTS. FROM THE JOURNAL OF HENRY D. THOREAU.... Boston: Houghton Mifflin, 1881. viii, 318 p.

   See next item.

SUMMER: FROM THE JOURNAL OF HENRY D. THOREAU. Edited by H.G.O. Blake. Boston and New York: Houghton Mifflin, 1884. vi, 382 p. Map.

See next item.

WINTER: FROM THE JOURNAL OF HENRY D. THOREAU. Edited by H.G.O. Blake. Boston and New York: Houghton Mifflin, 1888. vi, 439 p.

See next item.

AUTUMN: FROM THE JOURNAL OF HENRY D. THOREAU. Edited by H.G.O. Blake. Boston and New York: Houghton Mifflin, 1892. vi, 470 p.

See next item.

FAMILIAR LETTERS OF HENRY DAVID THOREAU. Edited, with an introduction and notes, by F.B. Sanborn. Boston and New York: Houghton Mifflin, 1894. xii, 483 p.

This and the four preceding items are now out of print. No paper editions are available.

THE HEART OF THOREAU'S JOURNALS. Edited by Odell Shepard. Boston and New York: Houghton Mifflin, 1927. xiii, 348 p. Frontispiece.

Available in a paper reprint edition.

Other, posthumous, selections from Thoreau's writings are primarily of literary, poetical, or political character and have not been included here. For a complete list, see the bibliographies listed in Section B2, above.

5. Biography and Criticism

Listed below are the major biographical and critical books dealing with Thoreau. For critical insights on the varying degrees of usefulness of these works, the reader is referred to Harding's THOREAU HANDBOOK and to Leary's bibliographic essay (see Section B2: Special Bibliographies, above). Both are in print and available in paper.

Atkinson, Justin Brooks. HENRY THOREAU, THE COSMIC YANKEE. New York: Knopf, 1927. 158 p.

Canby, Henry Seidel. THOREAU. Boston: Houghton Mifflin, [1939]. xx, 508 p. Frontispiece. Plates. Facsimiles. Bibliography, pp. [485]-91.

Channing, William Ellery. THOREAU, THE POET NATURALIST, WITH MEMORIAL VERSES. New ed., enl. Edited by F.B. Sanborn. Boston: Charles E. Goodspeed, 1902. xx, 397 p. Portrait.

Cook, Reginald L. THE CONCORD SAUNTERER: INCLUDING A DISCUS-

SION OF THE NATURE MYSTICISM OF THOREAU.... Original Letters by Thoreau, and a Check List of Thoreau Items in the Abernethy Library of Middlebury College compiled by Viola C. White. Middlebury, Vt.: Middlebury College Press, 1940. ix, 41 p. Illustrated.

_____. PASSAGE TO WALDEN. Boston: Houghton Mifflin, 1949. xvi, 238 p.

Glick, Wendell, comp. THE RECOGNITION OF HENRY DAVID THOREAU; SELECTED CRITICISM SINCE 1848. Ann Arbor: University of Michigan Press, [1969]. xxi, 381 p. Facsimile. Bibliographic footnotes.

Harding, Walter R. THE DAYS OF HENRY THOREAU. New York: Knopf, 1965. xvi, 472 p. xvi. Illustrated. Map. Bibliographic note, pp. 471-72.

_____, ed. THOREAU: A CENTURY OF CRITICISM. Dallas: Southern Methodist University Press, 1954. 205 p.

Hicks, John Harland, ed. THOREAU IN OUR SEASON. [Amherst]: University of Massachusetts Press, [1966]. 176 p. Illustrated.

Hough, Henry Beetle. THOREAU OF WALDEN; THE MAN AND HIS EVENTFUL LIFE. New York: Simon & Schuster, 1956. 275 p.

Krutch, Joseph Wood. HENRY DAVID THOREAU. [New York]: William Sloane, 1948. xiii, 298 p.

Murray, James G. HENRY DAVID THOREAU. New York: Washington Square Press, [1968]. 180 p. Bibliography, pp. 155-56.

Paul, Sherman. THE SHORES OF AMERICA, THOREAU'S INWARD EXPLORATION. Urbana: University of Illinois Press, 1958. xi, 433 p. Illustrated. Maps. Bibliographic footnotes.

Salt, Henry Stephens. THE LIFE OF HENRY DAVID THOREAU. London: Richard Bentley & Son, 1890. x, 315 p. Portrait. Appendix. Bibliography, pp. 300-307.

Sanborn, Franklin Benjamin. THE LIFE OF HENRY DAVID THOREAU, including Many Essays Hitherto Unpublished and Some Account of His Family and Friends. Boston: Houghton Mifflin, 1917. xix, 541 p. Illustrated.

Stowell, Robert F. A THOREAU GAZETEER. Edited by William L. Howarth. Princeton, N.J.: Princeton University Press, 1970. xi, 56 p. Illustrated. Maps. Portrait. Bibliographic footnotes.

Van Doren, Mark. HENRY DAVID THOREAU; A CRITICAL STUDY. Boston and New York: Houghton Mifflin, 1916. viii, 138 p. Bibliography, pp. [129]-32.

Whicher, George F. WALDEN REVISITED; A CENTENNIAL TRIBUTE TO HENRY DAVID THOREAU. Chicago: Packard & Co., [1945]. 93 p.

C. NATURE WRITING SINCE THOREAU

Abbott, Charles Conrad (1843-1919)

> Charles C. Abbott, naturalist, archaeologist, and author, grew up in and around Trenton, New Jersey, where he spent most of his life. Although Abbott wrote a number of serious works on the archaeology and Indian history of the Delaware Valley, he is known now for the short, semipopular, natural history essay, of which he wrote more than a hundred for popular periodicals. Many of these were later collected into books. For biographical information see the sketch by Wilmer Stone in the DICTIONARY OF AMERICAN BIOGRAPHY (volume 1, pp. 17-18).

A NATURALIST'S RAMBLES ABOUT HOME. New York: D. Appleton, 1884. 485 p.

DAYS OUT OF DOORS. New York: D. Appleton, 1889. 325 p.

OUTINGS AT ODD TIMES. New York: D. Appleton, 1890. x, 282 p.

RECENT RAMBLES; OR, IN TOUCH WITH NATURE. Philadelphia: Lippincott, 1892. 330 p. Illustrated.

TRAVELS IN A TREE TOP. Philadelphia and London: Lippincott, 1894. 215 p.

NOTES OF THE NIGHT, AND OTHER OUTDOOR SKETCHES. New York: Century Co., 1896. 231 p.

FREEDOM OF THE FIELDS. Philadelphia: Lippincott, 1898. ix, 233 p. Frontispiece. Plates.

CLEAR SKIES AND CLOUDY. Philadelphia and London: Lippincott, 1899. 316 p. Frontispiece. Illustrated, with plates.

IN NATURE'S REALM. Trenton, N.J.: Albert Brandt, 1900. 309 p. Frontispiece. Illustrated.

"American Mountain Series."

Between 1942 and 1952, Vangard Press published nine books in this series. The books are similar in content and scope and, with the exception of two, are edited by Roderick Peattie. All contain chapters on human history and exploration combined with natural history, scenery, camping, and outdoor sports. The contributors to the various chapters were or are specialists in the areas in which they wrote. Although dated in terms of factual information, all are well written and documented.

Atwood, Wallace W. THE ROCKY MOUNTAINS. New York: Vangard Press, 1945. 324 p. Illustrated, with plates. Maps (one folding) and diagrams. Bibliography, pp. 311–15.

Chapters on geography, scenery, geology, the art of camping, mountain building, mining history, and the national parks in the region. Contains "cross-section drawings" by Erwin Raisz and a "geologic calendar." Still a useful and interesting book.

Peattie, Donald Culross, ed. THE SIERRA NEVADA, THE RANGE OF LIGHT. Introduction by Donald Culross Peattie. New York: Vangard Press, 1947. 398 p. Illustrated.

Contributions by Charles A. Harivell, Weldon F. Heald, Idwal Jones, Oliver Kehrlein, Francois E. Matthes, Lester Rowntree, Richard Joel Russell, and Mary Tresidder.

Peattie, Roderick, ed. THE FRIENDLY MOUNTAINS: GREEN, WHITE, AND ADIRONDACKS. New York: Vangard Press, 1942. xii, 341 p. Illustrated.

Contributions by Robert Balk, Victor Conrad, Zephine Humphrey, Roderick Peattie, Henry Potter, Louis B. Puffer, Hugh M. Raup, and Katharine Toll.

_____, ed. THE GREAT SMOKIES AND THE BLUE RIDGE; THE STORY OF THE SOUTHERN APPALACHIANS. New York: Vangard Press, 1943. x, 372 p. Plates. Maps. Bibliography, pp. 353–59.

Contributions by Edward S. Drake, Ralph Erskine, Alberta P. Hannum, John Jacob Niles, Donald Culross Peattie, Henry S. Sharp, and Arthur Stupka. Contains chapters on mountain people, forest trees and wildflowers, folk-lore and music, crafts, and other subjects.

_____, ed. THE PACIFIC COAST RANGES. New York: Vangard Press, 1946. 402 p. Illustrated.

Contributions by Archie Binns, John Walton Caughey, Lois Crisler, Aubrey Drury, Idwal Jones, Donald Culross Peattie, Thomas Emerson Ripley, Richard Joel Russell, Judy Van der Veer, and Daniel E. Willard. Covers the coast mountains of Washington, Oregon, and California.

_____, ed. THE BERKSHIRES: THE PURPLE HILLS. New York: Vangard Press, 1948. 414 p. Plates.

Contributions by Walter Prichard Eaton, A. Kenneth Simpson, George J. Wallace, Bartlett Hendricks, Theodore Giddings, Haydn Mason, William S. Annin, and Margaret Cresson.

_____, ed. THE INVERTED MOUNTAINS: CANYONS OF THE WEST. New York: Vangard Press, 1948. x, 390 p. Illustrated. Maps.

Contributions by Weldon F. Heald, Edwin D. McKee, and Harold S. Colton. Geographically, this book covers the canyon country of southern Utah and northern Arizona. Some of the more familiar places considered are Grand Canyon, Zion, Bryce Canyon, Arches National Monument, Canyon de Chelly, Rainbow Bridge, Cedar Breaks, and the Petrified Forest. The contributors, all experts on the history, natural history, and scenery of the Southwest, have written chapters on the physiographical features, geologic history, fossil life, ecology, and human history, as well as the tourist attractions, of the various canyons. An excellent and absorbing book.

_____, ed. THE CASCADES, MOUNTAINS OF THE PACIFIC NORTHWEST. New York: Vangard Press, 1949. 417 p. Illustrated.

Contributions by Margaret Bundy Callahan, Harry W. Hagen, Weldon F. Heald, Charles D. Hessey, Jr., Ellsworth D. Lumley, Herbert Lundy, Grant McConnell, Walter F. McCulloch, and James Stevens.

_____, ed. THE BLACK HILLS. New York: Vangard Press, 1952. 320 p. Illustrated.

Contributions by Leland D. Case, Badger Clark, Paul Friggens, R.V. Hunkins, Clarence S. Paine, and Elmo Scott Watson. This volume, unlike others in the series, emphasizes the human history of the area, largely to the exclusion of nature and natural history.

Austin, Mary. THE LAND OF LITTLE RAIN. Boston and New York: Houghton

Mifflin, 1903. xi, 280 p. Frontispiece. Illustrated.

The locale of this beautifully evocative book is the borderlands
between Arizona and southern California, including the eastern
slopes of the Sierra Nevada, Owens Valley, Death Valley, and
the Mojave Desert. Mrs. Austin skillfully wove together elements
of scenery and natural history with portraits of the human inhabitants of the settlements and Indian villages of the area. The
book is an acknowledged classic of the literature of the Southwest.
It has been reprinted several times and is now available in a paper
edition published in 1961.

Bedichek, Roy. ADVENTURES WITH A TEXAS NATURALIST. Garden City,
N.Y.: Doubleday, 1947. xx, 293 p. Illustrated.

Meandering observations on the flora and fauna of Texas, especially east Texas, by an educator, outdoorsman, and conservationist.
In 1961, "a new revised" edition was published by the University
of Texas Press with an errata by the author correcting some typo-
graphical errors and some assertions in the first edition.

Beston, Henry. THE OUTERMOST HOUSE: A YEAR OF LIFE ON THE GREAT
BEACH OF CAPE COD. Garden City, N.Y.: Doubleday, Doran, 1928.
222 p. Frontispiece. Illustrated, with plates. Reprint ed., 1949. Paperbound ed., 1962.

For more than four decades this book has been recognized as a
classic of American nature writing. Beston spent a solitary year
in a house he built on the Cape Cod dunes near Eastham, Massachusetts, overlooking the North Atlantic. His observations of
dune and beach life, thunder of the surf, flights of sea birds, and
other natural phenomena are characterized by an uncommon vivid-
ness, a deep reverence for life, and a style informed by poetic
images of great beauty. In 1964, the "Outermost House" was
proclaimed a National Literary Landmark by the State of Massachusetts and the U.S. Department of the Interior.

_____. ESPECIALLY MAINE. THE NATURAL WORLD OF HENRY BESTON
FROM CAPE COD TO THE SAINT LAWRENCE. Selected and with introductions by Elizabeth Coatsworth. Brattleboro, Vt.: Stephen Greene Press, 1970.
198 p. Illustrated.

Selections from THE OUTERMOST HOUSE, WHITE PINE AND
BLUE WATER, HERBS AND THE EARTH, NORTHERN FARM, AMERI-
CAN MEMORY, THE ST. LAWRENCE (Rivers of America), and
from some lesser writings and poetry. Miss Coatsworth, Beston's
widow, provides introductions to the selections and has interpolated
excerpts from the author's letters to her and to friends and family.
Beston was not a prolific writer; indeed, his fame as a writer rests
largely upon one work, THE OUTERMOST HOUSE (see previous
item); yet within that work and others anthologized in ESPECIALLY
MAINE, there are some of the most beautiful and moving passages

to be found in the great body of nature writing in America.
Beston's particular concern, implicitly ecological, was that man
was becoming alienated from nature and had all but lost his early
reverence for the natural world.

Bolles, Frank. LAND OF THE LINGERING SNOW; CHRONICLES OF A
STROLLER IN NEW ENGLAND FROM JANUARY TO JUNE. Boston and New
York: Houghton Mifflin, 1891. 234 p.

> Bolles was a passionate lover of nature. During his short life of
> thirty-eight years, he tramped the regions around Cambridge and
> spent his summers in the White Mountains of New Hampshire.
> Encouraged by James Russell Lowell, Bolles published this, his
> first nature piece. Two books, FROM BLOMIDON TO SMOKY
> and CHOCORUA'S TENANTS (see below), were published post-
> humously. He died of pneumonia in 1894. LAND OF THE
> LINGERING SNOW went through several later editions.

_____. AT THE NORTH OF BEARCAMP WATER; CHRONICLES OF A STROLL-
ER IN NEW ENGLAND FROM JULY TO DECEMBER. Boston and New York:
Houghton Mifflin, 1893. 297 p.

> Several later editions are available. The 1917 edition includes
> photographic plates.

_____. FROM BLOMIDON TO SMOKY, AND OTHER PAPERS. Boston and
New York: Houghton Mifflin, 1894. 278 p.

> First appeared in periodicals during 1890-94.

_____. CHOCORUA'S TENANTS. Boston and New York: Houghton Mifflin,
1895. 68 p.

> Verse.

Borland, Hal G. (b. 1900)

> Borland is one of the most successful authors of essays about nature
> and country life writing today. He identifies himself with what he
> calls a diminishing breed, "the countryman." From his upland
> farm in the Berkshires, near Salisbury, Connecticut, Borland has
> conducted the outdoor column for the Sunday NEW YORK TIMES
> for over thirty years. He also writes regularly for the BERKSHIRE
> EAGLE (Pittsfield, Mass.) and THE PROGRESSIVE. Since 1967
> he has been a contributing editor of the AUDUBON MAGAZINE.
> Many of these essays form the bases for his nature books. In
> addition, Borland has written a number of well-received novels
> and several books for young people. He was awarded the 1968
> John Burroughs Medal for outstanding nature writing. Borland's
> prose is characterized by a quiet, dignified style that draws its

strength from a deep appreciation of the land and the seasons, and a serene belief in the importance of man's eternal relationship to the earth.

AMERICAN YEAR: COUNTRY LIFE AND LANDSCAPES THROUGH THE SEASONS. New York: Simon & Schuster, 1946. 200 p. Illustrated.

THIS HILL, THIS VALLEY. Philadelphia: Lippincott, 1957. 314 p. Illustrated.

THE ENDURING PATTERN. New York: Simon & Schuster, 1959. 247 p. Illustrated.

BEYOND YOUR DOORSTEP; A HANDBOOK TO THE COUNTRY. New York: Knopf, 1962. 400 p. Illustrated.

THE DOG WHO CAME TO STAY. Philadelphia: Lippincott, [1962]. 220 p. Illustrated.

SUNDIAL OF THE SEASONS; A SELECTION OF OUTDOOR EDITORIALS FROM THE "NEW YORK TIMES." Philadelphia: Lippincott, 1964. 350 p. Illustrated.

COUNTRYMAN: A SUMMARY OF BELIEF. Philadelphia: Lippincott, 1965. 160 p.

HILL COUNTRY HARVEST. Philadelphia: Lippincott, 1967. 377 p.

HOMELAND; A REPORT FROM THE COUNTRY. Philadelphia: Lippincott, 1969. 187 p.

BORLAND COUNTRY. Photographs by Walter Chandoha. Philadelphia and New York: Lippincott, 1971. 114 p. Color illustrations.

Boyle, Robert. THE HUDSON RIVER, A NATURAL AND UNNATURAL HISTORY. New York: Norton, 1969. 304 p. Illustrated. Bibliography, pp. 282-96.

An unusual book combining the human history, natural history, ecology, and sport-fishing history of the river, with a passionate expose of the individual and corporate polluters of the Hudson and its environs. Well written and documented by an editor of SPORTS ILLUSTRATED. Contains an excellent bibliography.

Brewster, William. OCTOBER FARM. FROM THE CONCORD JOURNALS AND DIARIES OF WILLIAM BREWSTER. Introduction by Daniel Chester French. Cambridge, Mass.: Harvard University Press, 1936. xv, 285 p. Plates.

The author, founder of the Nuttall Club and one of America's best field ornithologists, acquired a charming 300-acre farm near Concord, Massachusetts, which he called "October Farm." This book is a collection of diary and journal entries made in Concord from 1872-1919. The entries reflect the author's love of birds and the natural setting of his farm. OCTOBER FARM and its sequel, CONCORD RIVER, have achieved the status of minor classics among natural history and outdoor books. For an appreciative note about Brewster, see "In July--William Brewster," by Howard Zahniser (NATURE MAGAZINE 30, no. 1, July 1937, pp. 7, 60).

_____. CONCORD RIVER. SELECTIONS FROM THE JOURNALS OF WILLIAM BREWSTER. Edited by Smith O. Dexter. Cambridge, Mass.: Harvard University Press, 1937. [vii], 258 p. Illustrated.

Entries range from 1879 to 1918. Brewster died in 1919.

Brooks, Maurice. THE APPALACHIANS. The Naturalist's America. Boston: Houghton Mifflin, 1965. xvii, 346 p. Illustrated, with plates (some in color). Maps on endpapers.

This is popular natural history at its best. Brooks provides an integrated ecological survey of the Appalachian range from the Gaspe Peninsula in Canada to Springer Mountain in northern Georgia, including sidelights about its human inhabitants. A delightful and engrossing book.

Burroughs, John (1837-1921)

John Burroughs occupies the central place in the history of American nature writing. He was the originator of the modern "natural history essay," and his writings have been credited with stimulating the "nature-study" movement. During his long life, Burroughs published more than twenty-five books which sold over a million and a half copies, making him the most widely read naturalist in American history. Nearly all his nature essays and sketches first appeared in the ATLANTIC, SCRIBNER'S, CENTURY, OUTLOOK, OUTING, and other popular magazines. During the last fifteen years of his life, Burroughs became something of an institution in American letters. He was celebrated by fellow writers, and his immense popularity both as a writer and as a "grandfatherly figure of nature" drew hundreds each year to his Hudson River home near West Park, New York, and to his rural retreats, "Slabsides" on the Hudson and "Woodchuck Lodge" on his ancestral homestead in the Catskills. Burroughs had a large and loyal following of school children and college students who visited him regularly each summer. He numbered among his personal friends such luminaries as Walt Whitman, Theodore Roosevelt, John Muir, Henry Ford, Harvey Firestone, and Thomas A. Edison. Although Burroughs, unlike Muir, was never directly involved in the conservation movement, his writing helped to make several generations of Americans aware of the beauty of their natural environment and thus contributed to the movement by supporting, albeit tacitly, its goals for preservation. For information about Burrough's role in the "nature-faking" controversy, see Chapter 8, Section C: Nature Faking.

BIBLIOGRAPHIES

Blanck, Jacob. "John Burroughs, 1837-1921." In his BIBLIOGRAPHY OF AMERICAN LITERATURE, vol. 1, pp. 433-48. New Haven: Yale University Press, 1955.

A complete descriptive listing of books, pamphlets, and books containing selections from his writings. No listing of periodical articles.

Garrison, Joseph M., Jr. "John Burroughs: A Checklist of Published Literary Criticism, Including Essays on Natural History Containing Literary Criticism or Comment." BULLETIN OF BIBLIOGRAPHY 24, no. 4 (May-August 1964): 95-96, 94.

LITERARY HISTORY OF THE UNITED STATES: BIBLIOGRAPHY. Edited by Robert E. Spiller and others. 3rd ed., rev. New York: Macmillan; London: Collier-Macmillan, 1963. xxiv, 790 p. SUPPLEMENT I. xvii, 268 p.

_____. SUPPLEMENT II. Edited by Robert E. Spiller and others. New York: Macmillan; London: Collier-Macmillan, 1972. xxiii, 366 p.

The LHUS and its two supplements contain brief listings of Burroughs' complete works and a sampling of the more important biographical and critical works about him. Relevant material can be found on pages 427-28 in the BIBLIOGRAPHY, on pages 87-88 in SUPPLEMENT I, and on page 118 in SUPPLEMENT II.

COLLECTED WORKS

Burroughs's collected works appear in several editions and formats. The sequence of individual titles varies from edition to edition.

THE WRITINGS OF JOHN BURROUGHS. Riverside Edition. 23 vols. Boston and New York: Houghton Mifflin, 1895-1923.

THE WRITINGS OF JOHN BURROUGHS. Autograph Edition. 23 vols. Boston and New York: Houghton Mifflin, 1904-22.

THE WRITINGS OF JOHN BURROUGHS. Riverby Edition. 23 vols. Boston and New York: Houghton Mifflin, 1904-23.

THE COMPLETE WORKS OF JOHN BURROUGHS. 12 vols. Boston: Houghton Mifflin, 1921-22.

THE COMPLETE WRITINGS OF JOHN BURROUGHS. Wake Robin Edition. 23 vols. New York: William H. Wise, 1924.

This is a reprint of the Riverby Edition (above).

INDIVIDUAL WORKS

NOTES ON WALT WHITMAN AS POET AND PERSON. New York: American News Co., 1867. 108 p.

WAKE ROBIN. New York: Hurd and Houghton, 1871. 231 p.

WINTER SUNSHINE. New York: Hurd and Houghton, 1876. x, 234 p.

A second, enlarged edition appeared in 1877.

BIRDS AND POETS, WITH OTHER PAPERS. New York: Hurd and Houghton, 1877. 263 p.

LOCUSTS AND WILD HONEY. Boston: Houghton, Osgood, 1879. 253 p.

PEPACTON. Boston: Houghton Mifflin, 1881. 260 p.

FRESH FIELDS. Boston: Houghton Mifflin, 1885. 298 p.

SIGNS AND SEASONS. Boston and New York: Houghton Mifflin, 1886. 289 p.

INDOOR STUDIES. Boston and New York: Houghton Mifflin, 1889. 256 p.

RIVERBY. Boston and New York: Houghton Mifflin, 1894. 319 p.

WHITMAN, A STUDY. Boston and New York: Houghton Mifflin, 1896. viii, 268 p.

THE LIGHT OF DAY, RELIGIOUS DISCUSSIONS AND CRITICISMS FROM THE NATURALIST'S POINT OF VIEW. Boston and New York: Houghton Mifflin, 1900. 224 p.

"Alaska, Narrative of the Expedition." In HARRIMAN ALASKA EXPEDITION. ALASKA: NARRATIVE, GLACIERS, NATIVES, edited by C. Hart Merriam, pp. 1-118. Harriman Alaska Series, vol. 1. New York: Doubleday, Page, 1902.

> Burroughs was the historian of the expedition organized and financed in 1899 by Edward Harriman. The expedition, consisting of the Harriman family, a scientific party of twenty-five (including John Muir, C. Hart Merriam, G.K. Gilbert, George B. Grinnell, and Charles A. Keeler), a group of artists, photographers, stenographers, doctors, nurses, and a chaplain, left New York in May, crossed the country by rail, and took passage in a specially outfitted steamer. Burroughs was overwhelmed by the conditions of the trip and, although he was impressed with the scenery, it is apparent that he preferred the humanized landscape of the Catskills and his Hudson River home. His narrative, in a slightly modified version, also appears in FAR AND NEAR (below).

JOHN JAMES AUDUBON. Boston: Small, Maynard, 1902. xx, 144 p.

LITERARY VALUES, AND OTHER PAPERS. Boston and New York: Houghton Mifflin, 1902. x, 264 p.

FAR AND NEAR. Boston and New York: Houghton Mifflin, 1904. viii, 288 p.

WAYS OF NATURE. Boston and New York: Houghton Mifflin, 1905. x, 280 p.

BIRD AND BOUGH. Boston and New York: Houghton Mifflin, 1906. 70 p.

CAMPING WITH PRESIDENT ROOSEVELT. Boston and New York: Houghton Mifflin, 1906. 46 p. Frontispiece. Plates.

> An enlarged edition, entitled CAMPING AND TRAMPING WITH ROOSEVELT, was published by Houghton Mifflin in 1907.

LEAF AND TENDRIL. Boston and New York: Houghton Mifflin, 1908. 289 p.

TIME AND CHANGE. Boston and New York: Houghton Mifflin, 1912. 279 p.

THE SUMMIT OF THE YEARS. Boston and New York: Houghton Mifflin, 1913. 298 p.

THE BREATH OF LIFE. Boston and New York: Houghton Mifflin, 1915. 295 p.

UNDER THE APPLE TREES. Boston and New York: Houghton Mifflin, 1916. 316 p.

FIELD AND STUDY. Boston and New York: Houghton Mifflin, 1919. 337 p.

ACCEPTING THE UNIVERSE. Boston and New York: Houghton Mifflin, 1920. 328 p.

UNDER THE MAPLES. Compiled and edited by Clara Barrus. Boston and New York: Houghton Mifflin, 1921. 223 p.

THE LAST HARVEST. Compiled and edited by Clara Barrus. Boston and New York: Houghton Mifflin, 1922. 295 p.

MY BOYHOOD, WITH A CONCLUSION BY HIS SON, JULIAN BUR-ROUGHS. Garden City, N.Y., and Toronto: Doubleday, Page, 1922. 247 p. Illustrated.

> Consists of two sections: "My Boyhood," by John Bur-
> roughs (pp. 1-132), and "My Father," by Julian Burroughs
> (pp. 135-247). Burroughs's reminiscences of his boyhood
> on his family farm in Roxbury, New York, are interesting
> and revealing, particularly for their objective self-criti-
> cism. Julian Burroughs's essay on his father is also valu-
> able. He was unafraid to describe his father's weaknesses
> as well as his strengths, and he frankly describes the dif-
> ficulties that existed between his parents. A number of
> personal letters are included.

JOHN BURROUGHS AND LUDELLA PECK. New York: Hardold Vinal, 1925. 81 p.

> Ludella Peck, a professor of elocution at Smith College,
> became a good friend of Burroughs. Their correspondence
> is contained in this little volume. Some of the letters are

quoted in Clara Barrus's LIFE AND LETTERS OF JOHN BUR-
ROUGHS (below).

THE HEART OF BURROUGHS'S JOURNALS. Edited by Clara
Barrus. Boston and New York: Houghton Mifflin, 1928. xvii,
361 p. Frontispiece.

> Based on the early notebooks covering the period 1854-75
> and the journals written from 1876 to within a few weeks
> of his death in 1921. The complete journals, which oc-
> cupy about 2000 pages of typewritten transcription, have
> never been published. The selection made by Dr. Barrus
> is therefore a unique and valuable source for Burroughs's
> thoughts and ideas.

JOHN BURROUGHS' AMERICA. SELECTIONS FROM THE WRIT-
INGS OF THE HUDSON RIVER NATURALIST. Edited, with an
introduction, by Farida A. Wiley. Foreword by Julian Burroughs.
New York: Devin-Adair, 1951. 293 p. Illustrated. Paperbound
ed. New York: Anchor Books, 1961.

BIOGRAPHIES AND CRITICAL WORKS

Barrus, Clara. OUR FRIEND JOHN BURROUGHS. INCLUDING
AUTOBIOGRAPHICAL SKETCHES BY MR. BURROUGHS. Boston
and New York: Houghton Mifflin, 1914. vii, 287 p. Illustrated.

> Clara Barrus, a practicing medical doctor when she met
> Burroughs in 1901, was to become his companion, physi-
> cian, and adoring biographer. This book is not a biog-
> raphy, but an appreciation designed to acquaint Bur-
> roughs's large readership with the commonplace, personal
> details of his life. The "autobiographical sketches" com-
> prise a series of letters written to the author between
> 1903 and 1912. Although the book is poorly organized
> and is filled with trivia, it is nevertheless interesting
> and, in parts, valuable as a first-hand account.

_____. JOHN BURROUGHS, BOY AND MAN. Garden City,
N.Y., and Toronto: Doubleday, Page, 1921. ix, 385 p. Illustrated.

> Originally conceived as a boy's life of John Burroughs,
> but later "arranged" to be of interest to adults, the
> book suffers from lack of focus. Although it was pop-
> ular and received generally favorable reviews, the book
> is, as one perceptive critic termed it, "cheerfully con-
> descending and commonplace."

_____. THE LIFE AND LETTERS OF JOHN BURROUGHS. 2 vols.
Boston and New York: Houghton Mifflin, 1925. Illustrated.

Barrus was John Burroughs's literary executor and so had access to all his papers. She used these along with her own personal knowledge of the man to write his "official biography." The author was not, however, very critical in her choice of the many excerpts from his diaries, journals, and correspondence; too much trivial information was included. Although Barrus's volumes remain a valuable source, they point up the need for a new rendering of John Burroughs's life.

De Loach, Robert J.H. RAMBLES WITH JOHN BURROUGHS. Boston: Richard G. Badger at The Gorham Press, 1912. 141 p. Illustrated.

De Loach, who lived in Georgia, appears to have been greatly affected by Burroughs and his writings. He visited with Burroughs several times, both in New York and in De Loach's home. Apart from three chapters on Burroughs and Walt Whitman as poets and writers, the bulk of the book consists of De Loach's descriptions of his visits and reports of Burroughs's conversations which are attributed verbatim.

Foerster, Norman. "Burroughs." In his NATURE IN AMERICAN LITERATURE; STUDIES IN THE MODERN VIEW OF NATURE, pp. 264-305. New York: Macmillan, 1923.

Since Burroughs achieved fame as a man of letters, from the 1880s to the present a large body of criticism has been published; yet no single study of Burroughs as a writer has achieved a more balanced and judicious analysis than Foerster's.

Haring, H.A., ed. THE SLABSIDES BOOK OF JOHN BURROUGHS. Edited for the John Burroughs Memorial Association. Boston and New York: Houghton Mifflin, 1931. [xxi], [168] p. Illustrated.

Composed of reminiscences of John Burroughs, and his "Slabsides" retreat. Contains: "Finding the Slabsides Swamp," by Julian Burroughs; "John Burroughs's Own Story of Slabsides," edited by H.A. Haring; "Burroughs the Man," by Hamlin Garland; "With John Burroughs at Slabsides," by Clifton Johnson; "A Winter Day at Slabsides," by Clara Barrus; "Bird-Nesting with Burroughs," by Frank M. Chapman; "Visits to John Burroughs at Slabsides," by Clyde Fisher; "A Little Journey," by Elbert Hubbard; "A Boy's Visit to Slabsides," by Theodore Roosevelt; and "John Burroughs and Some Bird-Lovers From Vassar," by Caroline E. Furness.

Hicks, Philip Marshall. "John Burroughs." In his THE DEVELOP-
MENT OF THE NATURAL HISTORY ESSAY IN AMERICAN LITERA-
TURE, pp. 124-58. Philadelphia: University of Pennsylvania, 1924.

Hicks, seeking to assess Burroughs's role in the development of the natural history essay, saw his importance as
fourfold: Burrough's work was the culmination of previous
influences acting upon the field; he was an arbiter of
definite standards for the practice of nature writing; he
was a major contributor to the field; and he was "the
great popularizer of nature study." Hicks's analysis of
Burroughs's style, nature philosophy, standards, and the
influences on his writing is a valuable contribution.

Johnson, Clifton. JOHN BURROUGHS TALKS, HIS REMINIS-
CENCES AND COMMENTS AS REPORTED BY CLIFTON JOHN-
SON. Boston and New York: Houghton Mifflin, 1922. xvi,
358 p. Illustrated.

Johnson visited Burroughs for the first time in June 1894.
For the next twenty-four years he met irregularly with
roughs at Riverby, Slabsides, Woodchuck Lodge, and in
New York City. During these visits, Johnson kept notes
of Burroughs's comments and reminiscences. The conversations have been edited and rearranged to fit the chapters.
The subject matter ranges widely over trivial details of the
author's life and activities. It does, however, include
much interesting information about Burroughs's wife, family, and friends, as well as some significant material relating the author's views on nature, literature, and politics.

Kelley, Elizabeth Burroughs. JOHN BURROUGHS: NATURALIST;
THE STORY OF HIS WORK AND FAMILY BY HIS GRANDDAUGH-
TER. An Exposition-Banner Book. New York: Exposition Press,
1959. 263 p. Bibliography, pp. 261-63.

Kelley has written what she termed a family history rather
than a biography of her grandfather. Although she has
used private family letters and unpublished journal entries,
and therefore revealed some unknown details of his family
life, the book is not a major contribution to our knowledge of the writer.

Kennedy, William Sloane. THE REAL JOHN BURROUGHS, PER-
SONAL RECOLLECTION AND FRIENDLY ESTIMATE. New York
and London: Funk & Wagnalls, 1924. xvi, 250 p. Illustrated.

Kennedy knew both Burroughs and Whitman, the latter
intimately, and he was on friendly terms with many of
the New England literati contemporary with Burroughs.
He includes in this work a number of letters written to
him by Burroughs. Because of these facts, Kennedy's
book must be considered a primary source for a study of

Burroughs. The author was not averse to rather sharp criticism, both personal and literary, of the naturalist. Kennedy claims that Julian Burroughs was an adopted son--a statement allegedly based upon Burroughs's own admission. Mrs. Elizabeth Kelley expressly denies this in her biography of her grandfather (above).

Osbourne, Clifford H. THE RELIGION OF JOHN BURROUGHS. Boston and New York: Houghton Mifflin, 1930. x, 105 p.

"A study of the evolution of John Burroughs's stand on religion, showing the changes in his attitude from youth and early manhood to later years." Contains copious quotations from Burroughs's writings.

Sharp, Dallas Lore. THE SEER OF SLABSIDES. Boston and New York: Houghton Mifflin, 1921. 71 p. Frontispiece.

A friendly appreciation of Burroughs, the man and his work. Sharp was a devoted literary follower and a good friend of Burroughs.

Tracy, Henry Chester. "John Burroughs." In his AMERICAN NATURISTS, pp. 86-99. New York: Dutton, 1930.

A brief biographical sketch and assessment of his writing. Tracy asserts that Burroughs will always be remembered, not for his defense of real natural history nor his philosophy of nature, but for his "power to see freshly and report well."

Welker, Robert Henry. "'John O'Birds': John Burroughs." In his BIRDS AND MEN: AMERICAN BIRDS IN SCIENCE, ART, LITERATURE AND CONSERVATION, 1800-1900, pp. 125-35. Cambridge, Mass.: Harvard University Press, 1955.

A brief but valuable appraisal of Burroughs as a literary artist and naturalist. Welker asserts that Burroughs was a "whole-hearted evolutionist."

Cooper, Susan Fenimore. RURAL HOURS. Introduction by David Jones. Syracuse, N.Y.: Syracuse University Press, 1968. xxxviii, 337 p. Illustrated.

Cooper's work was first published in 1850. It appeared in England as JOURNAL OF A NATURALIST IN THE UNITED STATES. The present work is the "new and revised edition" published by Houghton Mifflin in 1887, when Cooper was seventy-four. Her reflections upon nature and country life, derived from experiences in and around Cooperstown, New York, in the late 1840s, are arranged as a seasonal journal. David Jones's introduction is a valuable contribution.

Douglas, William O. OF MEN AND MOUNTAINS. New York: Harper, 1950.

xiv, 338 p. Frontispiece. Maps on endpapers.

Douglas tells the story of his youthful discovery of nature and of the many adventures he had in the mountains of the Pacific Northwest.

_____. MY WILDERNESS: THE PACIFIC WEST. Garden City, N.Y.: Doubleday, 1960. 206 p. Illustrated. Maps on endpapers.

See next item.

_____. MY WILDERNESS: EAST TO KATAHDIN. Garden City, N.Y.: Doubleday, 1961. 290 p. Illustrated. Maps on endpapers.

In these two books, Justice Douglas describes his visits to twenty-two primitive areas in seventeen states and Canada, from the Brooks Range in northern Alaska to Mt. Katahdin in Maine. Each locale holds a particular attraction for the author and he writes of them with love, understanding, and an appreciation of their essential fragility. Both books are beautifully illustrated by Francis Lee Jaques.

_____. FAREWELL TO TEXAS: A VANISHING WILDERNESS. New York: McGraw-Hill, 1967. 242 p. Illustrated. Maps.

Charming descriptions of the Big Thicket, the Davis Mountains, and other ranges, along with folklore and a plea for conservation.

Dubkin, Leonard (b. 1904)

A large metropolitan area would seem an unlikely locale for a nature writer, but Leonard Dubkin has produced three notable books about nature in the city of Chicago. City parks, empty lots, lake and river fronts, lawns, yards, and roadside plantings are some of the places in which he has discovered the microcosmic workings of nature. In the three books, which span twenty-five years of observation, a gradual diminishment of the "natural" environment of Chicago can be seen. His last book, MY SECRET PLACES, is a wistful account of the loss--through urban growth, pollution, and industrial blight--of the places he held dear. In his introduction, Dubkin writes sadly of this loss and says that this book is probably his last about nature in a big city.

ENCHANTED STREETS: THE UNLIKELY ADVENTURES OF AN URBAN NATURE LOVER. Boston: Little, Brown, 1947. 210 p. Illustrated.

THE NATURAL HISTORY OF A YARD. Chicago: Henry Regnery, 1955. 208 p. Illustrated.

MY SECRET PLACES; ONE MAN'S LOVE AFFAIR WITH NATURE IN THE CITY. New York: McKay, 1972. xvii, 172 p.

Eaton, Walter Prichard (1878-1957)

Eaton was a curious phenomenon in American letters. He was a drama critic, professor of drama at Yale (1933–47) and a conservationist-minded author of country life and nature essays, gardening books, and juvenile stories for the Boy Scouts. Eaton was a friend of Benton MacKaye and a proponent of the Appalachian Trail, about which he wrote in SKYLINE CAMPS (1922). His two best books on nature are listed below.

GREEN TRAIL AND UPLAND PASTURES. Garden City, N.Y.: Doubleday, Page, 1917. xii, 303 p. Color illustrations.

IN BERKSHIRE FIELDS. New York and London: Harper, 1920. xiii, 312 p. Illustrated.

Flagg, Wilson (1805-84)

For a long period, Flagg wrote for the ATLANTIC MONTHLY and horticultural periodicals. He wrote several books on various subjects before he turned, in 1857, to nature writing, the genre that was to occupy him until his death. Flagg was a contemporary of Thoreau, and a predecessor of Burroughs. Although Thoreau applauded Flagg's enthusiasm for nature, he objected to the tameness of his writing and felt he needed "stirring up with a pole." Despite Thoreau's objection, Flagg was a sincere and devoted student of nature, and his better descriptive passages, especially those about trees and birds in THE WOODS AND BY-WAYS OF NEW ENGLAND, are well done. Although Flagg is not much read today, he made a definite contribution in his own time. A later critic described him as "the most voluminous and systematic of the writers who sought to popularize the facts of natural history down to the time of Burroughs" (see Hicks, Philip Marshall, above). For further information on Flagg, see Barton's essay (below) and the sketch by John D. Wade in THE DICTIONARY OF AMERICAN BIOGRAPHY (volume 6, pp. 450–51).

STUDIES IN THE FIELD AND FOREST. Boston: Little, Brown, 1857. vi, 330 p.

THE WOODS AND BY-WAYS OF NEW ENGLAND. Boston: James R. Osgood, 1872. xviii, 442 p. Illustrated, with plates.

This is a difficult work to classify. Flagg's intense love of New England pastoral scenery enlivens and informs this rather rambling description of its forest reserves.

Reissued through 1890. Later editions are entitled A
YEAR AMONG THE TREES; OR, THE WOODS AND BY-
WAYS OF NEW ENGLAND.

THE BIRDS AND SEASONS OF NEW ENGLAND. Boston: James
R. Osgood, 1875. vi, 457 p. Frontispiece.

Reissued in 1889 and 1890. Parts of this work were
reprinted in the following book.

A YEAR WITH THE BIRDS; OR, THE BIRDS AND THE SEASONS
OF NEW ENGLAND. Boston: Estes and Lauriat, 1881. iv,
324 p.

HALCYON DAYS. Boston: Estes and Lauriat, 1881. 316 p.

A selection from WOODS AND BY-WAYS and THE BIRDS
AND SEASONS.

Barton, William G. "Thoreau, Flagg, and Burroughs." HISTORI-
CAL COLLECTIONS OF THE ESSEX INSTITUTE 22 (1885): 53-80.

A comparative study. One of the very few critical
pieces on Flagg's nature writing.

Fuller, Raymond Tifft. NOW THAT WE HAVE TO WALK; EXPLORING THE
OUT-OF-DOORS. New York: Dutton, 1943. 256 p. Bibliography, pp.
253-56. Reprint ed., 1972.

The title alludes to gasoline rationing during World War II. The
author, an accomplished naturalist and author, presents in the
preface his rationale for yet another nature book: "to propagan-
dize the faith" of those like himself who have found a kind of
salvation in the observance of and reverance for nature. Fuller
tells us that nature writing is a way of maintaining "the morale
of all those who resist and oppose America's over-powering cult
of materialism and its high esteem of wealth...."

Gibson, William Hamilton (1850-96)

Gibson began his career as an illustrator, after study at Brooklyn
Polytechnic Institute, by contributing botanical and ornithological
sketches to natural history periodicals and illustrations to AMERI-
CAN AGRICULTURALIST, ART JOURNAL, and HEARTH AND HOME.
His work also appeared in William Cullen Bryant's PICTURESQUE
AMERICA (see Chapter 2, Section D2: The Appalachian Region,
General). Gibson's first essay was published in HARPER'S MONTH-
LY MAGAZINE and thereafter he contributed many nature articles
to HARPER'S, SCRIBNER'S, AND THE CENTURY, all illustrated with

his own drawings. Gibson achieved considerable success as an artist-illustrator and as an author. His books contain illustrated nature essays done originally for HARPER'S MONTHLY; all are handsome, gilt-edged volumes with attractive engraved illustrations. Gibson's writing reflects his own interest in the day-to-day observation of insects, flowers, and birds. His authorial stance was that of a nature study enthusiast, and his work suffers from somewhat sentimental, affected prose. Biographical information may be found in the sketches by Palmer and Adams and in the biography by Adams (all below).

PASTORAL DAYS, OR, MEMORIES OF A NEW ENGLAND YEAR. New York: Harper, 1881. 153 p. Illustrated.

HIGHWAYS AND BYWAYS, OR SAUNTERINGS IN NEW ENGLAND. New York: Harper, 1882. 157 p. Illustrated.

HAPPY HUNTING GROUNDS: A TRIBUTE TO THE WOODS AND FIELDS. New York: Harper, 1887. 202 p. Illustrated.

STROLLS BY STARLIGHT AND SUNSHINE. New York: Harper, 1891. 194 p. Illustrated.

SHARP EYES, A RAMBLER'S CALENDAR OF FIFTY-TWO WEEKS AMONG INSECTS, BIRDS AND FLOWERS. New York: Harper, 1891. xx, 322 p. Illustrated.

EYE SPY; AFIELD WITH NATURE AMONG FLOWERS AND ANIMATE THINGS. New York: Harper, 1897. xvi, 264 p. Illustrated.

MY STUDIO NEIGHBORS. New York and London: Harper, 1898. x, 245 p. Illustrated.

Adams, John Coleman. "William Hamilton Gibson." NEW ENGLAND MAGAZINE, n.s. 15, no. 6 (February 1897): 643-55.

_____. WILLIAM HAMILTON GIBSON, ARTIST-NATURALIST-AUTHOR. New York and London: Putnam, 1901. x, 275 p. Illustrated.

Mitchell, Catherine Palmer. "William Hamilton Gibson." In THE DICTIONARY OF AMERICAN BIOGRAPHY, vol. 7, pp. 259-60.

Halle, Louis J., Jr. BIRDS AGAINST MEN. New York: Viking, 1938.

228 p. Illustrated.

> Essays on bird life. The title does not reveal that the theme of the book is "bird personalities."

_____. SPRING IN WASHINGTON. Decennial Edition. Foreword by Roger Tory Peterson. New York: Harper, 1957. 234 p. Illustrated.

> First published in 1947. Observations on the coming of spring, bird life, and other natural phenomena, made by the author during bicycle excursions in and around the capital city. Halle, a distinguished public official and, later, professor of government at several universities, was at the time of this book a division chief in the U.S. Department of State.

Hay, John. NATURE'S YEAR: THE SEASONS OF CAPE COD. Garden City, N.Y.: Doubleday, 1961. 199 p. Illustrated.

> A record of the events observed by Hay in and around his Cape Cod home. The book received generally good reviews. See also next item.

_____. THE GREAT BEACH. Garden City, N.Y.: Doubleday, 1964. 131 p. Illustrated.

> THE GREAT BEACH may be considered a companion to Hay's NATURE'S YEAR. Both present his perceptions of the natural world of Cape Cod. It is inevitable that such a book be compared with Henry Beston's THE OUTERMOST HOUSE (above), and Hay's book is no exception. One critic felt this book was "thin" by comparison, while another argued that it was a far better book than Beston's. In any event, THE GREAT BEACH was awarded the John Burroughs Medal for distinguished nature writing in 1964.

_____. IN DEFENSE OF NATURE. Boston and Toronto: Little, Brown, 1969. x, 210 p.

> The author's ramblings along the Atlantic shore provide the background of this plea for man to treat his natural world and its nonhuman inhabitants with respect. Well written and stimulating.

Hay, John, and Farb, Peter. THE ATLANTIC SHORE; HUMAN AND NATURAL HISTORY FROM LONG ISLAND TO LABRADOR. New York and London: Harper, 1966. 246 p. Illustrated. Appendix, pp. 221-28. Bibliography, pp. 229-32.

> A popular ecological study of the Atlantic shoreline, including flora and fauna, with reference to human history and a plea for conservation of America's seascapes.

Heald, Weldon F. SKY ISLAND. Princeton, N.J.: D. Van Nostrand, 1967. ix, 166 p. Illustrated. Photos. Maps on endpapers.

> The fascinating story of a ranch in the Chiracahua Mountains of southern Arizona--an area of contrasts between high desert and alpine-like mountain tops.

Higginson, Thomas Wentworth. OUTDOOR PAPERS. Boston: Ticknor and Fields, 1863. 370 p.

> Higginson (1823-1911), a well-known reformer, soldier, and New England man-of-letters, was a casual writer on nature. His nature essays, all of which originally appeared in the ATLANTIC MONTHLY, were collected in OUTDOOR PAPERS. Included are "April Days," "My Outdoor Study," "Water-Lilies," "The Life of Birds," "The Procession of the Flowers," and "Snow." Higginson's essays are characterized by a pleasant, direct, readable style in the tradition of the familiar essay and are enhanced by literary allusions. OUTDOOR PAPERS appeared in several different editions and was included in Higginson's collected works.

Hough, Henry Beetle. SINGING IN THE MORNING AND OTHER ESSAYS ABOUT MARTHA'S VINEYARD. New York: Simon and Schuster, 1951. xii, 242 p. Illustrated.

> The author has been editor of the VINEYARD GAZETTE for many years. The essays that make up this book are short nature pieces which originally appeared in the columns of his paper.

Jaques, Florence Page (b. 1890)

> The author and her artist-illustrator husband, Francis Lee Jaques, collaborated on the six books listed below. All of their books are set in the north woods--the border country of northern Minnesota and Canada, Alaska, and the Yukon. Mrs. Jaques is a keen observer of the natural world of the north and her prose is highly evocative of the sharp contrasts of that region. Francis Lee Jaques, one of America's foremost nature artists and ornithologists, illustrated his wife's books with his characteristic black-and-white drawings. Three of their books--CANOE COUNTRY, THE GEESE FLY HIGH, and SNOWSHOE COUNTRY--are still in print. The last work was awarded the 1946 John Burroughs Medal for distinguished nature writing.

> CANOE COUNTRY. Illustrated by Francis Lee Jaques. Minneapolis: University of Minnesota Press, 1938. 78 p.

> THE GEESE FLY HIGH. Illustrated by Francis Lee Jaques. Minneapolis: University of Minnesota Press, 1939. 102 p.

BIRDS ACROSS THE SKY. Illustrated by Francis Lee Jaques. New York and London: Harper, 1942. xii, 240 p.

SNOWSHOE COUNTRY. Illustrated by Francis Lee Jaques. Minneapolis: University of Minnesota Press, [1944]. 110 p.

CANADIAN SPRING. Illustrated by Francis Lee Jaques. New York: Harper, 1947. xii, 216 p. Maps on endpapers.

AS FAR AS THE YUKON. Illustrated by Francis Lee Jaques. New York: Harper, 1951. x, 243 p.

Johnson, Josephine W. THE INLAND ISLAND. New York: Simon and Schuster, 1969. 159 p. Illustrated.

A chronicle of a year's observation of and reflection on an "abandoned" farm in Ohio. The author, a novelist, poet, and 1934 Pulitzer Prize winner, allowed her thirty-seven-acre farm to revert to wilderness where native animals flourish and she derives a measure of solace. Mrs. Johnson's intense bitterness toward the Vietnam War and modern technological society inform the book and make it unique among nature books.

Kieran, John. FOOTNOTES ON NATURE. Garden City, N.Y.: Doubleday, 1947. 279 p. Illustrated.

"This is a book about a few men and many walks in the woods and fields of New York and New England. It is, to a large extent, an account of the birds, trees, flowers and other forms of life that we encountered outdoors in that territory" (Foreword). This is a factual and informal book, charmingly written. The author includes memories of his boyhood in Dutchess County, New York.

_____. A NATURAL HISTORY OF NEW YORK CITY: A PERSONAL REPORT AFTER FIFTY YEARS OF STUDY AND ENJOYMENT OF WILDLIFE WITHIN THE BOUNDARIES OF GREATER NEW YORK. Boston: Houghton Mifflin, 1959. 428 p. Illustrated. Maps on endpapers.

A truly remarkable and fascinating book. John Kieran has made the region of New York City and its environs his special province of study and enjoyment for many years and his book is a valuable achievement in the area of popular natural history. It contains chapters on the geography, geology, history, botany, and zoology of New York City. Some emphasis is placed on the city's bird life.

King, Clarence. MOUNTAINEERING IN THE SIERRA NEVADA. Edited, with a preface, by Francis P. Farquhar. New York: Norton, 1935. 320 p. Illustrated. Bibliographic footnotes, pp. 317-20.

King was the first director of the U.S. Geological Survey. This book is a romanticized record of his ramblings and "naturalizing" through the Sierra Nevada during 1864-71. The book grew out of seven articles published in the ATLANTIC MONTHLY in 1871. The success of these essays encouraged the publication of the book, which appeared in 1872 under the imprint of James R. Osgood. MOUNTAINEERING has appeared in other editions since 1872, but the Norton edition contains Farquhar's valuable and informative preface which provides background information about King's travels and his later career. The bibliographical footnotes list King's published writings and a number of publications "collateral" to MOUNTAINEERING. The book has attained the status of a minor classic in nature writing.

Kirkham, Stanton Davis. IN THE OPEN; INTIMATE STUDIES AND APPRECIA-TIONS OF NATURE. San Francisco and New York: Paul Elder, [1908]. vii, 223 p. Illustrated.

Unusually well-written and sensitive study of nature. Kirkham's nature books received very good reviews upon publication, but the author is virtually unnoticed today. He also wrote a number of books concerned with philosophy and self-help.

_____. EAST AND WEST; COMPARATIVE STUDIES OF NATURE IN EASTERN AND WESTERN STATES. New York and London: Putnam, 1911. x, 280 p. Plates.

The setting of these essays ranges from the Adirondacks, Cape Ann seashore, and the Catskills through Arizona to Southern California and the Sierra Nevada.

_____. NORTH AND SOUTH; NOTES ON THE NATURAL HISTORY OF A SUMMER CAMP AND A WINTER HOME. New York and London: Putnam, 1913. vii, 286 p. Plates.

The summer camp was located on Lake Canandaigua, New York; the winter home was in South Carolina.

Krutch, Joseph Wood (1893-1970)

In 1962 the author published his autobiography with the title MORE LIVES THAN ONE, a very apt title for the life story of a man who had been an author, journalist, professor of English, drama critic, professor of dramatic literature, social philosopher, and naturist. Krutch occupies a unique niche in American letters, having written such diverse books as biographies (SAMUEL JOHN-SON, EDGAR ALLEN POE, and HENRY DAVID THOREAU), criti-cal works on the theatre, essays on culture and literature, philosophical works (THE MODERN TEMPER, THE MEASURE OF MAN, and HUMAN NATURE AND THE HUMAN CONDITION), and contemplative and interpretive books on American nature. These last are relevant here.

Beginning with his 1948 book on Thoreau, an author who profoundly influenced him, Krutch produced a number of essays on nature, country life, ecology, conservation, and gardening. In addition, he wrote many articles about nature for various magazines and, from 1955, he contributed to AMERICAN SCHOLAR a quarterly essay, "If You Don't Mind My Saying So," which was frequently about natural history or allied fields. Many of these essays were later collected and included in works containing criticism, drama, and other subjects.

The books listed below are his most important nature pieces. Krutch's contacts with physical nature were never communicated in purely descriptive terms. On the contrary, his narratives were often filled with metabiological speculation on the nature of man and his relationship to the cosmos, and with strongly argued pleas for the development of an ecological conscience in man. In 1952, Krutch moved to Tucson, Arizona, where he continued to write and to involve himself in conservation work. The author received many awards and honors, including the John Burroughs Medal in 1954, and, in the same year, the National Book Award for non-fiction. For biographical information, see his autobiography MORE LIVES THAN ONE (below), the bio-bibliographical sketch in CONTEMPORARY AUTHORS (volumes 1-4, revised edition, pp. 555-56), the articles by Atkinson and Dubos (below), and the article in THE NATION (below).

THE TWELVE SEASONS: A PERPETUAL CALENDAR FOR THE COUNTRY. New York: William Sloane, 1949. 188 p. Illustrated.

THE DESERT YEAR. New York: William Sloane, 1952. 270 p. Illustrated.

THE BEST OF TWO WORLDS. New York: William Sloane, 1953. 171 p. Illustrated.

THE VOICE OF THE DESERT. New York: William Sloane, 1955. 223 p. Illustrated.

THE GREAT CHAIN OF LIFE. Boston: Houghton Mifflin, 1956. 227 p. Illustrated.

GRAND CANYON, TODAY AND ALL ITS YESTERDAYS. New

York: William Sloane, 1958. 276 p. Illustrated.

Paper edition published as GRAND CANYON (Anchor Books, 1962).

THE FORGOTTEN PENINSULA: A NATURALIST IN BAJA CALIFORNIA. New York: William Sloane, 1961. 277 p. Illustrated.

MORE LIVES THAN ONE. New York: William Sloane, 1962. 378 p.

IF YOU DON'T MIND MY SAYING SO...ESSAYS ON MAN AND NATURE. Foreword by John K. Hutchens. New York: William Sloane, 1964. xiv, 402 p.

...AND EVEN IF YOU DO...ESSAYS ON MAN, MANNERS, AND MACHINES. New York: Morrow, 1967. ix, 341 p.

BAJA CALIFORNIA AND THE GEOGRAPHY OF HOPE. Photographs by Eliot Porter. Edited by Kenneth Brower. Foreword by David Brower. Exhibit Format Series, vol. 17. San Francisco: Sierra Club, [1967]. 174 p. Color illustrations. Folding map. 35 cm.

THE BEST NATURE WRITING OF JOSEPH WOOD KRUTCH. New York: Morrow, 1969. 384 p. Illustrated.

Available in a paper edition.

Atkinson, Brooks. "The Many Worlds of Joseph Wood Krutch." SATURDAY REVIEW 53 (July 25, 1970): 17.

Dubos, Rene. "The Despairing Optimist." AMERICAN SCHOLAR 40 (Winter 1970): 16-20.

"Joseph Wood Krutch." THE NATION 210 (June 8, 1970): 677.

Mills, Enos A. (1870-1922)

Mills won lasting fame as an author, lecturer, conservationist, and wilderness guide in the Colorado Rockies. As a youth, he roamed the area around Long's Peak, Colorado, and eventually homesteaded a quarter-section of land at the foot of that mountain. This homestead became the site of a resort which operated until his death. John Muir, whom he met on a trip to California, urged Mills to become a careful and sympathetic observer and to contribute to the literature of conservation and the popularization of nature study. Combining his careers as resort owner, lecturer, and author,

Mills became well known in Colorado and later throughout the nation. In 1907, Theodore Roosevelt appointed him federal lecturer on forestry. Mills was an outspoken advocate for a national park in the Rockies, and it was largely due to his efforts that the Rocky Mountain National Park was created. Much of his writing was first published in the popular eastern magazines. For biographical information, see the sketch by Charles O. Paullin in THE DICTIONARY OF AMERICAN BIOGRAPHY (volume 21, pp. 554–55) and the biography by Hawthorne and Mills below.

WILD LIFE ON THE ROCKIES. Boston and New York: Houghton Mifflin, 1909. xi, 263 p. Plates.

THE SPELL OF THE ROCKIES. Boston and New York: Houghton Mifflin, 1911. xi, 355 p. Plates.

IN BEAVER WORLD. Boston and New York: Houghton Mifflin, 1913. xiii, 277 p. Illustrated. Bibliography, p. 223.

THE ROCKY MOUNTAIN WONDERLAND. Boston and New York: Houghton Mifflin, 1915. xiii, 362 p. Plates. Map.

YOUR NATIONAL PARKS. With Detailed Information for Tourists by Laurence F. Schmeckebier. Boston and New York: Houghton Mifflin, 1917. xxi, 531 p. Illustrated, plates. Maps. Bibliography, pp. [417-21].

THE GRIZZLY: OUR GREATEST WILD ANIMAL. Boston and New York: Houghton Mifflin, 1919. ix, 288 p. Plates.

THE ADVENTURES OF A NATURE GUIDE. Garden City, N.Y.: Doubleday, Page, 1920. xiv, 271 p. Plates.

WAITING IN THE WILDERNESS. Garden City, N.Y., and Toronto: Doubleday, Page, 1921. xiii, 241 p. Plates.

WATCHED BY WILD ANIMALS. Illustrated from photographs and from drawings by Will James. Garden City, N.Y., and Toronto: Doubleday, Page, 1922. viii, 243 p. Plates. Diagram.

WILD ANIMAL HOMESTEADS. Illustrated from photographs and from drawings by Will James. Garden City, N.Y.: Doubleday, Page, 1923. xi, 259 p. Plates. Diagrams.

THE ROCKY MOUNTAIN NATIONAL PARK. Foreword by Robert W. Johnson. Garden City, N.Y.: Doubleday, Page, 1924.

xxvi, 239 p. Illustrated. Reprint ed., 1932.

> A memorial edition, enlarged from the author's THE STORY OF ESTES PARK. Includes two essays about Mills and his work: "A Champion of Wild Life," by Philip Ashton Rollins, and "Litigation Concerning the Rocky Mountain National Park," by Paul W. Lee.

Hawthorne, Hildegarde, and Mills, Esther B. ENOS MILLS OF THE ROCKIES. Boston and New York: Houghton Mifflin, 1935. 260 p. Plates. Portrait.

> This work was coauthored by Mills's widow. It is a popular biography and is not documented. Mills deserves better treatment.

Muir, John (1838-1914)

John Muir, along with Henry David Thoreau, George Perkins Marsh, and Aldo Leopold, has become one of the patron saints of the modern American ecology movement. His work as an author, naturalist, mountaineer, conservationist, and leader of the Sierra Club brought him fame during his lifetime and a continuing popularity today.

His writings communicate a poetic-mystical love of nature and a passionate defense of wilderness values. Most of his work first appeared in the popular press and effectively publicized the natural beauty of the western mountains--especially his beloved Sierra Nevada, "the Range of Light."

Throughout his life, Muir was closely associated with the national parks movement, and especially with the struggle to preserve Yosemite as a national park.

Muir's view of nature was informed by a religious impulse that caused him to see the world as a monumental design of the Creator. He had nothing but scorn for people who believed in a man-centered universe, but acknowledged that the universe would not be complete without man. Herbert Smith, in his study of Muir (below), has stressed the importance of this religio-ecological ethic to Muir's philosophical position, and at least one theologian has dwelt at some length on this same point (see Santmire, H. Paul, in Chapter 1, Section C: Nature and the Religious Impulse).

BIBLIOGRAPHIES

Blanck, Jacob, comp. "John Muir, 1838-1914." In his BIBLIOG-

RAPHY OF AMERICAN LITERATURE, vol. 6, pp. 387-403. New Haven: Yale University Press, 1973.

> A complete descriptive bibliography of Muir's books, writings published as parts of books, pamphlets, collections, collected writings, and a short list of works about Muir.

Bradley, Cornelius Beach. "A Reference List to John Muir's Newspaper Articles." SIERRA CLUB BULLETIN 10, no. 1 (January 1916): 55-59.

Doran, Jennie Elliott. "A Bibliography of John Muir." SIERRA CLUB BULLETIN 10, no. 1 (January 1916): 41-54.

> A very useful annotated bibliography. It includes all except his posthumously published books, with references to original publication of individual essays, a list of uncollected articles, chapters by Muir in books and pamphlets by others, and a list of articles and books about Muir.

COLLECTED WORKS

THE WRITINGS OF JOHN MUIR. Sierra Edition. 10 vols. Edited by William F. Bade. Boston and New York: Houghton Mifflin, 1915-24.

> There are no complete works. The Sierra Edition contains the following: Volume 1: THE STORY OF MY BOYHOOD AND YOUTH and A THOUSAND-MILE WALK TO THE GULF; Volume 2: MY FIRST SUMMER IN THE SIERRA NEVADA; Volume 3: TRAVELS IN ALASKA; Volumes 4-5: THE MOUNTAINS OF CALIFORNIA; Volume 6: OUR NATIONAL PARKS; Volume 7: THE CRUISE OF THE CORWIN; Volume 8: STEEP TRAILS; Volumes 9-10: THE LIFE AND LETTERS OF JOHN MUIR, by William F. Bade.

INDIVIDUAL WORKS

PICTURESQUE CALIFORNIA AND THE REGION WEST OF THE ROCKY MOUNTAINS, FROM ALASKA TO MEXICO. 2 vols. Edited by John Muir. San Francisco: J. Dewing, 1887.

> Muir contributed seven chapters to this work. (See the annotation for this item in Chapter 2, Section D 13: 'Yosemite).

THE MOUNTAINS OF CALIFORNIA. New ed., enl. New York: Century Co., 1911. xiv, 389 p. Illustrated, with plates. Paperback ed., 1961.

First edition, 1894.

OUR NATIONAL PARKS. New ed., enl. Boston and New York: Houghton Mifflin, 1909. x, 382 p. Plates. Map.

First edition, 1901. Primarily concerned with Yosemite.

"Notes on the Pacific Coast Glaciers." In HARRIMAN ALASKA EXPEDITION. ALASKA: NARRATIVE, GLACIERS, NATIVES, edited by C. Hart Merriam, pp. 119-35. Harriman Alaska Series, vol. 1. New York: Doubleday, Page, 1902.

STICKEEN. Boston and New York: Houghton Mifflin, 1909. [74] p.

Stickeen was a small mongrel dog that accompanied Muir on his glacial investigations in Alaska. Muir recounts their harrowing adventures while lost on a glacier.

MY FIRST SUMMER IN THE SIERRA NEVADA. Boston and New York: Houghton Mifflin, 1911. vii, 353 p. Illustrated, with plates.

Enlarged from sketches in the ATLANTIC MONTHLY for 1911, the book takes the form of a journal and, in fact, was developed from Muir's journal entries for June 3 to September 22, 1869. Illustrated with drawings by Muir and with photographs.

THE YOSEMITE. New York: Century Co., 1912. x, 284 p. Plates. 3 folding maps. Paperbound ed., 1962.

THE STORY OF MY BOYHOOD AND YOUTH. With Illustrations from Sketches by the Author. Boston and New York: Houghton Mifflin, 1913. 293 p. Illustrated, with plates. Portrait.

LETTERS TO A FRIEND. WRITTEN TO MRS. EZRA S. CARR, 1866-1879. Boston and New York: Houghton Mifflin, 1915. 194 p.

Mrs. Carr, a friend of Muir's from his days at the University of Wisconsin, had great influence on Muir's career. The letters are primarily concerned with his work in the Sierra Nevada and, specifically, in Yosemite. A substantial number of the letters were later included in the LIFE AND LETTERS, by William F. Bade (see Complete Works, above).

TRAVELS IN ALASKA. Boston and New York: Houghton Mifflin, 1915. ix, 326 p. Plates.

> Based upon several trips to Alaska, where Muir tested his theories about glacial action.

A THOUSAND-MILE WALK TO THE GULF. Edited by William Frederic Bade. Boston and New York: Houghton Mifflin, 1916. xxvi, 219 p. Frontispiece. Plates. Map. Facsimiles.

THE CRUISE OF THE CORWIN; JOURNAL OF THE ARCTIC EXPEDITION OF 1881 IN SEARCH OF DE LONG AND THE JEANNETTE. Edited by William F. Bade. Boston and New York: Houghton Mifflin, 1917. xxxi, 271 p. Illustrated.

STEEP TRAILS. Edited by William F. Bade. Boston and New York: Houghton Mifflin, 1918. ix, 391 p. Illustrated, with plates.

> These essays originally appeared in newspapers, magazines, and, in one case, in a letter written by Muir to a friend and published without his knowledge. All were written in the field and thus preserve an immediacy of impression. The locale varies and includes the mountains and deserts of Utah and Nevada, the mountains and forests of Washington and Oregon, the Grand Canyon, and the San Gabriel Mountains of southern California. Also included is a well-known essay on Mt. Shasta. Some of the essays were revised by Muir before his death.

JOHN OF THE MOUNTAINS: THE UNPUBLISHED JOURNALS OF JOHN MUIR. Edited by Linnie Marsh Wolfe. Boston and New York: Houghton Mifflin, 1938. xxii, 459 p. Plates.

> In 1867 Muir began keeping a journal which was later published as A THOUSAND-MILE WALK TO THE GULF. His second journal, begun in 1868 in California, was continued to 1911. It is this second journal that the editor has here assembled. Many of the entries were written in notebooks in the field, often in the evening before a small camp fire, and have an immediacy of impression of nature and other topics. An index is included, making the journal extremely valuable as a source of Muir's ideas.

STUDIES IN THE SIERRA. Edited by William E. Colby. Foreword by John P. Bulwada. San Francisco: Sierra Club, 1960. xxxviii, 103 p. Illustrated, with plates. Notes.

> "Studies in the Sierra" originally appeared as seven articles in the OVERLAND MONTHLY (1874-75) and was later re-

printed in the SIERRA CLUB BULLETIN (1915-21). It
was first published in book form by the Sierra Club in
1949. The present edition is revised to include a collection of contemporary photographs of Yosemite by
Eadward Muybridge (Muggridge). The "Studies" have
to do with glacial action in the High Sierra, and
especially with Yosemite.

SOUTH OF YOSEMITE; SELECTED WRITINGS OF JOHN MUIR.
Edited, with a foreword, by Frederic R. Gunsky. Photographs by
Philip Hyde. Sketches by John Muir. Garden City, N.Y.:
Published for the American Museum of Natural History, [by] The
Natural History Press, 1968. xiii, 269 p. Illustrated. Maps on
lining paper.

Gunsky, former editor of the SIERRA CLUB BULLETIN,
selected from Muir's writings passages dealing with the
Sierra Nevada south of Yosemite, notably the Sequoia
and Kings Canyon region. Many of the selections for
this collection were taken from the original periodical
articles and letters to newspapers which were written
in the 1870s and 1880s but revised for inclusion in
Muir's own books.

BIOGRAPHIES AND CRITICAL WORKS

Baker, Ray Stannard. "John Muir." THE OUTLOOK 74 (June
1903): 365-77.

A perceptive contemporary assessment of Muir's life and
work.

Foerster, Norman. "John Muir." In his NATURE IN AMERICAN
LITERATURE; STUDIES IN THE MODERN VIEW OF NATURE, pp.
238-63. New York: Macmillan, 1923.

The first half of this essay is devoted to a brief sketch
of Muir's life and scientific attainments, particularly as
a student of glaciers, while the second presents Muir's
views of nature and discusses his achievement as a literary artist. A valuable exposition.

Jones, Holway R. JOHN MUIR AND THE SIERRA CLUB: THE
BATTLE FOR YOSEMITE. San Francisco: Sierra Club, 1965.
xvii, 207 p. Illustrated. Photos. Maps. Appendices. Bibliography, pp. 195-200.

Traces the development of Yosemite, the founding of the
Sierra Club, and the fight for the preservation of Hetch
Hetchy valley. A very valuable and detailed account,
based heavily upon manuscripts and archival material.

Leighly, John, "John Muir's Image of the West." ANNALS OF THE ASSOCIATION OF AMERICAN GEOGRAPHERS 48, no. 4 (December 1958): 309-18.

> A carefully drawn exposition of Muir's powers of observation, his ecological point of view, and his love of nature.

Nash, Roderick. "John Muir: Publicizer." In his WILDERNESS AND THE AMERICAN MIND, rev. ed., chap. 8. New Haven: Yale University Press, 1973.

> An insightful study of Muir's "publicizing" of the western wilderness, particularly Yosemite and the Sierra Nevada, and of his efforts to preserve it. See also Chapter 10 in Nash's book for a description of the efforts to save Hetch Hetchy. Nash's footnotes to these chapters provide a valuable additional source for materials about Muir.

Rice, William R. "A Synthesis of Muir Criticism." SIERRA CLUB BULLETIN 28, no. 3 (June 1943): 79-95.

> This is an excellent comprehensive survey of Muir criticism from the 1890s through 1943.

Smith, Herbert F. JOHN MUIR. Twayne's United States Authors Series, vol. 73. New York: Twayne Publishers, 1965. 158 p. Selected Bibliography, pp. 152-53.

> An extremely perceptive and valuable analysis of Muir's writings. Smith asserts that Muir was a conscious artist, and that beneath the descriptions of physical nature and personal narrative, there lay a motive force of moral idealism which permeated his writing and made him a "Dangerous writer."

Tracy, Henry Chester. "John Muir." In his AMERICAN NATUR-ISTS, pp. 100-15. New York: Dutton, 1930.

> In this brief essay, Tracy concentrates on Muir the nature-mystic and rhapsodic lover of wilderness. "His best meanings would never be caught. They were above speech, as all must know who have been alone and glad in the high mountains...." Tracy saw Muir as a "mutant," like Thoreau and W.H. Hudson, and "not quite like other men."

Wolfe, Linnie Marsh. SON OF THE WILDERNESS: THE LIFE OF JOHN MUIR. New York: Knopf, 1945. xiii, 364 p. xvi. Plates. Facsimile. Bibliography and notes, pp. 349-64.

> This is the "official" biography, based largely upon information from the Muir family, his friends and Muir's papers and letters. It is the standard work on Muir. Although superceded, William F. Bade's THE LIFE AND

LETTERS OF JOHN MUIR (Volumes 9-10 of THE WRIT-
INGS; see Complete Works, above) is still useful,
particularly for Muir's letters.

Young, Samuel Hall. ALASKA DAYS WITH JOHN MUIR. New
York: Fleming H. Revell, 1915. 226 p. Illustrated.

> The author was a young Protestant missionary stationed
> at Wrangell. Muir met Young on his first trip to Alaska
> in 1879, and the two became good friends and companions
> on that and several of Muir's later trips. Young's de-
> scriptions of their expeditions to investigate glaciers
> are interesting and well drawn. The book is well writ-
> ten and is useful for the insights it gives into Muir's
> character and his views on God in nature. Young was,
> incidentally, the owner of the dog "Stickeen," made
> famous by Muir's story of the same name.

Olson, Sigurd F. (b. 1899)

> Olson was, for many years, a biology teacher and, later, Dean of
> Ely Junior College in Ely, Minnesota, where he makes his home.
> In his youth, he was a wilderness guide and explored by canoe
> much of the northern wilderness from Quetico-Superior to the
> Canadian Arctic areas. Since 1962, Olson has acted as a con-
> sultant to the U.S. Department of the Interior, and was also a
> consultant to the President's Quetico-Superior Committee and to the
> Izaak Walton League of America. He has been an active leader
> in a number of conservation organizations including the National
> Parks Association, the Ecological Society of America, Nature Con-
> servancy, the Wilderness Society, and the Sierra Club. This leader-
> ship role, especially in the wilderness preservation movement,
> coupled with his intimate, practical knowledge of the wilderness,
> has made him a forceful and articulate proponent of the esthetic
> and spiritual values of wild nature. He is a frequent lecturer
> and contributor to magazines as well as an author of seven best-
> selling books. Olson's books, all in print, are beautifully written
> in a personal narrative style, informed by a deep love for nature
> and sharpened by ecological understanding.

THE SINGING WILDERNESS. Illustrations by Francis Lee Jaques.
New York: Knopf, 1956. ix, 245 p. Map.

> In this perceptive and beautifully written book, the author
> tells of his experiences of more than thirty years in the
> Quetico-Superior wilderness area. Olson's efforts as a
> conservationist-writer were influential in the successful strug-
> gle to secure the Quetico-Superior as a wilderness preserve.

LISTENING POINT. Illustrations by Francis Lee Jaques. New
York: Knopf, 1958. x, 242 p.

RUNES OF THE NORTH. Illustrations by Robert Hines. New York: Knopf, 1963. xii, 254 p. Map.

OPEN HORIZONS. Illustrations by Leslie Kouba. New York: Knopf, 1969. xv, 227 p.

> A wilderness autobiography. Olson recounts his boyhood and youth in Wisconsin and Minnesota, his wilderness initiation, his experiences as a wilderness guide, his attempts at writing, and his conservation activities. A splendid book.

THE HIDDEN FOREST. Photographs by Les Blacklock. New York: Viking, 1969. 127 p.

> Contains 120 spectacular color plates.

SIGURD F. OLSON'S WILDERNESS DAYS. New York: Knopf, 1972. xxii, 233 p. Illustrations (some in color). Maps.

> A selection of passages from Olson's previous books, favorite chapters also especially favored by readers of his earlier work.

Packard, Winthrop (1862-1943)

> Packard was a New England journalist, editor, and naturalist. For a number of years he was a correspondent and columnist for several newspapers, including THE BOSTON TRANSCRIPT and the NEW YORK EVENING POST. From 1905-8 he served as editor of the NEW ENGLAND MAGAZINE. Nearly all of his nature essays originally appeared in the newspapers and popular magazines. In his later years, Packard became quite well known as a conservationist. He was active in the Massachusetts Audubon Society and served as its executive officer from 1914-36. All of Packard's prose is eminently readable, albeit a trifle "literary," today.

WILD PASTURES. Boston: Small, Maynard, 1909. x, 233 p. Illustrated.

WILDWOOD WAYS. Boston: Small, Maynard, 1909. 261 p. Frontispiece.

FLORIDA TRAILS AS SEEN FROM JACKSONVILLE TO KEY WEST AND FROM NOVEMBER TO APRIL INCLUSIVE. Boston: Small, Maynard, 1910. 300 p. Plates.

WOOD WANDERINGS. Boston: Small, Maynard, 1910. 222 p. Illustrated.

WOODLAND PATHS. Boston: Small, Maynard, 1910. 289 p. Illustrated.

LITERARY PILGRIMAGES OF A NATURALIST. Boston: Small, Maynard, 1911. xii, 220 p. Illustrated.

> In impressionistic prose, Packard describes his visits to the haunts of various New England literary figures, including Thoreau, Whittier, Emerson, Hawthorne, Webster, and Frank Bolles.

WHITE MOUNTAIN TRAILS. TALES OF THE TRAILS TO THE SUMMIT OF MOUNT WASHINGTON AND OTHER SUMMITS OF THE WHITE HILLS. Boston: Small, Maynard, 1912. xiv, 311 p. Illustrated.

OLD PLYMOUTH TRAILS. Boston: Small, Maynard, 1920. 351 p. Illustrated.

Peattie, Donald Culross (1898-1964)

Although Donald Culross Peattie wrote fiction, history, juveniles, and other books, he is rightly remembered for his many distinguished books on nature, natural history, and naturalists.

Peattie graduated from Harvard with honors in botany and served a short apprenticeship with the U.S. Department of Agriculture before traveling to France with his family to spend five years practicing the craft of writing. Two years after returning to the United States, he published his classic ALMANAC FOR MODERNS (1935). There followed a succession of a dozen or more adult books and innumerable magazine articles on nature and natural history. Later, he became associated with READER'S DIGEST as a "roving editor," in which capacity he and his wife, the novelist Louise Redfield Peattie, traveled frequently across the United States and to Europe doing research for his many contributions to that magazine.

Peattie brought to his nature writing the training and discernment of a scientist and "the vision of a poet." He was an intense student and lover of nature, and his prose style was characterized by a remarkable descriptive ability and lyricism.

AN ALMANAC FOR MODERNS. New York: Putnam, 1935. 396 p. Illustrated.

> Ruminations upon our natural world arranged in the form of an almanac. Out of print, but considered by many to be a classic, The book received the gold medal of the Limited Editions Club.

SINGING IN THE WILDERNESS, A SALUTE TO JOHN JAMES
AUDUBON. Illustrated with reproductions of Audubon Originals.
New York: Putnam, 1935. 245 p.

>An impressionistic and somewhat sentimental biography
>of Audubon and his times. It vividly recreates the flora
>of early Ohio.

A PRAIRIE GROVE. New York: Simon and Schuster, 1938.
289 p.

>Tells the story of frontier and pioneer life in a small
>section of Illinois prairie. Combines human history
>with natural history. Beautifully written.

FLOWERING EARTH. New York: Putnam, 1939. 260 p. Illustrated.

>Traces the evolution of the plant kingdom from its earliest
>beginnings to the development of modern plants. Includes
>glimpses of the author's botanical experiences. Available
>in a paper edition.

THE ROAD OF A NATURALIST. Boston: Houghton Mifflin, 1941.
viii, 315 p. Illustrated.

>This remarkable book is both the account of the author's
>automobile trip through the Southwest with his wife, and
>an informal, nonsequential autobiography told in a series
>of flashbacks. The episodes are skillfully woven together
>in what the editor believes to be Peattie's best book.
>It won a $2,500 publisher's prize.

A CUP OF SKY. By Donald Culross Peattie and Noel Peattie.
Boston: Houghton Mifflin, [1950]. x, 242 p. Illustrated.

>Twenty delightful essays by the author and his seventeen-
>year-old son, Noel. The book begins with a brief life
>of St. Francis of Assisi. The following chapters are con-
>cerned with those elemental things in the Saint's "Hymn
>to Creation"--"Sunlight," "Wind," "Water," "Hearth-
>fires," "The Moon," and other natural phenomena. This
>is pure nature writing and is beautifully done.

Peterson, Roger Tory, and Fisher, James. WILD AMERICA; THE RECORD OF
A 30,000 MILE JOURNEY AROUND THE CONTINENT BY A DISTINGUISHED
NATURALIST AND HIS BRITISH COLLEAGUE. Boston: Houghton Mifflin,
1955. 434 p. Illustrated.

>By two of the best-known English-speaking ornithologists in the
>world. Excerpts from Fisher's journal are followed by Peterson's

comments. Heavy and loving emphasis upon birds.

Peterson, Russell F. ANOTHER VIEW OF THE CITY. New York: McGraw-Hill, 1967. xiii, 220 p. Illustrated.

The author, a former staff mammalogist with the Museum of Natural History in New York, writes of his personal experiences with nature in a small enclave of "wilderness" near Sandy Hook, New Jersey, rapidly being encroached upon by suburban housing developments.

Porter, Gene Stratton. MUSIC OF THE WILD, WITH REPRODUCTIONS OF THE PERFORMERS, THEIR INSTRUMENTS AND FESTIVAL HALLS. Garden City, N.Y.: Doubleday, Page, 1911. 427 p. Illustrated.

Gene Stratton Porter (1863-1924), novelist, nature writer, and photographer, is best remembered as the creator of FRECKLES (1904), A GIRL OF THE LIMBERLOST (1909), and other popular novels--books which she referred to as "nature studies coated with fiction." Mrs. Porter was an enormously successful author; between eight and nine million copies of her books were sold during her lifetime. In addition to her novels, Mrs. Porter wrote a number of works of popular natural history. MUSIC OF THE WILD, profusely illustrated with her own photographs, is perhaps her best work in this genre.

Rich, Louise Dickinson. WE TOOK TO THE WOODS. Philadelphia and New York: Lippincott, 1942. 322 p. Plates. Maps on endpapers.

In the middle 1930s, the author married a Maine guide and took up residence in a cabin near the Rapid River in northwestern Maine. In this book and in HAPPY THE LAND and MY NECK OF THE WOODS, Mrs. Rich relates her family's experiences in an isolated, primitive, and roadless part of what was then the Maine frontier. The land and the people are charmingly portrayed by the author. After the death of Mrs. Rich's husband, she eventually and reluctantly decided to return to Connecticut. Among her later books, special note should be made of THE PENINSULA, a remarkably good study of the people and the land of Maine's Goldsboro Peninsula.

_____. HAPPY THE LAND. Philadelphia: Lippincott, 1946. 259 p. Plates.

_____. MY NECK OF THE WOODS. Philadelphia and New York: Lippincott, 1950. 255 p. Illustrated.

_____. THE NATURAL WORLD OF LOUISE DICKINSON RICH. New York: Dodd, Mead, 1962. xxvi, 195 p. Illustrated.

The author tells of her life-long love affair with the natural world of New England. Mrs. Rich divides her narrative into three parts--The Plain, The Highlands, and The Coast--each of which relates to a phase of her life. A fascinating and well-written work.

Rutledge, Archibald Hamilton (b. 1883)

Rutledge is one of South Carolina's most distinguished prose writers and, by legislative action, that state's Poet Laureate. He has made "Hampton," his Santee River plantation, familiar to thousands of his readers. The plantation with its two-thousand-acre tract has been in the author's family since 1686 and is the setting for many of Rutledge's thirty-odd books. After retiring from a teaching job in the North, the author returned to South Carolina in 1937 and undertook the restoration of his eighteenth-century home.

Combining a deep love for the natural setting with an intimate knowledge of plantation lore and local color, Rutledge's books are redolent of that mysterious charm so characteristic of much of the tidewater South. The author is the recipient of the coveted John Burroughs Medal for outstanding nature writing.

PEACE IN THE HEART. Garden City, N.Y.: Doubleday, Doran, 1930. xiv, 316 p. Reprint ed., 1956.

HOME BY THE RIVER. Indianapolis and New York: Bobbs-Merrill, 1941. 167 p. [28] p. of photos. Reprint ed., 1955.

> Reprint edition has an introduction by Frances Parkinson Keyes.

SANTEE PARADISE. Indianapolis and New York: Bobbs-Merrill, 1956. 232 p. [24] p. of photos.

THE WORLD AROUND HAMPTON. New York: Bobbs-Merrill, 1960. 192 p. Illustrated.

Schmoe, Floyd. FOR LOVE OF SOME ISLANDS. MEMOIRS OF SOME YEARS SPENT IN THE SAN JUAN ISLANDS OF PUGET SOUND. New York: Harper & Row, 1964. 226 p. Illustrated.

The author, a biologist and teacher, spent one summer with his family leisurely exploring and observing the flora and fauna of the islands. Well written and nontechnical.

_____. A YEAR IN PARADISE. Rev. ed. Rutland, Vt.: C.E. Tuttle, 1967. ix, 235 p. Illustrated, with plates. Maps.

First edition published by Harper in 1959. This is an exceptionally good book about Mt. Ranier National Park. Schmoe, an ex-ranger and naturalist, tells the story of his and his family's relationship to the mountain during a twelve-month period in the 1920s. A blend of natural history, ecology, and nature philosophy.

Sharp, Dallas, Lore (1870-1929)

Dallas Lore Sharp began his career as a Methodist minister, but within a few years he combined the careers of teacher, author, and amateur naturalist. In 1899 he became assistant librarian at Boston University and, later, professor of English. For three years, commencing in 1900, Sharp worked on the editorial staff of the YOUTH'S COMPANION, during which time he also taught at Boston University and began his writing career.

Sharp wrote hundreds of articles for periodicals, drawing upon many of them for his more than twenty volumes. Sharp's nature writing was very popular and several of his books sold over 100,000 copies. His personal friendship with John Burroughs, whom he took as his exemplar in nature writing, served as a cachet for his natural history endeavors and saved him from embroilment in the nature-faker controversy (see the headnote to Chapter 8).

Sharp's country place, "Mullein Hill," near Hingham, Massachu-setts, was the locale for much of his writing. For biographical information, see the sketch by Sidney Gunn in THE DICTIONARY OF AMERICAN BIOGRAPHY (volume 17, pp. 22-23). For an appreciation of his writing, see "Indoors and Out," by Howard Zahniser, in NATURE MAGAZINE (volume 30, no. 6, December 1937, pp. 327, 380).

WILD LIFE NEAR HOME. New York: Century Co., 1901. xvi, 357 p. Illustrated.

A WATCHER IN THE WOODS. New York: Century Co., 1903. xv, 205 p. Illustrated.

Reprinted in a 1911 school edition.

ROOF AND MEADOW. New York: Century Co., 1904. vii, 281 p. Illustrated.

THE LAY OF THE LAND. Boston and New York: Houghton Mifflin, 1908. 213 p. Illustrated.

THE FACE OF THE FIELDS. Boston and New York: Houghton Mifflin, 1911. 250 p. Reprint ed., 1967.

Contains several excellent and perceptive essays on John Burroughs.

THE FALL OF THE YEAR. The Dallas Lore Sharp Nature Series. Boston: Houghton Mifflin, 1911. xv, 126 p. Illustrated.

THE SPRING OF THE YEAR. The Dallas Lore Sharp Nature Series. Boston: Houghton Mifflin, 1912. x, 148 p. Illustrated.

WAYS OF THE WOODS. Riverside Literature Series. Boston: Houghton Mifflin, 1912. 119 p. Illustrated.

WINTER. The Dallas Lore Sharp Nature Series. Boston: Houghton Mifflin, 1912. x, 148 p. Illustrated.

SUMMER. The Dallas Lore Sharp Nature Series. Boston: Houghton Mifflin, 1914. x, 132 p. Illustrated, with plates.

WHERE ROLLS THE OREGON. Boston and New York: Houghton Mifflin, 1914. ix, 251 p. Plates.

THE WHOLE YEAR AROUND. Boston and New York: Houghton Mifflin, 1915. xvi, 503 p. Illustrated, with plates.

A combined edition of all the "seasonal" books.

THE HILLS OF HINGHAM. Boston and New York: Houghton Mifflin, 1916. ix, 221 p. Illustrated.

A delightful account of the Sharp family's life on their fourteen-acre farm near Hingham, Massachusetts, twenty miles from Boston.

SPIRIT OF THE HIVE; CONTEMPLATIONS OF A BEEKEEPER. New York and London: Harper, 1925. 250 p.

SANCTUARY! SANCTUARY! New York and London: Harper, 1926. 227 p. Illustrated.

Shepard, Odell. THE HARVEST OF A QUIET EYE: A BOOK OF DISGRESSIONS. Boston: Houghton Mifflin, 1927. 282 p. Illustrated. Reprint ed., 1971.

Records a leisurely two-week walking trip through rural Connecticut. An account of nature, people, and small towns. Received excellent reviews.

Teale, Edwin Way (b. 1899)

Teale has had a long and honored career as writer-naturalist and photographer. His first work was published in 1930; since then, he has written and edited more than twenty-five books, and contributed to more than 100 periodicals. The author has been honored by a number of awards, including the John Burroughs Medal, the Christopher Medal, and the Pulitzer Prize for general nonfiction in 1966. Several of Teale's books are now considered classics of nature writing. His masterwork, a four-volume survey of the natural history of the American seasons, is included in the selections below. For biographical information, see CURRENT BIOGRAPHY (1967), CONTEMPORARY AUTHORS (volumes 1-4, revised edition), and the biography by Edward H. Dodd, Jr. (below). See also "Trail Wood Trails With Edwin Way Teale," by Lawrence F. Willard, in AUDUBON MAGAZINE (volume 64, May-June 1962, pp. 136-41).

DUNE BOY, THE EARLY YEARS OF A NATURALIST. Illustrated by Edward Shenton. New York: Dodd, Mead, 1943. 255 p.

> Nostalgic and engrossing story of Teale's boyhood on his grandparent's farm in the dune country of northern Indiana, adjacent to Lake Michigan.

THE LOST WOODS, ADVENTURES OF A NATURALIST. Illustrated with 200 photographs by the author. New York: Dodd, Mead, 1945. 326 p.

NORTH WITH SPRING: A NATURALIST'S RECORD OF A 17,000-MILE JOURNEY WITH THE NORTH AMERICAN SPRING. Illustrated with photographs by the author. New York: Dodd, Mead, 1951. xviii, 358 p. Illustrated.

> This is the first of the four volumes in Teale's series, "The American Seasons." The author writes vividly of the natural world from Florida to the Canadian border. Also available in paper edition.

CIRCLE OF THE SEASONS: THE JOURNAL OF A NATURALIST'S YEAR. New York: Dodd, Mead, 1953. xiv, 306 p. Illustrated, with plates.

AUTUMN ACROSS AMERICA: A NATURALIST'S RECORD OF A 20,000-MILE JOURNEY THROUGH THE NORTH AMERICAN AUTUMN. New York: Dodd, Mead, 1956. xviii, 386 p. Illustrated. Maps on endpapers.

> From Cape Cod through the northern states to the Pacific Northwest and Monterey, California. Also available in a paper edition.

JOURNEY INTO SUMMER: A NATURALIST'S RECORD OF A 19,000-MILE JOURNEY THROUGH THE NORTH AMERICAN SUMMER. New York: Dodd, Mead, 1960. xviii, 366 p. Illustrated. Maps on endpapers.

The journey begins in the White Mountains, continues around the Great Lakes, into the North Woods, across middle America, and into the Rockies. Also available in a paper edition.

WANDERING THROUGH WINTER: A NATURALIST'S RECORD OF A 20,000-MILE JOURNEY THROUGH THE NORTH AMERICAN WINTER. New York: Dodd, Mead, 1965. xx, 370 p. Illustrated.

The last of the "American Seasons" books. It was for this work that Teale won the Pulitzer Prize. Also available in a paper edition.

Dodd, Edward H., Jr. OF NATURE, TIME AND TEALE. New York: Dodd, Mead, 1960. 63 p. Illustrated.

Thompson, Maurice (1844-1901)

Although he was born in Indiana, Thompson was raised in Kentucky and fought with the Confederate Army during the Civil War. After the war, he returned to Indiana where he worked as an engineer, a lawyer, and, from 1884-88, as the State Geologist. He wrote novels, poetry, geological treatises, several books for children, books on archery (of which sport he was a devotee), and three nature books (below). While growing up in the South, Thompson developed the interest in the outdoors which remained throughout his life. From 1890 until his death, Thompson served on the staff of THE INDEPENDENT.

BY-WAYS AND BIRD NOTES. New York: J.B. Alden, 1885. 179 p.

SYLVAN SECRETS, IN BIRD-SONGS AND BOOKS. New York: J.B. Alden, 1887. 139 p.

MY WINTER GARDEN; A NATURE-LOVER UNDER SOUTHERN SKIES. New York: Century Co., 1900. xiii, 320 p.

Torrey, Bradford (1843-1912)

Essayist, editor, and amateur ornithologist, Torrey developed an early and enduring love for nature. From 1886-1901 he was an editor of the YOUTH'S COMPANION. It was during these years that he found the leisure to develop his interests in nature, to travel, and to write his many essays, sketches, and books. His principal interest was in birds, although he also wrote of his experiences in fields and woods.

Torrey edited the fourteen volumes of the journal of Henry David Thoreau which were published as part of the twenty-volume Walden Edition (Houghton Mifflin, 1906).

When Torrey died in Santa Barbara, California, in 1912, John Burroughs wrote of his achievement: "He was a rare spirit and a maker of pure literature. His style has an ease and flexibility and a conversational charm that I wish I might inherit" (see THE LIFE AND LETTERS OF JOHN BURROUGHS, by Clara Barrus, volume II, p. 184, cited under Burroughs, John, above). For further information, see Zahniser's essay (below) and the sketch in THE DICTIONARY OF AMERICAN BIOGRAPHY (volume 18, pp. 594-95).

BIRDS IN THE BUSH. Boston and New York: Houghton Mifflin, 1885. 300 p.

A RAMBLER'S LEASE. Boston and New York: Houghton Mifflin, 1889. vi, 222 p.

THE FOOT-PATH WAY. Boston and New York: Houghton Mifflin, 1892. 245 p.

THE CLERK OF THE WOODS. Boston and New York: Houghton Mifflin, 1893. 280 p.

A FLORIDA SKETCH BOOK. Boston and New York: Houghton Mifflin, 1894. 242 p.

SPRING NOTES FROM TENNESSEE. Boston and New York: Houghton Mifflin, 1896. 223 p.

THE WORLD OF GREEN HILLS; OBSERVATIONS OF NATURE AND HUMAN NATURE IN THE BLUE RIDGE. Boston and New York: Houghton Mifflin, 1898. 285 p.

FOOTING IT IN FRANCONIA. Boston and New York: Houghton Mifflin, 1901. 251 p.

NATURE'S INVITATION: NOTES OF A BIRDGAZER NORTH AND SOUTH. Boston: Houghton Mifflin, 1904. viii, 300 p.

FIELD DAYS IN CALIFORNIA.   Boston: Houghton Mifflin, 1913.
234 p.   Illustrated.

Zahniser, Howard.   "In October--Bradford Torrey."   NATURE
MAGAZINE 30, no. 4 (October 1937):   199.

Van Dyke, John Charles (1856-1932)

Van Dyke, well-known art critic, librarian, professor, nature
writer, and cousin of preacher-naturist, Henry Van Dyke, wrote
several distinguished books on nature.   His family moved from
New Jersey to Minnesota when he was twelve and there he
developed a life-long love for the outdoors--fishing, hunting,
canoeing, and riding in a land that was still very much a frontier.
After college, Van Dyke secured a position as librarian in the
New Brunswick Theological Seminary where he found time to pursue the study of art.   Simultaneous with his library job, he held
the post of professor of art history at Rutgers College from 1891
to 1929.

Van Dyke's books on nature and landscape esthetics ("natural
appearances") were infused with a love of natural beauty and
informed by an artistic appreciation for American landscape.
His popular books on art subjects have been generally eclipsed
by more recent work, but his nature books are still read.   For
biographical information, see the sketch by Frank Jewett Mather,
Jr., in THE DICTIONARY OF AMERICAN BIOGRAPHY (volume
19, pp. 188-89).

NATURE FOR ITS OWN SAKE; FIRST STUDIES IN NATURAL
APPEARANCES.   New York: Scribner, 1898.   xx, 292 p.

> This is the first of the author's books on nature and
> "natural appearances."   In it, he discusses the natural
> elements such as light, sky, clouds, water, land, and
> foliage that give form and color to the landscape.   The
> volume went through several later editions.

THE DESERT; FURTHER STUDIES IN NATURAL APPEARANCES.
With illustrations from photographs by J. Smeaton Chase.   New
York: Scribner, 1918.   xii, 233 p.

> First edition (without illustrations) appeared in 1901.   The
> scene of the "studies" is the desert areas of southweatern
> California and southern Arizona.

THE MOUNTAIN; RENEWED STUDIES IN IMPRESSIONS AND
APPEARANCES.   New York: Scribner, 1916.   xvi, 234 p.

THE GRAND CANYON OF THE COLORADO; RECURRENT STUDIES
IN IMPRESSIONS AND APPEARANCES. New York: Scribner,
1920. xii, 218 p. Plates. Folding map.

> Views of the Canyon from the South Rim; a blend of geology
> and landscape appreciation.

THE OPEN SPACES; INCIDENTS OF NIGHTS AND DAYS UNDER
THE BLUE SKY. Scribner, 1922. vii, 272 p.

> A personal and engaging book filled with reminiscences
> of the author's early years in the "old Northwest," the
> plains of Nebraska, the Badlands, and the desert country
> of southeastern California, Arizona, and Mexico. Van
> Dyke writes with considerable feeling about his "lost
> youth" when nature was still largely untouched by civ-
> ilization.

THE MEADOWS; FAMILIAR STUDIES OF THE COMMONPLACE.
New York: Scribner, 1926. ix, 215 p.

> The location of the studies is near the Raritan River,
> New Jersey.

Chapter 8

NATURE STUDY IN AMERICA

Chapter 8

NATURE STUDY IN AMERICA

American nature study as a national movement began in the 1890s, after having "spontaneously" developed in the elementary schools in the latter part of the 1880s. Its most immediate aim was to acquaint young Americans with nature and may well be considered as concomitant to America's rediscovery of nature. During its heyday, roughly 1890-1925, nature study had many leading proponents, and detailed curricula were devoted to its development. Enormous quantities of books, articles, and curricular material were published during that period but, since about 1925, nature study has been eclipsed by the teaching of "elementary science" in the schools.

Included here are bibliographies, special studies, handbooks, studies of its history, philosophy, and purpose, a selected list of textbooks, popular writings on nature study, and a list of periodicals.

Related to nature study, and in part growing out of it, is the hobby of bird-watching. A selective list of materials from the considerable body of literature dealing with that genre has been included.

A colorful and humorous, if relatively unimportant, adjunct to the nature-study movement was the so-called "nature-faker" controversy that erupted in 1903 and lasted for a half-dozen years. John Burroughs began the argument with a polemic in the March 1903 issue of the ATLANTIC MONTHLY, in which he attacked popular nature writers for humanizing animal life and thus corrupting the study of nature. The controversy raged in the popular press for several years and is indicative of the seriousness with which otherwise reserved scientists and other professionals viewed the importance of nature study.

A. NATURE STUDY

1. Index

THE EDUCATION INDEX. New York: H.W. Wilson, 1932--.

A cumulative author and subject index to a selected list of educational periodicals, books, and pamphlets. Its coverage begins with January 1929. (For references to earlier work, THE READER'S GUIDE TO PERIODICAL LITERATURE should be consulted.) Each successive cumulation of the INDEX includes fewer references to "Nature Study"--from six columns in the 1929-32 cumulation to three-fourths of one column in the 1959-61 cumulation.

2. Bibliographies

Gordon, Eva L. "Bibliography of Nature Study." In THE HANDBOOK OF NATURE STUDY, by Anna Botsford Comstock, 24th edition, pp. [861]-908. Ithaca, N.Y.: Comstock Publishing Co., 1939.

> Also available as a paper off-print edition. See annotation for THE HANDBOOK in Section A4: Handbooks (below).

Hurley, Richard James. KEY TO THE OUT-OF-DOORS, A BIBLIOGRAPHY OF NATURE BOOKS AND MATERIALS. New York: H.W. Wilson, 1938. 256 p.

> A classified and graded list. Although it contains some adult books, its main emphasis is nature study for the child and the teacher.

Palmer, E. Laurence, and Gordon, Eva L. "A Nature Bibliography." In THE NATURE ALMANAC: A HANDBOOK OF NATURE EDUCATION, pp. 336-90. Washington, D.C.: American Nature Association, 1930.

> A valuable classified bibliography with annotations.

Underwood, Margaret H., ed. BIBLIOGRAPHY OF NORTH AMERICAN MINOR NATURAL HISTORY SERIALS IN THE UNIVERSITY OF MICHIGAN LIBRARIES. Ann Arbor: University of Michigan Press, 1954. 197 p. Paper.

> A listing of little-known, minor, and/or ephemeral periodicals devoted to the various aspects of natural history. Arranged in two alphabets--by state and, separately, by title. Each entry contains full bibliographic information on titles, title changes, dates of publication, names of editors and publishers, the holdings in the University of Michigan Libraries, and brief annotations by a cooperating scholar. This is an important source, especially for popular and semipopular periodicals dealing with natural history and nature study.

3. Special Studies

Bullough, William A. " 'It is Better to Be a Country Boy': The Lure of the Country in Urban Education in the Gilded Age." THE HISTORIAN 35, no. 2

(February 1973): 183-95.

At a time of increasing urbanization (1870-1900), there existed
an intellectual trend, a "lure of the country" or nature nostalgia,
among intellectuals, writers, orators, and politicians. Bullough
examines this phenomenon among urban educators. Of particular
relevance is his discussion of nature study.

Elson, Ruth Miller. GUARDIANS OF TRADITION: AMERICAN SCHOOL-
BOOKS OF THE NINETEENTH CENTURY. Lincoln: University of Nebraska
Press, 1964. xiii, 424 p. Illustrated. Bibliography, pp. 343-414.

For a fascinating description and thematic analysis of the place
of nature, farming, and country life in textbooks of the nineteenth
century, see Elson's Chapter 2: "Nature."

Krutch, Joseph Wood. "The Demise of Natural History." AUDUBON 69,
no. 5 (September/October 1967): 50-55.

Krutch laments the passing of natural history and the ascendance
of laboratory biology. Natural history as a formal course of study
is obsolete and is now considered the province of "nature lovers."
Its study and practice, says the author, give one both poetic and
scientific insight into the workings of nature. What we need, he
says, is a "generation that has not stopped with 'knowledge about'
nature, but has also learned to share the perennial joy and con-
solation which nature can provide."

Schmitt, Peter J. BACK TO NATURE: THE ARCADIAN MYTH IN URBAN
AMERICA. New York: Oxford University Press, 1969. xxiii, 230 p. Notes,
pp. 191-221.

For an interesting interpretation of nature study from 1890 to 1930,
see especially Chapters 3, 4, 7, and 8.

4. Handbooks

Comstock, Anna Botsford. THE HANDBOOK OF NATURE STUDY. 24th ed.
Ithaca, N.Y.: Comstock Publishing Co., 1939. xx, 947 p. Illustrated.
Bibliography by Eva L. Gordon, pp. [861]-908.

THE HANDBOOK, based upon the CORNELL NATURE STUDY LEAF-
LETS, has been in print continuously since its initial appearance in
1911. Although the 24th edition (still in print) was revised and ex-
panded by the publishers to bring it more into consonance with modern
knowledge, the greater part of Comstock's original treatment
and style has been retained. The work contains four parts. The
first part deals with definitions and the aims and methods of nature
study, while the other parts cover the major divisions of nature
study. These contain introductory sections on the classes of animals

and plants and are followed by specific treatments of individual members. Each subsection is followed by a "lesson," with suggested readings. Two hundred and thirty-two lessons are included. The bibliography by Eva L. Gordon is a valuable classified, graded, and briefly annotated list of books on nature study, including general works on nature, essays, and travel books. Although the nature study curriculum, as originally conceived by Mrs. Comstock and Liberty Hyde Bailey, has largely been transformed into the teaching of natural science in the nation's schools, the longevity of this book is a testimonial to its value and to the persistence of the original movement.

THE NATURE ALMANAC: A HANDBOOK OF NATURE EDUCATION. Washington, D.C.: American Nature Association, 1930. viii, 399 p. Illustrated. Bibliography, pp. 336-90.

This is a valuable source for the historian of American nature study. Included are the following: a statement of the purposes of nature education; sketches of associations and clubs interested in promoting nature education; a section on leadership training in normal schools and teachers colleges, including short descriptions of outdoor nature schools; a survey of nature education in the United States, arranged by state; a school nature outline with suggestions and references for teachers; a nature bibliography by E. Laurence Palmer and Eva Gordon; and a directory of "nature leaders." An earlier edition was published in 1927.

5.   History, Philosophy, and Purpose

Bailey, Liberty Hyde. "Nature-Study on the Cornell Plan." REVIEW OF REVIEWS (N.Y.) 23 (April 1901): 463-64.

"The Cornell nature-study movement seeks to improve the agricultural condition. It wants to interest the coming man in his natural environment, and thereby to make him content to be a countryman." Bailey also discusses the purpose of the CORNELL NATURE-STUDY LEAFLETS (below).

_____. THE NATURE-STUDY IDEA, BEING AN INTERPRETATION OF THE NEW SCHOOL MOVEMENT TO PUT THE CHILD IN SYMPATHY WITH NATURE. New York: Doubleday, Page, 1903. 159 p.

Bailey was one of the principal leaders of the nature-study movement and its most articulate spokesman. The movement, having "spontaneously" originated in the elementary schools, was fastened upon by Bailey and his Cornell University associates, notably Anna B. Comstock (see below). As Bailey saw it, nature study was to put the child into sympathy with nature, and, in the case of the farm child, make him more content to remain a "countryman." Bailey believed that the study of nature was fundamental to the evolution of popular education, and he therefore threw his support to its inclusion in the extension teaching being carried on at Cornell. In 1895, the College of Agriculture, through its extension publications, correspondence, and organization of pupils into junior naturalist clubs, made the University the exemplar of nature-study instruction in the United States. Although methodology is discussed to some extent, THE NATURE-STUDY IDEA is not a text but an exhortation. Nature study is defined by Bailey, its aims and purposes are cited and discussed, and its history is outlined. The author's deep personal commitment to the study of nature, and his belief in its importance to the nation's health and sanity, is made clear in the book. Bailey was undoubtedly atypical of the vast majority of agriculturists of the time in that he was, in addition to his many other attainments, a philosopher with a religio-poetic outlook on nature. THE NATURE-STUDY IDEA was reprinted several times, most recently in 1920. For other titles by Bailey see Chapter 10, Section A: Commentaries.

Bigelow, Maurice A. "Nature Study." In A CYCLOPEDIA OF EDUCATION, edited by Paul Monroe, vol. 4, pp. 389-91. New York: Macmillan, 1913.

A useful definition of nature study in the schools. The author differentiates between nature study in elementary schools and natural science in high schools and colleges. Bigelow, a professor at Columbia Teacher's College and founder of THE NATURE-STUDY REVIEW, felt that, although nature study must use books and other textual materials in the school, it should aim at teaching the pupil to study and appreciate nature in the absence of books.

Burroughs, John. "Nature Study." THE OUTLOOK 61, no. 5 (February 4, 1899): 326-28.

Burroughs argues against nature study by laboratory experiment. "Nature that comes through familiarity...fishing, hunting, nutting, walking, farming, that is the kind that...becomes a part of us." Very few of the nature study textbooks were worth much, in his opinion, because they did not excite the child's curiosity.

Comstock, Anna Botsford (1854-1930)

Mrs. Comstock, a naturalist, educator, scientific illustrator, and wood engraver, was married to Cornell entomologist John Henry Comstock. Although she received considerable recognition as a wood engraver and illustrator (primarily of her husband's entomological works), her principal contribution was to the nature-study movement of which she became one of its foremost proponents. In 1895 Mrs. Comstock assisted in the development of a nature-study program for New York State schools. The College of Agriculture at Cornell became the focus for much of the work, and she worked hard preparing leaflets, lecturing, and teaching. In 1897, she was appointed to Cornell's faculty and later became the first woman professor at that school.

She wrote a number of books for students and teachers of nature study; her major work, THE HANDBOOK OF NATURE STUDY, published in 1911, has gone through twenty-four editions and has been translated into eight languages. Mrs. Comstock was an associate director of the American Nature Association, founded in 1922, the editor (1917-23) of the NATURE-STUDY REVIEW, and poetry editor of COUNTRY LIFE IN AMERICA. For biographical information, see her autobiography (below) and the sketch by Kathleen Jacklin in NOTABLE AMERICAN WOMEN (volume 1, pp. 367-69).

"The Nature Club of America." COUNTRY LIFE IN AMERICA 10, no. 4 (August 1906): 439-40, 468.

> COUNTRY LIFE IN AMERICA was the "official organ" of the Nature Club of America, founded to advise its readers of the proper approach to nature study. With this number, the magazine began a continuing series devoted to the subject. In the September issue (p. 538) there appeared the following statement: "The Nature Club of America has been formed to stimulate and direct nature work by individuals or local chapters." The officers of the Club were Anna B. Comstock, National Secretary; Advisory Board: John Burroughs, E.T. Seaton, B.W. Evermann, A. Radclyffe Dugmore, Julia E. Rogers, L.O. Howard, and C. William Beebe.

THE COMSTOCKS OF CORNELL: JOHN HENRY COMSTOCK AND ANNA BOTSFORD COMSTOCK, AN AUTOBIOGRAPHY. Edited by Glenn W. Herrick and Ruby Green Smith. Ithaca, N.Y.: Comstock Publishing Associates, A Division of Cornell University Press, [1953]. xi, 286 p. Illustrated.

> Shortly before her death in 1930, Mrs. Comstock completed a narrative of the lives of her husband and herself and the manuscript was edited by Herrick and Green. The autobiography is a useful source of information about Mrs. Comstock's activities in the field of nature study.

CORNELL NATURE-STUDY LEAFLETS; BEING A SELECTION, WITH REVISION, FROM THE TEACHERS' LEAFLETS, HOME NATURE-STUDY LESSONS, JUNIOR NATURALIST MONTHLIES AND OTHER PUBLICATIONS FROM THE COLLEGE OF AGRICULTURE, CORNELL UNIVERSITY, ITHACA, N.Y., 1896-1904. Nature Study Bulletin No. 1. Albany: New York State Department of Agriculture, 1904. 607 p. Illustrated. Photos.

> First appeared as part of the Annual Report for 1903 of the College of Agriculture transmitted to the Commissioner of Agriculture by Liberty Hyde Bailey, Dean of the College. An excellent selection

and still useful source of study materials for children. Included
are three leaflets by Bailey: "What is Nature-Study?"; "The
Nature-Study Movement"; and "An Appeal to the Teachers of
New York State."

Curtis, Henry S. "Nature Study." EDUCATIONAL REVIEW (N.Y.) 63 (April
1922): 307-14.

Henry Stoddard Curtis was the organizer of the Playground Association of America. He was a frequent lecturer at universities and
normal schools. In this short article, he advocates direction of
the innate curiosity of young children as the way to interest them
in nature. Frankly enthusiastic about the value of studying nature,
Curtis felt that parents could do the most to interest their children
in the wonders of nature, and that formal instruction in the schools
should be a secondary resource.

Good, Harry G. "Nature Study." In his A HISTORY OF AMERICAN EDU-
CATION, 2d ed., pp. 221-28. New York: Macmillan, 1962.

Although short, the essay is an excellent source for details about
the movement and its history, and is particularly good for its discussion of early development in elementary schools.

Meyers, Ira Benton. "The Evolution of Aim and Method in the Teaching of
Nature-Study in the Common Schools of the United States." THE ELEMENTARY
SCHOOL TEACHER (Chicago) 11 (December 1910): 205-13, (January 1911):
237-48.

Meyers summarizes the various efforts of schools, from the earliest
decades of the nineteenth century, to develop the study of nature
for students "in such a way as to render the results educative."
Meyers's essay is valuable not only as a good outline of nature
study in the schools, but for its perceptive criticism of the influence
of specialists upon the curriculum. Meyers believed that the use
of specialist-dominated textbooks endangered the spirit of nature
study: "It [was] impossible to train teachers...through a system of
textbooks and libraries and expect them...[to] do strong, vigorous,
active original work with children...when they [had] never worked
from the standpoint of their own instinctive interests."

Mitchell, Dora Otis. A HISTORY OF NATURE STUDY. Ithaca, N.Y.:
Slingerland-Comstock Co., 1923. 45 p.

A good summary of the movement--particularly the New York phase--
up to 1920.

Palmer, E. Laurence. "Nature Study." In THE BOOK OF RURAL LIFE,
KNOWLEDGE AND INSPIRATION: A GUIDE TO THE BEST IN MODERN
LIVING, edited by Edward M. Tuttle, vol. 6, pp. 3760-63. Chicago:

Bellows-Durham Co., 1925.

> Palmer was a Cornell professor of rural education. He was active in the American Nature Association and the National Education Association, and was in charge of Cornell's publication of nature-study materials for schools after 1919. THE BOOK OF RURAL LIFE, a ten-volume encyclopedic treatment for farm families, was edited by Edward M. Tuttle, formerly identified with the Cornell nature-study program. In this brief section, Palmer discusses methods and aims, the social aspects of nature study, nature and economics, the esthetic value of nature study, its organization and teaching, and its relation to other subjects.

6. Textbooks

Hodge, Clifton F. NATURE STUDY AND LIFE. Introduction by G. Stanley Hall. Boston and New York: Ginn, 1902. xvi, 514 p. Illustrated.

Jackman, Wilbur S. NATURE STUDY FOR THE COMMON SCHOOLS. New York: Holt, 1891. vi, 438 p. 2nd ed., rev., 1892. x, 448 p.

> See next item.

————. NATURE STUDY FOR GRAMMAR GRADES; A MANUAL FOR TEACHERS AND PUPILS BELOW THE HIGH SCHOOL IN THE STUDY OF NATURE. New York and London: Macmillan, 1898. 407 p.

> Jackman (1855-1907) was one of the earliest educators to promote the teaching of nature study in the public schools. His early success in nature courses in Pittsburgh brought him to the attention of Colonel Francis Wayland Parker, principal of the Cook County Normal School in Chicago, who appointed him to the staff of his school. Jackman remained in Chicago, teaching and writing, and eventually became the first dean of the University of Chicago's College of Education. His books on nature study listed above were the first formal texts. He went on to write several manuals, syllabi, and articles on nature study and science education. Jackman was also editor of THE ELEMENTARY SCHOOL JOURNAL, begun in 1900. For biographical information, see the sketch by Charles H. Judd in THE DICTIONARY OF AMERICAN BIOGRAPHY (volume 9, p. 525).

Lange, Dietrich. HANDBOOK OF NATURE STUDY, FOR TEACHERS AND PUPILS IN ELEMENTARY SCHOOLS. New York and London: Macmillan, 1898. xvi, 329 p. Illustrated.

> Lange was a prolific writer of natural history guides and nature stories for children.

McMurry, Lida B. NATURE STUDY LESSONS FOR PRIMARY GRADES. New York: Macmillan, 1905. xi, 191 p.

> The "lessons" are arranged in two parts--animal life and plant life--each devoted to the learning of an object lesson about common animals and plants.

Schmucker, Samuel C. THE STUDY OF NATURE. Lippincott's Education Series, vol. 7. Philadelphia and London: Lippincott, 1909. 315 p. Illustrated. 3rd ed., enl., 1928. 349 p.

Scott, Charles B. NATURE STUDY AND THE CHILD. Boston: Heath, 1900. xxv, 618 p. Illustrated.

> Contains sections on philosophy, methodology, and course outlines.

7. Popular Books on Nature Study

Allen, Arthur A. AMERICAN BIRD BIOGRAPHIES, CONTAINING THE COMPLETE LIFE-HISTORIES OF FAMILIAR BIRDS WRITTEN IN AUTOBIOGRAPHICAL FORM. Ithaca, N.Y.: Comstock Publishing Co., 1934. ix, 238 p. Illustrated, with plates. Photos.

> Intended for use in school nature-study courses. Includes drawings and color plates by George Miksch Sutton and 190 photographs by the author. Allen was one of the nation's foremost ornithologists, a professor at Cornell, and an editor of BIRD-LORE.

Doubleday, Neltje Blanchan De Graff [Neltje Blanchan]. BIRD NEIGHBORS. AN INTRODUCTORY ACQUAINTANCE WITH ONE HUNDRED AND FIFTY BIRDS COMMONLY FOUND IN THE GARDENS, MEADOWS, AND WOODS ABOUT OUR HOMES. Introduction by John Burroughs. New York: Doubleday, McClure, 1896. viii, 234 p. Color plates.

> An extremely popular nature study by the publisher's wife. This work is available in a number of editions and was still in print in 1928.

Ingersoll, Ernest. WILD NEIGHBORS, OUTDOOR STUDIES IN THE UNITED STATES. New York: Macmillan, 1897. xii, 301 p. Illustrated, with plates.

> Ingersoll, naturalist and editor, was connected with the Hayden Survey and the U.S. Fish Commission and lectured at the University of Chicago. He wrote a number of books for children and animal studies for adults as well as two very popular travel books about the Rockies (see Chapter 2, Section D11: The Rocky Mountains). Ingersoll was a friend and neighbor of John Burroughs. WILD NEIGHBORS and WIT OF THE WILD are his two most famous animal books.

_____. THE WIT OF THE WILD. New York: Dodd, Mead, 1906. xi, 288 p. Illustrated.

Kieran, John. NATURE NOTES. New York: Doubleday, 1941. 112 p. Illustrated.

Fifty short essays on nature study. Elementary.

_____. AN INTRODUCTION TO NATURE. Garden City, N.Y.: Hanover House, 1955. 223 p. Illustrated.

Very elementary and intended for the novice.

Miller, Harriet Mann [Olive Thorne Miller] (1831-1918)

Mrs. Miller, who was better known by her pseudonym, was a highly regarded writer of nature books and children's stories. Mrs. Miller developed an early and enduring interest in birds and her summers were spent in the outdoors studying their habits. In her Brooklyn home she set up an aviary in order to observe them during the winter. Most of Mrs. Miller's twenty-five books (many about bird life) were written for children in a pleasant style informed by a fairly high degree of scientific accuracy resulting from close and careful observation. The passage of time has not dealt harshly with Mrs. Miller's juvenile bird books as it has for many other nineteenth-century children's writers. Her FIRST BOOK OF BIRDS, published in 1899, for example, remains a fresh, appealing, and instructive work. Her two best books, written for adults, are listed below. For biographical information, see the sketch by Robert H. Welker in NOTABLE AMERICAN WOMEN (volume 2, pp. 543-45).

Olive Thorne Miller. A BIRD-LOVER IN THE WEST. Boston and New York: Houghton Mifflin, 1894. vii, 278 p. Reprint ed., 1970.

_____. WITH THE BIRDS IN MAINE. Boston and New York: Houghton Mifflin, 1904. ix, 300 p.

Miller, Mary Rogers. THE BROOK BOOK. A FIRST ACQUAINTANCE WITH THE BROOK AND ITS INHABITANTS THROUGH THE CHANGING YEAR. New York: Doubleday, Page, 1902. xvi, 241 p. Illustrated, with plates.

The author, a lecturer on nature study at Cornell University, wrote this "series of pastoral idylls" as an instructive piece of nature study for adults. Although the author exhibits a tendency to "gush," the book presents good description in a pleasant style. Also published in London by William Heinemann, in 1903.

Seton, Ernest Thompson. WILD ANIMALS I HAVE KNOWN. New York:

Scribner, 1898. 359 p. Illustrated, with plates.

This was a best seller and went through many editions.

_____. LIVES OF THE HUNTED, CONTAINING A TRUE ACCOUNT OF THE DOINGS OF FIVE QUADRUPEDS AND THREE BIRDS, AND IN ELUCIDATION OF THE SAME, OVER 200 DRAWINGS. New York: Scribner, 1901. 360 p. Illustrated, with plates.

In a note to the reader, Seton states that he has tried "to empha-size our kinship with the animals by showing that in them we can find the virtues most admired in Man." Thus, "Lobo stands for Dignity and Love-constancy; Silverspot, for Sagacity [etc.]."

_____. WILD ANIMAL WAYS, WITH 200 DRAWINGS BY THE AUTHOR. Garden City, N.Y.: Doubleday, Page, 1916. xi, 247 p. Illustrated, with plates.

An abbreviated version of this popular work, consisting of only the first four chapters, was published by Houghton Mifflin in 1916.

Wright, Mabel Osgood, and Coues, Elliot. CITIZEN BIRD: SCENES FROM BIRD LIFE IN PLAIN ENGLISH FOR BEGINNERS. New York: Macmillan, 1897. xiv, 430 p. Illustrated.

Mabel Osgood Wright (1859-1934) belongs to a group of late nine-teenth- and early twentieth-century women who were famous for their activities in the fields of nature study and bird protection. Along with Olive Thorne Miller, Anna B. Comstock, Neltje Blanchan Doubleday, and Gene Stratton Porter, Mrs. Wright did yeoman service to promote the goals of these movements. She wrote a number of books about bird life, nature stories for children, and numerous magazine articles. CITIZEN BIRD, upon which she collaborated with the noted naturalist, Elliot Coues, was a very effective and successful juvenile. Mrs. Wright's efforts in bird protection included service on the magazine BIRD-LORE, of which she was a contributing editor from 1910 until her death. She helped found the Connecticut Audubon Society in 1898, and was a director of the National Association of Audubon Societies. For biographical information, see the sketch by Robert H. Welker in NOTABLE AMERICAN WOMEN (volume 3, pp. 682-84).

8. Nature Study Periodicals

BOYS AND GIRLS; A NATURE STUDY MAGAZINE. Ithaca, N.Y.: Stephens Publishing Co., 1903-7.

NATURE MAGAZINE. Washington, D.C., and Baltimore, Md.: American Nature Association, 1923-December 1959.

Absorbed by NATURAL HISTORY. See also next item.

NATURE-STUDY REVIEW. Ithaca, N.Y., and New York City: American Nature Study Society, 1905-December 1923.

Merged with NATURE MAGAZINE (above).

B. BIRD WATCHING

Baynes, Ernest H. WILD BIRD GUESTS; HOW TO ENTERTAIN THEM. WITH CHAPTERS ON THE DESTRUCTION OF BIRDS, THEIR ECONOMIC AND AESTHETIC VALUES, SUGGESTIONS FOR DEALING WITH THEIR ENEMIES, AND ON THE ORGANIZATION AND MANAGEMENT OF BIRD CLUBS. New York: Dutton, 1915. xviii, 326 p. Illustrated, with plates. Bibliography, pp. 312-14.

> Ernest Harold Baynes (1868-1925), writer, lecturer, and bird protectionist, was the organizer of the Meriden Bird Club and sanctuary in Meriden, New Hampshire, where he made his home. The Meriden Club was a showcase for bird enthusiasts; it was so successful in creating a sympathetic climate for birds in the town that Meriden became known as "the Bird Village." WILD BIRD GUESTS is a missionary work in which Baynes zealously pursues his theme of bird conservation in the United States. He claimed to have been instrumental in organizing more than 200 bird clubs in the country.

Beidleman, Richard G. "Bird Watching--Hobby of the Half Century." AUDUBON MAGAZINE 53, no. 5 (September-October 1951): 316-23, no. 6 (November-December 1951): 368-73.

> A brief history, interestingly told and illustrated with photographs of outings and famous bird watchers.

Broun, Maurice. HAWKS ALOFT: THE STORY OF HAWK MOUNTAIN. New York: Dodd, Mead, [1949]. xvii, 222 p. Illustrated.

> The director of Hawk Mountain Sanctuary (near Hamburg, Pennsylvania) tells the story of its founding, its tribulations, and its ultimate success as the most famous hawk refuge and counting station in the United States.

Deck, Raymond S. PAGEANT IN THE SKY; A BOOK OF THE MODERN SPORT OF BIRD WATCHING. New York: Dodd, Mead, 1941. 268 p. Illustrated.

> Adventures in bird watching by a naturalist who believes that birds should be "important to everyone."

Griscom, Ludlow. MODERN BIRD STUDY. Cambridge, Mass.: Harvard University Press, 1947. 190 p. Illustrated.

Developed from a series of lectures given at Lowell Institute in 1944. The author's main theme is that bird study should not be limited to the professional scientist, and that it contains much to interest the layman.

Pearson, Thomas Gilbert. THE BIRD STUDY BOOK. Garden City, N.Y.: Doubleday, Page, 1917. 258 p. Illustrated. Photos.

Pearson was the secretary of the National Association of Audubon Societies. Although much of the material is now dated, the book is still interesting.

Peterson, Roger Tory. BIRDS OVER AMERICA. New York: Dodd, Mead, 1948. xiii, 342 p. Illustrated.

This is one of the best popular books on bird watching available. Peterson, an artist and lecturer, is the best-known ornithologist living in America today. His FIELD GUIDES, articles, and pamphlets have done much to interest thousands of Americans in the hobby of bird watching. In BIRDS OVER AMERICA, Peterson relates many of his own experiences and comments on the people who make up the players in the game of "birding."

_____. "Birders: A More Civilized Breed." NEW YORK TIMES MAGAZINE, December 17, 1967, pp. 65, 67-68, 75, 77-78.

An interesting assessment of the modern sport and a description of the characteristics of its devotees.

U.S. Bureau of Sport Fisheries and Wildlife, and the Fish and Wildlife Service. BIRDS IN OUR LIVES. Edited by Alfred Stefferud. Washington, D.C.: Government Printing Office, 1966. 561 p. Illustrated.

Intended to "achieve public support for sensitive management and conservation of birds...through a widening public understanding of birds." Topics range from sports and recreation to conservation and birds in literature and art.

Welker, Robert Henry. BIRDS AND MEN: AMERICAN BIRDS IN SCIENCE, ART, LITERATURE, AND CONSERVATION, 1800-1900. Cambridge, Mass.: Harvard University Press, 1955. 230 p. Illustrated. Bibliography, pp. 213-20.

Historical exposition of American interest in and study of birds, their treatment in literature and art, and efforts to preserve them. Among the major figures covered are Mark Catesby, Alexander Wilson, Audubon, Thoreau, Emerson, Burroughs, and Theodore Roosevelt.

C. NATURE FAKING

Adams, J. Donald. "Speaking of Books." NEW YORK TIMES BOOK REVIEW, July 8, 1956, p. 2.

> Adams looks back to the controversy and, in a fair-minded assessment, finds that, although Long's animal stories were frequently "improbable," Long himself was not the "imposter" that Roosevelt alleged (see annotations for items by Clark, Long, and Roosevelt, below). The occasion for Adams's essay was the appearance of two books: Paul R. Cutright's THEODORE ROOSEVELT, THE NATURALIST (New York: Harper, 1956) and William J. Long's THE SPIRIT OF THE WILD (Garden City, N.Y.: Doubleday, 1956).

Burroughs, John. "Real and Sham Natural History." ATLANTIC MONTHLY 91 (March 1903): 298-309.

> This article was the opening attack in the controversy. Burroughs singles out William J. Long, Ernest Thompson Seton, and Charles G.D. Roberts for impeachment.

_____. "Fake Natural History: Gold Bricks for the Editors." OUTING 49 (February 1907): 665-68.

> Further protestations about "quack nature writers" and the editors who publish their work. A large part of this essay is devoted to Harold S. Deming's articles, "Briartown Sketches," which appeared in HARPER'S MONTHLY MAGAZINE (October 1905 and May 1906). Deming replied to Burroughs in OUTING (volume 50, April 1907, pp. 124-27).

_____. "The Credible and the Incredible in Natural History." THE INDEPENDENT 62 (June 6, 1907). 1344-47.

> More examples of nature faking, but here the "fakers" aren't named.

_____. "Imagination in Natural History: A Letter from John Burroughs on the Roosevelt-Long Controversy; and a Reply." THE OUTLOOK 86 (June 29, 1907): 457-60.

> In his letter Burroughs takes the editors to task for their criticism of President Roosevelt (see "The Roosevelt-Long Controversy," THE OUTLOOK, volume 86, June 8, 1907, pp. 263-64).

_____. "President Roosevelt as a Nature Lover and Observer." THE OUTLOOK 86 (July 13, 1907): 547-53.

Burroughs, a personal friend of Roosevelt, recounts examples of the President's skill as an observer of nature.

_____. "Seeing Straight." THE INDEPENDENT 64 (January 2, 1908): 34-37.

Another attack on the "nature-fakers." Burroughs sees the main object of nature study in the schools as the teaching of children to "see straight," and not to enthrall them with animal fables or romances.

Chapman, Frank M. "The Case of William J. Long." SCIENCE, n.s. 19 (March 4, 1904): 387-89.

The thrust of Chapman's article is that Long's observational talents are so conditioned by a poetic temperament and romantic imagination that his books should not be taken seriously. Chapman was a curator at the American Museum of Natural History and a noted ornithologist.

Clark, Edward B. "Roosevelt on the Nature Fakirs." EVERYBODY'S MAGAZINE 16 (June 1907): 770-74.

The result of an interview with the President held in the White House. Roosevelt criticized Long, Roberts, and Jack London for their preposterous animal stories. Reprinted in THE WORKS OF THEODORE ROOSEVELT, National Edition, volume 5, pp. 367-74 (New York: Scribner, 1926).

_____. "Real Naturalists on Nature Faking." EVERYBODY'S MAGAZINE 17 (September 1907): 423-27.

Clark presents excerpts from essays written especially for him by leading naturalists. A devastating critique of Long's nature romances.

Ganong, W.F. "The Writings of William J. Long." SCIENCE, n.s. 19 (April 15, 1904): 623-25.

Read before the Natural History Society of New Brunswick (Canada), March 1, 1904. Criticizes both Long and Charles D.G. Roberts for humanizing animals in their works.

Hayes, Ellen. ["William J. Long."] SCIENCE, n.s. 19 (April 15, 1904): 625-66.

A defense of Long's writings.

Long, William J. "The Modern School of Nature-Study and Its Critics." NORTH AMERICAN REVIEW 176 (May 1903): 688-98.

Long (1867–1952), a graduate of Harvard, Andover Theological Seminary, and a Ph.D. from Heidelburg, was a Congregational minister and a nature writer. He was a prolific author of children's books and nature romances, mostly about animals. His writings span the years from 1900 to his death in 1952. In this essay, he defends his writings against Burroughs's article in the ATLANTIC, and reasserts his belief in the individuality of animals within the same species.

———. "Animal Surgery." THE OUTLOOK 75 (September 12, 1903): 122-27.

Long recounts several examples he had seen or heard of animals and birds that practiced self–surgery to heal wounds or broken bones. Included is the woodcock story that caused such a furor among scientists.

———. "Science, Nature and Criticism." SCIENCE, n.s. 19 (May 13, 1904): 760-67.

An answer to the author's critics who wrote in previous numbers of SCIENCE. Long presents affidavits in the "woodcock surgery" controversy.

———. NORTHERN TRAILS. SOME STUDIES OF ANIMAL LIFE IN THE FAR NORTH. Boston and London: Ginn, 1905. xxv, 390 p. Illustrated.

In a nine-page preface, Long asserts that the animals portrayed were all "true to fact." He also claimed for his animals a natural intelligence beyond the simple instinct in which his critics believed. For a contemporary opinion of his writings, see the review of NORTHERN TRAILS in THE INDEPENDENT (volume 59, October 12, 1905, pp. 873-74).

Roosevelt, Theodore. "Nature Fakers." EVERYBODY'S MAGAZINE 17 (September 1907): 427-30.

A further denunciation along the lines of Edward Clark's interview with the author (see Clark, above).

Schmitt, Peter J. "Nature Fakers." In his BACK TO NATURE: THE ARCADIAN MYTH IN URBAN AMERICA, pp. 45-55. New York: Oxford University Press, 1969.

Schmitt sketches the history of the controversy and analyzes the significance of this amusing incident in terms of the urban back-to-nature movement.

Sullivan, Mark. OUR TIMES: THE UNITED STATES, 1900-1925, vol. 3, pp. 146-62. New York and London: Scribner, 1930.

An account of Theodore Roosevelt's involvement in the controversy. Interesting and well balanced.

Wheeler, William Morton. "Woodcock Surgery." SCIENCE, n.s. 19 (February 26, 1904): 347-50.

Wheeler takes Long to task for his account of a woodcock that cured its broken leg by creating a cast from mud and straw.

Chapter 9

CAMPING AND OUTDOOR LIFE

Chapter 9

CAMPING AND OUTDOOR LIFE

This chapter presents a highly selective listing of retrospective works which illustrate the growth of camping and outdoor life in America. Group camping and the theory and practice of recreational camping are not emphasized; the reader is referred to Barbara E. Joy's BIBLIOGRAPHY ON CAMPING (below) for a comprehensive list of materials concerned with these aspects. Hunting and fishing books are also excluded; for an excellent bibliography of such works (especially about hunting), see John C. Phillips's AMERICAN GAME MAMMALS AND BIRDS (below).

This listing is divided into six main sections: general works, bibliographies, books about outdoor life, guides and handbooks, the history of outdoor youth organizations such as the Boy and Girl Scouts, and periodicals specializing in camping and outdoor life.

A. GENERAL WORKS

Busch, Henry M. "Camping." In ENCYCLOPEDIA OF THE SOCIAL SCIENCES, vol. 2, pp. 168-70. New York: Macmillan, 1930.

> A brief but useful survey of the history and significance of camping, especially as a social function.

Nash, Roderick. "The Wilderness Cult." In his WILDERNESS AND THE AMERICAN MIND, rev. ed., pp. 141-60. New Haven and London: Yale University Press, 1973.

> A valuable essay on the wilderness cult that grew up in the United States during the early years of the twentieth century. Nash discusses Joseph Knowles and his expedition into the Maine woods, John Muir, mountaineering clubs, and the Boy Scouts. Of relevant interest are portions of Peter J. Schmitt's BACK TO NATURE: THE ARCADIAN MYTH IN URBAN AMERICA (New York: Oxford University Press, 1969).

B.   BIBLIOGRAPHIES

Joy, Barbara Ellen. ANNOTATED BIBLIOGRAPHY ON CAMPING. Minneapolis: Burgess Publishing Co., 1963. v, 126 p.

This is a remarkable labor of love by a long-time official of the American Camping Association. Based upon several earlier compilations by the A.C.A., this edition contains 1640 titles arranged topically by title. The thrust of the book is organized camping, and it is intended for use primarily by camp administrators, group leaders, and counselors. Contents include: administration and organization; camping-out, woodlore, and conservation activities; church camping--religious and spiritual emphasis; family camping; health, safety, and sanitation; leadership; outdoor cookery; programs and activities; school and outdoor education; standards; bibliographies, buying guides and directories; and agencies, associations, clubs, societies, etc. The section on camping-out is especially valuable for works on the history and significance of camping in the United States and contains many valuable late nineteenth- and twentieth-century works.

Phillips, John C., comp. AMERICAN GAME MAMMALS AND BIRDS: A CATALOGUE OF BOOKS, 1582-1925, SPORT, NATURAL HISTORY AND CONSERVATION. Boston: Houghton Mifflin, 1930. 639 p.

The title page announces that the book is presented "With the Approval of the Boone and Crocket Club." Reprinted from the same plates and retitled A BIBLIOGRAPHY OF AMERICAN SPORTING BOOKS; SPORT, NATURAL HISTORY, HUNTING, DOGS, TRAPPING, SHOOTING, EARLY AMERICAN TRAVEL, FISHING, SPORTING PERIODICALS, GUIDE BOOKS, FORESTRY, CONSERVATION, ETC. (Boston: Edward Morrill, n.d.). Although the overwhelming majority of books in this bibliography relate to hunting, travel, and natural history, a considerable number of titles about camping and woodlore are scattered throughout its pages. Unfortunately, there is neither a subject guide to the main listings (by author) nor an index; therefore, desirable titles are difficult to locate. Two separate sections on "Railroad Guides..." and "Other Guides, Advertising Pamphlets, Manuals of Woodcraft," although short, are useful. Another section, "Periodicals: Outdoor Sports, Shooting, Fishing and Camping" (pp. 613-30), contains a useful unannotated listing of popular magazines.

C.   OUTDOOR LIFE

Eaton, Walter Pritchard. SKYLINE CAMPS; A NOTEBOOK OF A WANDERER IN OUR WESTERN MOUNTAINS. Boston and Chicago: W.A. Wilde, 1922. 245 p. Illustrated.

Camping expeditions to Glacier Park, Crater Lake, and other points in the Cascade Mountains. Eaton writes also of his hopes for an Appalachian Trail and reservation.

Ferguson, Melville F. MOTOR CAMPING ON WESTERN TRAILS. New York and London: Century Co., 1925. xix, 300 p. Illustrated. Maps on endpapers.

The lively adventures of an easterner who, influenced by a magazine article on automobile touring, took his family of eight on an 18,000-mile trip through the United States and Hawaii. The family used two automobiles and two specially equipped trailers for the twelve-month trip. A remarkable story. Contains practical suggestions on camping, equipment, and methods.

Frazer, Elizabeth. "Young America Takes to the Wilds." SATURDAY EVENING POST 198 (May 22, 1926): 48-50, 68, 70, 72.

"The organized private summer camp is an institution peculiarly American." The article discusses the growth of these camps and changes in their organization and personnel. Camp activities emphasize land and water sports, arts and crafts, hiking, nature study, woodcraft, pack making, fire making, and trail marking. The main purpose of the program was to build character. The author gives an enthusiastic description of one day in a girls' camp.

Knowles, Joseph. ALONE IN THE WILDERNESS. ILLUSTRATED FROM DRAWINGS ON BIRCH BARK, MADE BY THE AUTHOR IN THE WOODS WITH BURNT STICKS FROM HIS FIRE, TOGETHER WITH PHOTOGRAPHS TAKEN BEFORE AND AFTER HIS EXPERIENCES. Boston: Small, Maynard, 1913. 295 p. Illustrated.

On August 4, 1913, Joseph Knowles entered the woods of northern Maine without clothes, tools, or implements and remained there, living off the land, until October 4. Knowles's experiences are related in this book. Despite critics who claimed that he was a fraud and that he had lived in a comfortable cabin for the two months, the book sold over 300,000 copies. Knowles himself was lionized, and he spent much time lecturing and promoting the primitive life. Regardless of the veracity of his experiences, Knowles's story, and its reception by the believing public, is an interesting sidelight on the cult of the primitive. An English edition appeared in 1914. For additional information, see the following articles:

Boyer, Richard O. "Where Are They Now? The Nature Man." NEW YORKER 14 (June 18, 1938): 21-25.

Holbrook, Stewart H. "The Original Nature Man." AMERICAN MERCURY 39, no. 156 (December 1936): 417-25. Reprinted in his LITTLE ANNIE OAKELY AND

OTHER RUGGED PEOPLE, pp. 8-18 (New York: Macmillan, 1948).

Lockley, Fred. "Interesting People: A Modern Cave Man." AMERICAN MAGAZINE 91, no. 1 (January 1921): 8.

Nash, Roderick. "The American Cult of the Primitive." AMERICAN QUARTERLY 18, no. 3 (Fall 1966): 517-37. Reprinted in a revised version in his WILDERNESS AND THE AMERICAN MIND, rev. ed., chap. 9 (New Haven: Yale University Press, 1973).

Rinehart, Mary Roberts. THE OUT TRAIL. New York: George H. Doran, 1923. x, 246 p. Illustrated.

Camping, fishing, and riding adventures in the United States, mainly in the West. Aimed at the women's market as a kind of "you can do it too" book.

Rowlands, John J. CACHE LAKE COUNTRY: LIFE IN THE NORTH WOODS. Illustrated by Henry B. Kane. New York: Norton, 1947. 272 p. Maps on endpapers.

An intimate and colorful picture of life through the seasons in the forest and lake country south of Hudson's Bay. The author, a timber cruiser for a lumber company, and his neighbors Tibeash, an old Cree Indian chief, and the artist Henry B. Kane, develop a north woods camaraderie thirty-two miles from the nearest settlement. The book combines natural history and woodcraft with wilderness survival, hunting, and fishing experiences. Kane's illustrations and marginal drawings enhance this remarkably good book.

Seton, Ernest Thompson. TWO LITTLE SAVAGES, BEING THE ADVENTURES OF TWO BOYS WHO LIVED AS INDIANS AND WHAT THEY LEARNED. With Over Two Hundred Drawings. New York: Doubleday, Page, 1903. xvii, 552 p.

Based on Seton's adolescent adventures in Canada during the 1870s, parts of this best seller are thinly veiled autobiography. Millions of copies of TWO LITTLE SAVAGES have been sold and the book remains in print. In BY A THOUSAND FIRES (below), Julia Seton told the story of how Seton came to write TWO LITTLE SAVAGES. It is probable that thousands of American children have been influenced by Seton's book.

. TRAIL OF AN ARTIST-NATURALIST: THE AUTOBIOGRAPHY OF ERNEST THOMPSON SETON. With illustrations by the Author. New York: Scribner, 1940. 412 p. Frontispiece. Plates.

During his long life, Seton became famous as an artist-illustrator, naturalist, author, outdoorsman, founder of the Woodcraft League,

and one of the early leaders of the Boy Scouts. His outdoor
books, mostly about animals, were very popular, although now
nearly all are out of print. He illustrated all of his own books
as well as books by others written before his own became popular.
In addition to his popular writing and illustrating, Seton also
published several natural history studies of wild birds and animals,
including one for the Smithsonian Institution. The autobiography
is a good source of information for events prior to about 1900,
but it compresses details thereafter and closes in 1930. No mention at all is made of Seton's role in the Boy Scout movement.
For other books by Seton see Chapter 8, Section A7: Popular
Books on Nature Study.

_____. ERNEST THOMPSON SETON'S AMERICA: SELECTIONS FROM THE
WRITINGS OF THE ARTIST-NATURALIST. Edited, with an introduction, by
Farida A. Wiley. Contributions by Julia M. Seton. New York: Devin-
Adair, 1954. xxiii, 413 p. Illustrated.

A useful selection enhanced by Miss Wiley's introduction. Illustrated with drawings by Seton. Includes a list of his books.

Seton, Grace Gallatin. A WOMAN TENDERFOOT. New York: Doubleday,
Page, 1900. 361 p. Illustrated.

The author, Seton's first wife, relates her outdoor experiences with
her husband in the Rocky Mountains and Canada. Included is a
long chapter addressed to the woman who goes hunting with her
husband.

_____. NIMROD'S WIFE. Pictures by Walker King Stone and Ernest Thomp-
son Seton. New York: Doubleday, Page, 1907. 406 p. Illustrated.

Hunting and camping experiences in the Sierra, the Rockies,
eastern Canada, and Norway. Nimrod, of course, is Seton.

Seton, Julia M. BY A THOUSAND FIRES; NATURE NOTES AND EXTRACTS
FROM THE LIFE AND UNPUBLISHED JOURNALS OF ERNEST THOMPSON
SETON. Garden City, N.Y.: Doubleday, 1967. xiv, 27 p. Illustrated.

A charming and nostalgic portrayal of Seton by his wife. Drawn
from his published and unpublished works and from personal reminiscences, the book gives interesting sidelights on Seton's career not
found in other sources.

White, Stewart Edward. THE FOREST. New York: Outlook Co., 1903.
276 p. Illustrated, with plates.

Stewart Edward White was a prolific writer, a novelist, and an
outdoorsman. His "wilderness" novels enriched him and made it
possible for him to indulge his passion for the outdoors. The four

outdoor books listed here are well written and were very popular.
THE FOREST is set somewhere in the "North Woods" and includes
information on how to camp, woodcraft, and "going light."

_____. THE MOUNTAINS. Illustrated by Ferdnand Lungren. New York:
McClure, Phillips, 1904. 282 p. Illustrated. Reprint ed., 1910.

The events related herein were based upon an actual trip taken
by White and some companions from the coast, near Santa Barbara,
California, over the Coast Range, through the arid lands south of
Bakersfield, and into the Sierra Nevada.

_____. THE PASS. New York: Outing Publishing Co., 1906. viii, 198 p.
Illustrated. Map. Reprint eds., 1912, 1925.

Based upon an actual trip made in 1905 by White and his wife.
The locale is the mountains and passes of the Kings Canyon area
of the Sierra Nevada. Illustrated with thirteen half-tones.

_____. THE CABIN. Illustrated with photographs by the author. Garden
City, N.Y.: Doubleday, Page, 1911. 282 p.

White and his wife Elizabeth (called "Billy" in the book) built a
rustic cabin in the central Sierra near the 6,500 feet elevation.
The book recounts their adventures with nature and visits with
forest rangers, lumber men, sheepmen, and casual visitors.

Whitney, Caspar. "What We Stand For." "Outdoor America" Section,
COLLIER'S WEEKLY 42 (March 13, 1909): 15.

Caspar Whitney was the editor of OUTING from 1900 to 1909. When
that magazine was sold to new owners, Whitney moved to COLLIER'S
where he edited a new monthly section, called "Outdoor America,"
which later became a magazine supplement in COLLIER'S and had
its own contributors. In "What We Stand For," Whitney's first
editorial, he tells his readers that "Outdoor America" aims at
nothing less than the conversion of Americans to outdoorsmen.
A fascinating and ebullient piece of outdoors propaganda.

D. GUIDES AND HANDBOOKS

There are many guides and handbooks to outdoor life, camping, woodcraft, and
wilderness survival. What follows is a highly selective list of the better-known
and significant works, with a heavy emphasis upon older titles.

Bangor and Aroostook Railroad Company. HAUNTS OF THE HUNTED; THE
VACATIONER'S GUIDE TO MAINE'S GREAT NORTH COUNTRY. Written
and Arranged by Fred H. Clifford. Bangor, Me.: 1903. 184 p. Illustrated,

with plates. Folding map.

As early as 1895, the Bangor and Aroostook Railroad began issuing
promotional guides to the Maine back-country, but in 1900 the
company brought out an attractive yearly series, "In the Maine
Woods," intended to draw affluent eastern outdoorsmen to visit
the scenic wonders of "B&A country." THE HAUNTS OF THE
HUNTED, the fourth in the series, is cited here not only as an
interesting work in its own right, but as an example of a large
body of promotional literature issued by American railroads.
Pages 130-84 contain advertisements.

Beard, Daniel Carter. THE BOY PIONEERS, SONS OF DANIEL BOONE.
New York: Scribner, 1909. xiii, 329 p. Illustrated.

This is the "official" manual for the Society of the Sons of Daniel
Boone, founded by Beard. It is, like all of Beard's books for
boys, a how-to-do-it book of woodcraft knowledge. Although the
Society dissolved after the Boy Scouts were established and Beard
became their Commissioner, this book was so popular that it was
reissued in 1914, 1919, 1925, and 1932.

_____. BUCKSKIN BOOK FOR BUCKSKIN MEN AND BOYS. Philadelphia
and London: Lippincott, 1929. 326 p. Illustrated.

Although written as a how-to-do-it book on camping, woodcraft,
and handicraft for both men and boys, its obvious appeal was to
youngsters. It contains twenty-five chapters about such skills as
the creation of buckskin clothing and making and setting traps,
all of which are illustrated with ninety-one drawings by Beard.

_____. HARDLY A MAN IS NOW ALIVE; THE AUTOBIOGRAPHY OF DAN
BEARD. New York: Doubleday, Doran, 1939. xii, 361 p. Illustrated, with
plates.

Dan Beard (1850-1941), affectionately known as "Uncle Dan"
to thousands of Boy Scouts, was one of the principal leaders in
the Scout organization. Before joining the Boy Scouts, Beard founded
the Sons of Daniel Boone and the Boy Pioneers. He began his
career as a surveyor but moved on to magazine and book illustration. After being invited to illustrate Mark Twain's A CONNECTI-
CUT YANKEE, he and Twain became good friends. Beard began
writing at the age of thirty-two and completed over twenty outdoor
books for boys. He was for many years National Scout Commissioner of the Boy Scouts of America. His autobiography is charming
and valuable, although he devotes less than ten pages to his
affiliation with the Scouts. His own illustrations adorn the volume.

Breck, Edward. THE WAY OF THE WOODS; A MANUAL FOR SPORTSMEN
IN NORTHEASTERN UNITED STATES AND CANADA. New York and London:
Putnam, 1908. xvii, 436 p. Illustrated, with plates. 18 cm.

A comprehensive manual for sportsmen and campers; highly recommended in contemporary reviews. It contains all the usual chapters
on camping, fishing, hunting, woodcraft, canoeing, trapping, and
hygiene; in addition, it includes a chapter for the novice on
photography. Most chapters have references to recommended books
and a final chapter on nature books is valuable for a contemporary
view of outdoor literature by a respected member of the "eastern
establishment." The author had an astounding career spanning
work as an editor, foreign correspondent, diplomat, U.S. Navy
secret agent during the Spanish-American War and World War I,
and as an author and lecturer. He was also a contributor to the
DICTIONARY OF AMERICAN BIOGRAPHY.

Brower, David R., ed. GOING LIGHT WITH BACKPACK OR BURRO. San
Francisco: Sierra Club, 1951. xiv, 152 p. Illustrated. Appendices. Bibliography, pp. 149-52.

Perhaps the best of the many handbooks for wilderness travel and
camping. The manual emphasizes those activities and practices
that are the least damaging to the environment.

Gibson, William Hamilton. CAMP LIFE IN THE WOODS AND THE TRICKS
OF TRAPPING AND TRAP MAKING. New York and London: Harper, 1881.
xvi, 300 p. Illustrated.

Based upon an earlier work, THE COMPLETE AMERICAN TRAPPER
(1876). Although this book was relatively successful, Gibson
was not a noted outdoorsman. His fame rests largely upon his
nature books (see Chapter 7, Section C: Nature Writing Since
Thoreau) and his illustrations, many of which appeared in well-
known books such as William Cullen Bryant's PICTURESQUE AMERI-
CA (see chapter 2, Section D2: The Appalachia Region, General).

Gould, John Mead. HINTS FOR CAMPING AND WALKING. HOW TO
CAMP OUT. New York: Scribner, Armstrong, 1877. 134 p. Illustrated.

The use of military phrases throughout this book and references to
the suitability of army tents, camp kits, etc., are evidence of the
author's military background. An air of gentility pervades the
book and makes it quaint by today's standards: "By all means
keep a diary"; "Be social and agreeable to all fellow travellers";
"Women should not depart so far from home as men do."

Hanks, Charles Stedman. CAMP KITS AND CAMP LIFE. New York: Scribner,
1906. xii, 259 p. Illustrated, with plates. 22 1/2 x 13 cm.

A popular handbook. The author wrote a number of outdoor books
under the pseudonym "Niblick."

Hough, Emerson. OUT OF DOORS. New York and London: D. Appleton,
1915. vii, 300 p.

A how-to-do-it book on camping addressed to the tenderfoot with
an amusing chapter devoted to the "woman in camp." In 1916
Appleton brought out a similar book by Hough, entitled LET US
GO AFIELD, on fishing, hunting, and game birds.

Jessup, Elon H. ROUGHING IT SMOOTHLY; HOW TO AVOID VACATION
PITFALLS. New York and London: Putnam, 1923. xiv, 274 p. Illustrated,
with plates.

The author, an editor of OUTING MAGAZINE, wrote a number
of books on camping, skiing, and other outdoor sports. This book
was aimed at the urban dweller with little or no outdoor experience.

Kephart, Horace. THE BOOK OF CAMPING AND WOODCRAFT; A GUIDE-
BOOK FOR THOSE WHO TRAVEL IN THE WILDERNESS. New York: Outing
Publishing Co., 1906. xiv, 321 p. Illustrated, with plates.

A vade mecum of outfitting, camping equipment, marksmanship,
cooking, first aid, woodcraft, living off the country, tanning
pelts, and many other topics. (See also next item.)

_____. CAMPING AND WOODCRAFT; A HANDBOOK FOR VACATION
CAMPERS AND FOR TRAVELLERS IN THE WILDERNESS. 2 vols. New York:
Outing Publishing Co., 1916-17. Illustrated.

Based upon Kephart's earlier work (above). The author, who was
famous as a writer on the outdoors, shooting, and camping, became
known as the "Dean of American Campers." Before moving to the
Smokies in 1904, Kephart had been a librarian at the St. Louis
Mercantile Library. He also became one of the principal founders
of the Great Smoky Mountains National Park. CAMPING AND
WOODCRAFT appeared in twenty editions between 1917 and 1960
and was, with G.W. Sears's book (below), one of the two most
popular books of its kind ever published in the United States.
For a good sketch of Kephart in the Smokies, see Michael Frome's
"Horace Kephart," Chapter 12 of his STRANGERS IN HIGH PLACES
(Garden City, N.Y.: Doubleday, 1966).

Murray, William Henry Harrison. ADVENTURES IN THE WILDERNESS, OR
CAMP-LIFE IN THE ADIRONDACKS. Boston: Fields, Osgood, 1869. vi,
236 p. Illustrated.

See annotation for this item in Chapter 2, Section D6: The
Adirondack Mountains.

Rutstrum, Calvin. THE NEW WAY OF THE WILDERNESS. New York: Macmillan, 1958. ix, 276 p. Illustrated.

A how-to-do-it book for wilderness travel, camping, and survival
by an experienced wilderness guide and author.

Sears, George Washington [Nessmuk] (1821-90)

Sears, better known by his pen name Nessmuk, is a remarkable phenomenon in the annals of American outdoor literature. His fame is largely derived from his one slender book on camping entitled WOODCRAFT (below). Although by no means the first manual on the subject, WOODCRAFT must be considered the most successful, since it has gone through more editions, and remained in print longer, than any other work in the field.

Sears was fifty-nine when he took his first trip to the Adirondacks, an area to which he was drawn by his reading of Verplanck Colvin's survey reports. Before his first visit to the Adirondacks, Sears had tramped around much of North America, served on a whaling ship, been a miner in Colorado, worked as a trail driver and cowboy in Texas, traveled in Arizona and Oregon, and hunted and fished extensively in the wilds of northern Michigan in the 1840s and 1850s. He had also made two trips to the jungles of the Amazon in 1867 and 1870.

Sears wrote outdoor material for the ATLANTIC, ALDINE'S, LIP-PINCOTT'S, PUTNAM'S, and other periodicals (all without signifi- cant profit) before he began his successful association with FOREST AND STREAM in the 1880s.

Nessmuk. WOODCRAFT. Forest and Stream Series, vol. 3. New York: Forest and Stream, 1884. vi, 149 p. Illustrated. 17 cm.

WOODCRAFT went through many editions (see headnote, above). An edited and slightly abridged version, pub- lished by Dover in 1963, is still in print.

THE ADIRONDACK LETTERS OF GEORGE WASHINGTON SEARS, WHOSE PEN NAME WAS "NESSMUK." With explanatory notes and a brief biography by Dan Brenan. Blue Mountain Lake, N.Y.: The Adirondack Museum, 1962. 177 p. Illustrated. (Distributed by Syracuse University Press, Syracuse, N.Y.)

Reprints eighteen letters that originally appeared in FOREST AND STREAM between 1880 and 1883. Of Sears's many contri- butions to that magazine, these letters describe three cruises in Adirondack waters in canoes especially built for him by America's foremost boat and canoe builder, J. Henry Rushton of Canton, N.Y. "Nessmuk's" letters are redolent of the North Woods. They describe his canoe trips, portages, camp- ing, fishing, and hunting experiences, and give excellent accounts of famous Adirondack guides, hotels, and camps. At the time of Sears' cruises he was already suffering from the early stages of tuberculosis, a condition (exacerbated by malaria contracted in Florida in 1886) that caused his death in 1890.

White, Stewart Edward. CAMP AND TRAIL. New York: Outing Publishing Co., 1907. vii, 236 p. Illustrated.

> Camping, hiking, canoeing, packing, and campcraft combined with anecdotes about White's personal experiences. Originally appeared in OUTING.

E. OUTDOOR ORGANIZATIONS FOR YOUTH

1. The Boy Scouts

The literature of the Boy Scouts is extremely voluminous, much of it issuing from the organization's own press. THE NATIONAL UNION CATALOG: PRE-1956 IMPRINTS (see Chapter 11, Section B: National Library Catalogs) contains over twenty-five three-column pages of entries for books published by the Scouts--outdoor crafts, hobbies, song books, sports, civil defense manuals, and books for scoutmasters and executives. All of this literature relates only to the Boy Scouts of America, and not to the international movement (which is not covered in this bibliography). Although there has been an enormous amount of popular periodical literature, scholars have shown little interest in the Scouting movement. Peter J. Schmitt devotes a chapter, "Backwoods Brotherhoods," in his BACK TO NATURE: THE ARCADIAN MYTH IN URBAN AMERICA (see Chapter 1, Section A: General Studies) to the movement, in which he briefly describes the founding and organization of the Boy Scouts, Woodcraft Indians, and related youth groups.

Arthurs, Frank B. "Boy Scouts Building for Manhood." OUTING MAGAZINE 57, no. 3 (December 1910): 276-84.

> See next item.

Beard, Daniel Carter. "The Boy Scouts of America." AMERICAN REVIEW OF REVIEWS 44 (October 1911): 429-38.

> This article and Arthurs's (above) give useful contemporary views of the aims and activities of the Boy Scouts.

Davis, Christopher. "The Boy Scouts." ESQUIRE 64, no. 1 (July 1965): 69-71, 102.

> A journalistic overview of the Scout movement, including brief looks at the people in the national headquarters.

Murray, William D. THE HISTORY OF THE BOY SCOUTS OF AMERICA. New York: Boy Scouts of America, 1937. vii, 574 p. Illustrated. Portraits. Diagrams. "Literature of the Movement," pp. 391-416.

> This is the official organizational history. Too often pedestrian

in style, and poorly structured, Murray's work leaves much to be desired.

THE NATURE ALMANAC: A HANDBOOK OF NATURE EDUCATION. Washington, D.C.: American Nature Association, 1930. 399 p.

Information about the program, current to 1930, history, and activities of the Boy Scouts, Girl Scouts, and Camp Fire Girls may be found on pages 46-55.

Oursler, William C. THE BOY SCOUT STORY. Garden City, N.Y.: Doubleday, 1955. 253 p. Chronology, pp. 239-50. Bibliography, pp. 251-53.

Although not a formally documented history, Oursler's story is more interesting and useful than Murray's earlier work (above). The main outlines of the Scout movement are made clear and the bibliography and chronology are helpful.

Seton, Ernest Thompson. BOY SCOUTS OF AMERICA; A HANDBOOK OF WOODCRAFT, SCOUTING AND LIFE CRAFT...WITH WHICH IS INCORPORATED BY ARRANGEMENT GENERAL SIR ROBERT BADEN-POWELL'S SCOUTING FOR BOYS. New York: Published for the Boy Scouts of America, by Doubleday, Page, 1910. xxi, 192 p. Illustrated.

For this first official handbook of the Boy Scouts, Seton drew upon his many articles on woodcraft and scouting which had appeared in periodicals during 1886-1905. The copyright statement indicates that the handbook is the ninth edition of Seton's BIRCH-BARK ROLL. Combined with Baden-Powell's SCOUTING FOR BOYS, it contains little original material apart from a special introduction and a preface. Seton was Chief Scout of the Boy Scouts, a position he held from 1910-14, after which time he resigned his position and turned his attention to his Woodcraft League.

Sheppard, R. Z. "Trustworthy, Loyal, Thrifty...and Relevant." TIME 100, no. 10 (September 4, 1972): 61.

A perceptive review of the eighth edition of the Boy Scout handbook, now called simply SCOUT HANDBOOK. The sections on nature and woodcraft have been de-emphasized and replaced by material on "relevant" contemporary problems such as drug use, water pollution, and family problems.

Tillery, Floyd. "Little Babbitts." THE FORUM 84 (December 1930): 338-42.

Highly critical of the Boy Scouts. Tillery said the movement was taken over from "men of vision" like Seton by "high pressure executives who could engineer programs and commandeer millionaires." The author claimed that the Rotarians and Kiwanians supported the

Boy Scouts in order to instill Americanism, and that outings were like "Sunday school picnics."

In addition to the titles listed above, the reader is here referred to some of the more important publications of the Boy Scouts of America (and to the book by Levy about the Scouts):

HANDBOOK FOR BOYS. New York: 1910--.

Title varies.

THE HOW BOOK OF SCOUTING. New York: 1917. 420 p. Illustrated.

Subtitle varies. In print unitl 1942.

ANNUAL REPORT TO THE CONGRESS. 8th report for the year ending 1917. Washington, D.C.: Government Printing Office, 1918--.

National Council. BIBLIOGRAPHY OF STUDIES ON SCOUTING. New York: [1938]. 25 leaves. Mimeographed.

Much of the material listed is of the nature of research reports, nearly all sociological.

Grant, Bruce, ed. THE BOY SCOUT ENCYCLOPEDIA. Text and illustrations prepared under the direction of the Boy Scouts of America. Chicago: Rand McNally, [1965]. 168 p.

Levy, Harold P. BUILDING A POPULAR MOVEMENT: A CASE STUDY OF THE PUBLIC RELATIONS OF THE BOY SCOUTS OF AMERICA. New York: Russell Sage, 1944. 165 p.

Michigan. University of. Survey Research Center. A STUDY OF THE BOY SCOUTS AND THEIR SCOUTMASTERS. Conducted... for National Council, Boy Scouts of America.... [Ann Arbor, Mich.]: 1959. viii, 418 p.

2. The Woodcraft League

Seton, Ernest Thompson. "Ernest Thompson Seton's Boys." LADIES HOME JOURNAL 19, no. 6 (May 1902): 15, 41; no. 7 (June 1902): 15; no. 8 (July 1902): 17; no. 9 (August 1902): 16; no. 10 (September 1902): 15; no. 11 (October 1902): 14; no. 12 (November 1902): 14.

Seton organized his first group of "Indians" on his Cos Cob,

Connecticut, estate in 1900. Two years later he wrote this series of articles, subtitled "The New Department of American Woodcraft for Boys," which was aimed at developing interest in a national movement. In the seven articles, all illustrated by Seton, he deals on a how-to-do-it level with animal behavior, trailing and tracking, hunting with bows and arrows, construction of teepees, making of Indian head dresses, and general woodcraft. Much of this material was incorporated into his BIRCH BARK ROLL.

_____. THE BIRCH-BARK ROLL OF WOODCRAFT. New York, 1902-31.

This is the manual of the Woodcraft Indians. Its title and imprint vary. The ninth edition appeared as BOY SCOUTS OF AMERICA; A HANDBOOK OF WOODCRAFT, SCOUTING AND LIFE CRAFT (above), which was the first official handbook of the Scouts. Other noteworthy editions of the manual are

THE BOOK OF WOODCRAFT AND INDIAN LORE WITH OVER 500 DRAWINGS BY THE AUTHOR. [11th ed]. Garden City, N.Y.: Doubleday, Page, 1912. xxi, 567 p.

MANUAL OF THE WOODCRAFT INDIANS; THE FOUR-TEENTH BIRCH-BARK ROLL, CONTAINING THEIR CONSTITUTION, LAWS, AND DEEDS, AND MUCH ADDITIONAL MATTER. Garden City, N.Y.: Double-day, Page 1915. xviii, 105 p. Illustrated.

THE BIRCH BARK ROLL OF WOODCRAFT, TWENTY-FIRST EDITION OF THE MANUAL, FOR BOYS AND GIRLS FROM 4 TO 94. n.p., 1927. xxxi, 493 p. Illustrated.

THE BIRCH BARK ROLL OF WOODCRAFT. THE 29TH EDITION OF THE MANUAL FOR BOYS AND GIRLS FROM 4 TO 94. Revised by Julia M. Buttree. New York: A.S. Barnes, 1931. xii, 268 p. Illustrated. Diagrams.

Julia Buttree's revision was the last edition of THE BIRCH BARK ROLL. Soon after it was brought out, Miss Buttree and Seton married.

_____. "The Boy Scouts in America." THE OUTLOOK 95 (July 23, 1910): 630-35.

This is an early account of the founding of the Woodcraft Indians. Parts of the account were used by Seton in his autobiography (above) and elsewhere. Only the last few paragraphs deal with the Boy Scouts.

_____. THE RISE OF THE WOODCRAFT INDIANS. Privately Published, [c.1928]. Pamphlet.

Reprinted as pages 344-54 of ERNEST THOMPSON SETON'S AMERICA (above). Describes how the "Indians" were formed by

Seton in 1900.

_____. "The Woodcraft League or College of Indian Wisdom." HOMILETIC REVIEW (N.Y.) 101 (June 1931): 434-39.

> Seton, from his Woodcraft League headquarters near Santa Fe, New Mexico, sets forth his vision of the League's purpose: to create "for my people, a figure of perfect manhood, a being physically robust, an athlete...wise in the ways of the woods, sagacious in council, dignified, courteous, respectful to all...." This ideal figure was, of course, based upon that of the American Indian. Seton discusses the League's aims of education (manhood, not scholarship), the rise of instincts in building character, and the adherence "to honors by standards, not by competition."

Sykes, M'Cready. "Let's Play Indian: Making A New American Boy Through Woodcraft." EVERYBODY'S MAGAZINE 23 (October 1910): 473-83.

> The author visited a meeting of the Woodcraft Indians at "Wyndy-goul," Seton's country place at Cos Cob, Connecticut. Sykes's description of the council fire, the awarding of "coups" and feathers for woodcraft achievement, and the heavy reliance upon Indian trappings and lore, is an excellent contemporary record. The author gives too much credit to Seton for organization of the Boy Scouts which were, at that time, in an embryonic stage of development.

3. The Camp Fire Girls

Buckler, Helen; Fiedler, Mary F.; and Allen, Martha F. WO-HE-LO, THE STORY OF CAMP FIRE GIRLS, 1910-1960. New York: Holt, Rinehart and Winston, 1961. x, 308 p. Illustrated. Bibliography, pp. 293-98.

> The principal founder of the Camp Fire Girls was Dr. Luther H. Gulick, then a member of the Russell Sage Foundation. Other early leaders were Mrs. Ernest Thompson Seton, Lina Beard (Dan Beard's sister), and Mrs. Gulick, who created the motto of the Camp Fire Girls, "Wo-He-Lo," taken from the first two letters of the words work, health, and love. This is a comprehensive and well researched narrative.

Camp Fire Girls. THE BOOK OF THE CAMP FIRE GIRLS. New York, 1913--.

> The official Camp Fire Girls' magazine, WOHELO, was published from July 1913 to July 1920 when the name was changed to EVERYGIRLS; this latter continued through June/July 1933; THE GUARDIAN, MAGAZINE FOR LEADERS, appeared from 1922 to September 1944, continuing as THE CAMP FIRE GIRL, 1944 to date.

Davis, Hartley. "The Camp Fire Girls." THE OUTLOOK 101 (May 25, 1912): 181-89.

> The Camp Fire Girls were organized in March 1912, two months
> before this article appeared. Davis wrote it in collaboration with
> Charlotte Vetter Gulick. It is a useful piece, though frankly
> promotional in nature. Although the Camp Fire Girls had a
> strong outdoor focus like the Boy Scouts, the girls had to keep
> to their natural "division." "Boys may be scouts; but girls are
> going to keep the place to which the scout must return," and
> that place was the campfire, an outdoor substitute for the hearth,
> the "natural" feminine habitat. Illustrated.

Gulick, Charlotte Vetter. "What the Camp Fire Girls Stand For." LADIES' HOME JOURNAL 29, no. 7 (July 1912): 51.

> Written by one of the founders. In this article Mrs. Gulick makes
> a comparison between the Boy Scouts and the Camp Fire Girls.
> "Scouting is a masculine activity; keeping the fire burning in a
> camp or home is a feminine activity." The ranks for the girls
> were called "Wood Gatherer," "Fire Maker," and "Torch Bearer."
> Laws and chants of the Camp Fire Girls are quoted and costumes
> are discussed and illustrated with photographs. "The Camp Fire
> Girls is an agency for showing girls how to form their own charac-
> ters." Play acting grownup roles (cooking, sewing, knitting, and
> other feminine duties) in the spirit of fun was to prepare the girl
> for adulthood.

Loomis, C. Frances. "The Program of the Camp Fire Girls." JOURNAL OF HOME ECONOMICS 24, no. 7 (July 1932): 588-94.

> The author discusses the aims of the founders of the movement.
> The emphasis is upon the educational value of "life situations"
> and "family relationships." The objective of the Girls was to
> "cultivate...an attitude of interest, responsibility, and self-respect
> regarding their homes and the activities that center in the home."
> The author credits Mrs. Gulick and Ernest Thompson Seton with
> seeing the educational possibilities of Indian trappings, primitive
> crafts, and "the cultural value of Indian tradition, music, folk-
> lore, arts and handicrafts."

4. The Girl Scouts

The founding of the Girl Scouts was due to the actions of one well-to-do
American woman from Savannah, Georgia, Mrs. Juliette Gordon Low. Having
lived in England for many years after her marriage, Mrs. Low became interested
in the Girl Guides, after becoming a friend of Sir Robert Baden-Powell and
his sister, Agnes Baden-Powell. The Baden-Powells were the founders of the
English Boy Scouts and the Girl Guides. Mrs. Low brought the idea to Savannah, where she founded several troops of the Girl Guides in 1912. She went

on to develop a national organization for her Guides, changing the name to the Girl Scouts in 1913.

Choate, Anne Hyde, and Ferris, Helen, eds. JULIETTE LOW AND THE GIRL SCOUTS; THE STORY OF AN AMERICAN WOMAN, 1860-1927. Garden City, N.Y.: Published for Girl Scouts, Inc., by Doubleday, Doran, 1928. xxv, 271 p. Plates. Portraits.

> A compilation of previously unpublished essays about Mrs. Low by members of her family and by associates in the Girl Scouts movement. The book was published a year after Mrs. Low's death as a tribute to a remarkable woman. Reissued in 1946 by the Girl Scouts.

Girl Scouts of the United States of America. SCOUTING FOR GIRLS; OFFICIAL HANDBOOK OF THE GIRL SCOUTS. New York: 1920-29. Later editions with title GIRL SCOUT HANDBOOK. New York: 1929--.

> See next two items.

Hoxie, W. J. HOW GIRLS CAN HELP THEIR COUNTRY, ADAPTED FROM THE HANDBOOK OF AGNES BADEN-POWELL AND SIR ROBERT BADEN-POWELL. New York: Knickerbocker Press, 1913. vi, 147 p. Frontispiece. Illustrated, with plates.

> This was the first "handbook" for the Girl Scouts. Shultz and Lawrence (below) claim that it is likely that Mrs. Low contributed some parts of the book, although her name does not appear in the book as a contributor. See also next item.

[Low, Juliette Gordon]. HOW GIRLS CAN HELP THEIR COUNTRY, ADAPTED FROM AGNES BADEN-POWELL AND SIR ROBERT BADEN-POWELL'S HANDBOOK. [Savannah, Ga.: Press of M.S. & D.A. Byck Co.], 1916. vi, 156 p. Frontispiece. Illustrated, with plates. Reading list, pp. 138-48. 17 cm.

> This is a revision by Mrs. Lowe of Hoxie's earlier work. Later editions follow the format established by the Boy Scouts.

Shultz, Gladys Denny, and Lawrence, Daisy Gordon. LADY FROM SAVANNAH: THE LIFE OF JULIETTE LOW. Philadelphia and New York: Lippincott, 1958. 383 p. Illustrated.

> This is a remarkably warm and perceptive biography of Juliette ("Daisy") Gordon Low. The coauthor, Mrs. Lawrence, is the niece of Mrs. Low, and "the first Girl Scout in America." Although the book contains neither bibliography nor footnotes, it is based upon family letters and other documents held by the Georgia Historical Society and the Southern Historical Collection at the University of North Carolina. See also the sketch by Kenneth Coleman in NOTABLE AMERICAN WOMEN (volume 2, pp.

432-34), and the following article:

> Addington, Sarah. "The First Girl Scout." GOOD
> HOUSEKEEPING 104, no. 2 (February 1937): 24-25,
> 183-84, 187-88.

In addition to the titles listed above, the reader may consult some of the more important publications of the Girl Scout national organization, listed below:

> CAMPWARD HO! A MANUAL FOR GIRL SCOUT CAMPS, DE-
> SIGNED TO COVER THE NEEDS OF THOSE UNDERTAKING TO
> ORGANIZE AND DIRECT LARGE, SELF-SUPPORTING CAMPS FOR
> GIRLS. New York: Girl Scouts, Inc., 1920. 192 p. Illustrated.
> Plans, charts, and diagrams. Bibliographies, pp. 178-80.

> THE GIRL SCOUT MOVEMENT, ITS ORIGIN, AIMS AND ACTIV-
> ITIES. New York: Girl Scouts, Inc., [1932]. 25 p.

> THE AMERICAN GIRL; A MAGAZINE FOR GIRL SCOUTS AND
> GIRLS WHO LOVE SCOUTING. New York: October 1917--.
>
> > Title varies. Published as THE RALLY, October 1917-May
> > 1920. This is the Girl Scouts' national periodical.

F.   CAMPING PERIODICALS

AD-I-RON-DAC. Albany, N.Y.: Adirondack Mountain Club, May 1, 1937--.

APPALACHIA. Brattleboro, Vt.: Appalachian Mountain Club, June 1876--.

BETTER CAMPING; FOUR SEASONS OF OUTDOOR LIVING. Highland Park, Ill.: 1960--.

CAMPING MAGAZINE. Boston and North Plainfield, N.J.: American Camping Association, January 1, 1930--.

FIELD AND STREAM. St. Paul, Minn., and New York: April 1, 1896--.

> See also next item.

FOREST AND STREAM. New York: August 14, 1873-July 1930.

> Subtitle varies. Merged with FIELD AND STREAM.

OUTDOOR LIFE. Denver, Colo., and New York: 1897--.

OUTING; SPORT, ADVENTURE, TRAVEL, FICTION. Albany, N.Y.: May 1882-April 1923.

Subtitle varies.

SIERRA CLUB BULLETIN. San Francisco: 1893--.

The reader is also referred to the brief listing of relevant periodicals in the following:

Phillips, John C. "Outdoor Sports, Shooting, Fishing and Camping." In his AMERICAN GAME MAMMALS AND BIRDS: A CATALOGUE OF BOOKS, 1582-1925, SPORT, NATURAL HISTORY AND CONSERVATION, pp. 613-30. Boston: Houghton Mifflin, 1930.

Chapter 10

"BACK TO NATURE":

REPORTS ON COUNTRY LIFE IN AMERICA

Chapter 10

"BACK TO NATURE":

REPORTS ON COUNTRY LIFE IN AMERICA

In his book, BACK TO NATURE: THE ARCADIAN MYTH IN URBAN AMERI-
CA (1969; see Chapter 1, Section A: General Studies), Peter J. Schmitt
described a "back to nature" movement which was characterized by land-hungry,
romantic urbanites seeking nostalgic communion with nature on plots ranging
from luxurious country estates to small abandoned farms. As a movement, this
phenomenon dates roughly from the last decade of the nineteenth century, and
its greatest philosophical articulation is found in the works of Liberty Hyde
Bailey. However, books glorifying rural life (often with ill-disguised dislike
of the city) were written much earlier, and some of these books are listed in
this chapter.

The movement itself can also be seen as a reflection of a distinct dissatisfaction
with urban-industrial values, held by many upper- and middle-class Americans,
and a concomitant desire to return to the simpler, more "natural" life espoused
by the romantic pastoralists like Emerson and Thoreau, and earlier, by Jefferson,
the "father" of American agrarianism. This phenomenon has been discussed by
a number of modern writers, including Leo Marx in his THE MACHINE AND
THE GARDEN: TECHNOLOGY AND THE PASTORAL IDEAL IN AMERICA,
Morton and Lucia White in THE INTELLECTUAL VERSUS THE CITY, and numerous other writers cited in this bibliography.

The phenomenal growth of cities after the Civil War also brought an incipient
suburbanization, fully developed and continuing today. At the turn of the
century, there began a steady stream of "back to nature" books and articles.
The theme of many of these was "how to live virtuously in harmony with nature in the country and make it pay." Practical books on choosing a country
home (usually aimed at the affluent), fictionalized country life essays like those
of Ray Stannard Baker ("David Grayson"), and the books by "literary commuters"
like Andrew C. Wheeler, Walter A. Dyer, and Lewis Gannett were printed.
This genre became quite popular with city dwellers filled with nature nostalgia.
Since 1900 there has been a continuing market for such books and, in recent
years, it has been increasing. The genre has broadened to overlap the natural
history essay, notably in the books by Hal Borland.

This chapter lists only the most significant works--books and articles, as well as the more important country life periodicals. There is no published bibliography of popular or literary works on living in the country. The best--indeed, the only--scholarly account of the urban country life movement is Schmitt's BACK TO NATURE, noted above. The first two chapters of Schmitt's book are devoted to the development of this theme.

A. COMMENTARIES

Bailey, Liberty Hyde (1858-1954)

Bailey had a long and honored career as horticulturist, botanist, teacher, administrator, author and editor, naturist, poet, and philosopher. He wrote hundreds of papers and dozens of books (several became standard works in their fields), chaired Theodore Roosevelt's Country Life Commission in 1909, edited COUNTRY LIFE IN AMERICA from 1901 to 1903, and became the first Dean of the New York State College of Agriculture at Cornell in 1903. As Dean of the College and Director of the State Experiment Station, Bailey became involved in promoting both the country-life and nature-study movements in the United States.

Through his many popular books, articles, and lectures, Bailey sought to bring Americans back to fundamentals and to an appreciation of the natural order of things. Though the movements he espoused ultimately failed to achieve the goals he set for them, the nature movement continued, largely with a suburban focus. See also Chapter 8, Section A5: History, Philosophy, and Purpose, for additional titles by Bailey. Biographical information may be found in the works by Dorf, Lawrence, Rodgers, and Tracy listed below.

"What This Magazine Stands For." COUNTRY LIFE IN AMERICA 1, no. 1 (November 1901): 24-25.

In his first editorial, Bailey outlined the goals of the new periodical. He saw it as a medium for disseminating practical advice to farmers, for leading country people to appreciation of the beautiful in nature, and as a vehicle for increasing interest in nature study. When it became apparent that the publishers had other goals, Bailey resigned as editor, saying that it should have been called "City Life in the Country."

THE OUTLOOK TO NATURE. New York: Macmillan, 1905. ix, 296 p. Rev. ed., 1911. xii, 195 p.

The first edition is made up of four lectures given in Boston under auspices of the Twentieth Century Club. They were entitled "The Realm of the Commonplace,"

"Country and City," "The School of the Future," and
"Evolution; The Quest of Truth." The revised edition
(reprinted in 1924) involved considerable rewriting as
well as reduction of "some of the incidental subjects."
The first two chapters are of primary relevance to this
bibliography. The chapter on "The Commonplace" discusses the "return to nature" and its efficacy for the
nation's moral fibre. The second chapter is an expression of Bailey's concern over the growing hegemony of
the city over the country and the resulting shift in
values. Bailey saw rural values as a corrective to the
urban influence in the nation.

THE COUNTRY-LIFE MOVEMENT IN THE UNITED STATES. New
York: Macmillan, 1911. xi, 220 p.

Topics include a discussion of the national movement,
relationships between city and country, decline in the
rural population, the need for reclamation and conservation, agricultural education, women and the farm,
community life in the country, the labor problem, and
Bailey's own suggestions for a revitalization of the rural
areas of the United States. For Bailey, the country-life
movement and the "back-to-the-land" movement were
quite distinct and in many ways "antagonistic." He
saw the latter as an escape mechanism for urbanites
that offered little or nothing to the pressing needs of
the countryman. The farm was not, in his view, a
refuge or a solution for city problems.

THE HOLY EARTH. The Background Books. New York: Macmillan, 1915. vi, 171 p. Reprint ed., 1943.

This is Bailey's most important and influential nontechnical book. In it he argues that the earth is divine "because man did not make it"; that our relationship with
it must be elevated to the "realm of the spirit"; and
that although we have a right to its use, our dominion
does not imply ownership but rather a cooperative "bio-
centric" association for the mutual welfare of all living
things. Bailey's emphasis upon the need for man to
recognize a moral obligation to the earth and its inhabitants places him solidly in the ecological tradition in
America. Aldo Leopold, the foremost exponent of the
land ethic and an ecological conscience, acknowledged
his debt to the ideas of Bailey. The book deserves to
be brought back into print.

WIND AND WEATHER. The Background Books. New York:

Scribner, 1916. ix, 216 p.

> A book of verse devoted to the themes of nature, country life, and farm values.

THE SEVEN STARS. The Background Books. New York: Macmillan, 1923. 165 p.

> A fictional character, "Questor," is the focus for an examination of the values and conditions of life. Nature plays an important thematic role.

THE HARVEST OF THE YEAR TO THE TILLER OF THE SOIL. The Background Books. New York: Macmillan, 1927. 209 p.

> A really remarkable little book along the lines of THE HOLY EARTH. In a series of short essays, Bailey seeks to define the farmer's role in life and society, and his relationship to nature. The second half of the book, entitled "The Incomes," is composed of beautifully evocative vignettes of the natural world of the farm.

Dorf, Philip. LIBERTY HYDE BAILEY, AN INFORMAL BIOGRAPHY. Ithaca, N.Y.: Cornell University Press, 1956. 259 p. Bibliography, pp. 247-50.

> Although shorter and less heavily documented than Rodgers's biography (below), Dorf's book reveals more of Bailey the man and is much more readable.

Lawrence, George H.M. "Liberty Hyde Bailey, 1858-1954." BAILEYA 3, no. 1 (March 1955): 27-40.

> A very good resume of Bailey's life, scientific achievements, and public service, written by a former associate. Lawrence was the Director of the Bailey Hortorium at Cornell from 1937-43 and from 1945-60.

Rodgers, Andrew Denny III. LIBERTY HYDE BAILEY, A STUDY OF AMERICAN PLANT SCIENCES. Princeton, N.J.: Princeton University Press, 1949. 506 p. Illustrated.

> The author has written several biographies of American plant scientists, and this work forms a part of that series. Published five years before Bailey's death in 1954, the book uses him as the focus for a study of the growth of American plant sciences through research in agricultural colleges and experiment stations. Rodgers's book is rich in detail; quotations are profuse and sometimes continue over several pages. There is no bibliography. Although useful, Rodgers's study is not as readable as Dorf's later

work (above).

Tracy, Henry Chester. "Liberty Hyde Bailey." In his AMERICAN
NATURISTS, pp. 208-14. New York: Dutton, 1930.

A brief appreciation of Bailey's contributions as a popular author and naturist.

Colby, Frank Moore. "Rusticity and Contemplation." In his CONSTRAINED
ATTITUDES, pp. 43-53. New York: Dodd, Mead, 1910. Reprint ed., 1968.

Colby (1865-1925), a one-time professor of history, became a full-
time writer in 1900. His writing for magazines won him a devoted,
if small, following. In this humorous essay, he discusses the then-
current growth of "commuter literature" for suburbanites.

Crandall, C.H. "Is Country Life Lonely?" THE NORTH AMERICAN REVIEW
159 (July 1894): 127-28.

A reassurance for the timid urbanite. "[One's] lonesomeness in
the country depends largely upon one's will, one's attitude toward
the country. If you begin country life feeling that you are a
foreigner to it, and never intend to be naturalized, then you
doom yourself to dislike it." The author claimed that there was
strength in loneliness, that when "a man is lonely, the eternal
Verities speak to him, as they may not speak in a crowd."

Erskine, John. "A House in the Country." CENTURY 112, no. 3 (July 1926):
373-76.

John Erskine (1879-1951) was a well-known novelist, poet, essayist, critic, professor, and amateur musician. He was also a literary commuter. In this brief piece, he gives his reasons for having
a house in the country.

Hungerford, Edward. "Our Summer Migration. A Social Study." CENTURY
42 (August 1891): 569-76.

A study of the social effects of the mass exodus each summer from
the cities of the eastern seaboard to the countryside.

Krutch, Joseph Wood. "The Best of Two Worlds: Some Reflections on a
Peculiarly Modern Privilege." THE AMERICAN SCHOLAR 19, no. 2 (April
1950): 141-48.

In this short but thoughtful essay, Krutch discusses the advantages
that accrue to an urbane and cultured individual living in the
country. Reprinted in THE AMERICAN SCHOLAR READER, edited
by Hiram Haydn and Betsy Saunders, pp. 176-83 (New York:
Atheneum, 1960).

"Out-of-Doors." INDEPENDENT 55 (April 16, 1903): 924-25.

> A short but valuable editorial devoted to the idea that Americans must become an "out-of-doors" people.

[Sargent, Charles Singer]. "The Effect of Country Life Upon Women." GARDEN AND FOREST 6, no. 254 (January 4, 1893): 1-2.

> "[To] most men of means their rural retreat rarely amounts to more than a place to smoke their cigars...or to drive their well-groomed horses over pleasant roads of a Sunday," and thus "the brunt [of] a prolonged residence in the country" was borne by women. Sargent was sure that the lesson that amusement was not the end of life, but "its exception," could be learned by the female sojourner, that simple pleasure like a walk in the woods, landscape gardening, and other rustic avocations would result in a "steadier habit of mind, a greater power of concentration."

The number of magazine articles published in the popular periodicals relating to country life is astounding, particularly from the 1890s through the 1930s. The titles selected above are representative of this profusion. For additional articles, the reader should consult periodical indexes (READER'S GUIDE, AGRICULTURAL INDEX, etc.; see Chapter 11, Section L: Periodical Indexes) under the subject headings "country life," "country homes," "rural life," and "farm life."

B. GUIDES TO COUNTRY LIVING

Borsodi, Ralph. FLIGHT FROM THE CITY; THE STORY OF A NEW WAY TO FAMILY SECURITY. New York and London: Harper, 1933. xv, 194 p. Illustrated. Bibliography, pp. 173-90.

> Dissatisfied with urban life and longing for independence and contact with nature, the Borsodi family moved to the country in 1920 and began a successful program of subsistence farming. Eventually, the Borsodis developed an almost completely self-sufficient home economy, raising animals for milk, meat, and wool, growing their own vegetables and fruit, and making most of their own clothing. The author recounts his family's adventures and argues forcefully for subsistence living as both a way of life and an answer to the exigencies of the depression years. The book has been reprinted many times and is now available in a paper edition. Later editions, beginning in 1935, are subtitled "An Experiment in Creative Living on the Land."

[Morris, Edmund]. TEN ACRES ENOUGH: A PRACTICAL EXPERIENCE SHOWING HOW A VERY SMALL FARM MAY BE MADE TO KEEP A VERY LARGE FAMILY. WITH EXTENSIVE AND PROFITABLE EXPERIENCE IN THE CULTIVATION OF THE SMALLER FRUITS. New York: James Miller, 1864. 255 p.

After a career as a newspaper editor and publisher, Morris (1804-74) moved to his home town of Burlington, New Jersey, where he purchased an eleven-acre farm. TEN ACRES ENOUGH is the record of Morris's successful efforts to make fruit and berry farming profitable. The book was immensely popular and exerted a noticeable influence upon other land-hungry city dwellers (see Hubert's LIBERTY AND A LIVING and Robert B. Roosevelt's FIVE ACRES TOO MUCH, both cited in Section C: Reports on Country Living, below). It had a printing history far longer than any other American agricultural tract of similar intent. The book remained in print during the 1860s and 1870s, was translated into several languages, and was reissued again in 1905, 1912, and 1928.

Nearing, Helen, and Nearing, Scott. LIVING THE GOOD LIFE: HOW TO LIVE SANELY AND SIMPLY IN A TROUBLED WORLD. Introduction by Paul Goodman. New York: Schocken Books, 1970. xx, 213 p. Illustrated. Bibliography, pp. 203-9.

This is a truly remarkable chronicle of "a twentieth century pioneering venture" by a man and wife who, after being denied their part in "public education" because of collectivist views, left the city and bought a Vermont farm in 1932. The Nearings turned to subsistence farming; they grew their own vegetables (they are vegetarians), erected their own dwelling, barns, and other buildings, and depended upon writing and maple sugar products for needed cash. This is a modern day WALDEN and, unlike Thoreau, the Nearings remained in the country in tune with both nature and man. After nineteen years of "experimental homesteading" in Vermont, the authors left Vermont and took up residence on a salt-water farm on the coast of Maine. The Nearings' example has influenced many young people who visited their Vermont and Maine farms over the years. This book is both a record of the authors' achievement and an invitation to others. The book was written for those considering a break with the city. "We maintain that a couple, of any age from twenty to fifty, with a minimum of health, intelligence and capital, can adapt themselves to country living, learn its crafts, overcome its difficulties, and build up a life pattern rich in simple values and productive of personal and social good."

_____. THE MAPLE SUGAR BOOK, TOGETHER WITH REMARKS ON PIONEERING AS A WAY OF LIVING IN THE TWENTIETH CENTURY. New York: Schocken Books, 1970. xiii, 273 p. Illustrated. Bibliography, pp. 265-68.

Originally published in 1950 by John Day with an afterword by the authors. This is an informal history of the home maple sugar industry and the story of how the Nearings made "sugaring" both a way of life and their livelihood.

Ogden, Samuel R. THIS COUNTRY LIFE; MAKING THE MOST OF THE SIMPLE LIFE. Emmaus, Pa.: Rodale Press, 1973. xi, 207 p. Illustrated.

The author has written a very practical and sensible book for people interested in making "a new life" in the country. A Vermont author, teacher, builder, blacksmith, and part-time public official (he has served in several local and state government positions including a term in the state legislature, 1935–47), Ogden has been a sincere advocate of country life for many years and has written several books. He presents a balanced advocacy in THIS COUNTRY LIFE, warning the would-be countryman of many special problems. In a prefatory admonition, he says that many people "are merely enamoured" with the idea of country living, and that, for them, it would be "grim reality." For the serious, however, he has encouraging advice on rural conditions, including community life, schools, what to look for in a country place and the effects on family life. Half of the book is devoted to a detailed exposition of various ways to make a living. The author sees contemporary treks to the hinterlands as nothing new, but rather as the increasing popularity of the "search for Walden." This is a remarkably good and useful book.

Powell, Edward Payson. "A Country Home for the Professional Man." INDEPENDENT 55 (May 14, 1903): 1131–34.

The author (1833–1915) was an untiring publicist for the "back-to-nature" movement. Ill-health forced him in 1877 to give up his successful Chicago pastorate and retire to his family homestead in Clinton, New York. Powell was a regular contributor to newspapers and magazines, an associate editor of the ARENA, and outdoor columnist for the INDEPENDENT. Powell wrote a series of books on gardening, landscaping, and other outdoor topics. Using the INDEPENDENT as a forum, he wrote a number of articles on how to select a country home. The cited essay is a representative and significant example.

_____. THE COUNTRY HOME. New York: McClure, Phillips, 1904. 383 p. Illustrated.

A how-to-do-it book for middle class urbanites. Includes chapters on selecting a home, water supply, lawns and shrubberies, orchards, crops, stock, and other topics.

_____. HOW TO LIVE IN THE COUNTRY. New York: Outing Publishing Co., 1911. 300 p. Illustrated.

Similar in content and tone to his earlier work cited above.

Wend, Milton. HOW TO LIVE IN THE COUNTRY WITHOUT FARMING; PLANNING AND ESTABLISHING A PRODUCTIVE COUNTRY HOME. Garden

City, N.Y.: Doubleday, Doran, 1944. viii, 316 p. Illustrated. Bibliography, pp. 305-10.

Like many--indeed, most--of such guides, this one was aimed at the middle- and upper-income families that were country minded and wished to reside there without farming. It is a thorough guide, generally honest and sincere, and the author doesn't minimize the obstacles encountered in country life. One hundred twenty "money earning urban occupations that can be practiced in small communities" are listed.

C. REPORTS ON COUNTRY LIVING

Baker, Ray Stannard (1870-1946)

Internationally famous as a crusading journalist, editor, reformer, and biographer of Woodrow Wilson, Baker was also creator of a series of reflective and charming country life books under the nom de plume of "David Grayson." The Grayson articles appeared first in the AMERICAN MAGAZINE, a journal in which Baker had both a financial and editorial interest. To his surprise, the pieces were an instant success. The fictitious Grayson, having suffered a physical breakdown in the city, retired to his farm, "Hempfield," to live the quiet and simple life. The Grayson books had a large popular following which remained undiminished after it was revealed in 1917 that Grayson was in fact Ray Stannard Baker. Baker gives an account of his creation of Grayson in his AMERICAN CHRONICLE: THE AUTOBIOGRAPHY OF RAY STANNARD BAKER, pp. 228-48 (New York: Scribner, 1945). See also Walter A. Dyer's DAVID GRAYSON: ADVENTURER (Garden City, N.Y.: Doubleday, Page, 1926).

Grayson, David. ADVENTURES IN CONTENTMENT. New York: Doubleday, Page, 1907. xii, 249 p. Illustrated.

_____. ADVENTURES IN FRIENDSHIP. New York: Doubleday, Page, 1910. 232 p. Illustrated.

_____. A DAY OF PLEASANT BREAD. New York: Doubleday, Doran, 1910. 25 p. Illustrated. Reprint eds., 1926, 1941, 1942, 1948, 1952.

A chapter from his ADVENTURES IN FRIENDSHIP (above).

_____. FRIENDLY ROAD; NEW ADVENTURES IN CONTENTMENT. New York: Doubleday, Page, 1913. ix, 342 p. Illustrated.

_____. HEMPFIELD; A NOVEL. Garden City, N.Y.: Doubleday, Page, 1915. ix, 335 p. Illustrated.

_____. GREAT POSSESSIONS; A NEW SERIES OF ADVENTURES. Garden City, N.Y.: Doubleday, Page, 1917. xii, 208 p. Illustrated.

_____. ADVENTURES IN UNDERSTANDING. Garden City, N.Y.: Doubleday, Page, 1925. xii, 273 p. Illustrated.

_____. ADVENTURES IN SOLITUDE. Garden City, N.Y.: Doubleday, Doran, 1931. 180 p. Illustrated.

_____. THE COUNTRYMAN'S YEAR. Garden City, N.Y.: Doubleday, Doran, 1936. viii, 270 p. Illustrated.

_____. UNDER MY ELM, COUNTRY DISCOVERIES AND REFLECTIONS. Garden City, N.Y.: Doubleday, Doran, 1942. x, 278 p. Illustrated.

Beecher, Henry Ward. STAR PAPERS; OR, EXPERIENCES OF ART AND NATURE. New ed., with Additional Articles, Selected from more Recent Writings. New York: J.B. Ford, 1873. ix, 447 p.

First edition published in 1855. The present work contains three sections. The first two, "Letters from Europe" and "Experiences of Nature," were taken from the columns of the NEW YORK INDEPENDENT, anonymously signed with a "star." The third section, original to this edition, is called simply "Late Papers," and was taken from the columns of the CHRISTIAN UNION. The last two sections deal with descriptions of nature, "rural affairs," and farm economy. According to Beecher, all were written in the country.

Beers, Lorna D. WILD APPLES AND NORTH WIND. New York: Norton, 1966. 219 p. Illustrated.

The author and her husband decided to return to Vermont and become year-round residents. Their country place, used for many years as a summer retreat, is the focus of the action and description. A very appealing and charming narrative.

Beston, Henry. NORTHERN FARM, A CHRONICLE OF MAINE. New York: Rinehart, 1948. vii, 246 p. Illustrated.

A deeply-felt, beautifully written chronicle of life on Beston's farm, "Chimney Farm." Available in a paper edition. For other titles by the author, see Chapter 7, Section C: Nature Writing Since Thoreau.

Borland, Hal G.

All of Borland's country life essays and nature books are listed in Chapter 7, Section C: Nature Writing Since Thoreau.

Bromfield, Louis. PLEASANT VALLEY. New York and London: Harper, 1945. vii, 300 p. Illustrated.

Part of the book consists of autobiographical reminiscences of Bromfield's life in the United States, France, and India; part is a narrative of his return to Ohio and the beginning of "Malabar Farm." Glimpses of nature and a great love of the land inform this book. See also next two items.

_____. MALABAR FARM. New York and London: Harper, 1948. viii, 405 p. Illustrated.

In PLEASANT VALLEY Bromfield recounted his return to Ohio in 1939 and the founding of Malabar Farm. He continues his narrative in this book. In it he tells of his agricultural experiments, of the planting of crops, of soil reclamation and organic farming. Bromfield first conceived of his 640 acres (later enlarged to 715) as a place of self-sufficiency, a goal he gradually and reluctantly had to give up. Much of the book is a record of Bromfield's experimentation and his sometimes controversial views of agriculture as a whole. About a third of the volume consists of entries from his diary from August 31, 1944, to August 31, 1945. Despite sections of purely technical content intended for agriculturists, and what is at times rather heavy moralizing, MALABAR FARM is an important book, reflecting the achievements of a significant American author-farmer and his attempts to create a successful utopian agricultural community. After Bromfield's death, Malabar Farm was acquired by the State of Ohio and is now run as a demonstration farm, open to the public.

_____. FROM MY EXPERIENCE; THE PLEASURES AND MISERIES OF LIFE ON A FARM. New York: Harper, 1955. viii, 355 p. Illustrated.

This is a more contentious and, in some ways, a more somber book than Bromfield's earlier "Malabar" books. In addition to further happenings in Ohio, the author describes the beginnings of his daughter's plantation in Brazil, called "Malabar-do-Brasil." There is much retrospective rumination about the author's life in Ohio, his views of the world's political and economic situation, and a summary of his feelings toward "man and nature," derived in part from notions expressed by Albert Schweizer and Liberty Hyde

Bailey.

Canby, Henry Seidel. "Nature." In his THE AGE OF CONFIDENCE: LIFE IN THE NINETIES, pp. 210-25. New York: Farrar & Rinehart, 1934.

Canby recalls with charm the quality of life in the small town of Wilmington, Delaware, in the 1890s. "Country" surrounded the town and the "town dwellers moved by instinct and tradition alike to reach back to the farm."

Damon, Bertha. A SENSE OF HUMUS. New York: Simon and Schuster, 1943. 250 p. Illustrated.

A humorous and anecdotal account of the author's experiences on her New Hampshire farm.

De Weese, Truman A. THE BEND IN THE ROAD AND HOW A MAN OF THE CITY FOUND IT. New York and London: Harper, 1913. [x], 208 p. Illustrated, with plates.

De Weese, a New York newspaperman, purchased a ten-acre farm in rural New York as a "summer playground." Here he remodeled the colonial house, cared for his orchard and grapevines, landscaped his grounds, and generally enjoyed his role as part-time gentleman farmer. De Weese saw his rural adventure as part of the "country-life movement," a movement made up of many other city men who, unlike him, had no previous experience with farming. Unlike the farmer, who had to make his living from the land, this urbanite took to the country "a refined and sensitive capacity for enjoying nature in all her moods and colors." This is a valuable and realistic account of one man's participation in the back-to-nature movement. It received excellent reviews.

Duryee, William B. A LIVING FROM THE LAND. New York and London: Whittlesey House, McGraw-Hill, 1934. xiii, 189 p. Illustrated. References, pp. 185-89.

A highly practical book addressed to the family wishing to purchase a small property (one to fifteen acres) without renouncing a city-based occupation. The author was New Jersey's Secretary of Agriculture.

Dyer, Walter A. "This Farm of Mine: I Want to Be a Countryman." THE CENTURY 114, no. 6 (October 1927): 739-44.

Dyer, friend and neighbor of Ray Stannard Baker ("David Grayson"; see above), was the managing editor of COUNTRY LIFE IN AMER-ICA from 1906-14 and a prolific writer. He published hundreds of articles on country life and outdoor subjects, as well as numerous books for children. In this essay, Dyer reflects upon the spiritual values accrued by his family from living on their Connecticut farm.

Follett, Muriel. NEW ENGLAND YEAR--A JOURNAL OF VERMONT FARM LIFE. Brattleboro, Vt.: Stephen Daye Press, 1940. 222 p. Illustrated. Reprint ed. Detroit: Gale Research Co., 1971.

An authentic, day-by-day portrayal of family life on a Vermont farm during a depression year. It is written in simple, direct, and unsentimental prose by a farmer's wife and has the earmarks of a minor classic.

Fuller, Edmund. SUCCESSFUL CALAMITY: A WRITER'S FOLLIES ON A VERMONT FARM. New York: Random House, 1966. 239 p.

Fuller, a well-known author, editor, critic, and teacher, tells of his family's less than entirely successful experiences on his Vermont farm.

Gannett, Lewis. CREAM HILL: DISCOVERIES OF A WEEKEND COUNTRYMAN. New York: Viking, 1949. 191 p. Illustrated.

The Gannetts came to Cream Hill (West Cornwall, Connecticut) in 1924 to visit their friends the Carl Van Dorens and bought an old farm near-by. As Gannett explains it, they didn't come with any dream of "five acres and liberty," but rather to find a cool, pleasant place for the children in the summer. Gradually, however, Cream Hill grew into an all-year week-end and summer residence and, finally, after Gannett's retirement from his literary work in New York City, it became their permanent residence. In this delightfully charming book Gannett recounts his family's growing involvement with their farm from gardening to woodcutting. He also details a considerable amount of the area's local history, including that related to his eighteenth-century ancestor, Ezra Stiles. The author assesses the effects of change in the hinterlands of western Connecticut since the turn of the century and, in a chapter entitled "Parasitic City Folk," he describes the role played by summer residents in his community and the gradual decline of active involvement by local residents in town politics. Although now dated, Gannett's book was a harbinger of the much greater changes that have occurred since 1949. The author's description of his family's enchantment with the farm, his historical asides and social commentary, make this a truly significant book. Gannett died in 1966.

Hall, Donald. STRING TOO SHORT TO BE SAVED. New York: Viking, 1961. 143 p. Illustrated.

In this book, the well-known poet tells the story of the enchanted summers he spent growing up on his grandparents' farm in New Hampshire. Beautifully written, it is nostalgic and reflective, but unsentimental.

Hall, Leonard. COUNTRY YEAR: A JOURNAL OF THE SEASONS AT POSSUM TROT FARM. New York: Harper, 1957. xiv, 208 p. Illustrated.

The author's farm lies in a high valley of the eastern Ozarks in Missouri. Like Bromfield's Malabar, Hall's Possum Trot Farm became a gathering spot for visiting conservationists, farmers, and naturalists. The journal of the seasons, combining a fine feeling for nature with the day-to-day operations of a working farm, originally appeared in columns of the ST. LOUIS POST-DISPATCH.

Hersey, Jean. THE SHAPE OF A YEAR. New York: Scribner, 1967. 243 p. Illustrated.

A well-written calendar-record of family life on the Hersey's Connecticut farm.

Hilles, Helen Train. FARM WANTED. New York: J. Messner, [1951]. xii, 236 p. Illustrated.

Mrs. Hilles, a "miscellaneous" writer and author of cookbooks, tells the story of how she and her husband bought a fifteen-acre farm in Dutchess County, New York, as a summer place. From that function, however, it gradually grew into a subsistence farm with a few money-making crops. The book is interesting and well written; but as an example for other land-hungry urbanites, it rings a bit hollow considering the amount of help available to the author and her family.

Hubert, Philip G., Jr. LIBERTY AND A LIVING; THE RECORD OF AN ATTEMPT TO SECURE BREAD AND BUTTER, SUNSHINE AND CONTENT, BY GARDENING, FISHING AND HUNTING. New York: Putnam, 1889. 239 p. Frontispiece.

Hubert (1852-1925), the son of a well-to-do architect, was a successful music critic and editorial writer for several New York papers. Drawn to the country life by a philosophic conviction buttressed by a close reading of Thoreau's WALDEN and influenced by Edmund Morris's TEN ACRES ENOUGH (see Section B: Guides to Country Living, above), Hubert moved his family to a one-acre country place on Long Island. Here he grew fruits and vegetables, hunted, fished, and gathered oysters, while maintaining the intellectual home atmosphere of a cultured New Yorker. Much of LIBERTY AND A LIVING is an espousal of rural values as opposed to what he considered the degenerative forces of the city. Hubert devoted a chapter to a discussion of Thoreau's philosophical position and, although he disagreed with the latter's ascetic posture, Hubert's own flight from the city may be considered as an attempt to achieve a less rigorous "Walden." Ironically, the author drew his primary sustenance from New York, where he went every winter for three months to further his journalistic endeavors. Hubert's

book is a classic statement of the "back-to nature" aspirations
inherent in American urban history. A second edition was published by Putnam in 1904.

Huston, Paul Griswold. AN OLD-FASHIONED SUGAR CAMP AND OTHER
DREAMS OF THE WOODS; A BOOK OF THE SEASONS. Chicago and New
York: Fleming H. Revell Co., 1903. vii, 203 p.

See annotation below.

_____. AROUND AN OLD HOMESTEAD; A BOOK OF MEMORIES. Cin-
cinnati: Jennings and Graham; New York: Eaton and Mains, 1906. 362 p.
Illustrated, with plates.

The homestead was that occupied in 1822 by the author's grandfather in Colerain Township, Hamilton County, Ohio. A book
of very nostalgic reminiscences of the author's life on the farm
and its environs, it includes reflections on country life, farm
and wild animals, the woods, hunting, orchards, and nature philosophy.
Quaint by today's standards, the book is still appealing, as is his
earlier book above.

Hutchinson, Frances Kinsley. WYCHWOOD; THE HISTORY OF AN IDEA.
IN THREE PARTS: OUR COUNTRY HOME; OUR COUNTRY LIFE; OUR FINAL
AIM. Chicago: Lakeside Press, 1928. xvi, 480 p. Plates.

In 1902, the Hutchinsons, wealthy Chicagoans, purchased seventy-
two acres of rolling woodland along the shore of Lake Geneva,
Wisconsin. Utilizing their substantial financial resources, they
transformed their woodland into a country show place. In 1908
the author reported the development of "Wychwood" in OUR
COUNTRY HOME (Chicago: McClurg) and in 1912 she published
a sequel, OUR COUNTRY LIFE (Chicago: McClurg). The present
work brings together the first two books, revised and shortened,
and adds a third part, "Our Final Aim." In 1926, Mrs. Hutchinson presented Wychwood to the State of Wisconsin, endowed with
a trust fund, as a permanent sanctuary for native plants, birds,
and small animal life.

McMillen, Wheeler. THE FARMING FEVER. New York, London: D. Appleton, 1924. 168 p.

McMillen, an editor of FARM AND FIRESIDE, wrote this book for
the land-hungry city dweller. It is filled with practical advice
as well as humorous anecdotes from the author's experience.

Mitchell, Donald Grant [Ik Marvel] (1822-1908)

Better known as Ik Marvel, Mitchell was a well-known essayist
and agriculturist. In 1855, after some newspaper work and diplo-

matic service in Europe, Mitchell purchased a large farm near
New Haven, Connecticut, which he called "Edgewood." Here
he lived quietly, combining literary with agricultural pursuits.
His farm became a show place and his Edgewood books reflected
a growing concern over the ugliness of urban life. Mitchell intended his books to persuade Americans of the beauty and virtue
in country life. His place and influence in American letters is
discussed by George S. Hellman in THE CAMBRIDGE HISTORY OF
AMERICAN LITERATURE, Volume 3, pp. 110-13 (New York: Putnam; Cambridge: At the University Press, 1921). A biographical
sketch, by Waldo H. Dunn, appears in THE DICTIONARY OF
AMERICAN BIOGRAPHY (volume 13, pp. 41-42). Dunn has also
written THE LIFE OF DONALD G. MITCHELL, IK MARVEL (New
York: Scribner, 1922), which contains an extensive bibliography.

MY FARM OF EDGEWOOD: A COUNTRY BOOK. New York:
Scribner, 1863. x, 319 p.

> Reprinted several times before 1894. Reissued in 1907
> as Volume 6 of the WORKS OF DONALD GRANT MIT-
> CHELL (15 vols. New York: Scribner, 1907).

WET DAYS AT EDGEWOOD: WITH OLD FARMERS, OLD GAR-
DENERS, AND OLD PASTORALS. New York: Scribner, 1865.
vii, 324 p. Illustrated.

> Large parts of this volume were previously published in
> the ATLANTIC MONTHLY. Reissued in 1884, 1894,
> and in the WORKS in 1907.

RURAL STUDIES, WITH HINTS FOR COUNTRY PLACES. New
York: Scribner, 1867. iii, 295 p. Illustrated.

> Reissued by Scribner in 1884 as OUT OF TOWN
> PLACES; WITH HINTS FOR THEIR IMPROVEMENT.
> Also published under this title as Volume 7 of the
> WORKS.

PICTURES OF EDGEWOOD; IN A SERIES OF PHOTOGRAPHS BY
ROCKWOOD, AND ILLUSTRATIVE TEXT, BY THE AUTHOR. New
York: Charles Scribner, 1869. 62 p. Frontispiece. Plates.
Photos. 33 x 25 cm.

> Three hundred copies printed.

Paine, Albert Bigelow. DWELLERS IN ARCADY: THE STORY OF AN ABAN-
DONED FARM. New York and London: Harper, 1919. 242 p. Illustrated.

A country life "novel." A young New York couple buy an abandoned farm in Connecticut for a summer home and are so entranced
by rural life that they remain permanently.

Pearson, Haydn S. NEW ENGLAND FLAVOR: MEMORIES OF A COUNTRY BOYHOOD. New York: Norton, 1961. 249 p. Illustrated.

The author grew up in Hancock, New Hampshire, in the years preceding the first world war. This is a fascinating and nostalgic portrayal of the many aspects of country living on a small backwoods farm.

_____. THE NEW ENGLAND YEAR. New York: Norton, 1966. 255 p. Illustrated.

A chronicle of country living similar to Pearson's NEW ENGLAND FLAVOR (above). Many of the sketches appeared earlier in the author's column in the BOSTON HERALD.

Peden, Rachel. RURAL FREE: A FARMWIFE'S ALMANAC OF COUNTRY LIVING. New York: Knopf, 1961. 382 p. Illustrated.

Grew out of columns written for the INDIANAPOLIS STAR and the MUNCIE EVENING PRESS. Mrs. Peden, a farmer's wife, tells the story of her life on an Indiana farm. See also next item.

_____. THE LAND, THE PEOPLE. New York: Knopf, 1966. xv, 332 p. Illustrated.

In this sequel to RURAL FREE, Mrs. Peden writes of Indiana farmers and farm life. Those portrayed are chiefly relatives and friends of her father and father-in-law, all of whom had an abiding love for the land they worked. This is a very interesting evocation of a rapidly changing way of life in rural America.

Pochman, Ruth Fonts. TRIPLE RIDGE FARM. New York: Morrow, 1968. 232 p. Illustrated. Maps on endpapers.

The fascinating and charming story of a Wisconsin family's struggles to reclaim 100 acres of central Wisconsin farmland.

Prime, Samuel Irenaeus. UNDER THE TREES. New York: Harper, 1874. 313 p.

Prime (1812-85), the brother of William Cowper Prime, was trained for the pulpit but forced by continual poor health into writing and journalism. For years he edited the NEW YORK OBSERVER, a Presbyterian paper and, from 1851 until his death, he conducted the "Editor's Drawer" in HARPER'S MAGAZINE. Roughly half of UNDER THE TREES, a collection of "miscellaneous letters and papers," is devoted to sketches of nature and country life. Of particular value are the two chapters on Prime's tour of the Adirondacks and the White Mountains. For biographical information, see the sketch by Robert Hastings Nichols in the DICTIO-

NARY OF AMERICAN BIOGRAPHY (volume 15, p. 228).

Robinson, Rowland Evans (1833-1900)

Robinson, well known in his day as a Vermont regionalist, wrote a number of books on country life, local customs, hunting, fishing, and nature appreciation. Many of his stories and sketches appeared first in magazines, most notably in FOREST AND STREAM. Several of his books had lengthy printing histories, and three works of fiction have been reprinted. His two nonfiction books are listed below. For additional information, see the article by Howard Zahniser, below.

IN NEW ENGLAND FIELDS AND WOODS, WITH SKETCHES AND STORIES. Edited by Llewellyn R. Perkins. Foreword by Sinclair Lewis. Bibliography by Harold G. Rugg. Centennial Edition. Rutland, Vt.: Charles E. Tuttle, 1937. 257 p. Illustrated. Bibliography, pp. 5-11.

First published by Houghton Mifflin in 1896. The sketches appeared first in issues of FOREST AND STREAM.

SILVER FIELDS AND OTHER SKETCHES OF A FARMER-SPORTS-MAN. Boston and New York: Houghton Mifflin, 1921. 261 p.

Collected sketches, published posthumously.

Zahniser, Howard. "In May--Rowland E. Robinson." NATURE MAGAZINE 29, no. 5 (May 1937): 263, 317.

An appreciation of Robinson's nature writing.

Rockwell, Frederick F. THE KEY TO THE LAND: WHAT A CITY MAN DID WITH A SMALL FARM. New York and London: Harper, 1915. xii, 213 p. Plates.

The author's experiences put into story form and somewhat sugar-coated.

Roosevelt, Robert B. FIVE ACRES TOO MUCH. A TRUTHFUL ELUCIDATION OF THE ATTRACTIONS OF THE COUNTRY, AND A CONSIDERATION OF THE QUESTION OF PROFIT AND LOSS AS INVOLVED IN AMATEUR FARMING, WITH MUCH VALUABLE ADVICE AND INSTRUCTION TO THOSE ABOUT PURCHASING LARGE OR SMALL PLACES IN THE RURAL DISTRICTS. New York: Harper, 1869. xvii, 296 p. Illustrated.

The author, a prominent New York political reformer, conservationist, and writer, was the uncle of Theodore Roosevelt. FIVE ACRES TOO MUCH is a humorous account of the author's farming experiences in Flushing, Long Island, and a semiserious rebuttal of Morris's TEN ACRES ENOUGH (see Section B: Guides to

Country Living, above).

Sanborn, Katherine Abbott [Kate Sanborn] (1839-1917)

Miss Sanborn, author, lecturer, and teacher, was a noted speaker on popular topics and current literature in clubs and schools, and an organizer of women's clubs. Between 1859-83, she taught in several girls' schools and at Smith College. During this time she was a frequent contributor to periodicals. When her health deteriorated in the late 1880s, she moved to a farm near Metcalf, Massachusetts, where she settled for the rest of her life. The two books listed below are her contribution to the "back-to-nature" genre; they are remarkable for the wit and gentle satire of the exigencies of country life. Although the author grew to love her rural retreat, she was able to see the drawbacks to farming, especially at the subsistence level, and particularly their effect on women.

ADOPTING AN ABANDONED FARM. New York: D. Appleton, 1892. 171 p.

ABANDONING AN ADOPTED FARM. New York: D. Appleton, 1894. 185 p.

Shute, Henry A. FARMING IT. Boston and New York: Houghton Mifflin, 1909. x, 248 p. Illustrated.

A semihumourous treatment of country life by a farmer-author. Shute (1856-1943) was primarily a writer of children's stories.

Smart, Charles Allen. R. F. D. New York: Norton, 1938. 314 p.

Smart, an editor, novelist, and essayist, moved to an inherited farm in southern Ohio in 1934. The book details his experiences after the first three years. In addition to purely agricultural topics, the author provides an interesting account of his neighbors, of his relations with county agents and the local Grange, and of his gradual acceptance into the social activities of the area.

Stadtfeld, Curtis K. FROM THE LAND AND BACK. New York: Scribner, 1972. xix, 202 p. Illustrated.

This a truly good book, destined to become a minor classic. Stadtfeld writes of his youth on his family's farm in central Michigan in the 1940s. Set against the sometimes harsh realities of an "indifferent nature," and finally swept away by technological change, that life was nevertheless filled with "great enrichment," "whole...organic and satisfying." The author looks back on his life with a nostalgia tempered by what one critic called "enlightened pessimism." The family farm is all but gone, not to be resurrected. To young people unhappy and confused by urban living and seeking a simpler life on the land, Stadtfeld addresses a warning that "it is not in nature to support man very well."

Streeter, John Williams. THE FAT OF THE LAND: THE STORY OF AN AMERICAN FARM. New York: Macmillan, 1904. xi, 406 p.

The author, a well-to-do Chicago physician, was forced by illness to give up his practice. He purchased several hundred acres of farm land and proceeded to farm it "scientifically." The book chronicles the doctor's experiences of farming with hired help.

Taber, Gladys B. (b. 1899)

Mrs. Taber published her first book in 1929. Since then, she has written novels, cookbooks, juveniles, animal books, and country life essays. As a writer, Mrs. Taber has been enormously popular and, although most of her books were written primarily for women, her country life essays based on her life on a Southbury (Connecticut) farm, "Stillmeadow," have been appealing to both sexes. Some of the essays appeared first in her column, "Diary of Domesticity," which ran in the LADIES' HOME JOURNAL, 1938-58.

HARVEST AT STILLMEADOW. Boston: Little, Brown, 1940. 261 p. Illustrated.

BOOK OF STILLMEADOW. Illustrated by Edward Shenton. Philadelphia: Macrae-Smith, 1948. 273 p.

STILLMEADOW SEASONS. Illustrated by Edward Shenton. Philadelphia: Macrae-Smith, 1950. 256 p.

STILLMEADOW AND SUGARBRIDGE. By Gladys B. Taber and Barbara Webster. Illustrated by Edward Shenton. Philadelphia: Lippincott, 1953. 359 p.

STILLMEADOW DAYBOOK. Illustrated by Edward Shenton. Philadelphia: Lippincott, 1955. 274 p.

STILLMEADOW SAMPLER. Illustrated by Edward Shenton. Philadelphia: Lippincott, 1959. 282 p.

THE STILLMEADOW ROAD. Illustrated by Edward Shenton. Philadelphia: Lippincott, 1962. 287 p.

THE STILLMEADOW CALENDAR; A COUNTRYWOMAN'S JOURNAL.

Philadelphia: Lippincott, 1967. 256 p. Illustrated.

STILLMEADOW ALBUM. Philadelphia: Lippincott, 1969. 126 p. Photos.

Tetlow, Henry. WE FARM FOR A HOBBY AND MAKE IT PAY. New York: Morrow, 1938. xii, 200 p. Illustrated. Bibliography, pp. 193-94.

Tetlow, a city-based businessman and part-time farmer, lived on thirty-eight acres within sight of Valley Forge, Pennsylvania. Here, with the benefit of a comfortable outside income and some hired help, he made his hobby pay, or so we are told. Much of the book is meant as an example for other urban would-be country gentlemen. See also next item.

_____. ON MEDLOCK FARM. New York: Morrow, 1940. 272 p. Illustrated.

A sequel to the author's earlier work. Tetlow offers advice on country living and observations about the rural landscape and its human history. F.F. Van de Water, himself the owner of a small farm, called this an "entertaining and occasionally irritating" book. It received generally favorable reviews.

Van de Water, Frederic F. (1890-1968)

Van de Water, an ex-newspaperman, columnist, and free-lance writer, gave up his New York City home in 1934 and took his family to a hillside farm in Vermont. Motivated by a persistent hunger for land, he and his wife had spent months seeking a country home close to Manhattan. It was with initial reluctance that they finally settled for a secluded Vermont farm.

Van de Water's books constitute a record of his family's life in the country. HOME IN THE COUNTRY is a witty account of the frustrations they suffered during endless bouts with realtors. In addition to his essays, Van de Water wrote novels, histories, and biographies.

HOME IN THE COUNTRY. New York: John Day/Reynal & Hitchcock, 1937. 198 p. Illustrations on endpapers.

WE'RE STILL IN THE COUNTRY. New York: John Day, 1938. 253 p.

CIRCLING YEAR. New York: John Day, 1940. 222 p.

MEMBERS OF THE FAMILY. New York: John Day, 1942. 190 p.

Wheeler, Andrew Carpenter [J.P. Mowbray]. A JOURNEY TO NATURE.
New York: Doubleday, Page, 1901. x, 315 p. Illustrated.

> Originally published in the NEW YORK EVENING POST, these
> essays were reworked by the author, and new material was added,
> to form the present work. Purportedly based upon real people,
> this is the story of a New York stock broker who spends a year
> on a broken-down farm north of New York City seeking renewed
> health. Superficial, but engrossing.

_____. THE MAKING OF A COUNTRY HOME. New York: Doubleday,
Page, 1901. viii, 258 p. Illustrated. Reprint ed., 1909.

> A country life novel. A young man and his family move to a
> worn out farm near New York City. Rural values triumph over
> city conveniences.

D. COUNTRY LIFE PERIODICALS

The following is a list of the leading periodicals devoted to promoting country
life in America. For the most part, these magazines were intended for urban
and suburban dwellers interested in moving to the country, and for the more
affluent "countrymen" already living there. Not included are general magazines that carried occasional pieces about rural living. Magazines devoted
to home design, gardening, and landscaping, such as BETTER HOMES AND
GARDENS, GARDEN AND HOME BUILDER, HOUSE AND GARDEN, and
HOUSE BEAUTIFUL, have also printed material to encourage the movement,
but they were, and are, aimed at a different market. Farm magazines are
also excluded.

COUNTRY CALENDAR. Harrisburg, Pa., and New York: May-December
1905.

> Merged with COUNTRY LIFE IN AMERICA (below).

COUNTRY HOME MAGAZINE.

> See FARM AND FIRESIDE (below).

COUNTRY LIFE IN AMERICA. New York: November 1901-January 1919.
Continued as COUNTRY LIFE. New York: January 1919-October 1937.
Continued as COUNTRY LIFE AND THE SPORTSMAN. New York: November
1937-December 1938. Continued as COUNTRY LIFE. New York: January
1939-December 1942.

THE COUNTRYSIDE MAGAZINE AND SUBURBAN LIFE. Harrisburg, Pa., and
New York: December 1902-December 1904. N.s., January 1905-July 1917.

> From 1903-17, appeared as SUBURBAN LIFE. Merged with THE

INDEPENDENT.

FARM AND FIRESIDE. New York: 1877-January 1930. Continued as COUNTRY HOME MAGAZINE. Springfield, Ohio: 1930-December 1939.

GARDEN AND FOREST: A JOURNAL OF HORTICULTURE, LANDSCAPE ART AND FORESTRY, New York: 1888-1897.

THE LAND. Baltimore, Md.: Friends of the Land, Winter 1941-1952. Continued as THE LAND AND LAND NEWS. Baltimore, Md.: Friends of the Land, January 1953-November 1954.

MOTHER EARTH NEWS. Madison, Ohio: January 1970--.

ORGANIC GARDENING AND FARMING. Emmaus, Pa.: January 1954--.

OUTING; SPORT, ADVENTURE, TRAVEL, FICTION. Albany, N.Y.: May 1882-April 1923.

    Subtitle varies.

RURAL AMERICA. New York: American Country Life Association, March/April 1923-May 1941.

RURAL AMERICAN. Boston: 1900-1904.

Chapter 11

GENERAL REFERENCE WORKS

Chapter 11

GENERAL REFERENCE WORKS AND PERIODICALS

The materials in this chapter do not duplicate bibliographies and reference works cited in earlier chapters. Because of the specialized nature of this volume, most of the more commonly known historical bibliographies, such as the HARVARD GUIDE TO AMERICAN HISTORY and WRITINGS ON AMERICAN HISTORY, were found not to be useful or relevant. They are not included for this reason.

Two works are recommended for detailed and comprehensive information on American reference books--bibliographies, sourcebooks, guides to manuscripts and collections, serial indexes, dictionaries, biographical sources, indexes to government documents, library and trade catalogs, specialized encyclopedias, handbooks, gazetteers, etc.: Constance M. Winchell's GUIDE TO REFERENCE BOOKS, 8th edition (Chicago: American Library Association, 1967) and the three supplements by Eugene P. Sheehy, and Helen J. Poulton's THE HISTORIAN'S HANDBOOK: A DESCRIPTIVE GUIDE TO REFERENCE WORKS (Norman: University of Oklahoma Press, 1972), written in bibliographical essay form (with complete indexes) and including some later titles not yet incorporated into the Winchell supplements.

What follows is a selective list of reference books which the editor found particularly useful, and a list of periodicals concerned with the environment which are not listed elsewhere in this bibliography. Introducing this list are a number of important periodical directories and indexes.

A. DIRECTORIES

THE CONSERVATION YEARBOOK. Edited by Erle Kauffman. Washington, D.C., and Baltimore, Md.: 1952-62.

> Subtitle varies. During the period of its publication, this annual contained more information about conservation and resource management--resources, agencies, organizations, people, and publications --than any other comparable directory. Federal, state, and regional governmental agencies, as well as national, regional, and state private organizations and industry groups are included. Statistical

data about renewable resources is offered in each volume. Many of the listings for agencies, offices, and groups are substantially annotated with material about their history, purposes, activities, officers, and publications. Includes listings of national parks and monuments, national forests, game preserves, state parks, and reclamation districts. A valuable directory and guide.

ENCYCLOPEDIA OF ASSOCIATIONS. Edited by Margaret Fisk. 9th ed. 3 vols. Detroit: Gale Research Co., 1975.

Volume 1 is a listing of national associations of the United States arranged by group ("Trade, Business and Commercial," "Agricultural Organizations and Commodity Exchanges," etc.), then by specific type (accountants, advertising, conservation, etc.). The information includes addresses, officers, size of membership, a statement of purpose and activities, and publications. Citizen action groups are included. Includes a section on "inactive, defunct or former names," which is indispensable for the field of conservation. An alphabetical index of associations is included. Volume 2 is a Geographic-Executive Index to the material in Volume 1. Volume 3 is a loose-leaf listing of quarterly reports on associations newly formed or newly identified by the editors. A valuable directory.

National Wildlife Federation. CONSERVATION DIRECTORY; A LIST OF ORGANIZATIONS, AGENCIES AND OFFICIALS CONCERNED WITH NATURAL RESOURCE USE AND MANAGEMENT. Washington, D.C.: 1953--.

Published annually. Supercedes directories issued by the U.S. Bureau of Biological Survey, the U.S. Fish and Wildlife Service, and several other federal agencies since 1900. Title varies; began as DIRECTORY OF ORGANIZATIONS AND OFFICIALS CONCERNED WITH THE PROTECTION OF WILDLIFE AND OTHER NATURAL RESOURCES. Contains sections on United States government departments and agencies, interstate commissions, international organizations, national nongovernmental organizations, state and territorial agencies and citizens groups, Canadian government agencies and citizens groups, and an appendix listing colleges and universities offering professional training in natural resources management. Includes a personal name index. Information about most agencies and groups is reasonably detailed and includes purpose, activities, officers, and publications. Not limited to wildlife conservation, the DIRECTORY also includes preservationist organizations.

B. NATIONAL LIBRARY CATALOGS

The printed catalogs of the United States Library of Congress form one of the most important sources of bibliographic information available to scholars. As an aid to locating and verifying materials, it is indispensable. Beginning in 1942, the National Union Catalog and several other book catalogs have been issued by the Library of Congress. Supplements are also issued to cover specific periods. Listed below are the master cumulations and earlier catalogs not as yet superceded by master cumulations.

THE NATIONAL UNION CATALOG: PRE-1956 IMPRINTS: A CUMULATIVE AUTHOR LIST REPRESENTING LIBRARY OF CONGRESS PRINTED CARDS AND TITLES REPORTED BY OTHER AMERICAN LIBRARIES. Compiled and edited with the Cooperation of the Library of Congress and the National Union Catalog Subcommittee of the Resources Committee of the Resources and Technical Services Division, American Library Association. London: Mansell, in progress since 1968.

> This is a projected 610-volume master cumulation of all previous Library of Congress catalogs. As of 1974, 344 volumes (up to "L") have been issued. When completed, this edition (commonly referred to as "Mansell"), will contain printed cards for all books cataloged by the Library of Congress, and by other American libraries participating in the National Union Catalog, published up to and including the year 1956.

Library of Congress. CATALOG OF BOOKS REPRESENTED BY LIBRARY OF CONGRESS PRINTED CARDS ISSUED TO JULY 31, 1942. 167 vols. Ann Arbor, Mich.: Edwards Brothers, 1942-46.

> Being replaced by Mansell (above). Only those volumes covering entries beginning with "Luce" to the end of the alphabet need be consulted.

LIBRARY OF CONGRESS AND NATIONAL UNION CATALOG AUTHOR LISTS, 1942-1962: A MASTER CUMULATION. A CUMULATED AUTHOR LIST REPRESENTING ENTRIES IN THE LIBRARY OF CONGRESS--NATIONAL UNION CATALOG SUPPLEMENTS TO "CATALOG OF BOOKS REPRESENTED BY LIBRARY OF CONGRESS PRINTED CARDS." 152 vols. Detroit: Gale Research Co., 1969-71.

> A cumulation of entries appearing in four previous cumulations. It is also being replaced by the Mansell edition, currently at "L."

THE NATIONAL UNION CATALOG, 1956 THROUGH 1967: A CUMULATIVE AUTHOR LIST REPRESENTING LIBRARY OF CONGRESS PRINTED CARDS AND TITLES REPORTED BY OTHER AMERICAN LIBRARIES. 125 vols. Totowa, N.J.: Rowman and Littlefield, 1970-72.

> This is a complete cumulation for the years indicated.

THE NATIONAL UNION CATALOG: A CUMULATIVE AUTHOR LIST REPRESENTING LIBRARY OF CONGRESS PRINTED CARDS AND TITLES REPORTED BY OTHER AMERICAN LIBRARIES, 1968-1972. Ann Arbor, Mich.: J.W. Edwards, in progress since 1973.

Ninety volumes (through "Stu") have been published. When
completed, it will replace the annual cumulations published by
the Library of Congress for the years 1968 to 1972, which must
still be consulted for entries after "Stu." For materials published
in 1972 or later, the paperbound quarterly cumulations of the
National Union Catalog Author Lists must be used.

LIBRARY OF CONGRESS CATALOG. BOOKS: SUBJECTS, 1950-1954. A
CUMULATIVE LIST OF WORKS REPRESENTED BY LIBRARY OF CONGRESS
PRINTED CARDS. 20 vols. Ann Arbor, Mich.: J.W. Edwards, 1955. Sup-
plement for 1955-1959. 22 vols. Paterson, N.J.: Pageant Books, 1960.
Supplement for 1960-1964. 25 vols. Ann Arbor, Mich.: J.W. Edwards,
1965. Supplement for 1965-1969. 42 vols. Ann Arbor, Mich.: J.W.
Edwards, 1970. Annual cumulation for 1970. 9 vols. Washington, D.C.:
Government Printing Office, 1971. Annual cumulation for 1971. 11 vols.
Washington, D.C.: Government Printing Office, 1972. Annual cumulation
for 1972. 15 vols. Washington, D.C.: Government Printing Office, 1973.

An invaluable source. An alphabetical subject arrangement of
entries printed in 1945 and later and which have been cataloged
by the Library of Congress and other libraries which participate
in the cooperative cataloging system. The catalog is issued in
quarterly paperbound cumulations. Issues for 1973 and 1974 are
at present in this format.

C   OTHER LIBRARY CATALOGS

Harvard University. Graduate School of Design Library. CATALOGUE OF
THE LIBRARY OF THE GRADUATE SCHOOL OF DESIGN. 44 vols. plus
supplements. Boston: G.K. Hall, 1968-70.

This library serves the fields of architecture, landscape architecture, and city and regional planning. The catalog is in dictionary
format with author, title, and subject entries filed in one alphabet;
cards for books and pamphlets and analytics for periodicals are
interfiled. A two-volume supplement covering the years 1968-70
was published in 1970.

U.S. Department of the Interior Library. DICTIONARY CATALOG OF THE
DEPARTMENT LIBRARY. 37 vols. plus supplements. Boston: G.K. Hall,
1967-70.

A very valuable library catalog for materials in the fields covered
by this bibliography. In addition to author, title, and subject
entries, periodical articles (primarily those published during the
nineteenth and early twentieth centuries) are analyzed. Archival
and unpublished materials are also listed here. The library is
especially strong in the fields of conservation, natural resources,
and reclamation. An excellent source for National Park Service

publications, particularly of the "in house" type. The first supplement (four volumes) appeared in 1969 and updates the catalog to August 1968.

U.S. National Agriculture Library. DICTIONARY CATALOG OF THE NATIONAL AGRICULTURE LIBRARY, 1862-1965. 73 vols. New York: Rowman and Littlefield.

A very useful source for materials on forests, forestry, conservation, and other areas of interest covered by activities of the U.S. Department of Agriculture. The publishers plan to issue annual and quinquennial cumulations.

Yale University. School of Forestry Library. DICTIONARY CATALOGUE OF THE YALE FORESTRY LIBRARY. 12 vols. Boston: G.K. Hall, 1962.

A catalog of one of the largest forestry libraries in the world.

D. TRADE BIBLIOGRAPHIES

The following list excludes early trade catalogs that do not offer a subject approach.

AMERICAN CATALOGUE OF BOOKS, 1876-1910. 9 vols. in 13. New York: Publisher's Weekly, 1876-1910.

This is the standard American trade list of books in print during the period covered. Includes both author-title and subject approaches. Although based on information supplied by publishers, it is generally comprehensive and reliable.

UNITED STATES CATALOG: BOOKS IN PRINT. New York: H.W. Wilson, 1899. 2nd ed., 1902. 3rd ed., 1912. 4th ed., 1928.

With the exception of the first edition, the CATALOG is arranged as a dictionary, with author, title, and subject entries in one alphabet. Beginning in 1898, the publishers supplemented the UNITED STATES CATALOG with monthly lists entitled CUMULATED BOOK INDEX. These lists, commonly called "CBI," are cumulated for 1902-5 and annually for the years 1906-10. Supplementary cumulations were issued for 1912-17, 1918-June 1921, June 1921-June 1924, and annually for the years July 1924-December 1927. "CBI" has been issued monthly in dictionary format since 1898. See also next item.

CUMULATED BOOK INDEX, A WORLD LIST OF BOOKS IN THE ENGLISH LANGUAGE. New York: H.W. Wilson, 1933--. Cumulation for 1928-32, 1933. Cumulation for 1933-37, 1938. Cumulation for 1938-42, 1945. Cumulation for 1943-48, 1950. Cumulation for 1949-52, 1953. Cumulation for

1953-56, 1959. Monthly (except July and August) with biennial cumulations, 1957--.

> This index is the successor publication to the UNITED STATES CATALOG (above). Volumes are arranged in dictionary format. Taken together, the UNITED STATES CATALOG and CBI form an indispensable listing of American publications since 1898. The scope of CBI varies. Since the 1928-32 cumulation, it has included English-language books and pamphlets published in the United States and Canada, and a selection from Australia, Great Britain, New Zealand, and South Africa. It omits government documents, maps, and paperback reprints. Because of its comprehensiveness and its detailed subject divisions, CBI is an excellent source for the compilation of subject bibliographies.

E. BIBLIOGRAPHIC FINDING AIDS

Besterman, Theodore A. A WORLD BIBLIOGRAPHY OF BIBLIOGRAPHIES AND OF BIBLIOGRAPHIC CATALOGS, CALENDARS, ABSTRACTS, DIGESTS, IN-DEXES, AND THE LIKE. 4th ed. 5 vols. Lausanne: Societas Bibliographica, 1965-66.

> The standard, authoritative guide in its field. It lists approx-imately 117,000 separately published bibliographies classified under some 16,000 subject-headings. The fifth volume is an alphabetical listing of authors, editors, translators, serial titles, and anonymous works. Each entry in the first four volumes has an estimate of the number of items in each bibliography listed.

BIBLIOGRAPHIC INDEX; A CUMULATIVE BIBLIOGRAPHY OF BIBLIOGRAPHIES. New York: H.W. Wilson, 1938--.

> A subject listing of bibliographies which have appeared in books, pamphlets, and periodicals. No author index; coverage is from 1937. Indexes about 1500 periodicals. Emphasizes bibliographies printed in English, with a few foreign titles. Prior to 1951, the cumulations have been irregular; since 1951, the INDEX has appeared semiannually and the December issue is the annual cumu-lation. The BIBLIOGRAPHIC INDEX is a very valuable tool, especially for research on minor American authors.

Havlice, Patricia Pate. INDEX TO AMERICAN AUTHOR BIBLIOGRAPHIES. Metuchen, N.J.: Scarecrow Press, 1971. vii, 204 p.

> Lists bibliographies of American authors that have appeared exclu-sively in periodicals. Covers 2,225 authors. Criteria for inclusion (other than nationality) are not given. A somewhat sketchy com-pilation, but useful.

F. SUBJECT BIBLIOGRAPHIES

Durrenberger, Robert W. ENVIRONMENT AND MAN; A BIBLIOGRAPHY.
Palo Alto, Calif.: National Press Books, 1970. x, 118 p.

An unannotated list of 2,225 numbered titles, including books,
parts of books, articles, and government documents. Coverage
is from about 1960, although a few earlier important works are
included. The arrangement is by author, or main entry in the
case of corporate authorship. A "guide" containing forty-six
categories, with reference to number of the titles in each, precedes the main listing. The bibliography is "strongest in the area
of relationships of man and environment [human ecology], the arid
lands of the world and...the atmosphere and the hydrosphere."
The bibliography's usefulness is diminished somewhat by the cumber-
some subject approach and the straight alphabetical arrangement.

McNamara, Katherine. LANDSCAPE ARCHITECTURE: A CLASSIFIED BIBLIOG-
RAPHY WITH AN AUTHOR INDEX. Compiled in the Library of the Schools
of Landscape Architecture and City Planning, Harvard University. Preliminary
Edition. Cambridge, Mass.: Harvard University School of Landscape Architecture, 1934. 209 p.

This is a valuable bibliography, particularly for the esthetic aspects
of landscape, landscape appreciation, public parks and reservations, conservation, roadsides and billboards, etc. The compiler
has construed landscape architecture in its widest meaning and
application, and includes many items in allied subjects. The
bibliography contains books, articles, parts of books, pamphlets,
government documents, fiction and poetry, and university extension bulletins and reports. Much historical material is included,
which makes the compilation especially useful. No unpublished
dissertations were noted. The major drawback to its use is the
lack of pagination keyed to a table of contents. A "Summary
Outline" precedes the bibliography, but without corresponding
page-number references. Considerable searching for desired sections is therefore necessary. It is unannotated, but has occasional
brief contents notes.

G. BOOK REVIEWS

BOOK REVIEW DIGEST. New York: H.W. Wilson, 1905--.

Indexes and quotes (on a selective basis) from reviews published
in over seventy-five periodicals, mostly general in nature, including a substantial number of social science journals. The
arrangement is by author and title with a subject index. It is
now published monthly (except for February and July) and cumulated semiannually and annually. Indexes for the preceding five

years began appearing with the volume for 1921 (which indexes
the volumes for 1917-21). Although the BRD is quite useful, it
is a selective digest, emphasizing best sellers and widely reviewed
works. Many books noted in this bibliography were not represented
in the DIGEST. See next item.

BOOK REVIEW INDEX. Detroit: Gale Research Co., 1965--.

This is a much more inclusive review index than the previous title.
Its intent is to index all reviews appearing in more than 200 periodicals. It covers the fields of the social sciences, humanities,
general fiction and nonfiction, librarianship and bibliography, and
children's books. Appears bimonthly with quarterly and annual
cumulations. Publication was suspended during 1969-71, but the
publishers are preparing retrospective indexes for those years.

INDEX TO BOOK REVIEWS IN THE HUMANITIES. Detroit and Williamston,
Mich.: Phillip Thomson, 1960--.

An annual index to some 600 periodicals. Subjects covered are
art, architecture, biography, drama, folklore, history, language,
literature, music, philosophy, travel, and adventure. In 1971,
social science periodicals previously indexed were dropped.

NEW YORK TIMES BOOKS REVIEW INDEX, 1896-1970. 5 vols. New York:
New York Times/Arno Press, 1973.

This valuable reference tool is the only book review index to a
major American paper. The five volumes are arranged by author,
title, byline, subject, and category, respectively. The INDEX
contains references to reviews of books not listed in BOOK RE-
VIEW DIGEST.

H.   BIOGRAPHICAL AIDS AND SOURCES

1.   Bibliography

Slocum, Robert B.   BIOGRAPHICAL DICTIONARIES AND RELATED WORKS;
AN INTERNATIONAL BIBLIOGRAPHY OF COLLECTIVE BIOGRAPHIES, BIO-
BIBLIOGRAPHIES, COLLECTIONS OF EPITAPHS, SELECTED GENEALOGICAL
WORKS, DICTIONARIES OF ANONYMS AND PSEUDONYMS, HISTORICAL
AND SPECIALIZED DICTIONARIES, BIOGRAPHICAL MATERIALS IN GOVERN-
MENT MANUALS, BIBLIOGRAPHIES OF BIOGRAPHY, BIOGRAPHICAL IN-
DEXES, AND SELECTED PORTRAIT CATALOGS. Detroit: Gale Research Co.,
1967. xxiii, 1056 p. SUPPLEMENT, 1972. xiii, 852 p.

A monumental and invaluable work. Arrangement is as follows:
universal biography, national or area biography, and biography by
vocation. Author, title, and subject indexes are provided. The

main volume contains 4,829 titles; 3,400 new entries and new editions of older works and a few corrected entries appear in the supplement. Bibliographical information is complete and brief annotations follow most entries.

2. Indexes

BIOGRAPHY INDEX: A CUMULATIVE INDEX TO BIOGRAPHICAL MATERIAL IN BOOKS AND MAGAZINES. New York: H.W. Wilson, 1947--.

An excellent index to biographical materials of all kinds published in many countries. It indexes material in the 1,500 periodicals currently indexed by all the H.W. Wilson indexes, plus books and parts of books "in the English language wherever published." It contains obituaries (including selected obituaries from the NEW YORK TIMES), autobiography, diaries, letters, as well as formal biographies. In addition to the location of the biographical material, the INDEX provides lifetime dates, professions, and nationalities of biographees.

NEW YORK TIMES OBITUARIES INDEX, 1858-1968. New York: New York Times Co., 1970. 1136 p.

The material in this index is taken primarily from the NEW YORK TIMES INDEX. It contains 353,000 names. Each entry includes the date of death and the date and location of the obituary in the TIMES.

3. Retrospective Biographical Sources

APPLETON'S CYCLOPAEDIA OF AMERICAN BIOGRAPHY. Edited by James Grant Wilson and John Fiske. 7 vols. New York: Appleton, 1887-1900.

For most names, this work was superseded by the DICTIONARY OF AMERICAN BIOGRAPHY (below), although Appleton's is still useful for some historical figures not included in the D.A.B. The articles are fairly long, with many portraits but, unfortunately, with little bibliography and many inaccuracies.

DICTIONARY OF AMERICAN BIOGRAPHY. Various eds. 22 vols. New York: Scribner, 1928-58. Index, vols. 1-20.

The D.A.B. is the standard scholarly biographical dictionary for the United States. Published under the auspices of the American Council of Learned Societies, it includes only those persons who have made some "significant contribution to American life." The biographee must have lived in the United States or the American colonies. Although it is narrower in scope than APPLETON'S

(above), and more limited in coverage than the NATIONAL
CYCLOPAEDIA (below), its articles are more thoroughly researched,
using primary sources wherever possible, and it contains useful
bibliographies. The biographies are 500 to 16,500 words long
and are signed with the author's initials. Each volume contains
a key to initials. The first twenty volumes contain 13,633 biographies; supplement one (Volume 21) added 652 biographies; and
supplement two (Volume 22) added another 585. The terminal
date for inclusion is 1940. The D.A.B. was the single most
important source for biographical information used in this bibliography.

NATIONAL CYCLOPAEDIA OF AMERICAN BIOGRAPHY. New York: J.T.
White, 1892--.

The value of this work lies in its comprehensiveness. It is much
less selective than the D.A.B., and therefore contains many more
biographical sketches, particularly of minor figures, than any other
similar general work. The N.C.A.B. is comprised of two series,
both in progress: the "Permanent" series (1892--), which now
consists of fifty-four volumes and contains information about deceased Americans, and the "Current" series (1930--), volumes
"A - L," which includes persons alive at the time of publication.
Two cumulated indexes exist--a revised index to Volumes 1-51
and a revised index to both Permanent and Current series, published in 1971. Since the contents of the volumes are not arranged alphabetically, the indexes must be used. No bibliographical data is included with the sketches.

NOTABLE AMERICAN WOMEN 1607-1950, A BIOGRAPHICAL DICTIONARY.
Edited by Edward T. James and others. 3 vols. Cambridge, Mass.: Harvard
University Press, 1971.

This is the first large-scale scholarly compendium of biographies
of American women. It is modeled after the DICTIONARY OF
AMERICAN BIOGRAPHY, the format of the sketches being the
same. The N.A.W. contains 1,359 names (compared to some 700
in the D.A.B.). Its coverage starts in 1607 and is restricted to
women who have died no later than 1950.

WHO WAS WHO IN AMERICA: HISTORICAL VOLUME, 1607-1896. A
COMPONENT VOLUME OF WHO'S WHO IN AMERICAN HISTORY. Rev.
ed. Chicago: A.N. Marquis, 1967. 670 p.

Subtitled "A compilation of sketches of individuals, both of the
United States of America and other countries, who have made a
contribution to, or whose activity was in some manner related to
the history of the United States, from the founding of the James-
town Colony to the year of continuation by volume 1 of WHO
WAS WHO."

WHO WAS WHO IN AMERICA; A COMPANION BIOGRAPHICAL WORK TO WHO'S WHO IN AMERICA. 5 vols. Chicago: A.N. Marquis, 1942--.

Contents: Volume 1: 1897–1942; Volume 2: 1943–50; Volume 3: 1951–60; Volume 4: 1961–68; Volume 5: 1969–73. Contains sketches of persons removed from WHO'S WHO IN AMERICA following their deaths. The form of the sketches follows that of WHO'S WHO IN AMERICA, with minor revisions.

4. Current Biographical Sources

CURRENT BIOGRAPHY. New York: H.W. Wilson, 1940--.

"Presents articles on people who are prominent in the news--in national and internal affairs, the sciences, the arts, labor and industry." CURRENT BIOGRAPHY utilizes many sources for biographical information, including the biographees themselves. Sketches often run to several double-column pages. Later volumes sometimes include revisions of previously published biographies. Published monthly (except August) with annual cumulations. Each annual volume contains a cumulated ten-year index to previous volumes (the 1950 annual volume includes an index for the 1940–50 volumes, etc.).

WHO'S WHO IN AMERICA. A BIOGRAPHICAL DICTIONARY OF NOTABLE LIVING MEN AND WOMEN. Chicago: A.N. Marquis, 1899--.

This is the basic biographical dictionary of currently prominent Americans and some outstanding foreigners and members of the United Nations. The information in most cases is supplied by the biographees and follows the established style, which includes addresses, marital data, education, occupation, honors, clubs, and in the case of authors, a list of publications. WHO'S WHO is the most useful of the current biographical works for basic information. It is published biennially.

In 1943 A.N. Marquis began a series of regional WHO'S WHOs to supplement the main series. Each of the series, listed below, follows the original format. The biennial volumes average about 14,000 names. There is some duplication between volumes of listings for people deemed especially noteworthy. The titles of some of the series vary and the frequency is slightly irregular.

WHO'S WHO IN THE EAST; A BIOGRAPHICAL DICTIONARY OF NOTEWORTHY MEN AND WOMEN OF THE MIDDLE ATLANTIC AND NORTHEASTERN STATES. Chicago: A.N. Marquis, 1943--.

Includes persons in eastern Canada.

WHO'S WHO IN THE MIDWEST; A BIOGRAPHICAL DICTIONARY

OF NOTEWORTHY MEN AND WOMEN OF THE CENTRAL AND MIDWESTERN STATES. Chicago: A.N. Marquis, 1949--.

Includes persons in central Canada.

WHO'S WHO IN THE SOUTH AND SOUTHWEST; A BIOGRAPHI-CAL DICTIONARY OF NOTEWORTHY MEN AND WOMEN OF THE SOUTHERN AND SOUTHWESTERN STATES. Chicago: A.N. Marquis, 1950--.

WHO'S WHO IN THE WEST; A BIOGRAPHICAL DICTIONARY OF NOTEWORTHY MEN AND WOMEN OF THE PACIFIC COASTAL AND WESTERN STATES. Chicago: A.N. Marquis, 1949--.

Includes persons in western Canada.

WHO'S WHO OF AMERICAN WOMEN; A BIOGRAPHICAL DICTIONARY OF NOTABLE LIVING AMERICAN WOMEN. Chicago: A.N. Marquis-Who's Who, 1958--.

Title varies. All the American women listed in WHO'S WHO IN AMERICA are listed here (in addition to Canadian entries) together with others judged to be of special reference value. Issued bi-ennially.

5. Author Biographies

Burke, William J., and Howe, Will D. AMERICAN AUTHORS AND BOOKS, 1640 TO THE PRESENT DAY. 3rd ed., revised and edited by Irving Weiss and Anne Weiss. New York: Crown, 1972. 719 p.

Two previous editions appeared in 1943 and 1962. This third edition updates entries and adds new ones to cover the 1960s. In one alphabet are included the following: brief author biogra-phies; titles of books, plays, poems, essays, short stories, songs, orations, etc.; magazines, publishers, societies, and a selected list of newspapers. The biographies give complete data concerning birth and death, occupation, and principal works. The coverage is broad and writers in many fields are included. Particularly useful for minor figures and writers not treated in such works as the LITERARY HISTORY OF THE UNITED STATES (see Chapter 7, Section A2: Histories and Special Studies).

CONTEMPORARY AUTHORS; A BIO-BIBLIOGRAPHICAL GUIDE TO CURRENT AUTHORS AND THEIR WORKS. Various eds. Detroit: Gale Research Co., 1962--. Rev. ed., Vols. 1-4 (4 vols. in 1), 1967; Vols. 5-8 (4 vols. in 1), 1969; Vols. 9-12 (4 vols. in 1), 1974.

Sketches in this work provide a timely and valuable source of

biographical materials for authors in many countries and many
fields. Included, along with standard biographical data, are
complete bibliographies, a list of works in progress, and, in some
cases, sources for additional biographical information. The frequency is semiannual, with annual cumulations. Plans call for revision
and cumulation of the annual volumes about five years later. A
cumulative index appears in every other volume; the latest indexes
Volumes 1–48 (1967–74).

Duyckink, Evert A., and Duyckink, George L. CYCLOPAEDIA OF AMERICAN
LITERATURE, EMBRACING PERSONAL AND CRITICAL NOTICES OF AUTHORS
AND SELECTIONS FROM THEIR WRITINGS. Edited by M. Laird Simons. 2
vols. Philadelphia: Wm. Rutter & Co., 1875. Illustrated. Reprint ed.,
Detroit: Gale Research Co., 1965.

Although the information about major authors has been largely
superceded by later, more critical works, this work is still useful
for minor writers. The essays vary in quality. A first edition
appeared in 1855.

Kunitz, Stanley J., and Haycraft, Howard, eds. AMERICAN AUTHORS,
1600–1900; A BIOGRAPHICAL DICTIONARY OF AMERICAN LITERATURE.
New York: H.W. Wilson, 1938. vi, 846 p. Illustrated.

Contains 1,300 biographical sketches of both major and minor
authors. The emphasis is upon professional writers--poets, novel-
ists, essayists, historians, biographers, critics, etc.--although some
writers whose primary occupations are in other fields are included.
The length of sketches varies from 150 to 2,500 words. Each
biography lists principal works and biographical sources. Portraits
of most figures are included.

. TWENTIETH CENTURY AUTHORS, A BIOGRAPHICAL DICTIONARY
OF MODERN LITERATURE. New York: H.W. Wilson, 1942. vii, 1,577 p.
Illustrated. FIRST SUPPLEMENT. Edited by Stanley J. Kunitz and Vineta
Colby. New York: H.W. Wilson, 1955. vii, 1,123 p. Illustrated.

TWENTIETH CENTURY AUTHORS contains 1,850 quite lengthy
biographies, written in an informal style, of authors of all nations
"familiar to readers of English." The supplement updates the
original (although some authors listed in the main volumes are
not included in the supplement) and adds 700 new biographies for
a total of 2,550 listings. The criteria for inclusion are virtually
the same as in earlier Kunitz volumes (see AMERICAN AUTHORS,
above), as is the format. The third and fourth printings of the
supplement (1963 and 1967) added a necrology of authors who
had died since 1955, and corrected the earlier text. For the
most part, the biographies were written by the authors.

Wallace, W. Stewart, comp. A DICTIONARY OF NORTH AMERICAN AU-

THORS DECEASED BEFORE 1950. Toronto: Ryerson Press, 1951. viii, 525 p.

> Gives dates and places of birth and death and occupation. References are made to eighty-four listed sources of biographical information.

I. GOVERNMENT PUBLICATIONS

United States government publications were not a major resource for the compilation of this bibliography, the emphasis of which is upon the nongovernmental, often popular, index to attitudes, such as the magazine article, memoir, or narrative. However, it is recognized that much important material may be found in the multitudinous reports, bulletins, and other publications issued by U.S. government agencies. For the student wishing to pursue this approach, there are two excellent specialized guides which may be used in addition to the works by Winchell and Poulton mentioned in the headnote to this chapter: Ann Morris Boyd's UNITED STATES GOVERNMENT PUBLICATIONS, 3rd edition, revised by Rae Elizabeth Rips (New York: H.W. Wilson, 1949) is still useful for publications issued up to the late 1940s, and GOVERNMENT PUBLICATIONS AND THEIR USE, by Laurence F. Schmeckebier and Roy B. Eastin (2nd rev. ed. Washington, D.C.: Brookings Institution, 1969) is both useful and more up to date. Both books describe basic guides, indexes, catalogs, and bibliographies of government publications.

The Congressional Edition (or Serial Set) of U.S. government publications contains the House and Senate journals through the 82d Congress (1952), House and Senate documents and reports, as well as a large number of executive department documents printed by order of Congress. Each volume of the set, beginning with the 15th Congress (1817), is given a serial number. In most libraries, the Congressional Edition is arranged serially; thus its contents can be used most effectively by one who knows the serial number of the desired document. For the period covered by this bibliography, the following indexes and catalogs are basic.

Poore, Benjamin Perley. A DESCRIPTIVE CATALOGUE OF THE GOVERNMENT PUBLICATIONS OF THE UNITED STATES, SEPTEMBER 5, 1774-MARCH 4, 1881, COMPILED BY ORDER OF CONGRESS, 48th Cong., 2d sess., Senate Miscellaneous Document, no. 67. Washington, D.C.: Government Printing Office, 1885. 1,392 p. Reprint ed., 1953.

> A chronological arrangement, giving full title, author, date of publication, a brief abstract, and the location of the publication. Although it contains a subject and name index, it is not easy to use because it lacks completeness and specificity. In spite of these drawbacks and certain inaccuracies, Poore's work is basic for the period covered.

Ames, John Griffith. COMPREHENSIVE INDEX TO THE PUBLICATIONS OF THE UNITED STATES GOVERNMENT, 1881-1893, 58th Cong., 2d sess.,

House Document, no. 754. 2 vols. Washington, D.C.: Government Printing Office, 1905.

> Supercedes an earlier edition by Ames published in 1894. It contains both documents in the Congressional Edition and those published by departments. Congressional documents are referenced by congressional session and serial number. It is arranged alphabetically by subject matter with a personal name index at the end of the second volume.

U.S. Superintendent of Documents. CHECKLIST OF UNITED STATES PUBLIC DOCUMENTS, 1789-1909. 3rd ed., rev. and enl. Vol. 1. Washington, D.C.: Government Printing Office, 1911. 1,707 p.

> Two volumes were planned: the first volume lists congressional and departmental publications; the second, never published, was to be an index. The CHECKLIST covers congressional documents through the 60th Congress, with serial number equivalents for early publications, and department publications to the end of 1909.

_____. CATALOG OF THE PUBLIC DOCUMENTS OF CONGRESS AND OF ALL DEPARTMENTS OF THE GOVERNMENT OF THE UNITED STATES FOR THE PERIOD MARCH 4, 1893 TO DECEMBER 31, 1940. 25 vols. Washington, D.C.: Government Printing Office, 1896-1945.

> This work, commonly called the DOCUMENTS CATALOG, is a comprehensive dictionary catalog of all congressional and departmental documents published from 1893 to 1940. It contains author (personal and agency), subject, and, when necessary, title entries. Entries are bibiographically complete, with serial set numbers following each item. Contents notes and analyses are given for many publications. An altogether valuable tool, especially since it covers most of the years relevant to this bibliography.

_____. MONTHLY CATALOG OF UNITED STATES GOVERNMENT PUBLICATIONS. Washington, D.C.: Government Printing Office, 1895--.

> Title varies. Lists current publications of all branches of the government published during any given month. Arrangement is by department and bureau, with an annual index. Three supplements, for the years 1941-42, 1943-44, and 1945-46, were published in 1947-48 and contain documents not listed previously in the MONTHLY CATALOG. Since 1947, all public documents appear in the CATALOG as received. There is a DECENNIAL CUMULATIVE INDEX, 1941-1950 (Washington, D.C.: Government Printing Office, 1953) and a DECENNIAL CUMULATIVE INDEX, 1951-1960 in 2 volumes (1968). Both are subject indexes. In 1971, Pierian Press published three personal name indexes to the MONTHLY CATALOG:

> U.S. Superintendent of Documents. MONTHLY CATA-

LOG OF UNITED STATES GOVERNMENT PUBLICA-
TIONS; DECENNIAL CUMULATIVE PERSONAL AU-
THOR INDEX, 1941-1950. Edited by Edward Przebienda.
Ann Arbor, Mich.: Pierian Press, 1971. 276 p.

_____. MONTHLY CATALOG OF UNITED STATES
GOVERNMENT PUBLICATIONS; DECENNIAL CUMULA-
TIVE PERSONAL AUTHOR INDEX, 1951-1960. Edited
by Edward Przebienda. Ann Arbor, Mich.: Pierian
Press, 1971. 351 p.

_____. QUINQUENNIAL CUMULATIVE PERSONAL
AUTHOR INDEX, 1961-1965. Edited by Edward
Przebienda. Ann Arbor, Mich.: Pierian Press, 1971.
293 p.

_____. NUMERICAL LISTS AND SCHEDULE OF VOLUMES OF THE REPORTS
AND DOCUMENTS OF THE 73RD CONGRESS, 1933/1934--. Washington, D.C.:
Government Printing Office, 1934--.

> Since the MONTHLY CATALOG does not list serial numbers of
> congressional documents and reports, the NUMERICAL LISTS
> must be used for this purpose. A separate volume is issued for
> each session of Congress. Prior to 1941, the CATALOG OF
> PUBLIC DOCUMENTS (DOCUMENTS CATALOG) should be con-
> sulted, since it does contain serial numbers.

J. DISSERTATIONS AND THESES

Only published sources have been cited in this bibliography; however, unpublished doctoral dissertations and master's theses do sometimes provide the scholar
with significant research findings and references to important bibliographic
sources. The degree of bibliographic control over these materials has never
been as thorough as for printed sources; indeed, even today, several major
universities do not report their dissertations to University Microfilms, publisher
of DISSERTATION ABSTRACTS (see below). In the case of master's theses,
bibliographic control is even slighter. The lists, indexes, and abstracts listed
below are the basic general sources for locating dissertations and theses.

1. Lists, Indexes, and Abstracts of Dissertations

The first three titles below are arranged sequentially by the dates of the dissertations described therein and are followed by DISSERTATION ABSTRACTS and
a cumulated index to all the titles.

U.S. Library of Congress. Catalog Division. A LIST OF AMERICAN DOC-

TORAL DISSERTATIONS PRINTED IN 1912-38. 26 vols. Washington, D.C.: Government Printing Office, 1913-40.

Cites only published ("printed") works. Each volume contains an alphabetical listing, a classified listing by Library of Congress classification scheme, a subject index, and an arrangement by issuing institution.

DOCTORAL DISSERTATIONS ACCEPTED BY AMERICAN UNIVERSITIES, 1933/34-1954/55. Compiled for the Association of Research Libraries. 22 nos. New York: H.W. Wilson, 1934-56.

This is an annual classified listing, subdivided by issuing institution and then by author. It is not a complete listing for the years covered and is superceded by AMERICAN DOCTORAL DISSERTATIONS (below).

AMERICAN DOCTORAL DISSERTATIONS. Compiled for the Association of Research Libraries. Ann Arbor, Mich.: University Microfilms, 1957--.

Title varies; began as INDEX TO AMERICAN DOCTORAL DISSERTATIONS. Beginning with the biennial cumulation for 1963-64 it assumed its present title. The coverage is from 1955/56. Its arrangement is first by subject and then by issuing institution with alphabetical author and subject indexes. It purports to be a complete listing of American and Canadian doctoral dissertations compiled from commencement programs; thus it includes titles not included in DISSERTATION ABSTRACTS. With Volume 16, number 13, AMERICAN DOCTORAL DISSERTATIONS became a subsidiary part of DISSERTATION ABSTRACTS which it indexes, although retaining its individual series title.

DISSERTATION ABSTRACTS; ABSTRACTS OF DISSERTATIONS AND MONOGRAPHS AVAILABLE IN MICROFILM. Ann Arbor, Mich.: University Microfilms, 1952-69. Continued as DISSERTATION ABSTRACTS INTERNATIONAL. Ann Arbor, Mich.: Xerox, University Microfilms, 1969--.

Title varies: Volumes 1-11 (1938-51) appeared as MICROFILM ABSTRACTS; with Volume 27, number 1, DISSERTATION ABSTRACTS began two sections: (A) humanities and social sciences, and (B) sciences and engineering; beginning with Volume 30, number 1 (July 1969), the title was changed to DISSERTATION ABSTRACTS INTERNATIONAL (the A and B sections are maintained). These compilations do not abstract all dissertations written in the United States; a list of cooperating institutions appears in the front of each monthly issue. In 1968, about 200 institutions sent their dissertations for microfilming; the coverage was increased to over 300 institutions with the advent of DISSERTATION ABSTRACTS INTERNATIONAL. The new series includes abstracts of dissertations from the United States and Canada and a few foreign universities. In each issue, the abstracts are arranged by subject and

then by university. Each abstract contains full bibliographic information and includes the name of the supervising professor, the
date, order number, and the prices of microfilm copies and photo-
copies. Author and subject indexes accompany each issue; there is
a cumulated author and subject index to each year.

COMPREHENSIVE DISSERTATION INDEX, 1861-1972. 37 vols. Ann Arbor,
Mich.: Xerox, University Microfilms, 1973.

This is an invaluable index to DISSERTATION ABSTRACTS (above),
AMERICAN DOCTORAL DISSERTATIONS, DOCTORAL DISSERTA-
TIONS, DOCTORAL DISSERTATIONS ACCEPTED BY AMERICAN
UNIVERSITIES, LIST OF AMERICAN DOCTORAL DISSERTATIONS
PRINTED IN 1912-38, and a large number of separate institutional
lists. The volume arrangement is by subject discipline. Within
each volume, a computer-generated keyword index is used; unfortunately, the difference in typographic density between the
keyword and the rest of the title is so slight that scanning of
titles is difficult. There is a cumulated author index.

2.   Subject Lists of Dissertations

Kuehl, Warren F. DISSERTATIONS IN HISTORY; AN INDEX TO DISSERTA-
TIONS COMPLETED IN HISTORY DEPARTMENTS OF UNITED STATES AND
CANADIAN UNIVERSITIES, 1873-1960. [Lexington]: University of Kentucky
Press, 1965. xi, 249 p. ..., 1961-June 1970. [Vol. 2.] Lexington:
University of Kentucky Press, 1972. x, 237 p.

Kuehl's works include only those dissertations presented to departments of history and so exclude dissertations prepared on historical
topics in other disciplines and area studies programs. The arrangement is by author with a subject index. The index, however, is
"not...a full index to all subjects...but an index to titles or
those subjects implicit within the titles." The work is based upon
entries appearing in general lists and indexes, as well as upon
questionnaires from departments of history which have been cross-
checked against university library catalogs for accuracy. No
distinction is made between published and unpublished dissertations.
This is an invaluable and monumental compilation.

Woodress, James L. DISSERTATIONS IN AMERICAN LITERATURE, 1891-1966.
Newly rev. and enl. with the assistance of Marian Koritz. Durham, N.C.:
Duke University Press, 1968. xii, 185 p.

First edition published in 1957. This edition lists some 4,700
doctoral dissertations from institutions in the United States, England,
France, Germany, New Zealand, and other countries. The primary
emphasis is upon American universities. Woodress interprets American literature broadly so as to include subthemes such as politics
in literature, religion, science and technology, periodicals, journal-

ism, etc.

3. Master's Theses

Black, Dorothy M. GUIDE TO LISTS OF MASTER'S THESES. Chicago: American Library Association, 1965. 144 p.

> This work incorporates references in an older guide by Thomas
> R. Palfrey and Henry E. Coleman, GUIDE TO BIBLIOGRAPHIES
> OF THESES: UNITED STATES AND CANADA (Chicago: American Library Association, 1940), and includes lists of master's
> theses from colleges and universities written through 1964. The
> book is divided into four parts: sources, general lists, lists in
> specific fields, and lists by specific institutions in the United
> States and Canada. Includes theses listed in various periodicals.

MASTER'S ABSTRACTS; A CATALOG OF SELECTED MASTER'S THESES ON MICROFILM. Ann Arbor, Mich.: University Microfilms, 1962--.

> Subtitle varies. This is a quarterly abstracting service that currently includes forty-six participating institutions. It does not
> contain all the theses accepted by these schools, but only those
> selected for microfilming. Abstracts are listed in a classified
> arrangement.

K. PERIODICAL DIRECTORIES

IRREGULAR SERIALS AND ANNUALS, AN INTERNATIONAL DIRECTORY. 3rd ed., 1974-75. A Bowker Serials Bibliography. New York and London: R.R. Bowker, 1974. 989 p.

> This work, planned as a companion supplement to ULRICH'S (below), first appeared in 1967. The present edition contains some
> 25,000 currently published titles "issued annually or less frequently
> than once a year, or irregularly; serials published at least twice
> under the same title, and those first publications which plan to
> have subsequent issues." This definition includes such publications
> as annual reviews, yearbooks, proceedings, transactions, handbooks,
> and monographic series. Excluded are such "administrative" publications as house organs and annual reports. It also contains a
> separate listing of over 800 titles that have ceased or suspended
> publication since the second edition.

THE STANDARD PERIODICAL DIRECTORY; THE MOST COMPLETE GUIDE TO UNITED STATES AND CANADIAN PERIODICALS...INFORMATION ON MORE THAN 62,000 PUBLICATIONS. 4th ed., edited by Leon Garry. New York: Oxbridge Publishing Co., 1973. 1,916 p.

> First edition published in 1964. Because it defines a periodical

as any publication issued at least once every two years, this is a very useful compilation. It includes titles not listed in other compilations: house organs, newsletters, government publications, directories, etc. It claims to include "every type of [American and Canadian] periodical with the exception of suburban, weekly and small daily newspapers; approximately 325 major city daily newspapers are listed." It is arranged alphabetically by subject, and then by title, with a separate index to titles. Some entries have short annotations.

ULRICH'S INTERNATIONAL PERIODICALS DIRECTORY; A CLASSIFIED GUIDE TO CURRENT PERIODICALS, FOREIGN AND DOMESTIC. 15th ed., 1973-74. A Bowker Serials Bibliography. New York and London: R.R. Bowker, 1973. 2,706 p.

The first edition of this standard periodicals directory was published in 1932. The fifteenth edition contains entries for about 55,000 currently published periodicals and 1,800 titles that have ceased or suspended publication since the fourteenth edition. Each periodical entry includes the following information: full title and subtitle; beginning date of publication (if known); frequency; name and address of publisher; editor's name; price; circulation; information about indexes and supplements; whether it carries book reviews or advertisements; and the titles of indexes or abstracting services in which the periodical is listed. Previous editions are still useful for information on titles no longer published.

L. PERIODICAL INDEXES

AMERICA: HISTORY AND LIFE; A GUIDE TO PERIODICAL LITERATURE. Santa Barbara, Calif.: American Bibliographic Center-Clio Press, 1964--.

This publication abstracts articles on American and Canadian history and culture from prehistoric times to the present. Abstracts come from 2,200 serials in about forty languages. Approximately 700 of these are published in the United States and Canada and include the publications of state and local historical societies, major historical periodicals, and journals covering generally the social sciences and humanities. It includes irregular serials, such as "Festschriften," and annuals. Foreign language articles appear with translated titles and abstracts in English. AMERICA: HISTORY AND LIFE is published in four numbers, the last of which includes an annual index, and there is a cumulative index to the first five years (1964-69). In 1972, the publishers issued a retrospective volume "0" (zero), containing 6,154 abstracts selected from its sister publication, HISTORICAL ABSTRACTS, covering the periodical literature from 1954 to 1963. The arrangement of each number is as follows: I. North America; II. Canada; III. United States: National history to 1945; IV. United States: 1945 to present; V. United States: Regional, state, and local history;

and VI. History, the humanities, and social sciences. Each of the six categories is divided into topical, chronological, or geographical sections as appropriate. Indexes include a list of abstractors, and a combined author, biographical, geographical, and subject index.

BIOLOGICAL AND AGRICULTURAL INDEX. New York: H.W. Wilson, 1916--.

Title and contents vary: from 1916 to August 1964 (Volumes 1-49), it appeared as AGRICULTURAL INDEX; in September 1964 the name was changed to reflect the increased emphasis upon biological periodicals and the decreased importance of agricultural materials. As AGRICULTURAL INDEX, it is particularly useful in the area of nature study and country life. During this period, it provided coverage of agricultural periodicals, including those of a popular nature, and reports, bulletins, and circulars of state agricultural departments and experiment stations. With the change of name, such magazines as ORGANIC GARDENING (now indexed in READER'S GUIDE, below) were dropped. Both series provide a subject approach.

CUMULATED MAGAZINE SUBJECT INDEX, 1907-1949. A CUMULATION OF THE F.W. FAXON COMPANY'S ANNUAL MAGAZINE SUBJECT INDEX. Edited by Frederick Winthrop Faxon, 1907-35, Mary E. Bates, 1936-44, and Anne C. Sutherland, 1942-49. Cumulated by G.K. Hall & Co. 2 vols. Boston: G.K. Hall, 1964.

A cumulated edition of the forty-three volumes of the ANNUAL MAGAZINE SUBJECT INDEX. While some general magazines were indexed, the emphasis of this work was upon history, particularly state and local, including the proceedings of many local historical societies. It gave "special emphasis to art, architecture, geography, travel, exploration and mountaineering, outdoor life, forestry, education and political science." As an example of this special emphasis, it indexed the SIERRA CLUB BULLETIN from 1902 to 1949.

NINETEENTH CENTURY READER'S GUIDE TO PERIODICAL LITERATURE, 1890-1899. 2 vols. New York: H.W. Wilson, 1944.

Indexes author, subject, and illustrator entries in fifty-one periodicals, primarily for the period 1890 to 1899; supplementary indexing of fourteen additional periodicals was carried on for 1900-22 before being taken over by other Wilson indexes. Indexed periodicals are mostly general and literary in character. The citations follow the style of other Wilson indexes and contain complete bibliographical information. See READER'S GUIDE TO PERIODICAL LITERATURE (below).

POOLE'S INDEX TO PERIODICAL LITERATURE, 1802-1881. Rev. ed. 2 vols. Boston: Houghton Mifflin, 1891. Supplements, January 1882-January 1, 1907. 5 vols. Boston: Houghton Mifflin, 1887-1908.

The original editor of this pioneer index was William F. Poole; it was continued by him and W.I. Fletcher in cooperation with the American Library Association. Because POOLE'S indexes about 590,000 articles in 479 American and British periodicals, it is an invaluable source for this early period. It is a subject index only and contains no author entries; however, Wall's CUMULATED AUTHOR INDEX (below) makes access by author possible. The subject entries in POOLE'S consist of title of article, author, abbreviated title of periodical, volume, and first page number. The date and exact pagination is not given; however, the work by Bell and Bacon (below) offers a "key" to the indexed periodicals, making possible a correlation between the volume and date. POOLE'S INDEX was reprinted in six volumes in 1938. The Wall compilation is a triple-column, alphabetical-order author index to POOLE'S. Citations refer to volume, page, and column, and state whether the reference is single ("s") or multiple ("m").

Bell, Marion V., and Bacon, Jean C. POOLE'S INDEX, DATE AND VOLUME KEY. Association of College and Research Libraries Monograph, no. 19. Chicago: Association of College and Research Libraries, 1957. 61 p.

Wall, C. Edward, comp. CUMULATED AUTHOR INDEX FOR POOLE'S INDEX TO PERIODICAL LITERATURE, 1802-1906. Ann Arbor, Mich.: Pierian Press, 1971. 488 p.

READER'S GUIDE TO PERIODICAL LITERATURE. New York: H.W. Wilson, 1905--.

This is the standard and most widely known and used cumulated periodical index. It appears in paper issues monthly from July to August and semimonthly, September to June, cumulating at intervals until the end of the volume year. The frequency of the permanent cumulations varies: from 1900-35, every three to five years are cumulated; from 1935 to date, two-year cumulations have appeared. The arrangement of the READER'S GUIDE is that of a dictionary catalog containing author and subject entries, and title entries when no author has been established. The bibliographic citations are complete, and the subject headings are sufficiently detailed and sophisticated to make location of entries easy. Book reviews were included through 1904. READER'S GUIDE indexes United States periodicals of a general, popular, and nontechnical character in the fields of science, the humanities, social sciences, and literature. Of all the periodical indexes, this work was the most fruitful in the compilation of this bibliography.

SOCIAL SCIENCES AND HUMANITIES INDEX. New York: H.W. Wilson, 1907--.

This index covers the standard scholarly journals in the social sciences and humanities published in the English language. Includes classics, folklore, languages and literature, philosophy, religion, and the theater arts, in addition to other areas subsumed by the social sciences and humanities. It presently indexes over 200 journals. The title varies: from 1907 to 1916-19 (Volumes 1-2), it appeared as READER'S GUIDE TO PERIODICAL LITERATURE, SUPPLEMENT; from 1920 to 1965, it appeared as INTERNATIONAL INDEX; A GUIDE TO PERIODICAL LITERATURE IN THE SOCIAL SCIENCE AND HUMANITIES; beginning in 1965 (Volume 19), it was published under the present title. The current numbers are issued quarterly with annual cumulations; previous cumulations have varied from four to two years.

M.   INDEXES AND ABSTRACTS OF ENVIRONMENTAL LITERATURE

THE ENVIRONMENTAL INDEX; A GUIDE TO THE KEY LITERATURE OF THE YEAR. New York: Environmental Information Center, Inc., 1971--.

This annual indexes the monthly issues of ENVIRONMENTAL ABSTRACTS (called ENVIRONMENTAL INFORMATION ACCESS, 1971-December 1973) by the same publisher. It indexes newspaper and magazine articles, reports, and government documents from over 1,500 American and foreign periodicals, heavily emphasizing scientific, engineering, and industry journals, with an admixture of general magazines, the publications of conservation organizations, and planning, architectural, natural resource, and business sources. The entries in THE ENVIRONMENTAL INDEX are arranged within subject categories by accession numbers (no author is given) which refer to the corresponding abstract in ENVIRONMENTAL ABSTRACTS. There is a separate author list to the access-numbered abstracts, a geographical index, a list of key environmental books and films, a section on major conferences held during the year, and a selection of environmental patents. The INDEX's coverage is suited to the informational needs of biological and physical scientists, engineers, planners, human ecologists, and behavioral scientists; however, scholars in the humanities, particularly historians, are not so well served. Major periodicals concerned with American history and culture are not covered; for example, FOREST HISTORY is indexed, but AGRICULTURAL HISTORY is not; counterculture publications like MOTHER EARTH NEWS are also not indexed. Traditional subject headings such as "nature," "country life," and "natural beauty," are not used and tend to be subsumed under headings like "General," and "Environmental Design." All in all, this is an important service, with much significant information; but its arrangement, lack of combined author-title entries, and subject indexing leave much to be desired.

ENVIRONMENTAL PERIODICALS BIBLIOGRAPHY: INDEXED ARTICLE TITLES.
Edited by Eric Boehm. Santa Barbara, Calif.: Environmental Studies Institute,
International Academy at Santa Barbara, 1972--.

> This is a bimonthly "current awareness" bibliography. It duplicates
> the tables of contents of some 260 United States and foreign peri-
> odicals on "environmental and related subjects." Six major sec-
> tions are arranged as follows: 1. General. Human Ecology
> (includes architecture, landscaping, education, environmental
> organizations, etc.); 2. Air; 3. Energy; 4. Land Resources
> (including conservation, preservation, wildlife and nature, nation-
> al parks, recreational and wilderness areas, and agriculture); 5.
> Water Resources; and 6. Nutrition and Health. Each issue con-
> tains a subject and author index. The subject index is sophisti-
> cated and analyzes articles for subject matter not explicit in the
> article titles. There is an annual index in the December issue.

N. LIST OF PERIODICALS

The periodicals below have not been listed in Chapters 4 (on conservation and
national parks), 8 (on nature study), 9 (on camping and outdoor life), or 10
(on country life). The list includes periodicals in which articles cited elsewhere have appeared, as well as some neither cited nor listed elsewhere, but
in which material regularly appears that is relevant to the theme of this bibliography. The titles are not annotated, but some have brief contents notes
explaining coverage, title changes, and frequency variations where necessary.

AMERICAN FORESTS. Washington, D.C.: American Forestry Association,
1895--. Bimonthly.

AUDUBON. New York: National Audubon Society, 1899--. Bimonthly.

> Title varies: appeared as BIRD-LORE, 1899-1940, and as AUDU-
> BON MAGAZINE, 1941-66.

CONSERVATIONIST. Albany, N.Y.: New York State Environmental Conservation Department, August 1946--. Bimonthly.

> Title varies: appeared as NEW YORK STATE CONSERVATION-
> IST, 1946-April/May 1960. This is an excellent regional publica-
> tion devoted to wildlife preservation, nature study, and conserva-
> tion of natural resources, including scenery.

CRY CALIFORNIA. Sacramento and San Francisco: California Tomorrow,
Winter 1965-66--. Quarterly.

ECOLOGY; ALL FORMS OF LIFE IN RELATION TO ENVIRONMENT. Durham, N.C.: Ecological Society of America, 1920--. Bimonthly.

ENVIRONMENT AND BEHAVIOR. Beverly Hills, Calif.: Sage Publishing Co., June 1969--. Quarterly.

GARDEN CLUB OF AMERICA BULLETIN. Baltimore, Md., and New York, July 1913--.

    Frequency varies; currently issued five times per year.

JOURNAL OF FOREST HISTORY. New Haven, Conn.: Forest History Society, Spring 1957--. Quarterly.

    Title varies: FOREST HISTORY NEWSLETTER, 1957-58; FOREST HISTORY, 1958-January 1974.

JOURNAL OF FORESTRY. Washington, D.C.: Society of American Foresters, 1902--. Monthly.

JOURNAL OF WILDLIFE MANAGEMENT. Menasha, Wis., and Washington, D.C.: The Wildlife Society, July 1937--. Quarterly.

LANDSCAPE; MAGAZINE OF HUMAN GEOGRAPHY. Santa Fe, N.M., and Berkeley, Calif., 1951-70 [suspended?].

    Subtitle varies slightly. This journal was published and edited by John B. Jackson as a quarterly from its inception to the Fall 1969 issue. With Volume 18, number 1 (Winter 1969), LANDSCAPE was published three times a year under the editorship of Boyd Blair. The last issue to appear was that of Winter 1970. Under Jackson's editorship, the magazine maintained a consistently high degree of excellence. Coverage included human geography, human ecology, landscape design, architecture, environmental perception, urban design, city planning, scenic preservation, conservation, recreation, and allied subjects.

LANDSCAPE ARCHITECTURE. Louisville, Ky.: American Society of Landscape Architects, 1910--. Quarterly.

    Contains a great deal of material on national, state, and local parks, scenic preservation, and recreational planning.

NATIONAL GEOGRAPHIC MAGAZINE. Washington, D.C.: National Geographic Society, 1888--. Monthly.

NATIONAL WILDLIFE. Washington, D.C.: National Wildlife Federation, December 1962-January 1963--. Bimonthly.

NATURAL HISTORY. New York: American Museum of Natural History, April 1900--. Ten issues per year.

> Frequency has varied. Absorbed NATURE MAGAZINE in 1960 (see Chapter 8, Section A8: Nature Study Periodicals). This is a popular journal of natural history, but its articles and features reflect considerable interest in conservation, national parks, wildlife, and ecology.

NATURE CONSERVANCY NEWS. Arlington, Va.: Nature Conservancy, 1951--. Quarterly.

NATURE STUDY. Homer, N.Y.: American Nature Study Society, 1946--. Quarterly.

NOT MAN APART. Albuquerque, N.M.: Friends of the Earth, December 1970--. Monthly.

> Tabloid format.

OUTDOOR AMERICA. Arlington, Va.: Izaak Walton League of America, 1922-23, 1935--. Monthly.

SNOWY EGRET. Williamsburg, Ky.: Edited and published by Humphrey A. Olsen, 1922--. Semiannual.

> Mimeographed; title and frequency vary. This "little magazine" contains articles, reviews, criticism, and poetry, primarily related to the cultural aspects of nature and natural history.

INDEX

INDEX

Indexed on the following pages are titles, authors, and subjects cited in this Guide. The subtitles of many books have been shortened or omitted to conserve space. Authors, editors, compilers, and illustrators of importance have been included. Geographical place names have been included in the index only when they are the major subject of a book.